WARRIORS of GOD

WARRIORS
OF GOD

the Great Religious Orders
and their Founders

by WALTER NIGG edited &
translated from the German by
Mary Ilford

London : SECKER AND WARBURG : 1959

Made and printed by offset in Great Britain by
William Clowes and Sons Ltd, London and Beccles
and first published 1959 by
Martin Secker and Warburg Ltd
7 John Street, London
W.C.1

CONTENTS

INTRODUCTION

A STRANGE POEM in Rainer Maria Rilke's *Stunden-Buch* tells of monks who "buried themselves deep down in the earth," returning, as it were, into the womb; of a life that was "as a thousand years" because it was no longer divided into night and day; of pilgrims who come to gaze with reverent eyes upon the "buried ones" whose bodies have never known decay.[1] Rilke was writing about the monks of a cave-monastery in Kiev which had become a famous place of pilgrimage; he was also—unwittingly, no doubt —creating an image of the fate of monasticism in modern times.

With the spread of the ideas of the French Revolution, the very concept of monasticism became increasingly unintelligible to the West. A purely utilitarian world had little place for otherworldly aspirations. Besides, monastic life must perforce be looked upon as contrary to nature. The objection, of course, was not new; it had been raised by men like Erasmus in the sixteenth century, as it had been raised by men like Jovinian in the fourth. But in the Age of Enlightenment the opposition to monasticism gathered into veritable frenzy, forcing the dissolution of numerous monasteries. And monasticism, like the monks in Rilke's mysterious verse, responded by retreating into the catacombs, hibernating, so to speak, in the caverns of the earth, the better to preserve its secret from impious eyes.

It had not disappeared for good; monasticism is far too deeply

[1] Rainer Maria Rilke: *Das Stunden-Buch* (Leipzig: Insel Verlag; 1936), p. 67.

1*

rooted in the human heart ever to disappear completely. Signs of a revival were already apparent in the nineteenth century. And just as St. Paul, speaking of the resurrection of the dead, cried out to the Corinthians: "Behold, I show you a mystery!" (I Cor. xv, 51), so we today must tell the world none the less urgently: see, monasticism descended into the bowels of the earth only that it might rise again! Indeed, the true significance of the descent lay in the patient preparation of an imminent reawakening.

The process is a hidden one unperceived by those whose concern is only with externals; from a religious point of view, however, it is one of the most significant developments of our time, and it requires of us a new encounter with monasticism. Here we may recall Franz Overbeck's dictum that monasticism is a phenomenon that neither Catholic nor Protestant theology is able to assess adequately, Catholic theology having long since lost the necessary purity of understanding, Protestant theology never having been sufficiently objective.[2] For all that it is so disputable, the statement sounds a warning that merits attention.

To grasp the reality of monasticism is clearly not as easy as it might appear to be. Well-nigh impassable mountains of prejudice have to be scaled first. And that means, to start with, that the whole subject has to be lifted right out of the context of sectarianism. For sectarianism—not to be confused with membership of the particular denomination in which Providence has been pleased to place a particular individual—is all too conducive to malice, and tends to blur one's vision of truth. It should be remembered, moreover, that the great monastic orders were founded in the marvelous climate of an as yet undivided Christendom. If only on ecumenical grounds, therefore, it is necessary to break through all narrow partisan attitudes in a Christian spirit that transcends polemics and keeps one mindful of the duty to serve all denominations. In such a spirit, we shall approach monasticism with a new open-mindedness, and we shall look upon this mighty edifice of Christian spirituality with loving veneration, though not, of course, uncritically.

Scholarship can provide some of the means of gaining a better

[2] Franz Overbeck: *Ueber die Christlichkeit unserer heutigen Theologie* (1903), p. 83.

understanding of monasticism. Historical methods have been invaluable in the assembling of source material, and the author re-
calls with sincere gratitude the numerous monographs he has read
on particular aspects of the monastic movement. Academic objectivity, however, often leads to an inner aloofness that blinds the
scholar to the essential. Although research is necessary, therefore,
it must remain peripheral to the subject and cannot be regarded as
constituting the final authority.

More than scholarly treatment is needed if there is really to be
a new encounter with monasticism. The academic approach has
to be completed and lifted to a higher plane by an altogether different approach, such as was formulated, for instance, in the very
heyday of rationalism, by the fascinating visionary who called
himself Novalis (1772–1802). That Johannine emissary of the
divine, having passed through the "Gothic arches of pure reason,"
was able to survey the world of sense from the vantage point of a
higher reality; in one of his most bewitching poems he speaks of a
future when "those who sing or those who kiss will know more than
all the great scholars." [3] The man who, "through tales and poems,
penetrates to the heart of things" can arrive at the deeper vision of
a Novalis. The supra-scholarly approach is not founded on mere
emotion; intuitive perception depends upon the illumination of the
Logos, and precisely this makes of the new inquiry into monasticism an act of living religion rather than an exercise in academic
hairsplitting.

II

In re-evaluating monasticism, we can adopt various points of view.
It is doubtless wisest to begin by considering the subject from the
point of view of history; we tend, nowadays, to be very conscious
of the importance of historical perspective. And history will at once
show us that monasticism is heir to a venerable tradition, and that
it is common to many religions.

The phenomenology of religious history shows us that there is

[3] Novalis: *Gesammelte Werke*, ed. Seelig, I, 343.

a deep connection between man's religious aspirations and the monastic life. India, with its extraordinary talent for religion and its profusion of monasteries, affords an interesting illustration of the point.

Indian monasticism is most strongly marked by the influence of the Buddha, that tremendous figure whose significance no Western mind has yet succeeded in comprehending to the full. Buddha opens his lapidary admonitions with the stereotyped "This, O monks, is the sacred truth," thereby indicating that he is addressing himself exclusively to men who have embraced the monastic state. And Buddha's true disciple is the radiant monk who passes through the world absolved and filled with inner peace: "His heart overflowing with loving-kindness, compassion, sympathetic gladness, and even-mindedness, he abides, raying them forth toward one quarter of space, then toward the second and third, then toward the fourth, above and below, thus all around. Everywhere, into all places the wide world over, his heart overflowing, streams forth, ample, expanded, limitless, free from enmity and all ill-will." [4]

Buddha sent forth his monks, freed from all worldly ties, for the salvation and joy of many, out of pity for the world and for the good of mankind, to announce a teaching that they were also to manifest by their own holiness, reconciling men wherever they went. Buddha's radiant monk is free of earthly dust; the love of his liberated heart transcends the baser preoccupations of the majority of men as the moonlight outshines the brightness of the stars.

Thus, the Buddhistic form of monasticism alone should give us pause: perhaps our opinion of monasticism was overhasty, and needs revision.

Monasticism is, above all, a valid development of Christianity. The single answer to the largely unfruitful discussions on the origins of Christian monasticism is that the monastic life is implicit in the Church, not the product of pagan influences. The eschatological teachings of Jesus brought about a turning-away from the world, an attitude that was already very marked in St. Paul. Christian monas-

[4] From Buddha's sermons to his disciples. See B. Brown, ed.: *The Story of Buddha and Buddhism* (Philadelphia: David McKay; 1927), chap. v, p. 114.

ticism is rooted in the New Testament, and the first hermits appealed to the Bible to justify their way of life. Oswald Spengler, whose philosophy of history was certainly innocent of all denominational bias, remarked that "Christian monasticism did not begin with Pachomius (320); he was merely the builder of the first cloister. The movement began with the original community in Jerusalem itself." [5]

. Historically speaking, Christian monasticism stemmed directly from the earliest Christian ascetics, a response to the danger that a secularized Christendom would stifle all genuine religious life. Monasticism and the teachings of the Fathers are the fairest flowers of the early Church. And it is logically impossible to recognize the fundamental importance of the early Church for all subsequent Christian generations and, at the same time, to reject as an aberration monasticism, which was an integral part of that Church. In the deplorable entanglement of ecclesiastical and political issues which was already apparent in the fourth century, the monks represented "as it were the other side of the Church," and, "thanks to their asceticism, preserved the balance." [6] That, in effect, is the ultimate significance of monasticism: to express most purely what is purest in Christian spirituality. We must focus our attention on this other, oft-neglected side of the Church.

The Eastern Church was molded by monasticism; indeed, it cannot be understood at all in isolation from its monastic life. "If you want to know what Christianity really means, you have to know monasticism," wrote Kirejewsky. [7] This is no isolated opinion; it is echoed, for instance, by Konstantin Leontiev. [8] And the legends of the Russian saints make abundantly clear that the Eastern Church is wholly penetrated by monasticism. The growing interest in Eastern Christianity, therefore, will be something more than a vague enthusiasm for the Russian soul only if it also extends to Eastern monasticism, which conceals a truly marvelous piety under its alien garb.

[5] Oswald Spengler: *The Decline of the West* (New York: Alfred A. Knopf; 1928), II, 254.
[6] Walter Dirks: *Die Antwort der Mönche* (1952), p. 115.
[7] J. Smolitsch: *Leben und Lehre der Starzen* (1936), p. 165.
[8] Cf. J. von Kologriwof: *Von Hellas zum Mönchtum* (1948), pp. 14 ff.

Religious Russians have always been convinced of the immense importance of monasticism in the life of their people. Gogol, for instance, himself a deeply religious man, testified to the intimate connection between faith and the monastic life in the Eastern Church when he wrote: "There is no higher vocation than the monk's. Please God that we may one day don the cowl for which my soul longs. Merely to think of it fills me with great joy. But by our own strength we can never attain to this; we can attain to it only if God calls us to it." [9] Even Tolstoy, for all his opposition to the Church, was to experience the loving-kindness of Russian monasticism. During his last flight, at dead of night, he knocked at a monastery door to ask whether he might spend the night there even though he had been excommunicated. "We receive everyone," was the doorkeeper's answer. Those simple words epitomize an attitude permanently characteristic of Eastern Christian monasticism.

It was in Western Christendom, however, that monasticism flourished most abundantly. During the barbarian invasions that engulfed the Roman Empire like a second Flood, the monasteries served as so many arks, salvaging the greater part of the writings of the classical authors, of the primitive Church, and of the Fathers. Monasticism reached its peak in the Middle Ages; nearly all the great religious figures of the time were members of orders, and it is mostly to them that we owe whatever great Christian achievements the period produced. The religious orders constituted the spiritual arsenal of the Church; monks were the mainstay of medieval Christendom.

Most of the orders were founded in pre-Reformation times, but only within the Catholic Church have they continued to receive the care and the encouragement they require. That is why one tends to identify monasticism with the Catholic Church. In any case, they are intimately connected, and have constantly enriched one another. For the Church the orders have been an inexhaustible well of holiness without which the Christian soil would long since have dried out. They have given the Church an abundance of saints whose

[9] N. Gogols sämtliche Werke, ed. Buek, V, 143.

lives have both demonstrated the transcendent character of Christianity and inspired other men to love it. Catholicism without monasticism is, indeed, unimaginable. It is not surprising, therefore,
that those who desire to deal a mortal blow to the Catholic Church
always begin by attacking the monasteries, the true powerhouses of
Catholicism.

Yet while the Catholic Church lives primarily by the spiritual
substance of her orders, and not by their political action, the progress of monasticism within the Church has been neither smooth
nor steady. The curve shows sheer ascents succeeded by steep de-
clines—but these latter are always made up again. New orders
have constantly sprung up, affording the best proof of the Church's
inner vitality. This fruitfulness certainly did not come to a halt
with the founding of the Society of Jesus, with which the present
work concludes. The founders of orders we treat in these pages are
only the outstanding ones; they are far from exhausting the list.

That Protestantism saw the light of day in the lonely cell of a
monastery is too often forgotten. For nineteen years Luther belonged to a religious order, and monasticism was an aid far more
than an obstruction in his path. His religious development, however, brought him into serious conflict with the monastic world,
and only at the very end of his life did he come to appreciate the
regenerated monasteries as fortresses of peace in a wicked world.[1]
But he arrived at this conclusion too late to prevent Protestantism
from inheriting his earlier antagonism to monasticism, and that
anti-monastic attitude has remained with it ever since. Luther's
tragic step is too often oversimplified, and there is a tendency to
forget that, in the depths of his soul, "he remained a monk, even
though he no longer belonged to an order." [2]

There are positive overtones even in Melanchthon's *Apologia
Confessionis Augustinae*, with all its attacks on monasticism; he
speaks, for instance, of a few monasteries that "do know the holy
Gospel of Christ," [3] and considers that "Bernard, Francis, and

[1] R. Thiel: *Luther* (Philadelphia: Muhlenberg Press; 1955).
[2] F. Parpert: *Das Mönchtum in der evangelischen Kirche* (1930), p. 55.
[3] *Die symbolischen Bücher der evangelisch-lutherischen Kirche*, ed.
Müller (1882), p. 272.

other" founders of orders should not be identified with the corrupt monasticism of his own day.[4]

In any case, early Protestantism was hardly in a position to debate these matters; it was in a state of active warfare, and was therefore obliged to combat monasticism in all its forms, eradicating it down to the last decaying institutions for ladies of noble birth. The modern Protestant attitude on this score was expressed by Adolf von Harnack: "The Reformation abolished monasticism, and was bound to abolish it. It rightly affirmed that to take a vow of lifelong asceticism was a piece of presumption; and it rightly considered that any worldly vocation, conscientiously followed in the sight of God, was equal to, nay, was better than, being a monk. But something now happened which Luther neither foresaw nor desired: 'monasticism' of the kind that is conceivable and necessary in the evangelical sense of the word disappeared altogether. But every community stands in need of personalities living exclusively for its ends. The Church, for instance, needs volunteers who will abandon every other pursuit, renounce 'the world,' and devote themselves entirely to the service of their neighbor; not because such a vocation is 'a higher one,' but because it is a necessary one, and because no Church can live without also giving rise to this desire. But in the evangelical Churches the desire has been checked by the decided attitude they have been compelled to adopt towards Catholicism. It is a high price that we have paid; nor can the price be reduced by considering, on the other hand, how much simple and unaffected religious fervor has been kindled in home and family life." [5]

Protestantism was the poorer for suppressing monasticism. The Baptists who attempted in their own way to remedy this loss were accused by Heinrich Bullinger of new monkery. Nevertheless, various attempts have been made to introduce monasticism within the framework of Protestantism, and these attempts should not be regarded as the product of mere romantic enthusiasm. We might mention the gentle Gerhard Tersteegen, who organized a Protestant

[4] Ibid., p. 275.
[5] Adolf von Harnack: *What Is Christianity?* (New York: G. P. Putnam's Sons; 1901), lecture xvi, p. 288.

monastic community on the Otterbeck estate, giving it rules that have become a revered document of Protestant monasticism. Following in the footsteps of the Mühlheim weaver, Jean de Labadie tried to organize a similar group in Holland. And Albrecht Ritschl noted the connection between monasticism and the sort of Pietism evident in the rule for German deaconesses.

Some individual Protestants, moreover, have shown quite unexpected leanings toward the monastic life. Sören Kierkegaard, in particular, makes repeated references to medieval monasticism in his principal work, Concluding Unscientific Postscript. It is characteristic that he should not only have been the first once again to regard Christianity as an existential doctrine, but also should have felt that he himself belonged to the monastic world. In his autobiographical work, The Point of View for My Work as an Author, he remarks that when he was writing Either-Or, in which he set out his views on ethics and esthetics, he was already, religiously speaking, in the cloister—as shown by his use of the name "Victor-Eremita." He saw himself as a man dwelling in a monastery, and Martin Thust in his monograph on Kierkegaard stresses the theme: "Kierkegaard was a Protestant monk in the sense that he was able to achieve a unique combination of what was deepest in the old monastic way of life with that vindication of life in the world which is characteristic of the Reformation." [6]

These different attempts in the direction of monasticism must not, of course, be overestimated; nevertheless, they are symptomatic of a deficiency in Protestantism. The problem has never been fully resolved in the Protestant Church, and it should, indeed, be kept alive. To deal with it is more than ever important, now, when it has become only too apparent that community consciousness by itself offers too narrow a basis for the Christian life. The tragedy occurs when the community, as one of Bernanos's characters has it, becomes a dead community. The Christian life has to be anchored in something deeper than church communities, and Christian brotherhood offers just such an anchorage.

[6] Martin Thust: Sören Kierkegaard (1931), p. 416.

III

A historical sketch of the development of Christian monasticism would be incomplete without a further analysis undertaken from the point of view of religion. This would be in the nature of an inquiry into the essential significance of monasticism, a weighing of it, as it were, on Job's scales, to assay its worth in the light of eternity.

We are reminded, in this connection, of the famous words of a sixteenth-century German general, Georg von Frundsberg: "My dear little monk, you are taking a step the like of which neither I nor many a commander in our fiercest battle would take. If you are sure of being right, thoroughly convinced that your cause is of God, then proceed in the name of God, and be of good cheer: God will never forsake you." [7] These words, spoken on a memorable occasion, could be applied validly to all monks. Nor has the diminutive "little" any derogatory intent; on the contrary, it betrays something akin to tenderness. For the path of the monk has never been easy or smooth; it leads to stark heights and somber depths, and keen courage is needed to tread it.

We shall not grasp the religious significance of monasticism by looking at it through rose-colored spectacles. Uncritical admiration is the principal defect, for instance, of the Comte de Montalembert's monumental study, *The Monks of the West;* it is doubtless to be ascribed to the author's personal inexperience of the monastic life. The seasoned religious speaks in very different tones from those of the French romanticist, but he loves his cloister none the less for that. What is needed is not insipid, sometimes downright dishonest, eulogy, but an altogether new language. And this means discarding completely the kind of apologetics which, like Job's friends, uses deceit in defense of God (Job xiii, 7); it means pointing frankly to shortcomings. Nor does such frankness derogate from the reverence that the subject deserves. It is quite unnecessary to gloss over the infirmities of monasticism. The reality of monasticism

[7] J. T. Kostlin: *Life of Luther* (Philadelphia: Lutheran Publication Society; 1883), chap. ix, p. 218.

encompasses both heroic fulfillment and pitiful failure, and it proves its Christian vitality precisely when it endures the hardest blows.

The monk is called to a life that is far from ordinary. Unfortunately, too many merely ordinary men have sought to embrace it and, being unequal to the hardships it entails, have failed lamentably. It is they who have given rise to the absurd notion that the cloistered are prisoners of their own making, gloomily wasting their lives and depriving their countries of useful citizens. It is they, too, who have created the repulsive character of the monk who seeks to deceive God by means of his tonsure, as Benedict of Nursia puts it in his rule. Such people, who have no vocation, would do better to "leap over the wall" like Monica Baldwin, but it is certain that no one who has really been called will leap after them. The saddest part of it is the general corruption to which such individual attitudes have led. The decline of monasticism in the late Middle Ages which resulted from the decay of monastic discipline had catastrophic consequences for the whole of Christendom.

The dark pages of monasticism, which its adversaries cite with glee, must not be mistaken for monasticism itself. At the same time, we have no intention of overrating the importance of monasticism by calling it the highest form of the Christian life. Monks themselves have warned against that kind of exaggeration. In the letters of the Russian *staretz* Feofan, for instance, we read: "It is best not to consider whether or not one is called to the cloister; that is not the point. If the cloister is in a man's heart, it is immaterial whether the building is actually there. The cloister in one's heart means only this: God and the soul." [8] How admirably put! In appraising the monastic life, we must not be more monkish than the monks.

Considered from the point of view of religion, monasticism cannot but impress one by its greatness. In certain periods its positive contribution far outweighs its deficiencies. Its cultural achievements are there for all to see, and their value is permanent.

And yet to consider only its cultural achievements is to miss the whole point of the monastic life. For Christian monasticism can be comprehended only in terms of its own premises, and they are of an eminently religious nature. If we do not see monasticism as

[8] Bubnoff, ed.: *Russische Frömmigkeit* (1947), p. 112.

an absolutely Christian phenomenon, we do not really see it at all. What is far more significant than all its external achievements is the love of God, a love directed straight to the eternal, a love that flourishes in the cloister like a rose.

The monk is the religious man *par excellence*, whose ardent desire to save his soul governs his every action. He sacrifices everything to his fervent love of Christ, which blazes in him like another burning bush. By means of the rule that he seeks to fulfill, he achieves discipline, and the Christian precepts to which he deliberately submits shape and illumine his whole life. His wholehearted submission to the supremacy of an absolute lends his life an aspect of order to which all confusion, internal or external, is wholly alien. This inner security gives the monastic life its aura of the divine.

By his deference to the rule, the monk is freed from the agitation and perplexity that harass the lives of other men. He knows where he wants to go, and he knows the way there; when he entered the cloister, he resolved to tread that way unfalteringly. The monk is a guide who does not simply tell others where to go, but goes there himself. It is hardly possible to predicate anything greater of a human being, and here we approach the permanent mystery of all monasticism. One of the main causes of the attraction that monasticism has never ceased to exercise lies precisely in the monk's spiritual power to draw from the rich storehouse of his superior religious experience a positive answer to the problems of our troubled lives. There is nothing we need more, in our cheerless times, than these people who can direct souls, and from whom a healing virtue goes forth.

The objection that this is not a life that suits everyone is easily dismissed. Of course it does not suit everyone. But is there any way of life that would? Nevertheless, monasticism possesses a mysterious power of irradiation capable of penetrating to the darkest recesses of man's being. There are few institutions, indeed, in which the power the Gospel can release in man is so clearly visible. We must learn once more to see monks with the eyes of Léon Bloy: "Those men of prayer, unlettered, uncomplaining under the goad of persecution, whom we, in our idiotic sufficiency, assume to despise, those men bore the heavenly Jerusalem in their hearts and in their minds. They translated their ecstasies, as best they could, into the stone of the cathedrals, into the burning windows of the chapels, into the parchments of the books of hours. And all our endeavor, if we have but a particle of genius, is to return to that source of light. . . ." [9]

IV

These words bring us to another point: the mission of contemporary monasticism, which we should consider in the light of our analysis of monasticism from the historical and religious points of view. There is no question, here, of championing a cause with single-minded passion; we are simply anticipating a particular result. The comments that follow should be regarded as the logical conclusion of the work as a whole; they are an epilogue offered as a prologue.

If we look squarely at the twentieth century, which refuses to learn from the experience of two world wars, we can hardly do otherwise than call it the century of destruction. Hurtling from one catastrophe into another, our world seems unable to find a way out of this vortex of death. The hideous symbol of this century is the man armed with a machine gun, stumping off over endless heaps of ruins. And every Christian who really takes his faith seriously is weighed down by the questions: What solution is there to this demonic apocalypse? Who is capable of offering effective challenge to the Beast from the Abyss? Who has the inner strength to meet the robot of our times and defeat him in spiritual combat? These are the tremendous questions that will run like a basic theme through Christian history in the coming decades.

To expect any solution from statesmen is vain. They cannot give what they do not possess. Governments think too exclusively in terms of politics and military strategy, to the total neglect of the spirit. That is why they are now so completely barren of any new ideas, and have to depend solely on diplomacy, which has constantly proved its inadequacy. Only Christianity can provide the means of reversing the tide that threatens to engulf civilization.

[9] Léon Bloy: *La Femme pauvre* (Paris: Mercure de France; 1913), chap. xxii, p. 158.

By Christianity we do not mean an interpretation of the Gospel which is itself tainted by corruption, but rather a renewed Christianity whose heralds will again go forth wholly unarmed, like sheep among wolves, truly obedient to the new commandment of love by which Christ's disciples are known, and constituting another little flock that has been granted the living hope of the kingdom.

Any attempt to achieve this renewal, to arrive at a Christianity free from compromise of any sort, must necessarily involve a return to the founders of the religious orders. Indeed, a renewal of the orders, in their original intent, would be one of the most effective aids in the spiritual conflict of our times. Such a reversion to the founders, unfettered by any preconceived ideas, would lead to a wonderful flowering of the noblest traditions of Western Christendom. The fundamental and timeless virtues of the primitive Church find their purest expression in the founders of the great orders, and those monasteries whose primitive zeal has ebbed will be reinvigorated only by hearkening to their founders. The founders of the orders can be likened to a seed able to germinate, quite unexpectedly, centuries later. That is why a return to the spirit of the founders is the precondition for the new mission of monasticism in our times. If their first coming had such powerful effect, how great will be the consequences of their second epiphany for the life of the world!

Another major possibility is the deliberate endeavor to create new orders. A seemingly fantastic undertaking, perhaps, until we consider that, at a time when the face of monasticism is so radically changing, it need be no utopia. Indeed, that idea is really the purpose of the present work. And the reader must therefore bear with the author if he sometimes presents in faltering tones thoughts to which he would rather have lent the accent of adjuration.

The Christian knows, of course, that the Almighty is able to fulfill His plans in a thousand different ways that man has not even dreamed of. Yet it is difficult not to believe that it will be new religious foundations that will transform our times. Salvation, one feels, will come from a new, transfigured monasticism.

In order to realize the need for new monastic foundations, we have only to recall the significance of the religious orders of knighthood for the Middle Ages. How much poorer Christendom became when these lines of communication between religion and the state disappeared! Nor will modern Christendom endure unless the spirit of monasticism is injected into our society anew. The urgency of this problem can no longer be ignored, but it must on no account be approached from a partisan, sectarian point of view, which never serves truth. Threatened Christendom needs new orders because only a new "brotherhood of those marked by pain," as Albert Schweitzer put it, can provide the antidote to the spiritual malady of our day.

The creation of new orders is by no means outside the realm of possibility, as modern skeptics would have us believe, arguing that nowadays people are no longer capable of such self-sacrificing renunciation, of such an otherworldly approach to life. To this doubt, faith makes answer in the words of Christ: with God all things are possible. And the first timid steps are already being made in that direction. We might mention, among the various indications of this kind, the Protestant venture of Taizé, near Cluny, even though it is still in its infancy. The development of similar communities of women in western Switzerland and Germany is proof that this undertaking is meeting a deep-seated need.

Deliverance from the distress of our times can come only from small groups with the courage to remain small, at first, so as not to be burdened by unsuitable elements. Their community life must be based on monastic rules that include binding vows and recognize the principle of religious sacrifice. In the new religious foundations the waters of mysticism are again beginning to flow. For the mystical life, which is one of the most essential conditions of a Christian renaissance, can flourish only in silence, and only in the mystical life can man achieve true union with God, without which there is no recovery.

But the new monasticism can bring about a real transformation in contemporary attitudes only if it does not remain entrenched behind a wall of traditional thinking. Instead of acting simply as the custodian of the past, it must deliberately turn toward the future. The new foundations must blaze new trails and not be satisfied with being mere replicas of earlier orders. Throughout monastic history, such daring ventures have been undertaken. For all that they are rooted in eternity, the new orders must wear the colors of the twentieth century, just as the eremitic movement was cast in a fourth-century mold.

However much we may long for new orders, they cannot be artificially created if they are not to be a mere sham. What is holy can never be commanded; it always grows like a living organism, and almost in silence. That the founders of the old orders were saints, sent by God at particular historical moments, is no coincidence. Holiness is as inseparably linked with the emergence of an order as is the order's providential mission in history. New orders can only be prayed for; their creation depends on the breath of the Spirit. The founders of orders were vessels of the divine choice, and their foundations were works of grace. Authentic orders are always creations of the Spirit; hence their irresistible advance in their own times. And that is why, too, a new order may come into being at any time.

Until such time, we might well recall Dostoevsky's Alyosha, that unique figure of holiness in an unholy setting. Surprisingly enough, Dostoevsky, who contributed so greatly to the understanding of the Russian monk, and who saw in him the bulwark against nihilism, does not let Alyosha, the beloved disciple, remain in Father Sossima's monastery, but expressly sends him out into the world, which needs him so very urgently. The intention is not that Alyosha should share in that "Karamazov vileness" which was the downfall of his brothers, Mitya and Ivan. On the contrary, Alyosha hastens off like an angel in human form to bring the message of salvation into the very heart of his brothers' pain-racked world. Inwardly, Alyosha is enclosed in Father Sossima's monastery, but outwardly he is in the world. By this duality he personifies the hidden cloister in the midst of the sinister world of the Karamazovs. By his mission, he appears as one of the first harbingers of that transfigured monasticism which we are waiting for and which will surely come. The Alyosha of our times will be a new kind of monk, proclaiming to the modern world a Christian message that alone can save it from its present peril.

Saint ANTHONY

and the Hermits of the Desert

O NE DAY late in the third century, an event took place which in itself was unremarkable, although it proved momentous in its consequences. The scene was a church in the little township of Coma, in Upper Egypt. There, during a service, the Gospel story of the Rich Young Man was read out, as it had been read out many times before, when its only apparent effect had been to fill the faithful with a pious glow. But on this occasion a young man named Anthony was listening, and it seemed to him, as his biographer wrote, that "the reading had been directed especially to him." [1] The texts of Holy Writ lie dormant, as it were, for long periods of time, till suddenly the power enclosed in them begins to stir in an individual heart, and the world is set on fire.

Jesus' reply to the Rich Young Man: "If thou wilt be perfect, go, sell that thou hast and give to the poor, and thou shalt have treasure in heaven; and come, follow me" (Matt. xix, 21), plunged Anthony into a state of mental anguish which marked the beginning of his spiritual awakening. The very foundations of his life seemed to be called in question, for he too had great possessions. But Anthony did not turn sorrowfully away, like the Rich Young Man whose boasting "all these things have I kept from my youth up" had ended in such tragic failure. He could not even wait for the service to end, but rushed out of the church to act on the command.

It was indeed a memorable occasion. For once, at a Christian

[1] R. D. Meyer, ed.: *Saint Athanasius' Life of Saint Antony* (Westminster, Md.: The Newman Press; 1950), chap. ii.

service, the story of the Rich Young Man was taken literally, un-
compromisingly, and that once was enough to launch a movement
of incalculable proportions. It was only the rich young man who
returned to the Master who could bring the Gospel scene to its
proper fulfillment.

But Anthony's religious crisis did not come upon him unexpectedly. He was born of Christian parents about A.D. 250 at
Coma, and was brought up in the Christian faith. He was a sensitive and retiring child, and rarely played with other children of his
age; in fact, he deliberately shunned their company. On the death
of his parents, he busied himself with the administration of their
estate, which he had inherited. This property made of him, too, a
rich young man, at the same time burdening him with multiple
cares owing to the vexing system of taxation which prevailed in
Egypt. These circumstances combined to prepare the way for the
crisis that now broke upon the twenty-year-old youth.

Jesus' requirement for attaining perfection was the renunciation
of property: "Sell that thou hast and give to the poor." Anthony
could not take those words as a diluted, "spiritual" exhortation or
as an invitation that Jesus had addressed only to one man long since
dead. He took them in their most radical meaning, as an unmistakable and inexorable command. Accordingly, he began to give
his possessions to the inhabitants of Coma. The rest he sold and
gave the proceeds to the poor, reserving only a small sum for the
benefit of his little sister.

This was a step of fundamental significance. Man clings with all
the fibers of his being to what he has, and it takes an almost superhuman act of self-conquest to surrender it. He has to cut right into
his living flesh, so to speak, if he is to respond to the absoluteness
of Jesus' behest. Eternal life is a prize for which a man must play
his highest stakes, and that, according to Jesus' teaching, includes
the renunciation of possessions. No one who hesitates between God
and Mammon will reach perfection. That is why a man must give
up his possessions, which bind his heart and thus prevent him from
achieving freedom. Yet only extraordinary individuals are prepared
to make such a radical break with the standards of the world. And
it was precisely because he had not been able to go that far that

the young man in the Gospel had turned sorrowfully away. Anthony, on the other hand, was one of those heroic figures, so that he could personify, as it were, on a higher level, the Rich Young Man returning to accept the Lord's invitation.

By giving away his possessions, Anthony cast off his golden shackles and entered upon the path of the extraordinary. This liberation from the bondage of possession was the astonishing and marvelously fruitful starting-point in Anthony's life. It enabled him to gain that immeasurable treasure in heaven of which Jesus had spoken, the positive fulfillment of the negative action of renunciation of property.

It is this encounter with Jesus' words to the Rich Young Man which throws most light on Anthony, and not his Egyptian background, although that, too, of course, must be borne in mind. In any case, he had received no education, and spoke only Coptic, and the Copts were less receptive than any other people to the Hellenic form of Christianity. Anthony's action can be explained primarily by his own greatness of soul, which led him to respond so literally and so wholeheartedly to Jesus' call to perfection. And only his own religious experience made him capable of introducing into Christendom an element that was absolutely new, or at least that had never before been present in such a form.

For Anthony, to follow Jesus was virtually synonymous with asceticism. He had taken Jesus' words as a personal invitation to distribute his goods, and asceticism was the logical corollary. So he moved to a hut at the edge of the village in order to cut himself off from the society of men. But he made the break gradually, avoiding any precipitate action. He took as his model an old man living the ascetic life in solitude not far from there, and from him he learned the rudiments of his new way of existence.

Anthony believed in the importance of manual work as such, deeming it to be the first step to sanctification. And asceticism he regarded in the light of St. Paul's teaching in I Timothy (iv, 16), as the "taking heed unto oneself" and the acquiring of the most stringent control over one's person.

He set out systematically on the path of asceticism which he had chosen. According to his biographer, "he observed the graciousness of one, the earnestness at prayer of another; studied the even temper of one and the kindheartedness of another; fixed his attention on the vigils kept by one and on the studies pursued by another; admired one for his patient enduring, another for his fasting and sleeping on the ground." [2] Whatever pious practices he observed in others, he sought to apply himself. He imposed ever harsher conditions on himself, and this ascetic training transformed him. "For instance, he kept nocturnal vigil with such determination that he often spent the entire night sleepless, and this not only once, but many times. . . . Again, he ate but once a day, after sunset; indeed, sometimes only every other day, and frequently only every fourth day did he partake of food. His food was bread and salt, his drink, water only." [3] He slept on a rush mat or simply on the bare ground.

By his ascetic labors, Anthony introduced the powerful theme that runs through the whole history of monasticism. The man who is filled with a blind appetite for the pleasures of this life tends to misunderstand the nature of asceticism, to regard it as an unprofitable exercise in self-torture. It runs counter to his instinct for life. But a little reflection will show that such an attitude is untenable for a Christian. Asceticism is indeed inherent in the Gospel, and the reality of asceticism is far removed from so superficial a conception of it. Essentially, it is the daily effort to give the mastery to the things of the spirit. Anthony believed that "the soul's energy thrives when the body's desires are feeblest." [4]

This magnificent energy of soul is the purpose of asceticism, nothing else. By the development of his spiritual powers, a man discovers a completely new world that external realities have obscured. But this discovery does not come as a matter of course; it can take place only when the soul's energy is at its peak.

Spiritual reality can be reached only at the expense of the flesh; nor can any spiritual man refuse to struggle with himself unceasingly if he does not want to backslide imperceptibly. It is easy to see whether a Christian is seeking to sublimate his natural appetites so as to make them fruitful for the life of the spirit, or whether he is simply surrendering to their demands, a position that always leads

[2] Ibid., chap. iv.   [3] Ibid., chap. vii.   [4] Ibid.

to the death of the soul. True asceticism is not the product of negation; the ascetic is one who has discovered a delectable treasure that
summons him from the lowlands of ordinary living to the exhilarat-
ing peaks of the spirit.

Asceticism, which heightens the energies of the soul, has always
been a creative element in human history, releasing tremendous
spiritual power. It has had its exaggerations, of course, destructive
of life and therefore uncreative. But such negative asceticism must
be regarded as a corruption, against which genuine ascetics issue a
warning. Anthony, for instance, said: "There be some that wear
out their bodies with abstinence: but because they have no discretion
they be a great way from God." [5] Misuse is thus counterbalanced
by proper use based on the view that ascetic discipline is a necessary means, not an end in itself.

But Anthony, for all his asceticism, did not achieve his goal
without a struggle. Because asceticism is the means to perfection,
he was soon faced with great temptations. As he dwelt alone in his
hut on the edge of the village, memories of his former possessions
crowded in on him; he remembered his little sister with a sudden
renewal of affection; he longed for the comforting companionship
of his fellow men. Greed for money surged in his heart, and
thoughts of the multiple pleasures of the palate and a thousand other
pleasures paraded tantalizingly before his soul. He thought how
hard was the practice of virtue, how great the exertions it required;
he was oppressed by the thought that his own body was so weak,
the time of trial so long. In addition, he was assailed by the noisy
clamors of sensuality: erotic images obsessed his mind; at night the
forms of lovely maidens seemed to advance toward him. According
to Athanasius, the Devil "raised up in [Anthony's] mind a great
dust-cloud of arguments, intending to make him abandon his set
purpose." [6] Anthony was delivered to the powers of temptation,
which closed in on him from every side in an attempt to destroy
his inner balance. Temptations surged over him like the waves of
a stormy sea, threatening to engulf him.

The elemental tumult that deafened his soul made of Anthony

[5] H. Waddell: *The Desert Fathers* (London: Constable; 1936), p. 138.
[6] Meyer, ed.: op. cit., chap. v.

the prototype of the man who suffers temptation. It is impossible to talk about him without referring to these raging temptations against which he battled so courageously, against which he put up the desperate resistance of an ascetic, with the weapons of fasting and prayer. His countless temptations have become legendary in the history of mankind.

Temptation is a Christian theme, and it recurs constantly throughout the New Testament. It is not some transitory phenomenon, but a part of the human condition. Man's lot is temptation, not security. To the extent that he has any self-knowledge, he realizes that he is always besieged by temptation, and ever and again he is forced to cry, from the depths of his heart: "Lead us not into temptation." And the religious man, more than any other, is a prey to temptation. Asked why there should be such a thing as temptation at all, Anthony gave an answer that is worth reflecting on: "Take away temptation, and no one will be saved." [7]

We should pause at these words, for they are the product of a religious experience accessible to very few. For this prototype of the man assailed by temptation had also grasped the permanent significance of all temptation; it gives the Christian the means of proving himself. In temptation, man is tried as gold in the fire; the dross falls away. Temptation is a test, and without it life would come near to a drifting into total indifference, where all spiritual combat ceases.

After fifteen years spent in self-conquest in his hut on the borders of the village, Anthony cut himself off still more from his fellow men by moving into one of the tombs that lined the stony ridges on the outskirts of the near-by desert. This second phase of his spiritual life was marked by even greater solitude; he permitted only one friend to bring him bread at very infrequent intervals.

What Anthony experienced in his tomb beggars the imagination; it was horrible beyond belief. One shrinks at so much as referring to it at all, yet it is impossible to see Anthony as the man he was if we ignore this episode. On the contrary, we have to draw attention to the sinister forces that threatened the very life of the father

[7] M. Viller and K. Rahner: *Aszese und Mystik in der Väterzeit* (1939), p. 119.

of hermits, for only against this somber background can we glimpse Anthony's achievement in its stark, unadorned reality. A man who strives so powerfully toward the kingdom of light must necessarily encounter opposition from the hordes of Satan.

Anthony did not wait for Satan to come to him; he sought the enemy out on his own territory. It was in order to seize the offensive himself that he had moved into the tomb, which was completely dark and, as the Egyptians believed, haunted by demons. He entered alone into the mortuary chamber and locked the door behind him, as his biographer takes care to note,[8] thereby emphasizing his complete separation from the world.

· No sooner was he in the tomb than he began to experience the Devil's presence physically. Because the hermit was pressing the enemy so hard and so defiantly, the Devil took up the challenge. It was no learned debate that these two adversaries engaged in, peacefully seated upon a bench. What the doughty ascetic undertook was a veritable duel with Satan, a fight to the death.

Satan, we are told, "came one night with a great number of demons and lashed him so unmercifully that he lay on the ground speechless from the pain. He maintained that the pain was so severe that the blows could not have been inflicted by any man and cause such agony."[9]

Being too feeble to stand, Anthony prayed lying down. When his prayer was finished, he called out to his assailants: "Here am I, Anthony. I am not cowed by your blows!"[1] And he proceeded to sing a psalm. But the demons, unabashed, only rushed at him with even wilder cries, determined to destroy him. The pandemonium was deafening, drowning out the psalm-singing and causing the whole place to rock and to quake.

But the worst was to come, and Anthony's titanic struggle with the powers of darkness threatened to end in his defeat. In the midst of the most terrible combat, the demons, according to his biographer, assumed the shapes of beasts and reptiles. "All at once the place was filled with the phantoms of lions, bears, leopards, bulls, and of serpents, asps, and scorpions, and of wolves; and each moved according to the shape it had assumed. The lion roared, ready to spring

---

[8] Meyer, ed.: op. cit., chap. viii.   [9] Ibid.   [1] Ibid., chap. ix.

upon him, the bull appeared about to gore him through, the serpent writhed without quite reaching him, the wolf was rushing straight at him; and the noises emitted simultaneously by all the apparitions were frightful and the fury shown was fierce. Anthony, pummeled and goaded by them, felt even severer pain in his body; yet he lay there fearless and all the more alert in spirit. He groaned, it is true, because of the pain that racked his body, but his mind was master of the situation" [2] and he jeered at his tormentors. And so he remained as ready for the fray as before, his faith unshaken in Christ's final victory over Satan.

And just as the onslaughts had reached their peak of frenzy, God took pity on his steadfast servant and bestowed on him a first revelation that dispelled the fearful darkness like the brightness of the sun. "For he looked up and saw as it were the roof opening and a beam of light coming down to him." [3] The demons disappeared and Anthony received the assurance that God had been with him from the start and had delayed helping him only in order to see how he would acquit himself in his utmost peril.

Anthony's struggles with Satan's hordes fall outside any category of normal human experience. For a moment, the carefully concealed recesses of man's spirit stand revealed, and we glimpse the warfare that the powers of darkness wage for the possession of man's soul. That is why Anthony's struggles with the Devil must not be glossed over as though they were indicative of some shameful weakness of his own. On the contrary, it is only in the light of this duel with the Devil that we can really understand Anthony at all. For this experience reveals the inmost depths of his soul, and we find ourselves in the presence of a reality before which the human tongue falters.

But only for a moment is this insight vouchsafed to us. A thousand objections immediately arise, obscuring the lightning-like clarity of our perception. It would be best, really, to reserve one's judgment concerning an event that shows so vividly what man is capable of. But this prudent reserve is exceptional. We are far more inclined either to complain that Anthony's biographer concedes too great a role to the Devil [4] or, as moderns, to dismiss all

---

[2] Ibid.   [3] Ibid., chap. x.   [4] Viller and Rahner: op. cit., p. 86.

talk of the Devil out of hand as crass superstition or as the product
of an overheated imagination and nervous disorder. Since the Renaissance, there has been a tendency to relegate stories involving the
Devil to the status of delusions wholly divorced from reality. Nevertheless, the last word has not been spoken concerning this somber
side of human life. Anyone who disputes the existence of evil spirits
merely closes the door to the magnificent world of the early Christian solitaries, and his thinking is thereby denied an essential dimension in depth.

Those who still think of the satanic monster in terms merely of
horns and a tail should let Denis de Rougemont open their eyes
concerning "the role of the devil in our culture." [5] Prophetic poets
and writers like Baudelaire, Strindberg, Dostoevsky, and Bernanos,
who, by their genius, have penetrated the obscure regions of the
spirit, have used far from poetic language to describe the reality of
the Devil. Their testimony gives the lie to the freethinkers' assumption that belief in the Devil is a mere survival from a primitive
mentality. They speak forthrightly of the horror of the satanic
forces, and, having themselves borne the Devil's cruel yoke, are
obliged to confess that it is hard, indeed, to shake off. Or should we
counter such statements with Nietzsche's comment that poets are all
too often liars? The Gospels, however, are full of stories of encounters with evil spirits, whose role was in fact to bear witness to
the mystery of the Messiah.

Anthony's struggle with Satan is simply the working out in detail of a truth only hinted at in the accounts of the casting out of
devils which we find in the Gospels; hence, it can be properly understood only in the light of the fact that "Jesus was led up of the
Spirit into the wilderness to be tempted of the devil" (Matt. iv, 1).
According to St. Peter, "the devil, as a roaring lion, walketh about,
seeking whom he may devour" (I, v, 8). And has he not in fact
devoured virtually the whole of our modern world, with its cult of
standardization and mechanization? The cosmic pictures of Satan
which we find in the Apocalypse acquire a more immediate significance in the light of these monstrous developments. The only

[5] Denis de Rougemont: *The Devil's Share* (New York: Pantheon Books;
1944).

2

consolation in this hour of the Prince of Darkness is to remember the joyful tidings announced by Jesus Himself: "I beheld Satan like lightning fall from heaven" (Luke x, 18).

But it is not easy to talk about this preternatural reality in language that properly applies to it. Evil spirits belong to a sphere concerning which we can form no adequate concepts. Reason is powerless indeed to grasp Anthony's struggles with the demons: it must regard them as fantasies called up by excessive fasting. A new language of symbolism is required. Only Martin Schongauer and Matthias Grünewald have interpreted Anthony's warfare with Satan with their hearts instead of with book knowledge, and thus have been able to look into the depths of human existence. Demonic manifestations, as Anthony himself stated in later years after mature reflection, are not of capital importance in themselves; their place is in that twilight of the indefinable which can be haltingly expressed only by symbols. For symbols are able to render, in terms the imagination can grasp, the supersensual truths that alone render human existence intelligible.

Anthony's own opinion can serve us as a guide in this new attempt to understand the satanic world not simply in a spirit of academic objectivity, but with an inner vision. For he, more than any other, could speak with authority of that world of darkness of which he had had such immediate personal experience. As a seasoned warrior against the powers of darkness, he had a unique insight into the ruses the Devil employs to snare his victims. His biography thus includes a complete demonology, a study that never degenerates into abstraction but is wholly therapeutic in purpose and therefore deserving of far greater attention than it usually receives. Although it bears the clear imprint of fourth-century attitudes, the timeless truth it conveys shines powerfully through. Only so pure a being as Anthony could conjure up the world of the Evil One without harm to his soul.

The father of monks warns us that legions of demons surround us, and he tells us that they are "daring and exceedingly shameless." [6] Not only are they cunning, but they have the power "to

[6] Meyer, ed.: op. cit., chap. xxiii.

undergo every change and transformation." [7] Often "they even pretend to sing psalms without appearing, and to quote sayings from Scripture. . . . At other times they put on the guise of monks and simulate pious talk." [8] A man who regards only edifying words and is not concerned with whether or not they proceed from a right intention is not proof against their deceits. We are also told that demons can go through locked doors, and that they love to indulge in boastful chatter.

The only weapons that Anthony recognized against Satan were prayer and asceticism. He who fears God need not be fearful of these apparitions, for, as Anthony surprisingly remarks: "they are nothing and quickly vanish, especially if a person fortifies himself with the sign of the Cross." [9] In this statement, Anthony gives us the key to the inmost secret of his teachings concerning the powers of darkness. And this certainty leads him to a final conclusion: "Let us, therefore, not give up and become despondent in mind. . . . No, we must not . . . grieve as though we were perishing. Let us rather be of good courage and rejoice always as men who are being saved. Let us ponder in our soul that the Lord is with us, He who put the evil spirits to flight and made them impotent. Let us think this over and ever bear in mind that as long as the Lord is with us, our enemies will do us no harm. For, when they come, they conduct themselves as they find us. . . . If they see us fearful and fainthearted, so much the more do they augment our faintheartedness in the form of phantoms and threats. . . . But if they find us rejoicing in the Lord, meditating on the good things to come and contemplating the things that are the Lord's, considering that everything is in the Lord's hands and that a demon has no power over a Christian . . . then, seeing the soul safeguarded with thoughts such as these, they are put to shame and they turn away." [1]

The joyous tone of these remarks is so striking that it calls for one more brief comment. In Anthony's account of his experiences, two contradictory points of view seem to traverse each other. On the one hand, demons can deal out invisible blows so violent that

---

[7] Ibid., chap. xxv.   [9] Ibid., chap. xxiii.
[8] Ibid.   [1] Ibid., chap. xlii.

their victim cries out with pain. It would seem, therefore, that they were real beings. On the other hand, Anthony regards them as mere phantoms without substance because, as he says, "they are nothing" and appear different according to the mood of each individual. These conflicting viewpoints do not reflect confusion or uncertainty on Anthony's part. On the contrary, they touch the heart of the matter. Demons, in Anthony's view, are both real and unreal beings; they must be regarded as real unrealities, for supreme reality belongs to God alone.

The terrible and victorious struggle that Anthony had waged against the demons did not dull his appetite for feats of daring. He now decided to embark upon one more adventure—retreat into the desert—which was to lead to the final phase of his life.

For Anthony's contemporaries, withdrawal into the desert was something completely new and incomprehensible. Fourth-century Hellenic man was not at all susceptible to the grandeur or the pathos of the wilderness; to him it was simply a thing of unimaginable horror. At best, he would speak of its mystery, of its parched and colorless flatness, of its terrors that the human tongue was powerless to describe. The desert was that soundless, boundless wasteland which stubbornly rejected cultivation at man's hands. It was a sinister place, with its stifling winds that scorched men's lips and its yellow sands that seeped through everything. The bleak wilderness that swallowed up the intruder like some microscopic organism was no friend to man. Neither spiritually nor physically was man capable of penetrating the mystery of this fearful thing which breathed only death, never joy of life. The desert was feared as Satan's own peculiar domain, and whoever entered it thereby cut himself off from the society of men.

The significance of Anthony's decision to withdraw to the desert escapes us at first as completely as the meaning of a chemical formula before we know its terms. The undertaking seems to savor of madness, and only in the light of a more profound understanding do we see it as the symbol of an undying devotion to the Lord. The desert impels strongly toward religion; it offers no distractions and disposes to the deepest concentration. By withdrawing to the desert, Anthony joined the ranks of those biblical figures like Elias, John the Baptist, Jesus, and Paul, for whom the wilderness had a religious significance. Henceforward, the desert was to play an important part in the development of monasticism.

Anthony's deepest desire was to live as a hermit; he could, indeed, pre-eminently be called a monk—"one who lives alone." This ardent thirst for total solitude prompted him to withdraw systematically from human society: first to the outskirts of his own village, then to the burial place on the fringe of the desert, and finally into the depths of the desert itself. Never could he have enough of solitude. And as he wandered on through the trackless wilderness, a heavenly voice directed him, showing him the way. To him this was a proof of God's sanction of his plan.

He arrived finally at an oasis, at the foot of a mountain, and there he stayed. At first he had to depend for his food on the bread that was brought him twice a year; later he began to cultivate a little patch of ground so that he could live by the fruits of his own toil. Inevitably, the wild beasts of the desert were attracted to his garden. Once, we are told, after they had trampled down his vegetables, the hermit gently rebuked them, saying: "Why do you do harm to me, when I harm none of you? Go away, and in the Lord's name do not come near these things again." [2] Nor did they come near again, for Anthony's words were filled with a spiritual power that not even dumb creation could withstand. And this mastery over the beasts, no less than his struggles with the fiends, testifies to his spiritual greatness. The man who dared explore regions that defy exploration towers giant-like above the rest of men.

We cannot follow Anthony into his retreat in the wilderness without asking whence he drew the strength to endure this life of total privation, decade after decade. The only possible explanation is that it flowed into him from his own mystical life. Anthony himself said little enough about it; he did not gossip about his inner experiences, but kept his secret to himself. That he was a mystic, however, is certain, and it is expressly stated that he was sometimes found in a state of ecstasy. He gave a clue to his mystical life when, in answer to a sage who had inquired how he could endure his solitude without the consolation of books, he said: "My book, phi-

---

[2] Ibid., chap. l.

losopher, is the nature of created things, and as often as I have a mind to read the words of God, it is at my hand." [3] According to Athanasius, Anthony "prayed unceasingly, because he had learned that one must pray constantly in one's heart." [4] Unceasing prayer is one of the great Christian mysteries. Anthony, initiated in that mystery, often prayed the whole night through, and called to the rising sun: "Oh sun, why dost thou disturb me by thy early rising, distracting me from the contemplation of the glory of the true light?" It is in such "mighty outbursts of his longing," as Adam Möhler puts it, that Anthony laid bare the heart of his mysticism. [5]

According to Cassian, Anthony once was asked what was the highest prayer, to which he answered that prayer was not perfect so long as a man was aware of himself or of his prayer. [6] That reply epitomizes all mysticism. It expresses the basic truth that in ardent prayer man goes forth from himself, his soul soaring to commune with God. Anthony's prayer was a prayer of ecstasy. He believed that all speech with God transcended human understanding. There is no question of prayer's being contrary to reason; prayer is above reason—wholly above it—sweeping man up into the supernatural.

This union with the eternal enabled Anthony, in his solitude, to withstand any temptation to misanthropy. His biographer tells us that he was never gloomy or discontented. There was nothing of the sour or the morose about him—qualities that do little to recommend Christianity. On the contrary, Athanasius affirms that "the joy in his soul expressed itself in the cheerfulness of his face." [7] The comment is significant: mysticism is closely allied to joy.

How often it happens that what a man desires most is denied him! It was not granted to Anthony to enjoy the fullness of solitude which was his goal. His disappearance into the desert was something so unique, so totally incomprehensible to his fellow men that they could not get him out of their minds. A steady stream of visitors followed him into his retreat, some merely curious, others impelled by weightier reasons. In Anthony's presence, they were conscious

[3] Waddell: op. cit., p. 182.
[4] Meyer, ed.: op. cit., chap. iii.
[5] Adam Möhler: *Gesammelte Schriften und Aufsätze* (1840), II, 177.
[6] A. Kemmer, ed.: *Weisheit der Wüste* (1947), p. 161.
[7] Meyer, ed.: op. cit., chap. lxvii.

of the reality of the divine, which is sought in vain among men caught up in worldly affairs. For a man must be both extraordinarily close to God and altogether removed from the cares of the world if he is to advance in the knowledge of the supernatural. Such knowledge Anthony possessed; according to his biographer, he was "initiated into sacred mysteries." [8] And only mysticism can explain how it was that from this man who had fled the world to live in the desert alone there could flow back into the world a saving power that brought such untold benefits to a distracted humanity.

At first Anthony tried to avoid his visitors; later, compelled by divine charity, he placed himself at their disposal as their spiritual guide. His concern for the sick and the afflicted disposes conclusively of the notion that the eremitic life is a mere cloak for egotism. And people's confidence in this venerable figure, as gentle as he was grave, was virtually boundless.

When someone was faced with an insoluble difficulty, his friends would say to him: "The great [one] is still alive, go to him. . . . And whatsoever word he shall say unto thee, thou shalt perform, for God shall speak unto thee through him." [9] The father of monks was held in such high esteem that his words were regarded as the infallible answer of the Almighty. It is unfortunate that so few of his spiritual counsels have been preserved.

The following delightful anecdote, told by a certain Abba Mathues, shows the unique regard in which he was held. "There were three brethren who were in the habit of coming to Abba Anthony, and . . . two of them used to ask him questions . . . whilst the third one held his peace continually. And after a long time Abba Anthony said unto him, 'Brother, thou comest here each year, and askest nothing!' And he answered and said to the old man, 'It is sufficient for me to see thee.' " [1]

More and more visitors flocked to see him, and his name was on all lips. His biographer gives this wonderful picture of Anthony's pastoral work: "it was as though a physician had been given by God to Egypt. For who came to him in grief and did not return in joy?

[8] Ibid., chap. xiv.
[9] E. A. W. Budge, ed.: *The Paradise of the Holy Fathers* (New York: Duffield and Co.; 1909), I, 194.
[1] Questions and Answers on the Ascetic Rule, no. 161, in ibid., II, 189.

Who came weeping for his dead and did not immediately forget his mourning? Who came in anger and was not transformed into friendliness?" [2] To be Egypt's spiritual physician—that was the charismatic function finally bestowed upon the hermit who had forsaken the world. He was indeed well able to fulfill it, for he never set his own convenience above the needs of his brethren.

The hermit who abode in solitude in the desert was one of the greatest spiritual healers of all times. The sick, too, turned to him for help, and his spiritual power proved superior even to the power of disease. Yet Anthony did not heal by command; he healed by making prayer and supplication to Christ. A number of stories have been handed down concerning the miracles worked at his hands, and they throw a marvelous light on his personality. He was able to work miracles from afar, to perceive events of the invisible world, to drive out devils, and to foretell the future.

Once Anthony left his retreat in the wilderness and appeared unexpectedly in Alexandria, in order to help Athanasius in his struggle with the Arians. For the inhabitants of the Egyptian capital he was a source of constant amazement; they looked on him as on a being from another world. Anthony, in consequence, returned as quickly as he could to the desert, for, as he said, "just as fish exposed for any length of time on dry land die, so monks go to pieces when they loiter among you. . . . Therefore we must go off to the mountain, as fish to the sea." [3]

The ones who profited most from Anthony's pastoral care were those who did more than pay him a fleeting visit. Many Christians were so impressed by his life in the desert that they desired to become his disciples. They saw in him the embodiment of something they had only guessed at, had obscurely longed for. Anthony did not hide from them the terrors of a life so far removed from normal human pursuits. They begged nonetheless to be allowed to stay with him, and in this way, Athanasius writes, "the desert was populated with monks who left their own people and registered themselves for citizenship in heaven." [4]

Anthony was an apt instructor; he had acquired great prowess in

[2] Meyer, ed.: op. cit., chap. lxxxvii.   [4] Ibid., chap. xiv.
[3] Ibid., chap. lxxxv.

the school of asceticism, and he knew that no one could enter upon the solitary life without preparation. He therefore devoted a great deal of time to his disciples. His teachings, as they appear in his biography, are doubtless couched in the language of the author, but the content bears the unmistakable stamp of Anthony's spirit. And here we have a proof that spiritual training accompanied monasticism from its birth.

The keynote of his admonitions was that one should so live as though he daily expected to die.[5] He warned his disciples against pride in their own achievements: "Neither let us look back upon the world and think that we have renounced great things. For even the whole world is a very trifling thing compared with all of heaven." [6]

There are timeless truths in Anthony's teachings concerning man's interior struggle. What wisdom there is in his teaching: "Let every man daily take an accounting with himself of the day's and the night's doings"! [7] His watchfulness over himself had taught him that a man is often blind concerning his own actions, and he counseled his disciples to busy themselves about their own souls, the interior wealth of Christians: "Let us each note and write down our actions and impulses of the soul as though we were to report them to each other; and you may rest assured that from utter shame of becoming known we shall stop sinning and entertaining sinful thoughts altogether." [8] The monk, he said, must strive to make progress daily; only in that way can he achieve uprightness of soul.

Anthony was more than a match, too, for the pagan philosophers who came to visit him. "Those who are equipped with an active faith have no need of verbal argument, and probably find it even superfluous. For what we apprehend by faith, that you attempt to construct by arguments; and often you cannot even express what we perceive. The conclusion is that an active faith is better and stronger than your sophistic arguments." [9]

An eremitic movement rapidly developed as a result of Anthony's teachings. Hermitages sprang up one after another, and the deserts

[5] Ibid., chap. xix.
[6] Ibid., chap. xvii.
[7] Ibid., chap. lv.
[8] Ibid.
[9] Ibid., chap. lxxvii.

of Egypt were soon filled with the cells of anchorites. "And truly it was like seeing a land apart, a land of piety and justice. For there was neither wrongdoer nor sufferer of wrong, nor was there reproof of the tax-collector. . . ." [1] That was how it appeared to a contemporary, and the words convey the very essence of the eremitic life: the creation of another world, governed by quite different laws. To create a new world is truly one of the most magnificent goals toward which a man can strive. It is a grasping at the highest, and it must give the greatest joy to every Christian who wants to be more than just like everyone else. Such an endeavor can issue only from an exceptional soul that aims at surpassing itself.

Inevitably, the fame of the Egyptian physician of souls spread far beyond the boundaries of his own country. His life was regarded as one of the wonders of the world, and stories about his desert retreat were carried to Rome, to Gaul, and to Spain. He was spoken of at the imperial court, and Constantine and his sons wrote to him. Anthony, however, "did not make much of the documents, nor did he rejoice over the letters." [2] It meant nothing, he believed, for a monk to be praised by worldly people; he was proof against the sweet poison of adulation.

St. John Chrysostom in his homilies described Anthony as the greatest man that Egypt had brought forth since the time of the Apostles, and added that his name resounded in every mouth.

It was that passionate champion of orthodoxy, St. Athanasius, who did most to spread Anthony's fame through his magnificent *Vita Antonii*, a powerful document that was widely read at the time and later, and the value of which is increasingly appreciated. Its authenticity, disputed for a time, is now universally recognized. [3] It has the invaluable merit of having been written by a man who knew the father of monks personally. As Athanasius writes, "I saw him often," and in writing the *Life* he was able to make use of the testimony of his own eyes as well as of the reports of Anthony's dis-

---

[1] Ibid., chap. xliv.
[2] Ibid., chap. lxxxi.
[3] See Stefan Schiwietz: *Das morgenländische Mönchtum* (1904), I, 52; and K. Heussi: *Der Ursprung des Mönchtums* (1936), p. 79. See also H. Dörries: "*Die Vita Antonii als Geschichtsquelle*," in *Nachrichten der Akademie der Wissenschaften in Göttingen* (1949).

ciples. Certainly the *Life* is not a historical document in the modern sense—any more than are the Gospels. Its purpose is to kindle enthusiasm, not simply to inform. It is an exaggeration, however, to say that it is devoid of historical truth.[4] An unprejudiced reader will agree with Karl Holl when he says: "We have to search far in antiquity to find any text that can compare with the *Vita Antonii* in point of sobriety of style or artistic brevity. A great theme runs through it from beginning to end, everything is exactly where it should be, and no irrelevancy interrupts the enthralling account." [5]

We are told that, to the end of his life, Anthony wore an undergarment of hair and a top garment of skins. And the simplicity of his death was of a piece with the austerity of his life. Athanasius tells us that, having reached a great age and feeling that he was about to die, he spoke in this wise to the two disciples who were with him at the time: "And now, my children, God bless you; Anthony is going and is with you no more." [6] And with that, he gave up his soul to his Maker. Before his death, he had given instructions concerning his burial in order to prevent any honors being paid to his corpse. He had enjoined upon his disciples that they tell no one where they had buried him, and they kept their word. Like Moses, the first leader of the Chosen People of the Old Testament, so Anthony, the founder of a new people of divine election, was laid to rest in an unknown grave.

Anthony must certainly be regarded as the real founder of the eremitic movement. With him, a completely new type of Christian came into being, whose aim was not to reconcile Christianity and culture, as men in his times were only too readily contriving to do, but to keep them apart. And the consequences were incalculable. No words can encompass all that mankind owes to monasticism.

Could Anthony's grave be discovered, the only epitaph truly appropriate to that contender with demons and physician of souls would be the one that Kierkegaard desired for himself: "the alone." It was alone that Anthony founded monasticism. He sought no help from others; he accomplished his task single-handed. The eremitic

[4] W. Bousset: *Apophthegmata* (1923), p. 91.
[5] K. Holl: *Gesammelte Aufsätze zur Kirchengeschichte* (Tübingen: Mohr; 1928), II, 254.
[6] Meyer, ed.: op. cit., chap. xci.

movement is one of the most telling examples of what a man is able to do alone. The concept of the individual alone, responsible to God, is Christian; it has no relation to an individualism of self-glorification.

The significance of this God-directed individualism is worth considering. Almost everything great in history has been achieved by personal action. Nor can modern man achieve anything worth while unless he seeks, alone, to keep unswervingly to the path of his own calling. The strength of the eremitic movement lay in this aloneness. None could prop himself up against another; each stood alone or fell alone. Each had undertaken his task alone and must accomplish it without the help of others.

Anthony, with his iron determination and a spiritual tautness rarely equaled in human history, should be regarded as the man divinely appointed to combat that dilution of Christianity for mass consumption which was making far-reaching inroads into the Christian Church of his time. He has rightly been described as the strongest witness against the lie of the Constantinian establishment, and if his tremendous influence for good is to be correctly assayed, he must be seen in the context of his age, with all its dualism, as Jakob Burckhardt has described it.

A pandering to the crowd spells mortal danger to Christianity; Anthony pointed to the remedy. In a Christianity of the crowd there ceases to be any genuine relationship between God and the soul, which, if it is to be real, must be personal. If fourth-century Christendom withstood that mortal peril, not the least of the credit must go to the movement initiated by Anthony, in which the cheerless cipher was confronted by the individual, not with much speaking, but by a way of life. That is why at the present time, too, when the steamroller of a mass civilization is crushing the individual, we should look to Anthony. For only "the alone" is spiritually superior to the moloch of an all-absorbing collectivism. We, in our times, too, need an Anthony.

As Karl Hase has put it, Anthony was the childless father of a countless progeny. For his contemporaries, the eremitic life upon which he had embarked spelled salvation from the decadence of the age. It matters a great deal, in the things of the spirit, whether men know of a path they can tread, or whether they are able to complain that no way was shown them. Anthony eliminated that tragic alternative, and at a time when, thanks to Constantine's religious policy, disastrous confusion prevailed concerning Christianity, he showed the means of remedying the evil. Men saw that it was still possible, despite the changed circumstances, to lead a genuinely Christian life.

The remedy discovered by the desert fathers was flight from human society. The hermit's aim was to renounce all the good things of this world, whether wife or child, money or learning. Nothing and no one might have any claim on his person. He sought to be free from all the appetites that prevent a man from serving God with all his heart. Flight was the battle-cry of the hermits, flight to escape the rising tide of corruption, and for close on a century men poured out of the cities, old and young alike, to take up their habitation in the silence of the desert.

The word "flight" does not have a particularly happy connotation; a person who takes flight would appear to be avoiding difficulties instead of facing them. And indeed, if monasticism were only a movement of flight, it would lose much of its importance. But this kind of flight is not simply a negative movement. There are circumstances when "flight from the times" becomes the only proper position. When corruption becomes too widespread, the Christian can avoid it only by turning his back on it completely. When Sodom was about to be destroyed, Lot received the divine command: "Haste thee, escape . . ." (Gen. xix, 22). He was to flee the doomed city of corruption without a backward glance. Jesus, too, urged flight to the mountains (Matt. xxiv, 16) to endure the distress of the last times. Everything has its proper time, flight as well as resistance.

The flight of the hermits in the age of Constantine was a movement from the outward to the inward, a preserving of the content of religion from the canker of superficiality, a withdrawal from futility into the center of being. The hermits had no need to apologize for their flight; theirs was the logical response to the needs of the hour.

It is most significant, too, that the hermits were primarily layfolk, as was their founder, Anthony. Not that they were anticlerical; there was tension, sometimes, between the first monks and the clergy, but never any basic opposition. Monasticism, however, was a lay movement, and was fed out of the ranks of the laity. The monks were in fact reviving the tradition of the religious laity of the first Christian community.

It would be wrong to regard the first monks as no more than a crowd of ignorant and credulous peasants. Even if their education had been neglected, they did not lack sagacity, and their lives were in themselves a practical demonstration of the very essence of eremit-ism—namely, a striving to attain to the center of Christian reality.

Nothing about their way of life was quaint or romantic. On the contrary, in order to attain their goal, they were prepared to scale the uttermost heights of human endurance.

Their housing, to start with, was extraordinary. There was no question of living in a pleasant cell in which a man could make himself at home. Their homes were holes dug in the ground or tiny huts barely large enough for a grown man. They deliberately made their cells so small that they could neither stand erect nor lie down at full length. The hermit's back was always bent as he sat in his cell, his chin resting on his knees. They refused any enlargement of their huts; one of them argued: "I fear that a widening of my earthly dwelling would mean a narrowing of my heavenly one." [7] Others shut themselves up in caves that had no openings to the light. The hermit Akepsimis, for instance, lived like that for over sixty years. He would stretch his hand through a narrow slit in the wall to take the food that was brought him; the slit, however, was cut at an angle, so that the curious should not be able to peer through or the hermit to look out. Another hermit lived in a dried-out cistern, yet another in a tomb.

The hermits' fare was as wretched as their quarters. Anything in the way of flavorsome foods was ruled out. A few edible herbs, bread, and salt made up their staples; their drink was water. Some hermits ate barley, lentils, peas, or beans soaked in water. Some

[7] Theodoret: *Historia Religiosa*, chap. ii, in J.-P. Migne, ed.: *Patrologiae Cursus Completus* (Paris; 1849), LXXXII, 1310.

did not even eat bread, but lived instead on flour moistened with water. They would make a month's supply of this dish at a time so that it should turn moldy and smell. A particular feat of asceticism was the non-use of fire, which meant that all foods were eaten un-cooked. The amount eaten was always very small. Some hermits ate only once a week. Never to eat one's fill, but always to be hungry and thirsty, was the hermit's way. "True fasting is constant hunger" [8] was one of the maxims of the desert.

Their clothing was equally meager. The hermit did not allow his body the comfort of so much as a change of clothing according to the season; winter and summer he wore the same garment, and he was forbidden to possess more than one. Footwear, even in the form of sandals, was out of the question. A hermit would often be garbed in skins, with sometimes only a small opening for the nose and mouth. Of certain hermits it was told that they sought out the shade when it was cold and the sun when it was hot.

Everything else about their life was just as austere. The strictest continence was of course required, and the calls of sensuality were ruthlessly suppressed. Sleep, too, was sacrificed; the hermit allowed himself as few hours of sleep as possible, and spent half the night standing in prayer. Some hermits altogether gave up the comfort of lying down.

To use the language of the desert fathers, all these practices were so many rungs in the ladder to heaven which they were making for themselves.

One condition that applied to all was absolute solitude. The hermit wished to be alone in order to remain in uninterrupted union with the Maker of all things. And in this solitude, complete silence was observed. Visitors, too, were subject to reprimand if they put questions out of mere curiosity or concerning unprofitable matters. Aspiring hermits were often obliged to follow their teachers from afar, so that there might be no opportunity for conversation. It is told of the hermit Solomon that he never spoke to any man. Be-cause the hermits realized how easily the tongue slips, total silence was the general rule.

[8] Ibid., chap. iii.

The monks spent their time in various minor occupations such as mat- and basket-weaving. From the earliest days of monasticism, manual work was regarded as a duty, albeit a secondary one. It was considered unseemly that a monk should sit idle while a man living in the world had to feed wife and children by his toil, pay taxes, offer the first-fruits to the Lord, and relieve the needs of the poor according to his means.

The solitaries considered it important to invent new ascetic practices. Certain hermits, for instance, acting on this principle, began to burden themselves with heavy weights. If one started with 120 pounds of iron, he would subsequently add another 50 pounds, and by the end of his life—if the reports are not exaggerated—he would be carrying around a weight of 250 pounds. Some would drag weights of this kind around day and night, never removing them at any time. They would fasten iron belts about their hips and heavy iron yokes upon their necks. Even women anchorites would load themselves with iron weights that a man could scarcely carry, so that their bodies were bowed down to the earth.

These penitential practices of weight-carrying were a manifestation of that negative asceticism of which the eremitic movement was not wholly innocent. An unhealthy spirit of competition all too frequently drove the hermits on to outdo one another in ever stranger feats of asceticism. Eccentricity undoubtedly took its toll among them, an unfortunate fact that there is no advantage in hiding.

Palladius, in his *Historia Lausiaca*, finds himself compelled to observe that "every monk leadeth the ascetic life as he wisheth and as he is able." [9] In that one sentence, the important eyewitness of the eremitic movement put his finger on the defect that could have brought it to complete disaster. Eremitism almost foundered on the rocks of excessive individualism. For the result was anarchy, a danger inherent in all uncontrolled individualism, which can flourish without pernicious effect only in an ordered society. Because each of the hermits wanted to do something different from his fellows, the oddest practices arose, and their peculiar antics often made them a laughingstock in the eyes of the world. Monasticism, ordained to preserve the essence of Christianity through the chaotic

[9] Budge, ed.: op. cit., I, 99.

times of the collapse of antique civilization, was itself almost destroyed by unbridled individualism.

We have to be cautious, nevertheless, in our verdict regarding
the sometimes curious customs of the desert fathers. The mere fact
that they, after all, dared to go off and live as they did, while their
critics remain comfortably at home, makes the value of the critics'
verdicts—which, in any case, are usually too lightly given—highly
questionable. An unprejudiced approach is essential. We have to
try, at least, to set aside an all too limited personal point of view and
to direct our thinking into new channels. How else should we understand a hermit like Simeon Stylites, who, known as "the mighty and
the great wonder of the world," exerted an inexplicable influence
on his contemporaries from the eminence of his pillar? In his *Historia Religiosa*, Theodoret observes: "I am convinced that he did
not choose this standing without divine dispensation, and therefore
I admonish all fault-finders to curb their tongue and not to give it
free rein." [1]

Both Rufinus and Palladius overemphasized the externals of
eremitism, which do not reflect the essential. And if we stop there,
too, we shall easily be led to regard eremitism as little more than a
curiosity. Certainly the way of life of the hermits must be taken into
account, but only as an indication that something extraordinary was
taking place.

The core of eremitism was an intense spiritual life. The desert
fathers sought to storm heaven by their constant, ardent prayer.
The divine presence was unimaginably real to those men, who spent
their days calling upon God. Not that they used many words in
prayer; they would stretch out their hands and say: "Lord, as thou
wilt and as thou knowest, have mercy upon me." Macarius, of
whom it is said that his whole occupation was silent prayer, told
Palladius of the following experience:

"Every kind and variety of rule of the life of self-denial and
fasting which I have desired to observe with all my heart have I
kept, but there came upon me the desire that my mind should be
with God in Heaven if only for five days, and that I should be
exalted above the anxious cares and thoughts of material things. And

[1] Theodoret: op. cit., chap. xxvi.

having meditated upon this thing, I shut the door of the courtyard and of the cell, and I constrained myself so that I might not give a word to any man. And . . . I commanded my mind, and said unto it, 'Thou shalt not descend from Heaven, for behold, there thou hast angels, and the princes of angels, and all the hosts which are in Heaven, and especially the good and gracious God, the Lord of all. Thou shalt not come down from Heaven.' And continuing thus, I was sufficient for this thing for two days and two nights, and I constrained the Evil One to such a degree that he became a flame of fire and burned up everything which I had in my cell, and at length the very mat upon which I stood blazed with fire, and I thought that I should be wholly consumed. Now when, finally, fear of the fire took hold upon me, my mind came down from Heaven on the third day, because I was unable to keep my mind collected in the state in which it had been. . . . And this happened so that I might not boast." [2]

This was clearly no ordinary experience; mystical rapture had taken the form of visible fire. Such scorching flames fed the men of God, whose souls had really ascended into heavenly regions.

They never wearied of considering God's eternal beauty, however greatly divine love wounded them. Their life of mystical prayer often led to ecstasy: "My mind departed and was carried away by contemplation," the hermit Isidore told Palladius,[3] and of another monk Palladius notes that "his mind was more often exalted unto God than it was concerned with the things which are in this world." [4]

Other hermits, again, were granted the gift of tears; their tears flowed whenever they spoke, and their cheeks were always moist. Theodoret wrote: "It is the ardent love of God that produces these tears, inflaming the spirit to heavenly contemplation, wounding with its darts and summoning the soul to abandon the world." [5] Such tears, then, were never the effect of a downcast spirit, but rather a sign of joy. Palladius wrote in his *Historia Lausiaca* that the hermits lived constantly in joy such as one did not find anywhere else in the world, and told of an abbot Apollo who used to say to his disciples

[2] Budge, ed.: op. cit., I, 121, 122.   [4] Ibid., I, 115.
[3] Ibid., I, 90.   [5] Theodoret: op. cit., chap. XXX.

that he who seeks his salvation in God and places his hope in the kingdom of heaven need not be sad.[6]

This joy was the immediate fruit of ardent prayer, and on that account the hermits were able to overcome occasional temptations to presumption. They were ever mindful that many people living in the world and fulfilling their duties out of the love of God took precedence in the sight of God over many a monk. Rufinus reports the hermits as saying that they ought not to despise anyone in the world, be he a robber or a trickster, a farmer or a merchant, married or single, for in every state there were people who secretly performed works pleasing to God; it followed, therefore, that it was not so much a man's outward state or his clothing that were agreeable to God, but rather a good and upright heart and righteous works.

The hermits of the desert realized that after the Christian has done everything he can, he still remains an unprofitable servant. Pambo, for instance, made this humble confession on his deathbed, and it could apply to them all: "From the day wherein I came into this desert and built this cell in which I have lived, I know not that I have ever eaten the bread of idleness or bread which did not come from the labor of mine own hands; and my soul repenteth not that I have ever spoken an empty word in my life; yet I go to God like one who hath, as yet, not made a beginning in the fear of God." [7]

At the same time, one is tempted to ask whether this extraordinary mode of life was not exaggerated, whether the hermits did not go too far. Such objections have been raised times without number, but they cannot dim the glory of the Christianity of the desert, that beacon of the divine on earth. Like a glowing sunrise, it broke through the surrounding shadows, spreading light and warmth. The desert fathers are unique figures in Christian history. They were men who hungered and thirsted for the supernatural. They strove with a veritable passion to surpass themselves, and no effort was too great if it helped them to reach their goal. They struggled and fought to enter through the strait gate; they were prepared to pay the price for taking the kingdom of heaven by storm. Their heroism is a fact that cannot be gainsaid. They were filled

---

[6] Palladius: *Historia Lausiaca*, in J.-P. Migne, ed.: op. cit., LXXIII, 1161.
[7] Budge, ed.: op. cit., I, 104.

with a longing for the absolute, and one is tempted to say that they were not made of flesh and blood, but of spirit and fire.

And without such burning zeal nothing worth while has been achieved in Christendom. Desert Christianity is the strongest anti-pole to a drawing-room Christianity, in which the Gospel is reduced to the level of an interesting conversation. In the post-Constantinian age, true Christianity was outside, in the wilderness, and not in the imperial palaces. And today? Is it not again being driven into the desert? Is it not at all times the voice of one crying in the wilder-ness? True Christianity, indeed, has seldom subsisted in any other way. So that, instead of dwelling on the aberrations of individual hermits prone, like everyone else, to error, we should rather re-member desert Christianity as a renewal of the spiritual springtime of the Church.

Unlike the rest of Christians, the hermits made no cleavage be-tween theory and practice; indeed, they lived their theory with an almost unbearable consistency. It was said of them that they sought to emulate the nature of angels, and that they honored the memory of the first Christians not by building monuments or penning phrases, but by becoming their living images through the cultivation of their virtues.[8]

Because they practiced an optimum Christianity, their falls, when they occurred, were correspondingly violent. They played the high-est stakes that a Christian can wager. This heroism gives desert Christianity its immortal glory. But fear of future terrors did not motivate their extraordinary way of life; they knew that Chris-tianity is based on love, not on fear. Their principal motive was love of the divine beauty. Thus, Theodoret wrote that love was their food and their drink and their clothing, love that lent them wings and taught them to fly so that they were able to penetrate to the highest heavens, love that gave them sight of the Beloved, stirred up greater longing through that vision, awakened joy of love, and fanned the flames of passion more mightily. And we find Theodoret reporting the holy man Marcianus as saying that the hermits prized fasting higher than food, and ate only at nightfall,

---

[8] Theodoret: op. cit., prologue.

but that they knew that love was more precious than fasting, for love was of God's ordinance, whereas fasting depended on man's own will.[9]

The hermits' way was not a way for every man, and it was as far removed as possible from the gloomy and tedious caricature of religion produced by mechanical observance. The men of the desert, who had deliberately turned their backs on the world, realized that the worst foe of the Gospels was not sensuality or greed for gain— that these are incompatible with seeking after perfection is obvious enough—but mediocrity. And against this subtler foe the hermits waged the bitterest and most unrelenting struggle. At no time were they prepared to come to terms with it, for mediocrity, however seemingly harmless, is the harbinger of catastrophe. Through mediocrity, men are led to accept Christianity only up to a point, never to embrace it wholeheartedly, but merely to use it as a respected ornament on certain occasions. Mediocrity leads inexorably to that lukewarmness of which it is said that, because a man is neither hot nor cold, he will be spewed from the mouth of the Lord (Rev. iii, 16).

The desert fathers fought the corrosion of mediocrity not in others, but in themselves, which is what made of them saints and not simply critics of civilization and preachers of penitence. Their greatness lies in their determination to break through the conventional and worldly concept of Christianity, to leave behind every kind of security and step out into the unknown, as the Bible constantly invites man to do. When Christendom forgets that it must wage ceaseless warfare against mediocrity in its own ranks, then its salt loses its savor and it sinks into stagnation.

The hermits regarded themselves as dead men; they could truly be called men "from the other side." They were athletes of the spirit, their minds set upon the absolute, delighting constantly in the eternal. They were an elite among Christians; seldom, indeed, has the Christian spirit scaled such heights. They deserve our profound respect, and their warning that mediocrity is the arch-enemy of Christianity is as apposite today as it was in the fourth century.

[9] Ibid., chap. iii.

This leads us to consider one last facet of desert Christianity. Questions of dogma had become a focal point of interest in the age of Constantine. Christological problems should not, of course, be underestimated, and they certainly required clarification at the time. Nevertheless, a grave danger lurks behind the passion for theological speculation: it is that Christianity may be taken as primarily an intellectual pursuit, that man's beatitude may be regarded as depending on his acceptance of dogmatic formulas. It is an ever present danger to religious men, and one to which fourth-century theologians were particularly vulnerable. And it was the desert fathers who constituted the mighty rampart against this fatal error. They, fortunately, were not intellectuals, and Anthony himself coined the saying that "one who has a sound mind has no need of letters." [1] Their message was righteous living, a message spurned by those who pay mere lip-service to Christianity. For it is much easier to teach rightly than to live rightly.

Monasticism was the corrective to the tendency of certain churchmen of the time to express Christianity exclusively in terms of philosophico-religious definitions. Beside the theologian elaborating complicated formulas stood the silent hermit expressing his faith in the simplicity of his life. Anthony summed up the position of the desert fathers in this matter when he said that "no one of us is judged by what he does not know, and no one is called blessed because of what he has learned and knows; no, the judgment that awaits each asks this—whether he has kept the faith and faithfully observed the commandments." [2] The hermits were concerned solely with practice; action was what they always stressed. A dying solitary indicated this rule as leading most directly to perfection: never to teach another what one has not practiced oneself. The desert fathers believed that Christian ideas spoil if not put into practice but permitted to lie fallow in men's minds.

Once, after many had embraced the eremitic life, one of Anthony's disciples asked him whether such zeal would endure forever. Whereupon Anthony's face grew sad, his eyes filled with tears, and he replied that indeed it would not, but that a time would come when monks, instead of seeking solitude, would seek their

[1] Meyer, ed.: op. cit., chap. lxxiii. [2] Ibid., chap. xxxiii.

abodes in the most populated cities; there they would build magnificent dwellings, eat good food, and be indistinguishable from men of the world in all but their clothing; nevertheless, he added, there would always be a few in whom the spirit of the primitive foundation would endure.[8]

[8] Quoted in F. Böhringer: *Die Kirche Jesu Christi und ihre Zeugen* (1842), I, 34.

Saint PACHOMIUS

and Cenobitism

Tʀᴀᴅɪᴛɪᴏɴ has it that whenever Pachomius wished to ford a river, he would summon a crocodile, which speedily ferried him to the farther bank.[1] The tale is calculated to disconcert even the most gullible, and his biographer's admonition that we should not doubt the report does not make it any more convincing.

The improbable crocodiles have made the whole Pachomian tradition more than suspect. And because it has been regarded as lacking in historical foundation, there has been scant interest in its subject, so that the second father of monks is almost unknown to modern Christians. Few have so much as heard of him, and even fewer have any clear idea about his personality. When a historian did decide, at the close of the last century, to go into the matter, he deliberately set out to debunk the extravagances of the hagiographers and to reduce Pachomius to his "proper proportions."[2] The figure that emerged from the operation was, of course, completely colorless and quite unattractive.

Yet it could have been no ordinary man of whom it was believed that he used such astonishing means for crossing a river.

---

[1] H. Mertel, ed.: *Leben des heiligen Pachomius*, chap. vii, in *Bibliothek der Kirchenväter* (Munich: Kösel Verlag; 1917), Vol. XXXI.

Translator's note. This version of the *Life of St. Pachomius* was translated into German from a Greek manuscript in the Vatican library. It would appear that neither the original Greek version nor any translation of it other than the German has ever been published. Other versions of the *Life* exist—in Latin, Coptic, French, etc.—but they differ markedly from the one selected by Mertel. I have therefore translated the passages that the author quotes from the *Life* directly from Mertel's version.

[2] Grützmacher: *Pachomius und das älteste Klosterleben* (1896), p. 23.

One is reminded, almost, of the fiery chariot that swept Elijah into heaven. Nor is there any reason, merely because a tale is strange, to reject it out of hand; it should rather be accepted as the timeless symbol that it is. And if we so accept it, we shall find ourselves ushered into the grandiose world of early monasticism, in which the figure of St. Pachomius towers up like a mighty pyramid against the Egyptian sky.

Even the remarkable crocodiles have their place in that prodigious world, bearing out, after their manner, the view that when man is one with God, paradise is in some sort restored, and the very beasts are again subject to man in trusting obedience. Only the glowing language of legend could preserve for posterity something of the greatness of Pachomius; the scientific, positivist approach is far too clumsy to pierce through to the essence of that mysterious personality. Indeed, the world of the desert fathers becomes accessible to us only if we are able to read the symbolism of its multifarious legends; only by an inward, spiritual penetration of the past can we hope to rediscover its meaning.

The author of the *Life of St. Pachomius* had no intention of writing a tale to suit the fickle taste of succeeding generations; his principal purpose was to edify. "We have written this so that, by reading, we may be inspired to emulate his life." [3] It is this pedagogical aim that gives legend, through its symbolism, the power to preserve historical reality from ossification.

Pachomius was born of pagan parents in the neighborhood of Esneh about the year 290. The family eked out a wretched existence as peasants, and the boy received no education. His language was Coptic; not until much later did he learn Greek. When he was twenty, he was conscripted into the imperial army. And it was then, as he was being marched off, in the company of other young men, to join the combat forces, that he had his first encounter with Christians. The kindness these people showed to the ill-treated conscripts, their compassion and active charity made a lasting impression upon Pachomius. And when, after the unexpectedly early conclusion of peace, he was discharged from the army, he at once set out to join the Christian community.

[3] Mertel, ed.: op. cit., chap. 1.

He had not long been a Christian when he was caught up in the eremitic movement, which was making great headway through-out Egypt. We are not told what caused him to flee the world; much in the *Life* is only hinted at, rather than explicitly stated. What we do know is that Pachomius desired to be received as a disciple by an old hermit called Palaemon, from whom he hoped to learn the rudiments of the ascetic life.

Palaemon, however, failed to welcome the aspirant with open arms. "You cannot be a monk, for it is no small thing to embrace the monastic life," was his reply.[4] The old man doubtless had had unfortunate experiences with youths who had embarked upon the eremitic life without the necessary strength or staying power. He knew just what it meant to be a hermit—the sacrifice of the whole man—and his answer to Pachomius could serve as a device for the entire history of monasticism. To embrace the monastic life means, in effect, to venture upon the path of the extraordinary. It is no everyday affair. That explains why Palaemon, instead of enticing candidates with promises, sought rather to discourage them.

Pachomius, however, was not to be deterred, and his insistence triumphed over Palaemon's opposition. The old man accepted him as his disciple and initiated Pachomius into the art of asceticism, which must be learned if physical health is not to be impaired. Dur-ing this first phase of his religious life, Pachomius lived as a hermit. The two solitaries spent most of their time in prayer, but also worked with their hands, selling what they produced and giving the proceeds to the poor. Their food was of the simplest; they used no oil and even dispensed with fire. Frequent fasts punctuated their wretched meals. As a result of these ascetic exercises, Pachomius became adept in vigils, wholly mortified as regards worldly beauty, and embued with the virtue of humility.

This hard life of ascetic training continued for a number of years, and, had it rested with Pachomius, he would have remained a her-mit to the end of his days. There is not so much as a hint in the *Life* that he was in the least dissatisfied with his lot; it probably never occurred to him that the eremitic life left anything to be desired as a form of monasticism. It was almost against his will that he was

4 Ibid., chap. iii.

led to embark on the great mission that was to be his life's work, and to which his years as a hermit had been merely the prelude.

The turning-point came with a spiritual experience that broke upon him with the force of a sudden storm. He was praying alone in the desert of Tabenna when he heard a voice call him by name, and a supernatural radiance flooded his soul. Then an angelic figure spoke to him: "Remain here, Pachomius, and found a monastery, for many will come to you who want to be saved. Direct them according to the rule that I shall give you." [5]

Pachomius neither doubted the angelic message nor asked for further explanation. We are told only that he set out to obey the heavenly command. The sparing account hardly satisfies one's curiosity, but the inward experience of vision is, in any case, not susceptible of investigation. What is certain is that the angelic visitation was the crucial event in Pachomius' life, and led to a revolution in his mode of existence. As to the reality of the vision, it would be foolish to question it, for Pachomius was a visionary. His first vision had been granted him at baptism, and later he was often rapt in ecstasy, during which he had sight of wondrous things and received the gift of prophecy.

Although so richly endowed with charismatic gifts, Pachomius never overrated these extraordinary experiences. When a monk told him of a vision he had experienced, Pachomius made this reply: "The most beautiful vision is a pious man, and the best revelation is this, when you see the invisible God in that visible man." [6] This apt rejoinder, which the simplest Christian can readily understand, is no argument against Pachomius' exceptional gifts. Only a great seer can be so detached about his raptures; John of the Cross might well have said the same.

No sooner had Pachomius recovered from his dread at sight of the angel than he told Palaemon of the charge that had been laid upon him. The old man recognized the heavenly character of the mission, and Pachomius began forthwith to build "a small cell-like dwelling in the form of a monastery." [7] A laconic statement, but laden with significance. For it meant nothing less than the founda-

---

[5] Ibid., chap. v.   [7] Mertel, ed.: op. cit., chap. v.
[6] Quoted in Grützmacher: op. cit., p. 72.

tion of the first Christian cloister. A new tree of life had blossomed near the "palms of Isis"; the Church had been enriched with the means whereby imperfect man could most effectively attain to a life of proximity to God. But at the time no one realized that something altogether new had come into being, something that was to have the greatest influence on the development of Christendom. Not even the exact date of the foundation is recorded; we know only that it was in the twenties of the fourth century.

It was no imposing edifice that rose up on the sands of Tabenna. Pachomius' biographer expressly says that it was an unassuming little building. Monasticism grew out of small beginnings, and it seems to be a fact that Providence grants permanence in history only to undertakings born in humility and simplicity.

In order to protect the religious life of the cloister from curious eyes, Pachomius built a wall around the monastery. That wall became symbolic of the monk's separation from the world, as well as of his determination to create a "world apart."

The building of the first monastery would have sufficed to establish Pachomius' fame, but that was far from being the whole of his achievement. According to his biographer, the angel gave him "a tablet on which was written all the instruction needful for those who were to come to him." [8] This rule may be regarded as the prototype of all monastic rules.

Doubt has been cast upon this part of the vision because it does not appear in all the versions of the original biography.[9] It was long believed, moreover, that the wording of the rule, as it appears in Palladius' *Historia Lausica,* should not be ascribed to Pachomius. A careful examination of the text, however, shows it to be of a piece with the *Life;* both documents reflect the selfsame features of the second father of monks. The whole tradition, of course, savors of legend more than of history, but a rule written at the behest of an angel is entirely in keeping with the picture of Pachomius as it emerges from his *Life.* For Pachomius was pre-eminently a man whose conversation was in heaven. Angels, indeed, were as much a part of early monasticism as demons, who plagued the second father

---

[8] Ibid.
[9] Stefan Schiwietz: *Das morgenländische Mönchtum* (1904), I, 167.

of monks as they had plagued the first, and both kinds of visitation testified to the monks' familiarity with the supernatural.

The "angelic rule" has been described as one of the major monuments of early Christian literature. "Its lapidary style," writes one authority, "its rapid movement from one point to the next, its freedom from casuistic detail, all show it to be the original, all other texts being the product of subsequent attempts to complete it." [1] Its lack of system is equally an argument for its authenticity. A few passages may havè been interpolated later, but in essence it coincides with what is known of Pachomius' spiritual doctrine.

The rule affords an insight into the life of the Pachomian monastery. A stranger might not be received without preliminaries into the inner sanctum of the monastery, so the aspirant was first taken to the guest house. Then, before receiving the simple monastic habit, he was taught the indispensable rudiments of the religious life. There was no question, as yet, of vows. Pachomius considered it necessary that all monks should learn to read, so that they might be able to take an active part in the offices held twice daily. Relatively few prayers were prescribed, the angel, we are told, having so ordained it—overruling the objections of the zealous founder—"so that even the monks who are small [i.e., weak] may be able to fulfill the canons, and may not be distressed thereby. For unto the perfect no law whatsoever is laid down, because their mind is at all seasons occupied with God." [2] The monks lived together in the monastery, but each had his own cell in which he slept at night on a pallet. The rule made provision for virtually all the needs of the monks, prescribing simple clothing, a moderate amount of food, and adequate rest.

Pachomius knew that a monastic community could not endure without absolute standards of conduct, and he therefore insisted on strict discipline among his monks. He was particularly conscious, writes his biographer, that order and discipline were greatly to be prized in the sight of God and men. [3] The originality—and perma-

---

[1] O. Zöckler: *Askese und Mönchtum* (1897), I, 200, 203.

[2] "The Paradise of Palladius," in E. A. W. Budge, ed.: *The Paradise of the Holy Fathers*, (New York: Duffield and Co.; 1909), Vol. I, Book I, chap. xxxiii, p. 146.

[3] Mertel, ed.: op. cit., chap. xx.

nent value—of the "angelic rule" lay precisely in its provision of
clear directives for the monastic life. Previously, would-be monks
had had to rely for their training on the injunctions of their seniors,
whose teachings were exclusively in the nature of counsels. The
monastic rule, on the other hand, was in the nature of a binding
commandment, akin to a law.[4] There is indeed something majestic
about a rule that a man freely accepts as an unalterable canon of his
life, and it was by virtue of his rule that Pachomius was able to give
form to the formless monasticism inaugurated by Anthony. The
founder of the first monastery was also the first monastic lawgiver.

Having regard to the circumstances of the establishment of the
first monastery and its "angelic rule," we might truly say that Christian cenobitism was born of Christian vision. For it was through
the grace of ecstasy that Pachomius was led to create this completely
novel type of religious life.

The modern mind balks at vision, which is probably one of the
chief reasons why it finds Pachomius so disconcerting. The reaction
is understandable enough, for vision introduces man into an unknown and fearsome realm in which the natural light of reason is
extinguished and through which he has to grope his way in an
impenetrable darkness filled with dread shapes and mysterious symbols of the kind St. John describes in his Revelation. Book-learning
is altogether inadequate to explain the content of vision; intuition
alone may perhaps glimpse something of what takes place in
ecstasy. The incredulous should frankly admit that with a rationalistic approach they are as little likely to grasp the nature of vision as
they are likely to probe the symbolism of the amenable crocodiles
of the Pachomian legend. For to regard visions as the excrescence
of an exuberant imagination, or simply as evidence of mental disorder, is to make one's own limitations the measure of all things.

In religious history, visions have served as unique catalysts,
bringing the apparently impossible into being. And the visionary,
mystical form of Christianity that led to the emergence of monasticism is undoubtedly superior to the merely ethical conception of the
Gospel, which allows only for experiences that fall within the pur-
view of human reason. The ecstatic, for his part, is in actual contact

---

[4] J. Herwegen: *Väterspruch und Mönchsregel* (1937), p. 12.

with the supernatural. It is no coincidence, therefore, that monasticism should have counted so many visionaries in its ranks.

Instead of approaching visions with skepticism, it would be fitting to ask what would have become of Christendom had it not brought forth its great seers. For Christian history is unthinkable without them. Genuine vision, which is the fruit of divine inspiration and totally unrelated to self-deluding fantasy, is a window upon the supernatural, giving man glimpses of another world and allowing light to stream in upon the darkness of his entangled existence. Vision is indeed a marvelous event in the history of Christian spirituality, a vehicle for the revelation of divine things to the faithful. And it may be that the modern denial of the very possibility of authentic vision is one of the principal causes of the darkness that beclouds our times.

But it would be too much to expect the contemporary mind to feel at home with the visionary Christianity of the desert fathers. And nowhere is the gulf between their mentality and ours more apparent than in Pachomius' fierce antagonism to Origen. It is possible, of course, that his venomous attacks on Origen should be attributed rather to his nameless biographer, but that is a conjecture. We are told that Pachomius inveighed against what he regarded as Origen's "foolish chatter" and even went so far as to say that anyone who read Origen's work and accepted his ideas would be consigned to the depths of hell.[5] According to his biographer, Pachomius could tell by a stranger's smell whether the man was of Origen's way of thinking. So far removed was the Coptic visionary from the subtle spirituality and unorthodox teachings of the great Alexandrian.

This passionate condemnation is, of course, regrettable, particularly as monasticism owed much to Origen's profound teaching on mystical prayer. At the same time, it should not be written off as mere fanaticism; it reflects a basic conflict between two opposing approaches to Christianity—that of the Coptic mystics of the desert, with their insuperable distrust of intellectual brilliance, offset by their vigorous and utterly uncompromising spirituality, and that of the Greeks, with their love of philosophical speculation. What the des-

---

[5] Mertel, ed.: op. cit., chap. xxxvii.

ert fathers lacked in subtlety they certainly made up for in elemental religious force.

The objection has been raised against Pachomius that the common life he instituted was purely external in character and put a premium on mediocrity, the rule presupposing that most of the monks would have no vocation to the religious life.[6] It is true that the common life of the first monks was primitive beyond belief, but it could hardly have been otherwise, corresponding as it did to the wretched conditions of the *fellahin* from whose ranks most of the monks were drawn. In regard to clothing, for instance, we are told that a monk never possessed a change of shirt; he would wear a different one only on those rare occasions when, because his own was particularly dirty, he had arranged to wash it.[7] Life in the Pachomian monastery was certainly rugged; nevertheless, it was inspired by the noblest ideals and it did in fact bear the distinctive features of all subsequent monasticism: the common life of brethren under a rule. It is easy enough, after the event, to say that anyone could have done what Pachomius did; it was infinitely hard to be the one who actually took the initiative.

It would also be erroneous to applaud Pachomius merely as a great organizer, or to lay too much stress on the work aspect of the monastic life he inaugurated. It is true that a multitude of tailors, dyers, tanners, braziers, shoemakers, and other craftsmen filled his monasteries, marching in rank and file to and from their appointed workbenches, and that he formed them into a great producers' association.[8] But nothing could be further from the truth than a belief that his primary motive in promoting trade was an economic one. He was undoubtedly a remarkable organizer, but organization is not a merely external affair; the interior life of the individual may well suffer from a faulty division of labor. But he was also far more than an organizer, and, for all his soldierly temperament, he did not create a monastic barracks or a factory. Pachomius, first and foremost, was an enlightened shepherd of souls. His monastery, with its

[6] Jakob Burckhardt: *Die Zeit Konstantins des Grossen* (1924), p. 424.
[7] Mertel, ed.: op. cit., chap. vi.
[8] Grützmacher: op. cit., p. 132.

"angelic rule," aimed at nothing but the salvation of souls, as his biographer expressly states.[9]

Pachomius' attitude is very apparent in the manner of his teaching. According to the *Life*, Pachomius proceeded to gather around him "those men who, after their conversion, desired through him to come to God. After much testing, he bestowed the monastic habit upon them. He forbade them to concern themselves with the things of the world, but instead led them on, step by step, along the path of asceticism. Above all things, he admonished them to renounce the world, their families, and even, in accordance with the Gospel, themselves, so that they might take up their cross and follow the Saviour." [1] We see here the exclusively Christian motive governing Pachomius' action.

Cultural purposes lay wholly outside his orbit. Later the monasteries were to do much to promote culture, and it is this aspect of their action which well-intentioned critics usually cite first in their favor. The civilizing achievement of the monasteries must not, indeed, be underestimated, but it has all too often led monasticism away from its true purpose, which, fundamentally, is the salvation of souls, and nothing else. That strictly religious aim is of far greater significance than all the cultural effects of the monastic life, and if we do not understand this straining toward God, we shall never even begin to fathom the secret of monasticism.

By gathering his disciples together in a single community under a common roof, Pachomius inaugurated the cenobitic life. His biographer even records the names of his first disciples—Pserrthaisis, Surus, and Opsis. Anthony, too, had had disciples, but he had not lived with them; indeed, his aim had been rather to withdraw from them. It was almost accidentally that a number of lauras [2] had grown up subsequently in the neighborhood of Anthony's cell; there had been no connection between them. Pachomius, on the other hand, systematically gathered together and trained his disciples, realizing that this was essential if his monastery was to have permanence. His

[9] Mertel, ed.: op. cit., chap. xxxvi.
[1] Ibid., chap. viii.
[2] A *laura* was a group of cells situated at some distance from one another.

3

merit was to have united the scattered hermits in a many-celled single house that received the name of monastery, and to have emphasized the need for training, which is inseparable from monasticism.

Pachomius taught his disciples that "neither prayer nor the society of holy men would profit monks if inwardly they were careless" of their salvation.[3] And he insisted on strict submission to monastic discipline. We are told in the *Life* that "he enjoined upon them all to obey gladly, admonishing them never to seek their own will, that they might ever be mindful of God's good pleasure and not their own."[4] Those who desired to cultivate self-will had no place in his monastic community.

For Pachomius, religious obedience—which has no analogy with military obedience—was the highest law. It was a law that the hermits had known only in very general terms. But in the common life of a monastery, obedience is of fundamental importance, and it plays a decisive part throughout monastic history. All eccentricity was to be shunned, Pachomius taught; the best monk was the one who conformed most readily and most inconspicuously. To a brother who was overfond of his own ways, Pachomius said: "Conform to the rule! When the rule calls you to meals, then do not remain without nourishment, but go with the rest of the brethren and partake in moderation of the bread and the cooked food that are set before you."[5]

We find it hard, in our day, to understand the sacrifice of obedience, let alone to make it so wholeheartedly. The grandeur of the act of renunciation of self-will, despite its fundamental importance for the religious life, largely escapes us. The reason for this incomprehension is doubtless that religious obedience has too often been mistaken for cringing subservience, an unfortunate error that has inflicted untold harm on Christendom. Mere docility to constituted authority is often nothing more than cowardice, and has no relation to the exalted virtue of religious obedience which Pachomius required of his monks.

The *Life* has preserved a striking example of the manner in which Pachomius reacted to any infraction of the freely assumed obligation

[3] Mertel, ed.: op. cit., chap. xiv.   [5] Ibid., chap. xxix.
[4] Ibid., chap. x.

of obedience. On the grounds that the brethren would not eat much, some of the monks had failed to take their turn of duty in the kitchen, and had decided instead to weave mats. Pachomius wasted no words. "How many mats have you made?" he asked them. "Five hundred," they replied. "Bring them here," he ordered. When he saw the work of disobedience lying there before his eyes, his indignation knew no bounds, and he ordered that all the mats be thrown into the fire, regardless of their value. Then he turned to the offenders, saying: "Just as you have neglected the rule which was given for the sake of all the brethren, so I, with equal careless-ness, have burned the fruit of your labor, that you may know that it is not right to despise the commandments of the elders, which have been given for the sake of the salvation of souls." [6]

On another occasion, when a brother had sold some sandals at a higher price than the one agreed upon, Pachomius sharply reproved him. "You have done grievous wrong, because you have loved gain. Go quickly, now, and return what was in excess of the price to those who paid you, and then come back and repent your fault." [7]

This incident is also indicative of Pachomius' concern lest any breath of covetousness taint his monks; the cloister was not to be a place for the amassing of riches. On the contrary, the monastery's surplus supplies were to be distributed among the poor. The monas-tery thus initiated a new approach in economic relations, and in this respect, too, it was to prove the seed of a new social order. And whenever monasteries have departed from that strictly Christian line of conduct, as they have departed all too often, to their shame, their betrayal has spelled their own doom.

What Pachomius established was something completely new in the Christendom of his day. But novelty easily provokes opposition; it disturbs people's cherished ideas, which they are most reluctant to change. That was also Pachomius' experience, and he had to com-bat strong resistance before his foundation could be securely estab-lished. We should be painting a distorted picture of the world of early monasticism if we were silent on this point.

The first opposition, after that of the local population of Esneh, came from his brother, John, who had joined him in his foundation

[6] Ibid., chap. xxxvi.   [7] Ibid., chap. xli.

and was closely associated with him in his work. As an immediate relative, John believed he had more rights than the rest of the brethren, and he took it upon himself to meddle in Pachomius' administration of the community. Owing to the great influx of subjects, it had become imperative to enlarge the little monastery, but John objected and tried by every means to obstruct the building operations, going so far as to pull down the walls that were going up. As a result, a violent altercation broke out between the two. There was little to show, at that particular moment, that either of them had undertaken to seek perfection; both were consumed with anger, and the air resounded with their recriminations. John did not scruple to tell his brother to stop his "silly humbug and putting on airs," [8] and Pachomius, for his part, was unprepared to give way for the sake of peace. Later, however, he bitterly reproached himself, and with tears, for having allowed himself to be carried away by anger. His entire mission was at stake, and he believed himself to be in the right. He succeeded, therefore, in breaking his brother's resistance, and proceeded along his chosen path without a backward glance, regardless of all obstacles.

Many further trials awaited him, not the least of which were the ones arising out of his ecstasies. The conception of Christianity that Pachomius derived from his visions caused his dogma-conscious contemporaries to suspect him of heresy, and this suspicion could well have spelled ruin for his whole undertaking. The exact sequence of events in this regard is not clear, because here there is considerable variation between the Greek and Coptic versions of the *Life*. The most plausible account is that his bishop regarded the monastic foundation as an undesirable and suspicious novelty, particularly as it was purportedly based on a supernatural command, and summoned Pachomius to appear before the synod at Latopolis. There he was accused of presumption, on the ground that he had said that he had been in heaven and could read men's hearts. According to one version, a wild tumult arose; according to the other, Pachomius succeeded in convincing his accusers that their charges were unfounded. Whatever the truth of the matter, this unfortunate incident had no lasting effects and failed to prejudice his mission.

[8] Ibid., chap. vi.

Pachomius was too great of soul to allow such experiences to drive him into a position of hostility to the clergy, as they might well have done. On the contrary, and especially after the Latopolis incident, he was careful to conduct himself with particular deference toward the clergy. He would not accept priests in his monastery, and insisted on maintaining its purely lay character. He did not wish, he said, "that there should be any among the brethren with the power to impose hands"; on the contrary, he explained, it was better and altogether more profitable for the monks not to seek to be honored, respected, or esteemed, particularly when they were living in community, so that neither jealousy nor discord might arise among them.[9] It is expressly stated, moreover, that Pachomius occasionally requested a neighboring priest to come to the monastery to celebrate the eucharistic sacrifice, and he exhorted his monks to visit churches with all decorum and to show fitting submission to priests.

Pachomius' foundation was subjected to constant harassments, but nothing could halt its progress. In his own lifetime, he was to witness the establishment of several monasteries, each subject to the mother house. There were also two convents of women, directed by Pachomius' sister. Soon there were hundreds of monks and nuns, for at that time no formalities were required for admission and there was no novitiate. This monastic community could truthfully be described as a giant hive humming with activity—at the expense, inevitably, of solitude.

By the end of the fourth century, Egypt was *par excellence* the homeland of Christian monks. Later, however, monasticism suffered a decline even in Egypt, till finally it became virtually extinct. That is why not so much as a trace is left of the first monastery or even of its exact location. But this sad circumstance cannot dim Pachomius' memory. The Coptic hermit gave Christendom a priceless gift— the first monastery and the "angelic rule." That was his essential significance: to have effected the transition from the eremitic to the cenobitic form of monachism. It was not the spiritual needs of his times which prompted him to take that step, nor had he been brooding on the deficiencies of the eremitic life. His undertaking was certainly no reflection upon Anthony, whom he revered as the

[9] Ibid., chap. ix.

founder of the monastic movement. It was his vision that showed him the cenobitic life, which he regarded as a second form of monasticism alongside the first. In giving up his life as a hermit, he realized that he was giving up something very great, but in order to gain something greater still.

Its heavenly origin gave the new foundation an authority that placed it beyond the range of human criticism. At the same time, it constituted the most radical and the most productive transformation in monastic history, for monasticism owes its entire subsequent development to the cenobitic way of life.

Only a man of altogether exceptional stature could have been capable of such an achievement. The *Life of St. Pachomius* may not be on an artistic level, as a biography, with Athanasius' *Life of St. Anthony*, but its pages nevertheless reveal the features of a strong personality endowed with prodigious and supernatural powers. It is useless to try to explain Pachomius in terms of his origins or of the pagan influences to which he was exposed; we can begin to understand him only if we see him as a man graced with heavenly vision. Pachomius was first and foremost a man of prayer. His biographer tells us that he would stand rapt in prayer the whole night long, his arms extended wide in imitation of the Crucified.[1] The gift of tears was his, too; even at mealtimes he was unable to restrain his tears, which gushed forth like rivers from his eyes.

His Christlike spirituality gave him an almost uncanny authority over his monks. They submitted willingly to him, realizing that beneath his stern exterior he was filled with love for them and desired only their salvation. Men, he would say, must be treated like tender young trees; and when strife broke out among the brethren, he would quell it by reminding them of the virtue of Christian charity, which, he told them, consisted in bearing with one another.[2] His marvelous dignity resulted from the unity of theory and practice in his own life.

Pachomius was about sixty years old when a pestilence broke out in Egypt, carrying off many of the monks. Pachomius too was struck down, but refused to be treated in any way differently from the rest of the brethren. Seeing that he was in the grip of fever, his

[1] Ibid., chap. vi.   [2] Ibid., chap. xvi.

attendants tried to cover him with a blanket, but he immediately ordered them to take it away and to cover him instead with a rush mat, as was customary in the monastery. And so he lay, awaiting death.

In the light of what tradition tells us about the man, it is perhaps not so astonishing, after all, that he should have been credited with rendering even crocodiles submissive to his will, and with many other marvelous powers. It was said, for instance, that he could understand all languages, that he could heal the sick and drive out devils. Yet this Coptic wonder-worker, who in the eyes of his contemporaries was already clothed in a supernatural aura, made this humble confession of his faith: "My struggle and my whole ambition is not to walk dry-shod over rivers or to soar on wings over mountains or to command the wild beasts, which God from the beginning made subject to man, but rather to prepare myself for the judgment of God and to confound the hordes of Satan through the power of the Saviour." [8]

Saint BASIL

and Eastern Monasticism

WHEN Basil died, on January 1, 379, he was only forty-nine, yet his tremendous personality had so impressed his contemporaries that they forthwith surnamed him "the Great." It is a tribute paid to few ecclesiastics, but one that Basil fully deserved, not only because of his personal sanctity but even more because of his achievements.

For us of the twentieth century, however, it is not easy to bridge the gulf that separates us from the great Basil, whose fame, we are told, once echoed to the ends of the earth. True, his brother, St. Gregory of Nyssa, and his friend, St. Gregory of Nazianzus, composed funeral orations in his honor, but their exuberant rhetoric, so far from illuminating the man, tends only to obscure him. On the other hand, Basil's own style is not so removed from contemporary usage, and his letters give us a vivid picture of his personality.

The Basil of Christian tradition was no narrow-minded bigot. He was a man of outstanding intellect combined with rare practical ability; a man of impressive appearance whose very aspect struck fear into his adversaries' hearts, a man who knew what he wanted to do and did it, a man who was sure of himself and equal to every situation.

For this self-assurance, Basil was indebted in no small measure to his upbringing. He came of a wealthy family in which Christianity and culture alike were held in high esteem. His childhood was a very happy one, spent in the company of his mother, Emmelia, whose father had died a martyr's death; of his father, Basil,

a man of liberal ideas and education; and of his grandmother, Macrina, who earlier had chosen exile rather than forswear her faith.

The cultivated atmosphere of his home was to make itself felt
again and again in Basil's life. Never was he prepared to see Christianity surrender to barbarism, or learning to paganism. He gave
short shrift to those who claimed to despise letters, himself believing
that philosophy was the reflection of the eternal light.[1] It is significant, for instance, that one of his homilies should have been addressed to students and entitled "On the Right Use of Pagan Literature."[2] Nor is it surprising that Origen should have been his
favorite author, and that he should have published a selection of
Origen's writings. With his ingrained sense of harmony, Basil sought
constantly to reconcile Christian thought with Greek philosophy.

Basil's personality stands out even more strikingly in his ecclesiastical activities. Together with the two Gregorys, he was a tireless
champion of Athanasian orthodoxy, and paved the way for the
downfall of Arianism. As bishop of Caesarea, an office that carried
with it the title of Metropolitan of Cappadocia, Basil fearlessly up-
held the faith, daring to oppose even the emperor Valens in his
struggle against the Arians.

Once, when the imperial prefect, Modestus, threatened him with
confiscation of his goods and with exile, torture, and death, Basil
calmly replied: "If there is anything else, threaten me with that
too, for none of these you mentioned can affect me." The prefect,
apparently, did not understand the bishop's attitude, and so Basil
proceeded to explain: "The man who possesses nothing is not liable
to confiscation, unless you want, perhaps, these tattered rags, and a
few books, which represent all my possessions. As for exile, I do
not know what it is, since I am not circumscribed by any place, nor
do I count as my own the land where I now dwell or any land into
which I may be cast. Rather, all belongs to God, whose passing
guest I am. And as for torture, how can they rack a body that exists
no longer, unless you refer to the first stroke, for of this alone you
are the master? Death will be a benefit, for it will send me to God

[1] J. Sellmair: *Humanitas Christiana*, p. 103.
[2] E. R. Maloney, ed.: *Saint Basil the Great to Students on Greek Literature* (New York: American Book Co.; 1901 [Greek text, annotated]).

sooner. For Him I live and order my life, and for the most part
have died, and to Him I have long been hastening."

Stunned by such imperturbability, Modestus said: "No one up
to this day has ever spoken in such a manner and with such boldness
to me." To which Basil retorted: "Perhaps you have never met a
bishop. . . ." [3]

This was far more than a triumph in debate; Basil's words were
a statement of fact. How seldom is it given to men to meet a bishop
of that kind!

Basil was the very embodiment of the early Christian ideal of a
bishop, with scant time for merely ceremonial functions. His chari-
table works bore testimony to his zeal. He built a hospital and
personally helped look after the sick. During a time of famine in
Cappadocia, the bishop of Caesarea was to be seen standing in the
market place, girt with an apron, ladling pulse and salt meat into
the pots of the poor. This was no bid for popularity: Basil's concern
for his people's welfare stemmed from his Christian charity, just as
did the courageous stand he took against usurers. A magnificent
orator, he thundered against the rich:

"So, you are not a miser, nor do you rob, yet you treat as your
own what you have received in trust for others! Do we not say that
a man who steals the coat of another is a thief? And what other
name does he deserve who, being able to clothe the naked, yet
refuses? The bread you keep belongs to the hungry; the clothes
you store away belong to the naked; the shoes that molder in your
closets belong to those that have none; the money you have buried
belongs to the needy. Therefore you have wronged all those to
whom you could have given and did not." [4]

Such denunciations inevitably made him unpopular in certain
circles, but that did not trouble him; his sole responsibility, he felt,
was to the dictates of his Christian conscience. He used all his eloquence in favor of the socially underprivileged; with equal courage
he championed the right of youngsters to choose their professions
and insisted that slaves be treated humanely. Gregory of Nazianzus

[3] St. Gregory of Nazianzen: *Funeral Orations* (New York: Fathers of
the Church, Inc.; 1953).
[4] St. Basil: "Homily on Avarice," in J.-P. Migne, ed.: *Patrologiae Cursus Completus* (Paris, 1885), XXXI, 275.

called Basil the most important man of his century, even though Ambrose and Chrysostom were among his contemporaries, and it is not hard to understand the Church's veneration for this great prelate.

Yet Basil's action as a bishop shows us only one aspect of his personality. There was another Basil, a figure less familiar but perhaps even more significant than that of the seasoned ecclesiastical statesman: a suffering, anguished man, beyond the reach of the glaring spotlight of history but all the more intensely alive in the depths of his soul. We do not really know Basil if we do not see him as a man who, alone with his thoughts, could be "struck by a kind of shuddering fear," [5] a man whose sensitive features were often clouded with grief, a man who could weep.

Disregard of this aspect of Basil's personality led to the erroneous notions current about his student days in Athens. It was claimed that he had known only two roads in Athens, one leading to the church, the other to the school. Such exemplary conduct sounds highly edifying, and fits into the stereotyped picture of a Basil intent from youth upon treading the paths of holiness. But that is mere rhetorical hyperbole. It must by any objective standards be clear that Athens, whose eminence was already waning, exerted a most unfortunate influence upon the young man. Knowledge made him conceited and filled him with a sense of his own importance. His brother, Gregory of Nyssa, in a letter describing the life of their sister, Macrina, wrote that Basil had returned from Athens puffed up with intellectual pride, despising all authorities and, in his arrogance, believing himself superior to all illustrious men.

This attitude was in marked contrast with the deep piety of Macrina, who was quite unimpressed by what she regarded as mere pompousness in her brother, and a discussion took place between the two in which Basil came off considerably less brilliantly than he was later to do in his encounter with Modestus. The vain young rhetor could not hold his own against his sister, whose arguments, inspired by deep religious conviction, mercilessly shattered his complacency. The result was a spiritual crisis that proved wholly salutary. Basil wrote about it later, in one of his letters:

[5] St. Basil: The Long Rules, rule no. 2, in *Ascetical Works* (New York: Fathers of the Church, Inc.; 1950).

"I had wasted much time in vanity and had spent nearly all my youth in the vain labor in which I was engaged, occupying myself in acquiring a knowledge made foolish by God, when at length, as if aroused from a deep sleep, I looked upon the wondrous light of the truth of the Gospel and saw the futility of the wisdom of the rulers of this world who are passing away. Having mourned deeply my piteous life, I prayed that guidance be given me for my introduction to the doctrines of religion. And before all things else, I was careful to amend my ways, which for a long time had been perverted by my companionship with the indifferent." [6]

There and then, Basil gave up his career as a rhetorician. But as yet he did not know his vocation. The metropolitan who was later to steer the little barque of the Church so surely through the treacherous currents of his times was himself beset by uncertainty. Like St. Paul, he asked the burning question: "Lord, what wilt thou have me to do?" Not knowing where to turn for an answer, he decided to visit some of the monasteries of Asia Minor. His journey had only one aim: to find his bearings in the shipwreck of his life. The learned rhetorician, able to discourse wittily on any subject, was not too proud to knock at the doors of countless cloisters of Egypt, Palestine, and Syria, and to sit at the feet of unlettered monks in order to learn from them how to be a Christian. He had become as a little one; his pride had given place to an eager humility.

For over a year he journeyed, and during that time a previously unknown world opened up before him, giving his life a completely new direction. In those remote monasteries he met a living Christianity that surpassed anything he had expected or dreamed of; even today we can hear the echo of his wonder as we read his account of his travels:

"Accordingly, having read the Gospel and having seen clearly there that the greatest means for perfection is the selling of one's possessions, the sharing with needy brethren, the complete renouncing of solicitude for this life and the refusing of the soul to be led astray by any affection for things of earth, I prayed to find some one

[6] St. Basil: *Letters* (New York: Fathers of the Church, Inc.; 1955), Vol. II, letter no. 223.

of the brethren who had chosen this way of life, so as to pass with him over life's brief and troubled waters.

"And in truth I found many in Alexandria and many throughout the rest of Egypt, and others in Palestine and Coele Syria and Mesopotamia, the self-discipline of whose manner of life I admired. I marveled, too, at their endurance in toil; I was amazed at their attention at prayers, their victory over sleep, being overcome by no physical necessity, always preserving lofty and unconquered the resolution of their soul, in hunger and thirst, in cold and nakedness, not paying attention to the body or consenting to waste any thought on it, but, as if living in flesh not one's own, they showed by their deeds what it is to dwell among those on this earth and what to have their citizenship in heaven. I admired these things and I considered the life of the men blessed because they show by their works that they bear around in their body the dying of Jesus. And I prayed that I, also, as far as was possible, might be a zealous follower of those men." [7]

Basil returned from his travels a changed man. He was twenty-eight years old, and he had discovered a timeless verity: the road leads inward. Novalis' aphorism sums up the fruits of Basil's pilgrimage to the monasteries: the world of sense had lost its importance for him, inner reality had taken its place. But Basil was not a man to be satisfied with merely admiring the heroism he saw in others. He deliberately refrained from employing his rhetorical arts to laud the beauties of Christianity in fine phrases; what he wanted was to put into practice what he had learned. He felt called to become a monk, and he established a small monastery in the Pontine hills.

What is most immediately striking about that foundation is the site he chose. For all his ascetic fervor, he had clearly not lost his fine sense for scenic beauty. Basil described the lovely country surrounding his hermitage in an exquisite letter to his friend, Gregory of Nazianzus.[8] A mountain stream, he wrote, rushed foaming into a near-by gorge, and the sight filled him with joy. From his references to the abundance of flowers and the song of the birds, it is

[7] Ibid., Vol. II, letter no. 223.   [8] Ibid., Vol. I, letter no. 14.

quite clear that his inner preoccupation in no way blinded him to natural beauty. An atmosphere of idyllic charm lay over the monastery, and Basil soon began to feel that the monastic life had been expressly designed for him. Yet he was in bitter earnest about being a monk. He slept on the ground and ate the most wretched food; the bread was so hard that the monks were in danger of breaking their teeth on it, and more than once the community was near starvation.

Love of solitude was the guiding principle in Basil's plans for the monastic life. In persuasive tones he urged his friends to give up their life in the city—"that breeding-ground of innumerable ills." For what does a man have in the city but "wild desires, unruly impulses, and passionate yearnings"? All too many distractions harass him there: "the longing for children, if he is childless; the solicitude for their training, if he has children; the watchfulness over his wife, the care of his home, the protection of his servants, the losses on contracts, the contentions with his neighbors, the lawsuits, the business risks, the farm work. Each day, as it comes, brings its own shadow for the soul, and the nights, taking over the troubles of the day, beguile the mind with the same fantasies." [9]

For Basil there was only one way to escape these manifold troubles—to flee the world. And that meant, in the first place, to liberate the soul from its attachment to the body, to despise home and country, property and society. Nothing was excluded from this total renunciation, not even "spiritual assemblies," where, even then, little was to be heard but "clever speeches and fictitious tales told for the deception" of the hearers. Basil therefore shunned such gatherings, and indeed all crowds, preferring solitude. For in solitude the Lord had dwelled: "Here is the oak of Mambre, here is the ladder leading to heaven and the companies of the angels which Jacob saw; here is the desert in which the people, having been purified, were given the laws, and, thus entering the land of promise, saw God." [1]

Solitude is the greatest treasure, "quieting our passions and giving leisure to our reason to uproot them completely from the soul." [2]

[9] Ibid., Vol. I, letter no. 2.
[1] Ibid., Vol. I, letter no. 42.
[2] Ibid., Vol. I, letter no. 2.

It was a sweet, captivating song that Basil sang in praise of solitude, one that stirs an answering chord even in our own times.

Peace was Basil's goal, solitude the means. An atmosphere of divine tranquillity—the Greeks called it *hesychia*—was the secret of this architect of a new way of life who was yet so tireless in his efforts to refashion the clay of his own being. But the peace that held Basil's soul was what St. Paul, in his Epistle to the Hebrews, calls the rest of the people of God (Heb. iv, 9), not the immobility of the magnificent statues of the gods which Winckelmann admired. Stillness was all his striving. Everything about him must be so still that one might hear the air quiver. All noise must be muted, all agitation calmed, so that the voice of God might be heard in the soul.

Basil finally achieved a tranquillity so absolute that it never abandoned him; in the midst of the most heated theological controversies he was tranquil enough to remember that even his own arguments were but the shadow and not the substance of the truth he was defending.

Basil's reform of the liturgy, which is still in effect in the Eastern Church, was also aimed at producing inner peace. "We should try to keep the mind in tranquillity," he wrote.[3] This constant longing for peace was not the fruit of weariness or disappointment; what Basil sought was to taste the peace of heaven on earth, within the confines of his cloister. Blissful indeed is that eminent tranquillity through which a man attains to the purest peace of soul.

Clearly, therefore, this emphasis on peace was not some personal eccentricity of Basil's; peace is of fundamental significance for religion. Basil regarded tranquillity as the door through which a man must pass if he is to lay hold of the eternal. The presence of heavenly things cannot be perceived in the midst of a deafening din. Only the man who has withdrawn from the bustle and tumult of the world is able to encounter the divine. Stillness, Basil believed, was the first step to the soul's sanctification. How should a man take the next steps if he had not taken the first?

Because of this ceaseless emphasis on the striving for peace, monastic communities under Basil's influence deliberately began to lay

[3] Ibid., Vol. I, letter no. 2.

more stress on the interior life. A monastery became something far deeper than a merely external association of monks; the mechanical process of living side by side gave way to an organic process of living together. One might say, indeed, that Basil breathed a soul into cenobitism; that is his lasting merit, the achievement ever associated with his name. And for that reason he did not want his monasteries to be large like those of Egypt, with their multifarious enterprises that could easily breed a spirit of something akin to commercialism among the brethren; Basil of set purpose built small cloisters.

This spiritualizing of the monastic life constituted a genuine advance over eremitism, and not merely an external substitution of one form of the religious life for another. Basil could laud solitude in well-nigh intoxicating strains, but if we listen carefully we realize that he was not talking about the solitude of the hermit. In Basil's writings we find the first serious criticism of the anchoritic life: "Therefore, I urge, cast out of your mind the thought that you stand in need of union with no one." [4] Christ's words forbid man to seek his own, yet the hermit lives only for himself. In the Pauline metaphor, Christians are one body whose head is Christ—but the hermit has cut himself off. And if he is cut off from the body, how can he remain united to the head?

In Basil's view, the anchorite no longer remains in living association with the Christian organism, from which he has deliberately severed himself in order to indulge a refined egotism. How can the hermit fulfill the Apostle's injunction to rejoice with those that rejoice and to weep with those that weep, since he knows nothing of the lives of his fellow men? The eremitic life, Basil believed, is in accordance neither with human nature, which is essentially social, nor with the spirit of the Gospel.

Basil conceived of monasticism as a striving toward a new community, a new kind of living together. Superficially speaking, the movement of flight from the city appeared to be aimed at just the opposite—escape from society—but Basil was not deceived by appearances. He realized what it was that was straining to the light from below the surface; it was the suppressed cry for community,

4 Ibid., Vol. I, letter no. 65.

for a new "I-thou" relationship, about which antiquity in its decline was no less concerned than we are today.

Community usually remains a topic of conversation; Basil put it into practice. He created a radically new society, characterized by "a common roof, a common table, and a common mind," [5] thereby meeting the unconscious need of his own fast-decaying civilization. Eremitism could not supply the solution because, in its inordinate individualism, it was necessarily devoid of any spirit of community. The monastery, on the other hand, was based on the idea of man as a social being, and in itself, therefore, constituted an answer. For what was needed was the building of a really new society in accord with Christianity, not just the restoration of the old pagan social structure. And a community is not created, as so many tend to think, by the mere fact of people being together.

The Basilian form of monasticism embraced the essential features of both eremitism and cenobitism, as Gregory of Nazianzus realized from the outset:

"The solitary life and the community life were then in conflict and dissension in many ways, and neither completely possessed advantages or disadvantages that were unmixed. The one is more tranquil and stable and leads to union with God, but it is not free from pride, because its virtue escapes testing and comparison. The other is more practical and useful, but does not escape turbulence. Basil reconciled and united the two in the most excellent way. He caused hermitages and monasteries [6] to be built, not far from his cenobites and his communities of ascetics. He did not divide or separate them from each other by any intervening wall, as it were. He brought them close together, yet kept them distinct, that the life of contemplation might not be divorced from community life or the active life from contemplation. . . ." [7]

In Basilian monasticism we find that concept of true community which men in every century have struggled so desperately to achieve. For community can come into being only on a religious basis. Never

[5] F. Heiler: *Urkirche und Ostkirche* (Munich: E. Reinhardt; 1937), p. 370.

[6] Used here in the literal sense of abodes for solitaries.

[7] St. Gregory of Nazianzen: op. cit., pp. 79, 80.

should society be sacrificed to the individual, or the individual to the collectivity; the individual needs society, and, conversely, a true community can be formed only through the union of individuals grounded in God. The proper relation between individual and community is mutual fulfillment, and the solitude in community and community in solitude that Basil the Great called forth was predicated on the individual who was prepared to incorporate himself, in a spirit of service, into a whole higher than himself.

Basil's new community made possible the practice of fraternal charity, for which the hermit in his solitude had scant opportunity. For Basil, love of one's neighbor was of paramount importance and indispensable to perfection. His monastery was expressly intended to help the brethren live together in charity. The emphasis was not so much on material works, as the needs of the brethren were normally provided for; Basil's first concern was with the cure of souls. At the same time, he believed that monks should assume the responsibility of spiritual direction only within the monastery. A brother must feel himself responsible for another, and they must take pains to give each other the guidance which a man always needs if his interior life is to prosper.

Every monk, he ordained, must confess his thoughts and, in particular, his faults either to one or to more members of the community. Thus he laid down in his rules:

"Every subject, if he intends to make any progress worth mentioning and to be confirmed in a mode of life that accords with the precepts of our Lord Jesus Christ, ought not to conceal within himself any movement of his soul, nor yet utter any thoughtless word, but he should reveal the secrets of his heart to those of his brethren whose office it is to exercise a compassionate and sympathetic solicitude for the weak." [8]

The mandatory disclosure of what is hidden in the recesses of the conscience leads logically to auricular confession. This was no innovation; the idea goes back to St. James—"confess your faults one to another" (v, 16). Basil was simply the first to make the ascetical practice of confession of sin an integral part of monastic discipline.

[8] St. Basil: The Long Rules, rule no. 26, in *Ascetical Works*.

The reformer of the Eastern liturgy was at the same time one of the architects of the institution of auricular confession in Christendom.[9]

Examination of conscience and confession were at first incumbent only upon the cloistered, and were not generally practiced outside the monastic community. The deliberate revealing of the secrets of the heart to one another, as Basil puts it, contributed to an incalculable degree to the development of the spiritual life of the whole community. Moreover, the opportunity of unburdening one's soul affords a relief wholly beneficial to the soul which has been recognized as of great therapeutic value, whereas the process of introspection develops mental poisons that can endanger even the health of the body. "For vice kept secret is a festering wound in the soul," [1] Basil wrote in his rules, thus anticipating one of the major findings of medical psychology.

But confession, according to this penetrating master of the spiritual life, does not end with the telling of faults; the recognition of a problem does not automatically bring about its disappearance. An example will illustrate what "compassionate and sympathetic solicitude" meant in a Basilian monastery. A monk came in great trouble to the abbot Lot and told him that he had committed a grave sin but had not been able to reveal it to the senior brethren. Thereupon the abbot spoke to him encouragingly, and said: "Confess it to me, and I will bear it." [2] Instead of merely listening, the abbot was declaring himself ready to take upon himself the load that lay upon his brother's conscience; greater solidarity is hardly conceivable. This evangelical substitution gives an idea of the religious power of monastic confession.

In order to provide a sound foundation for his monastery, in which the brethren were to attain to supernatural tranquillity through solitude and were to experience a new kind of community life through mutual spiritual assistance, Basil drew up a rule that, significantly enough, he wrote before his ordination to the priesthood. It consists

[9] K. Holl: *Enthusiasmus und Bussgewalt im griechischen Mönchtum* (Leipzig, 1898), p. 262.
[1] St. Basil: The Long Rules, rule no. 46, in *Ascetical Works*.
[2] E. A. W. Budge, ed.: *The Paradise of the Holy Fathers* (New York: Duffield & Co.; 1909), II, 90.

of the "long rules," divided into fifty-five chapters, and 313 summary rules, which may be regarded as complementary to the former. Both are in the form of questions and answers.

Basil's rule is still authoritative in Eastern monasteries, and the fact that it should have served as a guide to countless monks for almost sixteen centuries is some indication of its worth. Its authenticity is beyond dispute.[3] Its importance is usually considered as residing in the firm framework it gave to monastic fervor, but first and foremost it is a spiritual textbook of the monastic life.[4]

At the summit of his rule, Basil set the love of God, which is the first duty of the monk; he was mindful, however, that "the love of God is not something that is taught." [5] Nevertheless, he exhorted his monks "to avoid ever losing the thought of God" and "to carry about the holy thought of God stamped upon our souls as an ineffaceable seal." [6]

The rule consists of detailed teachings on the conduct befitting monks. Basil's conception of monastic life was derived directly from the Scriptures, and he deliberately refused to give his rule the character of a law. "It is not possible . . . to include under one rule all who are in the school of the devout life. In setting the norm for healthy ascetics, we allow for appropriate deviation on the part of superiors according to particular circumstances." [7]

The humility of the monk, whom Basil calls a soldier in God's service, must be apparent even outwardly in his downcast glance. His gait must not be sluggish, for that would denote spiritual indolence. His clothing must serve his need: it must be a covering suited to the season, and it must never serve vanity. In the matter of food, too, need is the determining factor. For healthy men, bread and water suffice. Occasional vegetable dishes give the body the necessary strength for work. Only one hour in the day may be devoted to eating. Whatever is in excess of need must be regarded as luxury, and therefore as abuse.

[3] F. Laun: *"Die beiden Regeln des Basilius,"* in *Zeitschrift für Kirchengeschichte* (1925).

[4] J. Herwegen: *Väterspruch und Mönchsregel* (1937).

[5] St. Basil: The Long Rules, rule no. 2, in *Ascetical Works.*

[6] Ibid., rule no. 5.

[7] Ibid., rule no. 19.

For Basil, the monk is a man who has complete control of himself. "Perfect renunciation, therefore, consists in not having an affection for this life and keeping before our minds the answer of death, that we should not trust in ourselves (II Cor. i, 9)." [8] The soul is purified through the purification of the body; it is a reciprocal relationship: the soul increases as the body decreases and, when the body waxes overbold, the soul is lost.

The monk must have nothing whatsoever to do with money, which is the enemy of the interior life. He must be neither anxious nor petulant. His duty is to free himself of his passions. He must also rid himself of the habit of raucous laughter; the Lord himself did not laugh, else He would not have pronounced His doom upon them that laugh. To renounce buffoonery does not mean to advocate gloom; Basil admonished his brethren to be ever joyful: "it is not unbecoming to give evidence of merriment of soul by a cheerful smile." [9]

His comments on property are also of interest. Recalling that "the Scripture absolutely forbids the words 'mine' and 'thine' to be uttered among the brethren," [1] he endorses the early Christian communism of love, radically separating it from the pagan cult of Mammon.

Basil desired his monks to be industrious: "We must toil with diligence and not think that our goal of piety offers an escape from work or a pretext for idleness, but occasion for struggle, for ever greater endeavor, and for patience in tribulation." [2] Nevertheless, all types of work are not suited to the cloister: "Those trades should be chosen which allow our life to be tranquil and undisturbed." [3] For his first concern was ever to make of the monastery a haven of supernatural peace. The purpose of the work was to assist the poor, but Basil believed it preferable to lower the price of articles made in the monastery rather than to peddle them for the sake of a small profit. [4]

Basil believed that a man could not fulfill the rule by his own unaided powers, but only with the assistance of God's grace. For a man cannot, merely by exerting himself, attain to the summit of the

[8] Ibid., rule no. 8. [1] Ibid., rule no. 32. [3] Ibid., rule no. 38.
[9] Ibid., rule no. 17. [2] Ibid., rule no. 37. [4] Ibid., rule no. 39.

ascetic life; he cannot be expected to break with his past all at once, but must depart step by step from his erroneous ways. "Therefore be this known to you, brother, that not he who begins well is perfect, but he who ends well is approved by God," Basil wrote in one of his letters.[5] The Christian must advance from day to day, and he must never be satisfied with the progress he has achieved.

Though Basil's rule would appear to be primarily a series of spiritual counsels, it nevertheless entitles him to a place among the great monastic lawgivers. His ascetical program, for all its severity, is filled with an admirable humanity and devoid of all exaggeration. The measured quality of his spirituality has given his rule its permanence. He was the first, with his handbook on asceticism, to attempt a philosophical discussion of the problem of monasticism. He succeeded in attracting many people to his monastery, and he wrote enthusiastically to his friend, Gregory of Nazianzus: "What, then, is more blessed than to imitate on earth the choir of angels; hastening at break of day to pray, to glorify the Creator with hymns and songs, and, when the sun is brightly shining and we turn to our tasks, to accompany them everywhere with prayer, seasoning the daily work with hymns, as food with salt?" [6]

Basil's reputation also rests on what he did to clarify the relationship between the Church and monasticism, which in his time was still very confused. The earliest monasticism was directed against the tendency in the Church to compromise with the world, to water down the strong wine of the Gospels to suit the vulgar taste. Some Christians in the post-Constantinian age went so far as to doubt the possibility of salvation within the Church, believing it to have become too corrupt. Instead of seeking the divine in the hallowed precincts of the churches, the anchorites sought it in the inhospitable wastes of the desert. For some anchorites, the mediacy of the priest was set aside and perfect asceticism almost took the place of the sacraments. Many hermits, it would seem, were completely cut off from the eucharistic sacrifice; they did not take part in the sacraments, and indeed could not have done so in their desert fastnesses.

Monasticism, in its development, was unmistakably on the defensive against a worldly Church; there was consequently an under-

[5] St. Basil: *Letters*, Vol. I, letter no. 42.   [6] Ibid., Vol. I, letter no. 2.

current of tension between the clergy and the first monks; there were differences, arguments, and animosities. The monks were not directly opposed to the Church, but lived a separate existence alongside it, and were sometimes in danger of falling into heresy. And had they in fact become heretics, the Church would have had to reject eremitism, as it rejected other movements of enthusiasm. Thanks to Basil, this unfortunate eventuality was avoided. What Athanasius had begun as Anthony's friend, the bishop of Caesarea brought to its consummation—namely, the incorporation of monasticism into the organism of the Church. Basil preserved monasticism from being merely a movement of protest, which in the long run would have ceased to be productive. And in so doing, he won monasticism back for the whole of Christendom.

Because of its integration into the Church, monasticism had to free itself of its radical opposition to culture. Basil, at his conversion, was fully aware of the vanity of intellectual pride, and he concluded that men who desired to devote themselves to the ascetic life could properly pursue philosophy only in solitude. It is significant that he regarded the ascetic life as synonymous with the philosophical life. The wholeheartedness of his conversion did not cause him to forget his Greek grounding, and his concern with learning remained a permanent characteristic that he carried over into the monastic life.

Basil sought to instill into his monks a love of the things of the mind. He was not altogether successful; nevertheless, both he and his closest friends continued their scholarly work within the monastery. He set his monks the task of penetrating the mysteries of Christianity and putting them into personal practice, and in this he was the prototype of something quite new: the educated monk.

In this twofold pursuit of scholarship and asceticism Basil was following in the footsteps of Origen. A last breath of Greek philosophy lingered in Basil's monastery. It is true that in this way Basil was also introducing the seeds of worldliness into cenobitism. That danger could not be avoided, and it has always menaced Christian undertakings. But it was by making the monastery a center of intellectual activity that Basil rendered monasticism capable of development.

For learning should not be regarded as inimical to religion, al-

though on occasion it may be so, and when Christians sever themselves from culture they deprive themselves of influence on their fellow men. Just as culture, without religion, must sink into barbarism,
so religion needs culture to achieve its purpose. The question is
simply whether Christianity should welcome culture into its orbit or
become its servant. And Basil's masterly solution to the problem
was to develop a religious culture, to give a Christian humanism a
home in his monastery.

The problem is one that Christians have faced time and again.
Early monasticism tended to isolate Christianity from civilization;
the first monks chose solitude because they felt that it was their one
means of preserving the content of Christianity from corruption.
Basil, with his own love for solitude, could well understand this
withdrawal from human society. At the same time, with his background of Greek culture, he regarded it as a duty to make Christianity universally accessible. For Christianity, preaching as it does
the doctrine of creation at the hands of God, in fact embraces all
that is, not excluding whatever is good in the secular world.

Basil's greatness lies in his recognition of the necessary play of
diastasis and synthesis in Christian spirituality. The man who was
both metropolitan and monk sympathized deeply both with the
movement toward isolation and the tendency to universality; he
combined both positions in his own person, not as two conflicting
poles but as elements contributing to depth and breadth of vision.

Basil has been described as a man with whom others could live.[7]
And his was indeed a most attractive spirituality, which to this day
has not been assessed at its true worth. He was the kind of person
who cultivated friendship, and he wrote of himself that he had always had many good friends. His personality radiated a kindness
that warmed his companions like the rays of the sun. There is not
enough charity, he was wont to say. And he was entitled to say so,
because he himself possessed love to a rare degree.

The bishop of Caesarea never lost his longing for tranquillity,
and allowed nothing to disturb him; neither agitation nor tension nor

---

[7] J. Wittig: *Leben, Lebensweisheit und Lebenskunde des heiligen Me-
tropoliten Basilius des Grossen von Caesarea*, in *Ehrengabe deutscher Wis-
senschaft* (1920), p. 619.

any other such unhealthy attitude had any place in his philosophy. At the same time, he was one of the most effective exponents of a Christian humanism that offered a synthesis for apparently conflicting tendencies. Basil more than deserves his title of father of Greek monasticism, which to this day bears the imprint of his spirituality.

II

Eastern monasticism developed and bore its own characteristic fruits. Its emphasis was always on religious duty: we are but sojourners, it taught, on our pilgrimage to eternity; we come today, and tomorrow others will take our place; let us, then, be assiduous at prayer and attendance at the offices of the Church, for all else is superfluous. The Eastern monasteries were peopled by men who often succeeded in committing large portions of the Bible to memory, who practiced rigorous self-discipline, and who sought to cultivate a genuinely Christian attitude. Much has been written about Eastern monasticism, but perhaps the most satisfactory statement is that of Simeon, surnamed "the new theologian," an eleventh-century Byzantine monk, who wrote: "The true monk shuns worldliness. His conversation is ever with God alone. He regards Him and is regarded by Him. He becomes a light that sheds a light that words cannot describe. The more he is praised, the more he looks upon himself as a beggar, and though many are united to him in friendship, he still remains as a guest and a stranger. In a word, this is an inexpressible marvel." [8]

Because these monks lived such hidden lives, wholly removed from the gaze and the affairs of the world, Eastern monasticism has had relatively little history. One might even be tempted to regard it as a static phenomenon. But this would be quite erroneous; Eastern monasticism is no mummy preserved through the centuries. Such a notion is born of the bias of the West, which is unwilling to make the effort to understand a monastic life so different from its

[8] Translated from a work by Simeon published in German in 1930 under the title *Licht vom Licht*, p. 24.

own. Certainly there has not been the variety of monastic life in the East that there has in the West, and the historical process there has been considerably slower. Yet Eastern monasticism has had its transformations, too, and has found varying forms of expression. Basilian monasteries were established in the Near East, in the Balkans, in southern Italy, and later in Russia, and in all these countries they have exerted a beneficent influence.[9]

Eastern monasticism erected its own most imposing memorial in the monastic republic of Mount Athos, which has survived into our own times. These monastic settlements are staggering to the Western mentality and unlike anything else of their kind. To this day the shores of this Greek promontory are lined with silent fortified monasteries, and the Greek railroad system stops short of Mount Athos. Unbroken quiet reigns over these citadels of worship and of silence. In the words of Jakob Philipp Fallmerayer, "neither woman, nor the lust of the eyes, nor wedding feasts, nor sumptuous entertainment, nor celebrations, nor any tumult that stirs the senses are permitted within the precincts of the holy community. There is no breeding of domestic animals, there are no fairs, no speculation, no usury, no court, no pride of judgment. On Mount Athos there is neither master nor servant, and there alone is true freedom and the right measure of all things human. No living creature is born on the holy mountain; there is only death, but without tears and without monuments."[1]

The place itself is impressive enough, its pristine beauty preserved, it seems, as it came forth from the hands of the Creator, but even more impressive is the religious life that has flourished during the past thousand years in the twenty-one monasteries, making the holy mountain an outstanding witness to the Christian spirit. Its uniqueness lies in its total severance from the world. However unbelievable it may sound, a monk of Mount Athos never sets foot in the outside world again. The monks of Mount Athos have never taken part in questions of ecclesiastical rule or worldly politics, or even in doctrinal controversies. Such matters are wholly outside their

[9] M. Heimbucher: *Die Orden und Kongregationen der katholischen Kirche* (1933), I, 93.
[1] Jakob Philipp Fallmerayer: *Der heilige Berg Athos*, p. 35.

province, their sole concern being to bring to fruition the seeds of salvation implanted in their souls by Christ. The monk of Mount Athos is not, in the first place, a penitent, but one who has overcome the world.

Although time seems to stand still in that consecrated haven of natural beauty, an evolution has taken place imperceptibly over the centuries, at times giving rise to stormy incidents.

For instance, certain monks inaugurated the practice of leaving the monastery and the common life in order to live in complete seclusion, and thereby aroused considerable opposition. A fierce controversy arose, too, out of the development of Hesychasm. This was a movement aimed at achieving by mystical experience that peace of soul for which Basil had always striven. Gregory Palamas, the central figure of the controversy, who is venerated as a saint on Mount Athos, was in fact only the protagonist, not the originator, of Hesychasm, for the seeking after spiritual tranquillity is as old as monasticism itself. Only the ignorant can shrug off the Hesychasts as mere contemplators of their navels. These deeply religious men practiced a prayer of quiet which brought them to the highest peaks of contemplation, to the marvelous vision of the uncreated light of Tabor which flowed into the world from the very substance of the transfigured Saviour.

One of the most glorious products of Eastern monasticism was the institution of the *startzi* (elders), which originated on Mount Athos but bore its finest fruits in Russia. At first the Russian monasteries regarded the development with suspicion, but they accepted it finally, and the *staretz* cannot really be understood save in his Russian context. Through the *staretz*, monasticism shared with the world the blessings of the spiritual care enjoyed by the monks themselves. In a unique manner, the *staretz* combined renunciation of the world with service to the world, and, while he remained physically within the monastery, his compassion went out far beyond the cloister walls.

As a result, the *staretz* became central to the life of Russian Christianity. His profound sense of religious responsibility moved him to place himself simply at the disposal of the suffering, serving them freely, neither exacting payment nor seeking to win their allegiance to any special ecclesiastical interest. The spiritual direction he gave was unmarred by the slightest trace of authoritarianism. These men of interior action "blessed the world and prayed for the world and guided men, even the simplest and most ignorant, to a life of constant standing before God, anchored to the Cross of Christ." [2] The *staretz*, whose loving solicitude excluded no man, was eminently fitted for this task, for his own life was unshakably anchored in the divine.

Usually such a spiritual father would spend years in silence in his monastery before opening his cell to visitors, as is told of Seraphim of Sarow, a most attractive figure among the *startzi*. From then on, his little wooden shack would become a popular shrine to which people from every walk of life would journey in the hope of receiving the counsel for which their souls hungered.

The life of the *staretz* was one of such transparent piety that it was able to silence the last objections of those who questioned the very purpose of monasticism. No one, not even an opponent of the Church like Tolstoy, could object to the *startzi* once he had come into direct contact with one of them. The chapter entitled "The Russian Monk" in Dostoevsky's *The Brothers Karamazov* is, perhaps, a literary representation of a *staretz*, but it is largely based on the life of a *staretz* of the monastery of Optina. It needed the descriptive power of one of the greatest Russian writers to create that marvelous picture of genuine holiness.

The *startzi* represented what was closest to the Gospels in Eastern monasticism. We should realize, in any case, that only monks, men completely unfettered by the world, can be in a position to exercise the supremely consoling spiritual direction that the *startzi* gave. The institution of the *startzi* was a direct creation of the Spirit; it could never be imitated by organizational methods, and to foster it is one of the main functions of monasticism. Such havens of light are vital to the religious health of mankind, and though they may temporarily recede into the background, they can never disappear completely.

Before the First World War, the importance of the Eastern

[2] N. V. Arseniew: "*Das Mönchtum und der asketisch-mystische Weg*," in *Der christliche Osten* (1939), p. 205.

Church was largely ignored in the West. Subsequently an attitude of uncritical enthusiasm has sought to compensate for the earlier neglect. But this attitude is no more conducive to understanding than was the former. There is nothing picturesque or romantic about genuine monasticism; it is a sober thing that can properly be understood only from the standpoint of a God-centered realism. And that kind of realism is a far cry from the irreligious naturalism of the later nineteenth century.

The man whose approach is grounded in religion is capable of embracing the whole complex of reality, and his universe does not suddenly fall apart because of some individual aberration that he encounters, however distressing it may be. He is mindful of what the Bible tells us about Noah: that God had made a covenant with him, but that he was nonetheless found lying drunk in his tent; and that his temporary weakness did not deprive him of his archetypal character of the restorer of mankind who alone with his family survived the Flood.

In all periods of human history, light and shadow have been terribly close together; indeed, they are often inextricably interwoven. As long as the world shall last, the heavenly will at times be transformed into the satanic, but the man who looks at these things from the standpoint of a divine realism will not on that account lose faith in the final triumph of the eternal.

Eastern monasticism has had its shadow side, too. With a way of life that kept tension at fever pitch, it was beset by a multitude of dangers which it was unable to ward off, and to which many of its adherents succumbed. Cassian's famous "catalogue of faults" [3] itself reveals the aberrations to which individual monks fell prey. It speaks of gluttony and fornication, of vainglory and pride. The very mention of the catalogue introduces a jarring note into the picture of Eastern monasticism. It has to be mentioned, nevertheless, and not merely as a clue to monastic psychology. It was not, after all, the foes of monasticism who published it, but the monks themselves, in order to indicate the perils which beset the monastic life.

Those who are ill disposed toward monasticism and want to dis-

[3] J. Cassian: *The Institutes*, Book V, in *Library of the Nicene and Post-Nicene Fathers* (New York, 1894), Vol. XI.

credit it usually emphasize the moral lapses that have occurred in its ranks. And because fornication is included among the eight principal faults, it may be assumed that not all monks were always immune to the lusts of the flesh. The existence of dual monasteries constituted a danger, and their establishment was therefore forbidden. The public knowledge of such moral trespasses was damaging to monasticism as a whole, for individual actions too easily gave rise to facile generalizations. Nevertheless, though a brother's fall is certainly a sad event, it can never be made the basis for serious objections to the monastic life.

Monkish fanaticism—which belongs under the heading of "anger" in the catalogue of faults—was far more dangerous in its effects. Monks acted at various times as passionate and stubborn champions of the narrowest forms of orthodoxy, unhesitatingly identifying dogmatic opinion with divine truth. They took part ruthlessly in the struggles of their age against paganism, and many temples and ritual objects were destroyed by their fanaticism. Nor did their hate stop short of the lives of their fellow men; the persecutions of the heathen are among the darkest chapters of Church history. Monks were involved in the most horrible murders; the noble female philosopher Hypatia, for instance, was literally torn to pieces. Heretics, too, were made to feel the monks' malevolence. The monks' part in the shameful calumny of Origen was considerable and doubly heinous because monastic piety owed so much to the spiritual teachings of the great Alexandrian. But neither should actions of this sort be laid at the door of monasticism as a whole.

Another monastic fault, according to the catalogue, was dejection, defined not as a spiritual malady but as a sin. This comes as something of a surprise to the modern mind, accustomed as it is to regard a tendency toward dejection as an excuse for indulging it. In the monastic view, dejection was simply evidence of lack of faith.

And closely related to dejection was the sin of accidie—or spiritual sloth—the greatest foe of Eastern monasticism. Whole monasteries fell into a state of lethargy, often as a reaction to the performance of high feats of asceticism. After frequent fasts lasting many days, natural hunger took its revenge, and the monk would be possessed by an overpowering craving for food which stopped short of nothing he could lay his hands on. Record performance would be succeeded by insuperable lassitude, in which an outraged nature would go on strike.

Accidie—also known as the "noonday devil"—is a characteristic malady of the monastic life, far more insidious than fornication, for it renders any spiritual progress wholly impossible. Without the utmost vigilance, a debilitating negligence sets in and slowly seeps away the foundations of the Christian life. An inner weariness settles like a fine layer of mildew upon the soul, so that the monk abandons the religious combat and sinks into a state of semi-somnolence. Only a conscious struggle against accidie can save the monk from vegetating in a sleepy indifference that spells death to the spiritual life.

The phenomena to which we have referred helped to discredit Eastern monasticism in the eyes of later generations and to make it appear as an institution hostile to culture. Should we try to disprove the accusations leveled against the monastic life of the Eastern Church? It has been done often enough, but such apologias usually show scant comprehension of the underlying forces that make history and cannot be disposed of by the dialectic of thesis and antithesis for the simple reason that they do not operate on the level of thought. The catalogue of vices only expresses in words what belongs to the province of power. The abuses it lists are really another name for the frightful incursions of the Devil against monasticism. Unchastity and ire, dejection and apathy must not be regarded as minor temptations that at most gave the monks some occasional trouble; they were satanic attacks that descended like a rain of shells upon these warriors who were storming heaven.

At the birth of monasticism we find the dreadful struggles between St. Anthony and the Devil, and these struggles in no wise came to an end with Anthony's death; they rage through the entire history of monasticism, a history of men fighting with real powers and not with abstract theories. Not all monks have emerged victorious from the satanic onslaught; many have been vanquished on the battlefield, drugged by the sweet poison of apathy, unable to withstand the lusts of the flesh, succumbing to the demons of fanaticism.

But it would be grossly unfair to judge Eastern monasticism

solely by the satanic devastation wrought in its ranks. Divine powers have always been present alongside individual aberrations, and
the light that streams forth from the Christian East is far more potent
than the shadow.

The lives and teachings of the first of the Eastern Christian monks
—the fathers of the desert—probably best epitomize, as they inspired, the spirit of Eastern monasticism. And we are fortunate in
possessing an account of those teachings in the *Sayings of the Fathers*,[4] compiled by contemporaries, which reveal the inner features of
the men of the desert.

An authority has written of the *Sayings of the Fathers* that they
were never intended as a literary work; the different compilers
sought to write an unvarnished, impersonal account of what they
had seen and heard, and thus to present what are in fact a series of
vignettes of the monastic life of the desert.[5] Yet in content the *Sayings* are more than that: each is complete in itself; together they
trace the path of monastic perfection. "The doctrine of the Fathers
is not of this world; it is born of the Spirit of God. It must not idly
be consigned to parchment and stored away in a cupboard. It is in
the nature of an oracle, and must be treated as a word of divine
revelation." [6]

In fact, the *Sayings* contain insights into unfathomable depths that
deliver their mystery only to men of religious desire. The monks
themselves made it clear that such things could not be transmitted by
merely writing them down. All the Christian can do is to return
time and again to these priceless words, trying in a receptive spirit
to appropriate them to himself, for therein the spirit of Eastern monasticism continues to live in its purest and most concentrated form.

The *Sayings* contain neither daring speculations nor profound
musings nor elaborate philosophical systems. Preoccupation with
such matters was wholly alien to the monks. What we find in the
Sayings is the fruit of years of experience of the spiritual life, and

---

[4] A complete English translation from the original Syriac version ap-
pears in Budge, ed.: op. cit., Vol. II. Extracts translated from the original
Greek version are contained in H. Waddell: *The Desert Fathers* (London:
Constable; 1936).

[5] M. Viller and K. Rahner: *Aszese und Mystik in der Väterzeit* (1939),
p. 116. (Cf. Waddell: op. cit., p. 83.)

[6] Herwegen: op. cit., p. 12.

this lends them the character of inspired utterances. They must, of course, be understood with the heart rather than with the reason. Nor is it only modern man to whom they open vistas at which he had never so much as guessed before; even in those early days they were considered as being addressed only to extraordinary souls aspiring to things far removed from the ways of the world.

At the threshold we are faced with the prophetic warning that a time will come when men will be mad, so that when they see one who is not mad they will turn against him and say "thou art mad" because he is different from them.[7] It is a calamity that modern Christians know so little about the inestimable treasure of the *Sayings of the Fathers*, for today, more than ever, we have need to turn to one of those ancients and to beg: "Father, speak unto us some word of life."

Basically, the *Sayings* are a manual for the attainment of perfection, the whole aim of monasticism. On this subject, Macarius, one of the greatest figures of Eastern monasticism, wrote in one of his spiritual homilies: "Some imagine that because they abstain from marriage and other visible things, they are already saints. That is not so. Evil still lives and lifts itself up in the mind and in the heart. The saint is one who is cleansed and sanctified in the inner man. . . . How can the ordinary man say, 'By fasting, and making myself a stranger, and dispersing my property, I am a saint already'? Mere abstention from evil things is not perfection—only if thou hast entered into thy ruined mind, and hast slain the serpent that lies under the mind beneath the surface of the thoughts, and burrows into what we call the secret chambers and storehouses of the soul and murders thee—for the heart is a deep gulf—only, I say, if thou hast killed him, and cast out all uncleanness that was in thee."[8]

What is most important is that a man should never weary in his striving for perfection, and that after every setback he should struggle on again. "Abba Poemen used to say that John Colob, who made entreaty unto God, and his passions were removed from him,

[7] K. Heussi: *Der Ursprung des Mönchtums* (1936), p. 153.
[8] A. J. Mason, ed.: *Fifty Spiritual Homilies of Saint Macarius the Egyptian* (New York: Macmillan; 1921), homily no. 17, pp. 148, 149.

and he was set free from anxious care, went and said unto a famous old man, 'I perceive that my soul is at rest, and that it hath neither war nor strife to trouble it.' Then the old man said unto him, 'Go and entreat God to let war and strife come unto thee again, for it is through war and strife that the soul advanceth in spiritual excellence.' And afterwards, whensoever war stood up before him, he did not pray, 'O Lord, remove striving from me,' but he made supplication unto God saying, 'O Lord, give me patience to endure the strife.' " [9]

For this struggle, the monk must have solitude. Abba Allois was wont to say: "Unless a man shall say in his heart: 'I alone and God are in this world,' he shall not find quiet." [1]

In order to reach perfection, the monk, it was said, "should be like the cherub—all eyes." [2] And the first thing he must do is guard against presumption, which threatens him most strongly, for nothing bars the way to heaven more effectively than pride. "Whilst Abba Sylvanus was sitting down and the brethren with him, he dropped into a stupor which was of God, and he fell upon his face; and after a long time, when he was standing up, he wept, and the brethren entreated him, saying, 'What aileth thee, O father?' but he held his peace, and they continued to press him to tell them. . . . Then he answered and said unto them, 'I have just been snatched away to the place of the judgment of God, and I have seen many who belonged to our order, that is to say, Christians, going to punishment, and many men who have lived in the world going into the kingdom.' " [3]

From this it is clear that the monks did not regard their way of life as the only acceptable form of Christian living, as is often charged; on the contrary, they believed that the life of Christians in the world could also be pleasing to God. The saying that "if thou hast a heart, thou canst be saved" applies to all men alike. And true monks were not smug about their own achievements. As Pambo told his brethren before he died, he had not spoken an

[9] Budge, ed.: op. cit., saying no. 215, Vol. II, p. 47.
[1] Waddell: op. cit., p. 152.
[2] Questions and Answers on the Ascetic Rule, no. 285, in Budge, ed.: op. cit., II, 216.
[3] Ibid., no. 219, Vol. II, p. 200.

empty word in his life, and yet "I go to God like one who hath, as yet, not made a beginning in the fear of God." [4]

With the renunciation of pride went the exaltation of humility, which should make a monk regard himself as the lowest of all. Macarius the Egyptian taught that "he who is rich in the grace of God ought to be very humble and contrite of heart, and to consider himself as poor and having nothing." [5] And one of the fathers, asked by a brother, "What is the perfection of a monk?" replied, "Humility, for when once a man hath arrived at humility, he can reach forward to the goal." [6] It is also told that a brother asked an old man: "By what means may a man go forward?" and the old man said to him: "The greatness of a man consisteth of humility, for in proportion as a man descendeth to humility, he becometh exalted to greatness." [7] Humility," John Colob would say, "is the door which leadeth into the kingdom. . . ." [8]

Humility must extend, too, to questions of theodicy, as we see from the following story: "The abbot Anthony, being at a loss in his meditation on the depth of the judgments of God, prayed, saying, 'Lord, how comes it that some die in so short space of life, and some live to the further side of decrepit old age: and wherefore are some in want, and others rich with various means of wealth, and how are the unrighteous rich and the righteous oppressed by poverty?' And a voice came to him saying, 'Anthony, turn thine eyes upon thyself: for these are the judgments of God, and the knowledge of them is not for thee.' " [9]

Out of humility, the monks sought never to prefer their own opinion. It is told of one father that he never defended his opinion against that of an elder, but always praised and approved another's more than his own. This attitude is again apparent in the humility of Abba Apollo, who believed that in bowing before the brethren he was in fact bowing before God, for "when thou seest thy brother, thou seest Christ." [1] We also read of a brother who came to Abbot

4 Ibid., I, 104.
5 Mason, ed.: op. cit., homily no. 41.
6 Budge, ed.: op. cit., saying no. 520, Vol. II, p. 118.
7 Ibid., saying no. 459, Vol. II, p. 108.
8 Ibid., saying no. 510, Vol. II, p. 117.
9 Waddell: op. cit., p. 164.
1 Budge, ed.: op. cit., I, 350.

Sisois, saying: "I know this of myself, that my mind is intent upon God." To which the old man retorted: "It is no great matter that thy mind should be with God: but if thou didst see thyself less than any of His creatures, that were something." [2]

Out of the humility that made of the monk the servant of all flowed the boundless compassion that he must show to all living creatures. One of the most beautiful of the *Sayings of the Fathers* is contained in the answer given to a certain Isaac by an old man whom he had asked what it meant to have a merciful heart. The old man replied that a man of mercy was one who had ardent charity toward all creatures—men, birds, and animals, and even the demons—and who, at the sight or the thought of them, was moved to tears through the power of his compassion. Then his heart would grow tender and he would not wish to hear of any injustice done to any creature or of so much as the slightest harm suffered by any creature. And therefore he would offer supplication and tears at all times even for those who had injured him, that they might be preserved and strengthened. And he would pray even for all creeping things, out of the great compassion that was poured into his heart without measure, after the example of the Lord.[3]

Love, according to the *Sayings of the Fathers*, is the substance of the Gospels. A monk, we are told, urged his brethren to attain to the highest good, which, he said, was love. For, he added, fasting is nothing, watching is nothing, toiling is nothing without love, for it is written that God is love.[4] Love caused them to regard their neighbor's lot as their own and in all things to suffer with him and rejoice with him and so to live as though they bore his body in their own. This attitude forbade them to judge their neighbor. It is a sure sign, wrote Cassian, that a man is not yet purged of the lees of sin if he does not show pity, out of a merciful heart, for another's faults, but rather the severity of a judge.[5] For it is usually true that a man is subject to the selfsame vices that he condemns so harshly in another. And Cassian says that we must on no account reproach

[2] Waddell: op. cit., pp. 168, 169.
[3] Arseniew: *Der christliche Osten*, p. 157.
[4] Arseniew: *Die Kirche des Morgenlandes*, p. 65.
[5] *Weisheit der Wüste* (1948), p. 105.

a man with the passions he displays or harbor the slightest feeling of contempt for him, hard pressed as he is.[6]

The fathers taught that if a man would find peace both in this world and in the next, he ought on every occasion to ask himself the question, "Who am I?" that he might judge none; and again, that a man should despise none, condemn none, nor say any evil thing to anyone, and then God would give him peace and his life in his cell would be undisturbed.

One of the most consoling of spiritual counsels is contained in the following story: "A brother asked the Abbot Pastor, saying, 'I have sinned a great sin, and I am willing to do penance for three years.' But the Abbot Pastor said, 'That is a good deal.' And the brother said, 'Dost thou order me one year?' And again the old man said, 'That is a good deal.' And then he added, 'I think that if a man would repent with his whole heart and would not reckon to do again that for which he now repents, God would accept a penance of three days.' " [7]

Many of the *Sayings* concern prayer, which the fathers regarded as the true work of the monk. "The brethren asked the Abbot Agatho, saying, 'Father, which virtue in this way of life is most laborious?' And he said to them, 'Forgive me, but to my mind there is no labor so great as praying to God: for when a man wishes to pray to his God, the hostile demons make haste to interrupt his prayer, knowing that their sole hindrance is in this, a prayer poured out to God. With any other labor that a man undertakes in the life of religion, however instant and close he keeps to it, he hath some rest: but prayer hath the travail of a mighty conflict to one's last breath.' " [8]

The heavenly conversation that it was their constant aim to cultivate was the reason for their silence, and a marvelous spiritual joy flowed from it. It was considered very important that a monk should have interior delight, and it was even said that a man could not be a monk if he did not become as burning fire.[9] Concerning ardent prayer, we read this in the *Sayings:* "There came to the Abbot

[6] Ibid., p. 170.
[7] Waddell: op. cit., p. 144.
[8] Ibid., p. 157.
[9] Heussi: op. cit., p. 187.

Joseph the Abbot Lot, and said to him, 'Father, according to my strength I keep a modest rule of prayer and fasting and meditation and quiet, and according to my strength I purge my imagination: what more must I do?' The old man, rising, held up his hands against the sky, and his fingers became like ten torches of fire, and he said, 'If thou wilt, thou shalt be made wholly a flame.' " [1] The old man's gesture is the most vivid symbol of prayer, which mounts like flame toward God.

It is said of a certain monk named Anthony that he told a hunter to place an arrow in his bow and to draw the string taut. When the hunter had done so, Anthony told him to tighten it still more, and the hunter again obeyed. Whereupon Anthony again repeated his command. This time the hunter told him that if he drew it any tighter, the bow would break. To which the old man observed that so it was with the work of God; if the rule imposed was too severe, the brethren would speedily break under the strain, and therefore, for a time, some concession must be made to them. A similar idea was expressed by Abba Poemen: "If a man observeth his grade, he will not be troubled." [2] They deliberately cultivated sobriety of life, believing that if a man does not live soberly, he cannot defend his soul from danger, and they warned men of three things that open the way to all vices: forgetfulness of God, negligence, and greed.

It would be possible to go on quoting from the *Sayings of the Fathers* indefinitely without ever wearying of them. They constitute an interesting parallel to the marvelous stories of the Jewish *hassidim* collected by Martin Buber. The *Sayings* sound depths that had been magnificently revealed in the aphorisms of the Old Testament. They are full of a spiritual wisdom far removed from mere learning, which even a vain and frivolous man is able to impart.

But what is wisdom? It is that rare understanding of life and that inner composure which enable its possessor to face every situation with equanimity. It is granted only to the man who seeks to place his entire experience of life at the service of religion, who does not

---

[1] Waddell: op. cit., pp. 157, 158.
[2] Questions and Answers on the Ascetic Rule, no. 223 in Budge, ed.: op. cit., II, 202.

harden himself against the dispensations of Providence but looks always to the causes of things. The *Sayings of the Fathers* partake of that heavenly wisdom of which the New Testament speaks; they glow with the brightness of eternity, for nothing is more beautiful than a wise and understanding heart. It is through the wisdom of the fathers that Eastern monasticism has made its greatest contribution to mankind; the truth of their sayings has streamed like light out of the desert, encouraging and consoling multitudes of Christians caught in the toils of the world. Wisdom, the Bible tells us, was God's first creature, made at the beginning of time, before the world was, and her delight is to be with the children of men.

How can we adequately sum up the immeasurable significance of Eastern monasticism? Perhaps by recalling the prophetic words —they still await fulfillment—which Dostoevsky put in the mouth of the *staretz* Zossima: "How surprised men would be if I were to say that from these meek monks, who yearn for solitary prayer, the salvation of Russia will come perhaps once more. For they are in truth made ready in peace and quiet for the day and the hour, the month and the year. Meanwhile, in their solitude, they keep the image of Christ fair and undefiled, in the purity of God's truth, from the times of the fathers of old, the Apostles and the martyrs. And when the time comes they will show it to the tottering creeds of the world. That is a great thought. That star will rise out of the East." [3]

[3] Fyodor Dostoevsky: *The Brothers Karamazov* (New York: The Modern Library; 1929), p. 388.

Saint AUGUSTINE

and the Communal Life
of the Clergy

Now the heavenly Father has His hunting hounds everywhere —in convents and monasteries, in our homes and in cities, and in the forest; and you may be certain that all chosen friends of God are going to be sorely hunted by all created things. As the hart is driven by the hunters, tormented with thirst, so must thou be driven on till thou findest thy refuge in God. To make us thirst for God alone in time and in eternity—that is the divine purpose in allowing us men to be thus hunted, each one according to his special circumstances of life. Go forward, then, in all humility, patience, and mildness, for without doubt thou shalt at last come to our Saviour's sweet fountains, which will refresh thee beyond the power of words to describe." [1]

These words of Johannes Tauler's strike the keynote of Augustine's life: he was a man hunted by God. His own analysis of himself reveals a man pursued, always driven onward and seldom granted a breathing-space. "And You sent Your hand from above," [2] he writes, to indicate who was responsible for the ceaseless movement that filled his life. God was the cause of his restlessness.

[1] Johannes Tauler: *Sermons and Conferences*, translated by Walter Elliott, C.S.P. (Washington, D.C.: Apostolic Mission House; 1910), p. 377.

[2] St. Augustine: *Confessions*, ed.: F. J. Sheed (New York: Sheed & Ward; 1952), Book III, section xi.

As the hunted hart is driven out whenever it takes cover, so was Augustine harassed by an invisible power. No sooner did he think himself safe than the breathless chase was renewed, and he fled panting on. "My soul turned and turned again, on back and sides and belly, and the bed was always hard. For thou alone art her rest. And behold Thou art close at hand to deliver us from the wretchedness of error and establish us in Thy way, and console us with Thy word: 'Run, I shall bear you up and bring you and carry you to the end.' " ³ Augustine's life thus becomes a symbol of man's life on earth. The worst fate that can befall a Christian is not to be pursued by God, for then he is bound to sink into the morass of the commonplace and to lose his own best self.

The counterpart of this untiring pursuit is the ceaseless search that stamps Augustine's life. Monica's son had an unquenchable thirst for truth, and he did not seek merely for seeking's sake. He sought in order to find, and this made his wresting meaningful.

"Let us give our mind's best attention, and, with the Lord's help, seek after God. . . . Let us search for that which needs to be discovered, and into that which has been discovered. He whom we need to discover is concealed, in order to be sought after; and when found, is infinite, in order still to be the object of our search. Hence it is elsewhere said, 'seek his face evermore' (Ps. cv, 4). . . . For we do not say that it will not be so always, because it is only so here; but that here we must always be seeking, lest at any time we should imagine that here we can ever cease from seeking. . . . Let us be walking always in the way, till we reach the end to which it leads; let us nowhere tarry in it till we reach the proper place of abode: and so we shall both persevere in our seeking and be making some attainments in our finding, and, thus seeking and finding, be passing on to that which remains, till the very end of all seeking shall be reached in that world where perfection shall admit of no further effort at advancement." ⁴

God's hunt began in the little African town of Tagaste, where young Augustine sowed his wild oats. Like most of those born un-

³ Ibid., Book VI, section xvi.
⁴ St. Augustine: *Homilies on the Gospel of St. John*, in *Library of the Nicene and Post-Nicene Fathers* (New York, 1888), tract no. 63, Vol. VII, p. 314.

4 *

der the sun of the dark continent, he was a sensual man, and he confessed his inclinations with a disarming honesty: "I was tossed about and wasted and poured out and boiling over in my fornications." [5]

He was too hot-blooded to lead a life of continence, and became involved in several love affairs. Yet in the midst of his passions Augustine was aware of an aching dissatisfaction, and each new pleasure awakened fresh desire. For a long time he lived with a concubine; then, though a gifted son had been born of this union, he perfunctorily severed the relationship and dismissed his companion, oblivious even of the laws of courtesy. Despite his resolution to lead an honorable life, he had not the strength to renounce love altogether. Soon afterward he proposed marriage to a girl who was still under age, while at the same time he maintained another concubine. But neither did this engagement culminate in marriage.

These irregular love relations left him with a prejudice that was common enough in the early Church: because he had never known the purity of conjugal love, he developed a lifelong, festering, hatred for the unruly flesh.

Yet Augustine was more than a hot-blooded sensualist responding only to the lusts of the flesh. The main motivation of his life was a burning desire for truth, which he sought with the whole strength of his belief. His blind groping for it developed into a spiritual odyssey that occupied the first half of his life. He was driven constantly by his passionate yearning for fulfillment, but never wearied of the search.

Cicero's *Hortensius* brought about a radical transformation, awakening in him a keen interest in philosophy. The philosopher's thirst for knowledge cured Augustine of his earlier tendency simply to take life for granted, and God's hunt could at last begin.

First he turned to the Persian sect of the Manichees, whose teachings he drank in thirstily, believing himself at the end of his quest. For almost nine years he steeped himself in the Manichean heresy, and its dualism remained etched on his mind for the rest of his life. Eventually, however, he began to doubt some of the tenets of the doctrine; he asked questions and received no answers that satisfied

[5] St. Augustine: *Confessions*, Book II, section ii.

him. Once again the old restlessness came over him; God's hounds unearthed him from his cover and relentlessly drove him on.

This time he was even unluckier, for in his despair he fell into the waiting arms of the skeptics, according to whom there was no truth that men could discover and the search for it was labor lost. In this blind alley, from which there was no hope of escape, the quarry was very nearly run to earth, for to deny the existence of truth means to embrace nothingness, and the inevitable consequence is spiritual death.

Apparently Augustine had to go through this wholly negative phase, which brought him to the very edge of the abyss, before he was vouchsafed the experience of internal evidence: "But how should I know that what he said was true? And if I did know it, would it be from him that I knew it? No: but within me, in the inner retreat of my mind, the Truth, which is neither Hebrew nor Greek nor Latin nor Barbarian, would tell me, without lips or tongue or sounded syllables: 'He speaks truth.' " [6]

Such comforting experiences saved Augustine from giving up even in the utmost danger. The first ray of light in the darkness that surrounded him came from Plotinus' *Enneads,* which taught him spiritual understanding of spiritual things, and whose esthetic approach to philosophy appealed to his sense of beauty. Neo-Platonism became part of his way of thinking, although he did not accept it as the final goal of his searching. [7]

"I was much exercised in mind," Augustine says, "as I remembered how long it was since that nineteenth year of my age in which I first felt the passion for true knowledge." And here he was, "still sticking in the same mire," still asking: "But where shall I search? When shall I search?" [8] The situation caused him profound anguish, but he had not the strength to resolve it. His spiritual wanderings had been much more than mere esthetic dabbling; they had stirred up the bitter lees of his whole life, and he shed as many tears as Odysseus, who in the end had longed for home.

He stood on the threshold of a decision that he was utterly unable

[6] Ibid.. Book XI. section iii.
[7] Cf. J. Nörregaard: *Augustins Bekehrung* (Tübingen, 1923), p. 62.
[8] St. Augustine: *Confessions,* Book VI, section xi.

to make, as he so graphically describes: "And I tried again and I was almost there, and now I could all but touch it and hold it: yet I was not quite there, I did not touch it or hold it. I still shrank from dying unto death and living unto life. The lower condition which had grown habitual was more powerful than the better condition which I had not tried. The nearer the point of time came in which I was to become different, the more it struck me with horror; but it did not force me utterly back nor turn me utterly away, but held me there between the two." [9] Who can read these words, which have the ring of psychological truth, and fail to recognize in the fury of this life the pursuit of God? It is so palpably there, for all who have eyes to see and ears to hear.

At the peak of his soul's agony, when tension had reached the breaking-point, Augustine discovered monasticism—and with it salvation. One day, when he was at home with his friend Alypius, he received the visit of an African compatriot, Pontitian, who told them "the story of the Egyptian monk Anthony, whose name was held in high honor among Your servants, although Alypius and I had never heard it before that time. When Pontitian learned this, he was the more intent upon telling the story, eager to introduce so great a man to men ignorant of him, and very much marveling at our ignorance." [1]

This tale of the first desert father made an overpowering impression on Augustine; it shook him to the roots of his being. He was astounded to learn that such things had happened "so recently, practically in our own times." [2] Anthony had died at a great age when Augustine was yet an infant. Pontitian went on to tell of the first monasteries, which were then being founded in the West, and Augustine could only repeat, in helpless wonder: "And we had not heard of it!" [3]

After the visitor had taken his leave, Augustine turned to Alypius, the anguish of his soul writ large upon his features, and exclaimed: "What is wrong with us? What is this which you heard? The unlearned arise and take heaven by force, and here are we with all our learning, stuck fast in flesh and blood! Is there any

[9] Ibid., Book VIII, section xi.   [2] Ibid.
[1] Ibid., Book VIII, section vi.   [3] Ibid.

shame in following because they have gone before us? Would it not be a worse shame not to follow at once?" [4]

A violent inward conflict raged in Augustine's soul. The brilliant intellectual life he had thus far been leading was crumbling about him like a house of cards, threatening to bury him under its ruins. That obscure, unlettered monks should be translating into deeds what he and his highbrow friends had merely been theorizing about was not to be borne. The spiritual storm gathered strength till even the company of Alypius was too much for him, and he stumbled out into the garden alone. There he threw himself on the ground under a fig tree, as if in the extreme anguish of his soul he would flee to the bosom of mother earth. He let his tears flow freely, no longer trying even to check them, and able only to moan: "How long, how long shall I go on saying 'tomorrow' and again 'tomorrow'? Why not now, why not have an end to my uncleanness this very hour?" [5]

In this most bitter sorrow of his heart, he heard a child's voice chanting: "Take and read," and he arose and went to open a book that lay on his table. Here again the father of monasticism providentially came to his aid, for, as Augustine relates, "it was part of what I had been told about Anthony, that from the Gospel which he happened to be reading he had felt that he was being admonished as though what he read was spoken directly to himself." [6] The memory of that "spoken directly to himself" caused Augustine to open St. Paul's Epistles and to rely on the Apostle's words as on an oracle. In silence he read a passage from Romans xiii, and "a light of utter confidence shone in my heart, and all the darkness of uncertainty vanished away." [7]

This experience, so often and so unsatisfactorily termed "Augustine's conversion," cleared his path to a new life. This unexpected illumination from on high has often been described as Augustine's "road to Damascus," but it has never been brought out sufficiently that his spiritual transformation had been caused by his encounter with monasticism.

Freed from the darkness of uncertainty, bathed in the light of

[4] Ibid., Book VIII, section viii.
[5] Ibid., Book VIII, section xii.

[6] Ibid.
[7] Ibid.

faith, Augustine at last came to know Christian mysticism. The title
of mystic has been denied to him, but denied unjustly. Mysticism
does not mean solely the experience of ecstasy; it means also the
response of the human heart to the divine—and in this Augustine
has had few equals. Without this mysticism, which echoes like a
deep musical accompaniment through the second half of his life,
the course of that life cannot be comprehended. It was a mystical
emotion that he experienced as he stood together with his mother
at a window in Ostia: "And while we were thus talking of His
wisdom and panting for it, with all the effort of our heart, we did
for one instant attain to touch it." [8] Once the marvelous melody of
the divine had sounded in his soul, it never died away.

Again and again Augustine asked himself what it was that he
loved when his heart was aflame with the love of God, and this was
his imperishable answer: "Not the beauty of any bodily thing, nor
the order of seasons, nor the brightness of light that rejoices the eye,
nor the sweet melodies of all songs, nor the sweet fragrance of
flowers and ointments and spices: not manna nor honey, not the
limbs that carnal love embraces. None of these things do I love in
loving my God. Yet in a sense I do love light and melody and
fragrance and food and embrace when I love my God—the light
and the voice and the fragrance and the food and embrace in the
soul, when that light shines upon my soul which no place can contain, that voice sounds which no time can take from me, I breathe
that fragrance which no wind scatters, I eat the food which is not
lessened by eating, and I lie in the embrace which satiety never
comes to sunder. This it is that I love, when I love my God." [9]

In the *Confessions*, Augustine describes God's hunt that led him
to this point—that seemingly cruel pursuit which was in fact an act
of divine mercy. The language he speaks is a Christian language
far removed in content from the textbook jargon of philosophy, and
in divinely inspired pathos sets a model virtually beyond imitation.
Nor shall we do Augustine justice, as Guardini writes, if we fail to
recognize the artist in him or the quality of his artistry. [1] He had a

[8] Ibid., Book IX, section x.
[9] Ibid., Book X, section vi.
[1] R. Guardini: *Die Bekehrung des heiligen Augustin* (1935), p. 164.

poet's feel for the shape and texture of life, and only the dull of heart can mistake the melodiousness of his phrases for mere rhetoric.

St. Augustine dealt with every question from a religious rather than an esthetic point of view; his *Confessions* are the product of life rather than of thought, of suffering rather than of literary invention. They are penetrated with a sense of God; they are the work of a man who saw the reality of the eternal as Israel had seen the pillar of fire in the desert at night. Only a man who has himself been hunted and pursued by God can speak of the eternal in such a fashion. In writing his *Confessions*, Augustine was not making some kind of psychological experiment; his purpose was to purify his soul, and that is why his true and painful account is so free from any vain posturings of the ego. "To what purpose do I tell it? Simply that I and any other who may read may realize out of what depths we must cry to Thee." [2] A man may speak of his poor life with such proud humility only when his recital is meant in praise of God's mercy and not as a plaintive pouring out of his own woes.

Augustine's dignified account of his dealings with his God has never lost its hold on men. This Christian saw himself as the riddle of all creation: "Here are men going afar to marvel at the heights of mountains, the mighty waves of the sea, the long courses of great rivers, the vastness of the ocean, the movements of the stars, yet leaving themselves unnoticed. . . ." [3] Augustine, on the other hand, even while he recognized himself to be a mystery beyond solution, knew himself in the light of God. As a result, his profound understanding of human psychology was illumined by supernatural insight.

The life of the young Augustine is as exciting as any novel. Monica's questing son has captivated the whole world, which is apt to regard the many wrong turns he took as a justification for its own sins. But Augustine the Christian is a figure no less powerful than the brilliant young seeker, nor any less enthusiastic or passionate in spirit. There is a prejudiced view of him as sunk in his ecclesiastical duties and desiccated by virtuous living. But to try to

[2] St. Augustine: *Confessions*, Book II, section iii.
[3] Ibid., Book X, section viii.

play off the young pagan against the old Christian argues a lack of insight. The spiritually significant figure is the mature Augustine who has given us so vivid a picture of his earlier phase.

In his ripe age, Augustine appears as a man of worldly experience, one who has himself been embroiled in many difficulties and has overcome them all, who has long blundered and has at last come to the light. A hard-won peace characterizes the latter part of his life and lends it a dignity that was lacking in the first. In the mature Augustine, the thirsting after God is intensified to a point at which nothing matters to him but knowledge of God and of man's soul. The divine hunt has by no means given way to stultifying boredom; it has merely become a deeper, more inward experience.

We are all too ready to overlook the fact that Augustine continued to feel insecurity in the midst of his religious "security." This is because the only material available concerning the second half of his life is the official biography written by his disciple Possidius. For many years Possidius lived in the same community with Augustine, whom he venerated, and whom he had every opportunity to observe close at hand. But his was a prosaic nature, and his writings are simply not to be compared to Augustine's *Confessions*, which give the reader the feeling of being caught up in the stream of world history. The impression that Augustine's life as a Christian was dull and dreary derives from Possidius' lusterless *Vita*, for, lacking the gift to describe the indescribable, he failed utterly to capture and portray his hero's passionate spirit.

"And a new life begins"—these words of Dante's might well serve as a heading for Augustine's Christian phase. He was not one of the many converts who, having undergone a spiritual transformation, turn dour. In his new existence he came face to face with the problem to which there is no final solution—that of putting the Gospel into actual practice. It is a problem that can be solved only by a great spiritual effort and a readiness to commit oneself. With his new clarity of vision, Augustine realized that his most vital task was to apply his religion to his daily life.

It is amazing that so little attention has been paid to Augustine's endeavor to live according to the Gospel. The omission is in part explained by excessive concentration on his doctrine. As Etienne Gilson says, a true philosopher speaks always of things; it is only the professors of philosophy who speak of ideas.[4]

Accordingly, Augustine's purpose in meditating on intellectual problems was to discover what a true Christian's way of life should be. It is not true that in his Christian stage he had no experiences deserving our consideration. The mature Augustine's efforts to live his religion are of a far deeper religious significance than the young man's odyssey, and they form the enduring groundwork of his religious and philosophic work. The bases of his philosophy are to be found in his new way of living, and afford convincing proof of the genuineness of his conversion. There could hardly be a more striking contrast than that between the life of Augustine the pagan and that of Augustine the Christian. The blundering search of the earlier years had become a purposeful and noble journey, bringing him to an ever deeper knowledge of Christian truth, leading him ever closer home.

Augustine's conversion had been brought about by his encounter with monasticism. This it was that had made him decide to embrace the ascetic life—a decision that until then he had not had the strength of mind to take. That memorable hour of his life remained engraved on his memory and kept his resolution alive. Everything connected with the monastic life aroused his almost feverish sympathy. The key to Augustine the Christian lies in his inner relation to monasticism. The story of Anthony as told to him by his friend lodged deep in his heart, and from that time on he became an ardent admirer of the desert hermits, even though, in his estimation, such an existence was altogether beyond human endurance and the anchorites could not serve as models for ordinary men. Augustine considered that monks came closest to putting the Christian ideal into practice, and he resolved to do likewise. He joined their ranks and became, in the end, one of the great fathers of monasticism.

The first way-station in his new, godly life was Cassiciacum, near Milan. The weeks he spent there would have to be painted in soft pastel tones. As a new convert, Augustine was in a singularly gentle

[4] Etienne Gilson: *Introduction à l'étude de Saint Augustin* (Paris: Librairie philosophique J. Vrin; 1931).

mood. He was nursing the plan of withdrawing with his friends from the tumult of the world and leading a life of leisure like the philosophers of antiquity. The weeks he spent at Cassiciacum were like a romantic holiday. The Christian life was still a mere bud, waiting to unfold. But such a plan was too idealistic, and Cassiciacum was hardly more than a debating society, a sort of nursing-home for convalescent souls.

When Augustine saw that his enterprise was doomed to failure, he broke off his stay at Cassiciacum and visited several recently founded monasteries on the outskirts of Rome. Soon, however, he returned to Africa, after a five-year absence, settled down in Tagaste, the town of his birth, and established a little monastery in his own house. Possidius records this decisive step in the following dry fashion: "On arriving at Tagaste and settling down with these companions, he cast off all worldly care. He persevered there for nearly three years, living for God in fasting, prayer, and good works, and meditating day and night on the laws of the Lord." [5]

If we ponder this unvarnished statement, we will note two features. First, withdrawal from the world: as soon as he became a Christian, Augustine fled the world, even as the early monks had done. Second, abandonment of personal property: following Anthony's example, he divided his possessions among the poor, keeping only his parents' house to serve as a joint dwelling-place for himself and his friends. Withdrawal from the world and surrender of all worldly goods are the two prerequisites to a true monastic life, and Augustine the Christian had the resolution to take both steps.

With the founding of his own monastery in Tagaste, Augustine became the father of monasticism in North Africa. The establishment was small, and at first only six brothers lived in the house. Yet it represented an earnest attempt to lead a monastic life, and was no mere playing at monasticism on the part of a few world-weary esthetes. Together they led a life of prayer and study, for which Augustine drew up some regulations. This gave participation in the community an obligatory character, and in this lies its superiority over the Cassiciacum attempt. "Tagaste is a landmark in the development of Western monasticism. Here, under the hot sun of North Africa, near the edge of the Sahara, was to come into being —for the first time, perhaps, in history—a monastery that was truly Western in spirit." [6]

Small as the monastery was, the townsfolk of Tagaste were filled with admiration and wonder by this example of Christian communal life. It meant more to them than a mere novelty. And in this little monastery Augustine entered upon his career as a religious writer. For the first time in his hunted and hounded existence, he found himself at peace and able to put his thoughts on paper. He was accorded only three years of this withdrawal from the world, but they sufficed to mark him as one of the world's great thinkers, who strongly influenced Christendom and was hailed by it as "the genius of the West." His books cannot be divorced from the monastic ideal; and, indeed, only when we bear in mind that they were written by one of the fathers of monasticism does their purpose become wholly clear.

His quiet seclusion in the little monastery came to an abrupt end. Possidius relates that Valerius, Bishop of Hippo, was preaching one day to his people and exhorting them to provide a candidate for ordination to the priesthood. Augustine happened to be in the church at the time. "And now the people, finding him amongst them, laid hands upon him and, leading him to the bishop, according to their custom, presented him as a candidate for ordination." [7] Neither tears nor arguments availed to change the swift procession of events. Valerius ordained him, and, against his will, Monica's son was now a priest.

Before his ordination, he had earnestly asked himself whether a man with such a past dared accept the office of priest; above all, he shuddered at the thought that he might again give way to the passions of his youth. Priesthood to him was a burden, and he could not keep from sighing: "Nothing is finer than, in quiet, to seek for the rich treasure of the divine mysteries; that is sweet and good. But to preach, admonish, punish, build, be available to everyone: that is a great weight, a heavy load, a hard burden. Who would not

---

[6] A. Zumkeller: *Das Mönchtum des heiligen Augustinus* (1951), p. 10.
[7] St. Possidius: op. cit., chap iv.

flee from such work? But I fear the Gospel." He made his acceptance subject to the condition that even in his new role he should
be allowed to continue to lead a monastic life, for that he was unwilling to surrender. Bishop Valerius showed great understanding,
and even made him a gift of a tract of arable land, on which the
new priest built a monastery and a garden. This was his third home
since he had become a Christian. By clinging to the monastic life,
Augustine proclaimed to the whole world that the callings of monk
and priest were not mutually exclusive.

When Bishop Valerius died, Augustine was the logical successor. And it was as Bishop of Hippo that the author of the *Confessions* reached the last step of his public career. Our picture of
Augustine will not be complete without some knowledge of his episcopal activity. He was forty-two years old when he was raised to
that office, and he exercised it for over thirty years, until his death,
with never flagging energy. The people with whom he had to deal
as bishop were far from measuring up to his spiritual stature. His
community consisted for the most part of small-minded people,
spiritually unalert, such as one might find in any port city. Nor
were any of his African colleagues capable of appreciating his gigantic mind. At the same time, Augustine himself never made them
feel their inferiority.

Slight of build, with his closely cropped head always uncovered,
sharp-featured and clean-shaven, he approached all men with the
same friendliness. He would apologize to his congregation, which
according to the usage of the time listened standing to the sermon
that he delivered sitting, for having kept them for so long in such
an uncomfortable position. He was capable of great courtesy and
charm, enhanced by the fact that he never sought to make an impression.

He had no taste for admiration; he lived only for his work. It
was not unusual for him to dictate letters far into the night. He had
a dislike of time-consuming administrative duties, and regarded
them, according to Possidius, as troublesome occupations that took
him away from more important things.[8] Nevertheless, he conscientiously discharged all his episcopal obligations, devoting partic-

[8] Ibid., chap. xix.

ular attention to preaching and to the guidance of the souls committed to his care. "Consultation and cure of souls, administration of ecclesiastical discipline and awarding of justice in the episcopal court—one duty succeeded another. The turbid waters of human weakness flowed endlessly through the channel of Augustine's life." [9]

But never once did he try to lay aside the heavy burden. He had completely rid himself of his youthful arrogance; the lofty thinker spent his life in dealing with humble Christian folk as if that were the most natural thing in the world. The greatest man of the century did not condescend to his community—he simply put himself on the same level with it. Nor did he make any display of his episcopal rank, wearing neither ring nor cross. He was not fond of his sumptuous episcopal robes, and he was capable of ordering precious church vessels melted down in order to ransom prisoners. His great humanity made him accessible to all, and he endeavored to live in accord with his own unforgettable remark: "God humbled himself, and yet man is proud!" As he advanced in years, the modesty of his demeanor increased, and in his boundless humility there is perhaps even more greatness than in his philosophical writings.

In the midst of his varied ecclesiastical labors, Augustine remained faithful to monasticism. Although he had had to leave his "garden monastery" and, in order to discharge his duties, move into the bishop's residence in the immediate vicinity of the church, he neither gave up his monastic life nor allowed himself to drift gradually away from it. Instead, he established his third monastery in the bishop's palace. When he had been chosen to succeed Valerius, Augustine had set the condition that he be left in peace on certain days of the week so that he might be alone with God. He did not want to become one of those overworked men who are too busy even to think. The condition was not respected, for in those turbulent times the people made excessive demands upon their bishop. Nevertheless, Augustine felt an overpowering need for a few hours' peace each day, which are as vital to a religious person as the air he breathes. He sounded this warning to himself and to all Christians who have no time to spare for higher things: "No man has a

[9] F. van der Meer: *Augustinus der Seelsorger* (1951), p. 308.

right . . . to be so immersed in active life as to neglect the con-templation of God." [1]

Augustine urged all the clerics under his authority to live in the new monastery. He was keenly aware of the dangers to which a clergy moving freely about a seaport would be exposed. Moreover, he wanted to build a community with his fellow workers so that their unity might be proclaimed not only in their preaching but also in their very mode of life. Augustine said in that connection that those who lived with him would possess God [2]—a bold state-ment, and one that is hard to accept. He did not force his clergy to espouse the communal life, but gradually succeeded in persuading them all, down to the youngest deacon, to enter his monastery. In the end, he would not ordain any man not prepared to accept com-munal life.

His disciples soon became much sought-after priests, many of them rising to the rank of bishop, but without abandoning their mo-nastic way of life. The union of priesthood and monasticism, already discernible under Basil, reached its peak under Augustine. The clerical monastery in Hippo thus represents a turning-point in the history of monasticism. Until then, monks had sought to flee the world; but in the bishop's monastery the order of the day was: "The Church needs us! Preach for it, save the souls of its members! We may not shirk its tasks. It is our duty to serve the Church." By applying these principles, Augustine brought about a radical change: the monastery turned its face to the world. This was a new development that had untold consequences of immense benefit to the Church.

To gain a true picture of Augustine's third monastery we must try to visualize the actual life that the bishop led there with his fellow workers. For all his love of solitude, Augustine had always felt the need to gather men about him in order to form them in the communal life. Like all the fathers of monasticism, he had a strong pedagogical streak, and the communal life he led "with his breth-

---

[1] St. Augustine: *City of God*, Book XIX, chap. xix, in *Library of Nicene and Post-Nicene Fathers* (New York, 1907), Vol. II.
[2] Quoted in Van der Meer: op. cit., p. 242.

ren" in "God's garden"—his name for the monastic community—
gave him every opportunity for molding human beings.

The style of living in the bishop's monastery was of noble moderation. Clothing, footwear, and bedding were modest but appropriate, neither too fine nor too poor. "With regard to cutlery, the
spoons only were of silver; the vessels in which the food was served
were of clay, wood, or marble; and this was not out of necessity,
but because it was his wish." [8]

Augustine was an enemy of excessive asceticism, but he also
frowned on gluttony and would have nothing to do with the common pronouncement that the priest, denied the joys of marriage,
must find his pleasure in a good meal. The food in the bishop's
monastery was simple, but meat was occasionally served because of
guests or because someone was ill, and there was always wine on
the table. None of his priests was permitted to miss a meal, and
eating outside was forbidden.

Augustine would not tolerate unkind remarks about absent persons, seeing in them a violation of the commandment "Thou shalt
love thy neighbor as thyself," and he had the following inscription
carved into the table: "If anyone in his conversation attempts to
injure the character of some absent one, let him consider himself
unwelcome to this table." On one occasion, when some visiting
bishops were guilty of such a breach, Augustine pointed admonish-
ingly to the inscription. His guests, however, felt that it did not
apply to them. Whereupon Augustine became very angry, rose,
and said with severity: "Either these words must be effaced, or I
shall have to leave you in the middle of your meal and retire to my
room." [4] A moment of painful silence followed. But Augustine was
indifferent to the embarrassment he had caused his guests: he had
seen the Christian spirit of his monastery in danger and had sprung
to its defense. Possidius, who witnessed the incident, was deeply
impressed by the spectacle of Augustine's wrath. His narrative shows
how deep and earnest was Augustine's desire to apply Christian
teachings to his daily life.

The clerical monastery at Hippo had a far-reaching influence for

[8] St. Possidius: op. cit., chap. xxii.   [4] Ibid.

good. At the same time, to give the impression that it was a paradise on earth would be wrong. After all, it was inhabited by all
kinds of men, and they often rubbed each other the wrong way.
Some of the members failed dismally to live up to Augustine's expectations. He wrote in one of his letters: "I confess openly to your
charity before the Lord our God, who has been the witness of my
soul from the time when I began to serve him, that, just as it is
hard to find better men than those who live virtuously in monasteries, so I have not found worse than those who have fallen into
sin in monasteries. . . ." [5] One such failure was so scandalous
that Augustine felt it his duty as bishop to air the entire matter
from the pulpit lest there should be serious trouble in the community and the entire monastery should fall into disrepute. But the
fact that a few had fallen by the wayside was no reason, he believed, for condemning the whole venture. A monastery is not an
isle of the blessed, safe from all storms; nowhere is there absolute
security. The haven of the cloister, he wrote, is open to the sea,
and the winds can blow into it; and even if there are no cliffs, ships
can collide with one another and be damaged. [6]

He himself is not immune from this judgment. The great Church
father was capable of extreme harshness, as witness his severe
pronouncement against pagans, whose very virtues he deemed to be
glittering vices, and his sternness toward the Donatists. As the leading figure among the bishops of North Africa, he had expended
much time and effort on negotiations with the Donatists, but to
small purpose. Finally he felt that other methods must be used, and
in that connection cited the famous words of the parable: "Compel
them to come in." His arguments in defense of the use of force
were ambiguous, and have earned him the epithet of "the first
dogmatist of the inquisition." [7] The reproach, however, is undeserved, for Augustine had always had a horror of bloodshedding
by the Church, and he was not, in fact, advocating any form of
cruelty.

[5] St. Augustine: *Letters*, Vol. I (New York: Fathers of the Church,
Inc.; 1951), no. 78, p. 384.
[6] J. Mausbach: *Die Ethik des heiligen Augustin* (1929), I, 356.
[7] H. Reuter: *Augustinische Studien* (1887), p. 51.

With advancing age, he became unable to bear even the least contradiction, and a certain rigidity gripped his mind. The dogmatic controversies in which he had engaged led him into the ways of authoritarian thinking which dulled his perception of truth and which he vainly attempted to shake off. Augustine is such an outstanding figure in Christian history that he can easily bear these truths to be voiced. In the hour of his death no one would have been readier to admit these failings than Augustine himself, who had a keen sense of his own sinfulness.

Life in the clerical monastery was governed by a rule written by Augustine himself. He had already laid down a few principles binding upon the inmates of his own monastery in Tagaste. For his "garden monastery" and his episcopal monastery he worked out a formal rule in twelve chapters. For a long time it was thought that the document had originated several centuries later, but Winfried Hümpfner's investigations have shown that there is no ground for doubting Augustine's authorship of it.[8] It is his work, the oldest monastic rule of the West.

The remarkable contents of this document should not be underestimated because of its brevity. Augustine's rule contains an inexhaustible wealth of precepts, more than it is humanly possible to carry out. It contains directions about the singing of psalms, about fasting, about other monastic practices. Augustine's clergy were not yet required to observe uniformity of dress, but their clothing was not to be in any way conspicuous. Since they had many priestly duties to perform in the area, Augustine could not forbid them to go out, but he wished them, whenever possible, to go together rather than alone. He instructed them to read the rule once a week in order to keep it fresh in their minds.

Augustine's rule laid down a clear and meaningful line of conduct which could be adhered to. Moreover, its application was not limited to the clerical monastery. Other monasteries were soon founded, now in this city, now in that, through Augustine's direct intervention or indirect influence, and at last a great many were

[8] H. U. von Balthasar: *Die grossen Ordensregeln* (Einsiedeln: Benziger; 1948), p. 101.

scattered over North Africa. A women's convent, directed by Augustine's sister, was established in Hippo. He gave them all advice and active help.

Augustine headed his rule with the sentence: "Above all things, dearest brethren, love God, and after him your neighbor. For these are the main commandments given to us." [9] To Augustine, the love of love was the most important thing in life. The brothers should live together in an atmosphere of love, and love should be the motivating force of all their actions. As Augustine writes further in his rule: "Let charity, which abides forever, reign supreme in all things required by the passing needs of this life." [1]

The Augustinian monastery did not arise out of weariness of the world or rejection of life. To enter a monastery because of disgust with earthly things would be to enter it for the wrong reason. Communal life should be founded wholly on love of God—all other considerations are merely secondary. Augustine's whole thinking was molded by the new commandment of the Gospel of St. John. There welled in him a stream of loving-kindness which prompted all his magnificent utterances about the human heart.

According to Augustine, a Christian can attain to God only through charity, and to him the Gospel was the religion of charity *par excellence*. Charity is what distinguishes the children of God from the children of the Devil. Satan, too, has faith, but he does not love. He who has charity is God's own, and to him it may be said: "Love, and do as you will." Where love is, man can do no wrong; where it is not, how can he do good? Augustine made charity the supreme rule of his monastery, and his words on the subject might well be regarded as a sequel to St. Paul's exhortation to the Christians of Corinth: "Let charity be preserved above all things: charity is the rule in eating and in speaking, in clothing and in demeanor. All are resumed in a single love, breathe the same love. To wound love is to wound God. Whatever is opposed to charity is overcome and cast out; nothing that offends against love can endure but a single day. We know that Christ and the Apostles

  [9] St. Augustine: *Rule*, chap. i. For the text of the rule, see *Jordani de Saxonia Liber Vitasfratrum*, ed. R. Arbesmann and W. Hümpfner (New York: Cosmopolitan Science and Art Service Co.; 1943), Appendix C, p. 494.
  [1] Ibid., chap. viii.

have made charity so binding that without it, all is vain; with it, all is fulfilled." [2]

In this timeless wisdom of love we hear the very beating of Augustine's heart. True, the early hermits fled into the desert for love of God, and that love was the motive power of the entire monastic movement; but Augustine was the first to formulate the principle of love with such shining clarity and to give it absolute primacy. Love and the heart are inseparable; they are the focal point of Augustine's Christian philosophy, and that is why he has so often been shown by artists holding a heart in his hand. With his religion of love, he opposed and conquered the intellectualism of the ancients and proclaimed to posterity that man is what he loves, not what he thinks. This truly Christian appraisal of man led Pascal to write these memorable words: "Jesus Christ and St. Paul possess the order of charity, not of intellect, for they desired to enkindle, not to instruct. The same is true of St. Augustine." [3] These short words are perhaps the greatest tribute that could be paid to Augustine.

Augustine's lucid description of the purpose of the monastic life is closely linked with his concept of love. To understand this purpose wholly, however, one must grasp his philosophy of history, which he set forth in his gigantic work, *The City of God;* in it, like Daniel the prophet and St. Paul, he portrays the cosmic drama in the light of divine revelation. Scholz calls the twenty-two books of *The City of God* "a farewell discourse to a declining era and a prolegomenon to a new one." [4]

What prompted Augustine to undertake this work was, in the first place, Alaric's capture of Rome in 410. He analyzes the event in great detail, reminding his readers that life is fleeting and that the Christian's striving must be for the Eternal City. Augustine speaks of the hoary world in which all grows old and to which the Christian, his youth renewed in Christ, should not attach himself.

He did not take for granted that Rome would perish; perhaps it was merely being chastised by God so that it might mend its ways.

[2] St. Augustine: *De moribus Ecclesiae catholicae,* in J.-P. Migne, ed.: *Patrologiae Cursus Completus* (Paris, 1877), XXXII, 1341.

[3] Blaise Pascal: *Pensées* (Paris: Nelson; 1942), no. 283, p. 172.

[4] H. Scholz: *Glaube und Unglaube in der Weltgeschichte* (1911), p. 195.

Nevertheless, it did not escape his keen perception that society in the world that had embraced Christianity had not been regenerated. Social relations had not conspicuously altered and, world circumstances being what they were, the social problem could not be resolved.[5]

Since Christianity could not be put into effect in the world, monastic communities must undertake the task, and in his rule Augustine set them this lofty goal: "The first purpose for which you have been brought together is that, living in one house, you be of one mind, and that you have one heart and one soul in God. Do not call anything your own, but let all things be in common. Let food and clothing be distributed to each one of you by your superior, not in equal measure to all, because you are not all of the same strength, but so as to provide for each one according to his need. For thus you read in the Acts of the Apostles: they had all things in common, and distribution was made to everyone according to his need." [6] These words restate with even greater clarity the principle he had already applied in the little monastery of Tagaste: "We desire to live in the manner of the Apostles." [7] There can be no mistake; the aim of this monastic life in common was to revive the spirit of the primitive Church.

The first Christian community, unlike most later ones, differed radically, and deliberately, in its way of life from that of the pagans who surrounded it. In order to prevent excessive regard for property, the first Christians instituted and practiced community ownership; this was one of the most striking features of their way of life, to which St. Luke twice draws attention in his Acts. True, theirs was not a communism of production, but only of consumption; nevertheless, it was unquestionably an attempt to resolve social problems by the application of Christian principles. The system was entirely voluntary; no compulsion was involved, as we see from St. Peter's words to Ananias (Acts v, 4). Through this "communism of love," the first Christians demonstrated beyond all cavil

[5] Reuter: op. cit., pp. 391, 392.

[6] St. Augustine: *Rule*, chap. i.

[7] Balthasar: op. cit., p. 122. Quoted from St. Augustine's first rule, para. 4.

that men could make a wholly fresh start by living together in the spirit of the Gospel.

Augustine recognized community ownership as an essential element in the life of the early Church, and sought consistently to apply the same "communism of love" in his monastery, all of whose members really desired to emulate the Apostles. It was possible, he felt, to reproduce the life of the first Christians in a small society, as it was not in the profit-minded world of traffic and trade. Augustine, it has been said, was "deeply penetrated by this idea of a Christian communism, and convinced that private property was the source of many ills." [8]

The drastic measure of community ownership of the early Church led to the radicalism of the first monks, who had not yet become docile supporters of the existing social order, and who, like Augustine, often expressed highly unpopular views, regarding states as "great dens of robbers" which knew nothing of true justice.

At the same time, Augustine avoided any trace of that systematic leveling which is the inevitable concomitant of non-religious communism. In his rule he stated expressly that food and clothing should not be the same for all, as the needs of individuals differed, but rather that each should receive what he required. This provision ensured individual treatment for every member of the community and closed the door to uniformity.

The revival, within Augustine's monastery, of a communism based on love, and the fact that he kept nothing under lock and key, and indeed refused several legacies to his church,[9] show clearly that for him primitive Christianity was not simply an object of mild enthusiasm. The community ownership practiced in his monastery is proof positive of the sincerity with which the brethren pursued their purpose, and in itself constituted a return to primitive Christianity. Not that all the features of the first Christian community were reproduced in Augustine's monastery. But, however imperfect the imitation, it gives us considerable food for thought. For later Christian communities have all too often adapted themselves to the social standards of the surrounding pagan society and, having

[8] Zumkeller: op. cit., p. 138.   [9] St. Possidius: op. cit., chap. xxiv.

cut the bonds of a "communism of love," have been ensnared in the toils of a communism of compulsion.

Augustine is often portrayed as a man who was a riddle unto himself. But Augustine did not fear to face this riddle and come to this conclusion about the inner conflicts of his youth: "It is therefore no monstrousness, partly to will, partly not to will, but a sickness of soul." [1]

The same clear-sightedness is apparent in his theological writings, which show Augustine to have been anything but a mere theorist. For all his acumen in debate, his capacity for getting to the root of a problem, and his refusal to be satisfied with superficial solutions, he never regarded thought as an end in itself. He sought to present religion in terms acceptable to reason, but this never led him to indulge in dialectical games, using Christian problems as the ball. From such perils, which commonly beset the man who deals in philosophy and religion, Augustine was protected by his monastic way of life. Never did he forget, as one authority has put it, "that true Christianity is something far more than mere 'doctrine.'" [2] Augustine was marvelously adept at living the Gospels as well as at meditating deeply upon them.

This urge to give practical form to his belief merits Augustine the title of a Christian existentialist—in the sense in which Kierkegaard used the term. Thought, for him, was at the service of being. What he grasped with his mind, he was determined to bring into existence; this was his constant endeavor. This practical approach made him an inspired teacher and clothed him with a greatness that no argument can gainsay. For while theoretical pronouncements are always open to objection, a Christianity that is lived is not.

Augustine's behavior in the face of death fits perfectly into this picture of a monastic existentialist. Possidius relates that in intimate conversations with his clergy the bishop used to say that even tried and true Christians should not depart this life without sufficient atonement. When sickness compelled him to take to his bed, he withdrew to his own chamber. Having no possessions, he refused to make a will; but he had four penitential psalms inscribed on a parchment

[1] St. Augustine: *Confessions*, Book VIII, section ix.
[2] Reuter: op. cit., p. 494.

that he fastened to his wall so that he could read and reread them from his bed.[3] As his end neared, this powerful thinker concentrated wholly on the words of the psalms. Ten days before his death he gave orders that no more visitors should be admitted, so that no sound of the busy world might penetrate the stillness in which he lay. With prayers and tears, he prepared in solitude to meet the Almighty.

There have, of course, been more heroic deaths, and there have been Christians who have suffered far greater martyrdom, yet it would be hard to find a more human death than Augustine's. His silent earnestness and simplicity are deeply moving. As Augustine lay on his deathbed, the city was being besieged by the Vandals, and from time to time the noise of the beleaguering army penetrated into his sick-chamber and mingled with his feverish visions. He asked himself whether the end of the world was not at hand, and whether the final battle between the kingdom of God and the kingdoms of earth was not even then being joined. Yet he decided that the day of days had not yet come, and, trusting in the world's salvation, he closed his eyes forever on August 28, 430, at the age of seventy-six. Shortly after his death, the Vandals broke into the city, which was by then deserted after a defense that had lasted fourteen months, and razed it to the ground.

Standing, as it were, at Augustine's bier, we cannot help but look for a scriptural text that would sum up this unusual life, and we shall hardly find any more applicable than these words of Jesus: "When ye shall have done all those things which are commanded you, say, We are unprofitable servants: we have done that which was our duty to do" (Luke xvii, 10).

As a religious thinker, St. Augustine may be likened to a mountain range in which one can roam endlessly. A scholar could devote his entire life to assimilating Augustine's work and reading all that has been written about him; and even then it is doubtful whether he would have mastered his subject. A thinker of Augustine's stature does not appear more than once in many centuries. In the history of the human mind, Augustine lives on as a theologian whose all-embracing thought structure has survived the ravages of time. There is

[3] St. Possidius: op. cit., chap. xxxi.

hardly a theological problem with which this greatest of the Western fathers of the Church did not concern himself. His works include treatises on the Trinity, on predestination, on biblical exegesis; but his greatest service is to have revived interest in the Pauline Gospel.

At the same time, Augustine was a born philosopher. He gave deep thought to the problems of being and time, free will and cognition, to say nothing of his luminous work on the philosophy of history, which it took him twelve years to produce. It is hard to name a philosophical problem to the solution of which Augustine did not make a major contribution.

His dynamic and passionate mind fortunately prevented his cosmic philosophy of religion from forming a closed system that could be accepted or rejected as a whole. The living Augustinianism is still in the process of becoming. It rests on the idea that religious truth cannot be wholly attained through thought alone, and that all statements are but signs of the inexpressible. This very incompleteness of Augustine's thinking—which was a method rather than a system—has made him the constant companion of Christians in all ages. Not only was he the mainstay of the Middle Ages; the Reformation and our own day are also deeply in his debt. Whenever serious consideration is given to the basic problems of Christianity, St. Augustine's name comes to the fore.

Truly, Augustine did not stint his efforts, but gave of his best and was not easily satisfied with himself. What he succeeded in accomplishing in a lifetime of hard work staggers the imagination. And yet, after all his achievements, on his deathbed he thought of himself as an unprofitable servant. He literally did not dare to echo the words of the dying Ambrose, who had not been ashamed of his life and had had no fear of appearing before the supreme Judge. Augustine thought of himself as a debtor who had no choice but to pack up his miserable belongings and to come empty-handed before the Almighty. This humility was genuine; he was deeply conscious of his own sinfulness, and his eyes were filled with tears as he read the penitential psalms affixed to his wall.

No man has ever done more than his duty; even he who has lived the best of lives is in God's debt, and may not presume on fame or merit. A Christian can only trust in God's mercy, which alone can save him from perdition. This fervent belief in salvation through grace is a focal point of Augustine's faith, and in the very hour of his death he clung to this doctrine, which he had passionately defended in his writings against Pelagius, and which is the most important thing he had to teach.

II

After Augustine's death the flourishing communal life in North Africa was shattered by the invading Vandals, and its sorry remnants were wiped out two centuries later by Islam. It would seem as though all his great work lay in ruins. But the truth is that no seed of eternal life is ever lost; it merely rests for a while beneath the earth and then begins to sprout anew. And so the seed sowed by Augustine has come up and borne fruit, thirty-, sixty-, and a hundred-fold.

His work cannot be seen apart from the spiritual life of the Western world; to consider his influence is to evoke whole epochs in the history of Christianity. Widely different movements have claimed him as their authority. A saying of St. Augustine's can be found to support nearly every religious interpretation, so inexhaustible is the source. The Church and heretics have both claimed him as their own, and both with some justice. Yet there can be no doubt that Augustine was a true son of the Church. He believed that whoever did not have the Church for his mother could not have God for his father, and he once said that without the authority of the Church he would not believe in the Gospels. The Bishop of Hippo cannot be divorced from the Church, and any attempt in that direction is doomed to failure. Yet Gottschalk, Calvin, and Jansen came closer to some of his ideas than the official Church doctrine, which has not assimilated his teachings in their entirety.

Owing to the Vandal invasion, Augustine's institution of communal life for the clergy was not imitated until much later. Chrodegang, Archbishop of Metz, established a monastery for his clergy, but Augustine's rule was not applied in it. The imperial synod of

Aix issued 817 stipulations for clergy, which did not, however, have the desired effect, especially as members of the clerical communities retained their right to private property. The attempt miscarried because reform was being imposed from without rather than carried out voluntarily from within.

It was not until the eleventh century that the monastic reform movement spread also among the clerics, resulting in notable changes. Leaders of the movement reopened the battle against private dwellings and private property and deliberately revived the rule of St. Augustine. At the Roman council of 1050, Pope Nicholas II recommended to priests, deacons, and subdeacons "that they live together near the churches for which they had been ordained and that there they have in common their table, sleeping quarters, and church revenues." [4]

Compliance with these instructions led to the formation of the order of Canons Regular, who were governed by the rule of St. Augustine and who therefore came to be known as Augustinian Canons. They maintained various establishments, which at first were not in close contact with one another, but which played an important part in inducing the clergy to adopt a strictly religious mode of life. Unfortunately, not all clerics assumed it to be their duty to live as true Christians, and the Augustinian Canons acted as a bulwark against a worldly priesthood.

The Augustinians have been a blessing to Christianity. Many outstanding men have emerged from their ranks. On various occasions the order was threatened with dissolution, but it was always able to produce the right men to save it from that fate. It was among the Augustinians that Victorine mysticism, based on the doctrine of Richard of St. Victor, took firmest root, to the great profit of many Christians. One of the great members of the order was Nicholas of Cusa, the eminent religious philosopher of the fifteenth century, who put posterity in his debt by collecting Meister Eckhart's sermons, and whose own writings are only now receiving their due. Many establishments of Augustinian Canons were dissolved during the Reformation, and secularization inflicted even greater casualties

[4] F. Mourret: *A History of the Catholic Church* (St. Louis, Mo.: Herder Book Co.; 1941), VI, 347.

on them. Nevertheless, a few were able to weather every storm, and the order persists to this day.

Another fruit borne by St. Augustine's work was the order of Augustinian Hermits, various communities of whom existed in the Middle Ages, and who, at the Pope's bidding, in 1256 formed a religious order that later became a mendicant order and is still active. The name has only a historical value, for they have long since abandoned the eremitic life; in fact, the communal life is to them not merely a means, but an end in itself. They are still forbidden to accept any office outside the order, and their purpose remains unchanged: to revive the manner of life of the primitive Christians as an example to the world. They are an active rather than a contemplative order, and, like their patron, they work in parishes, in the missions, and in a variety of other fields, including that of science. They have produced many eminent men, among the best known, perhaps, being Johannes Staupitz and Abraham a Santa Clara.

But the religious impact of men like these has been far surpassed by another member of the order, Martin Luther. We can gauge how deeply the young Luther was steeped in the spirit of monasticism from this little-known passage, which he wrote at a time when he was already fired with his new ideal of reform: "I believe that it is better to be a monk now than it has been in the past two hundred years, for this reason, that up till now monks have shrunk back from the cross, and it has been an honorable thing to be a monk. Now, however, they are again beginning to incur men's displeasure. For that is what being a monk means: to be hated by the world and to appear foolish in its sight." [5]

Luther's ceaseless endeavor to attain to a merciful God was typical of a monk whose conscience is deeply stirred. All his life, his thinking was colored by monasticism, and this puts him closer in spirit to the Middle Ages than to our own times. And whenever Protestantism has forgotten that it saw its birth in a monastic cell, it has grown shallow. That is why Kierkegaard, who fought hardest in the nineteenth century against the identification of Protestantism with bourgeois respectability, made this pronouncement, which is

[5] Martin Luther: *Vorlesung über den Römerbrief*, ed. Ellwein (1927), p. 472.

even more apposite today than it was in his own times: "A return to the monastery from which Luther broke out: that is what Christianity has to achieve first of all!" [6]

As soon as we regard Luther from a religious rather than from a historical point of view, we see him as a man who strove with might and main to restore a Christianity centered in the naked cross, and therefore as a man who put new life into what had often become a rather theoretical form of Augustinianism. Luther himself recognized that "after the Apostles, Christendom had found no better teacher than Augustine." [7] He regarded St. Augustine as "a noble and devout man, who would have been on our side had he lived now. . . . Augustine was the most earnest, the bravest, and the purest of all, but he could not do everything singlehanded." [8] The greatest Augustinian of the sixteenth century saw in Augustine a herald of the selfsame gospel that he was announcing, and as the Church father who had understood the Scriptures better than any other.[9] Luther could regard St. Augustine as his mighty forerunner in his teachings on grace. And he was also justified in seeing in his own controversy with Erasmus on the subject of free will a repetition of Augustine's debate with Pelagius. There was much of Augustine in Luther, and we might get a startlingly new picture of the reformer if we approached him without bias and in the spirit of Augustine himself.[1]

At first Luther was hailed by his order with great enthusiasm as a man who was bringing the deepest religious problems into the open once again. Soon, however, his fellow Augustinians realized that his action was leading in a direction far removed from the aims of their order, and they broke with him. And it is a fact that Luther, with his determination to set aside sterile, man-made regulations in order to achieve a more immediate union with God, destroyed the very concept of the monastic life which had been central to Augustine's thought. A terrible inner struggle led the monk in Luther to rise up against monasticism. He had to turn against what he held

[6] Sören Kierkegaard: *Tagebücher*, ed. Haecker (1923), II, 353.
[7] Luther, M. (Erlanger edition—German), pp. 30, 107.
[8] Ibid., pp. 62, 111.
[9] A. Hamel: *Der junge Luther und Augustin* (1935), II, 155-8.
[1] Cf. J. Hessen: *Luther in katholischer Sicht* (1947), p. 8.

most dear for the sake of what he held most dear—and the result, inevitably, was a profound Christian tragedy, a tragedy that cannot be explained merely by the historical circumstances. We may understand it, perhaps, by analogy; in terms, for instance, of the image St. Paul uses in his Epistle to the Romans of branches that are broken off in order that new ones may be grafted on.

However similar his doctrine of grace, Luther cannot be considered as having continued or completed St. Augustine's work. He is to be regarded rather as Augustine's prodigal son, whom the father, according to the parable, welcomes home with redoubled love. Only when the sons of Luther join the sons of Augustine in a Christendom made whole once more will the eternal day of God's rest, with which grandiose vision St. Augustine concludes his *City of God*, dawn upon the earth: "This 'seventh day' will be our sabbath and . . . it will end in no evening, but only in the Lord's day— that eighth and eternal day which dawned when Christ's resurrection heralded an eternal rest both for the spirit and for the body. On that day we shall rest and see, see and love, love and praise—for this is to be the end without the end of all our living, that Kingdom without end, the real goal of our present life." [2]

---

[2] St. Augustine: *City of God*, Book XXII (New York: Fathers of the Church, Inc.; 1954), XXIV, 510–11.

Saint BENEDICT

and His Rule

Benedict" means "the blessed," and the patriarch of Western monasticism was indeed blessed as few men have ever been. At first, however, the fruits of the divine bounty were hidden from men's eyes. In his own century Benedict went almost unnoticed, nor did a single contemporary so much as take the trouble to commit his name to paper. Pope Gregory I, two generations later, was the first to write an account of the prodigious events of Benedict's life. Gregory devoted the second book of his *Dialogues* to the story of Benedict, and this, together with the rule, are our only sources for Benedict's life. Gregory, moreover, as he remarks in his preface, had not personally known Benedict: "All the notable things and acts of his life I could not learn; but those few, which I now mind to report, I had by the relation of four of his disciples." [1]

It is often objected that what Gregory tells us consists, in the main, of tales of miracles that clearly follow the biblical pattern. And the value of Gregory's account as a strictly historical piece of writing is certainly open to question. However, this objection is of no great consequence, for what Gregory set out to write was not biography in the modern sense of the word, but a portrait of the "man of God," of the fabulous wonder-worker. And the portrait reflects the reaction of Benedict's immediate disciples and their successors to the life and person of their spiritual father.

Owing, however, to the nature of Gregory's account, we are

[1] *The Dialogues of Saint Gregory the Great* (London: Philip Lee Warner; 1911), Book II, Introduction.

able to reconstruct Benedict's life only in very summary form, without any indication of the whys and wherefores of his action. His personality remains for the most part shrouded in obscurity; occasionally, and only momentarily, it stands out in clear view, and then it is again lost to sight. But the mystery about him only serves to make him more attractive. We cannot trace the path of his psychological development; all we have is individual scenes from his life, separated by long intervals of silence. The portrayal of the essential Benedict is a task that challenges every generation anew.

Benedict came of an honorable family of Nursia, in the Sabine country. When he was still very young, he was sent to Rome to complete his studies, but the Eternal City held no attractions for him. Instead of admiring the ancient monuments, he was appalled at the mounting evidence of social and moral disintegration which surrounded him, and feared, as Gregory writes, lest he too should fall headlong into "the dangerous and godless gulf" if he remained there longer. Accordingly, he broke off his studies and, "instructed with learned ignorance, and furnished with unlearned wisdom," [2] he fled to the solitude of the Sabine hills. There he sought out a cave and entered upon the life of a hermit, "desiring rather the miseries of the world than the praises of men," [3] as Gregory significantly adds.

Contrary to the usual notion, Benedict's first spiritual kinship was with the desert fathers of the East, and even in the subsequent phases of his life he observed the strictest seclusion from the world. His solitary life in an inhospitable region soon turned the youth of gentle birth into something more like a wild creature than a man. In the thickets near his cave, shepherds once caught a glimpse of him clothed in matted skins, and took him at first for an animal. One can hardly avoid a sense of revulsion at the young hermit's utter deprivation. And the animal-like figure of the youthful Benedict seems to have little enough in common with the poised and dignified patriarch of Western monasticism as he is usually portrayed. Benedict was far indeed from what he was later to become. Nor was his withdrawal from society merely external; he had cut himself off so completely that he no longer knew the day on which Christendom celebrated Easter. [4] In his total seclusion he had lost sight

<hr />

[2] Ibid., p. 51.   [3] Ibid., chap. i.   [4] Ibid., p. 54.

even of the life of the Church. The man with whose name we as-
sociate the most fruitful liturgical development was no longer mindful even of the day of the Lord's resurrection.

Like the desert fathers of old, Benedict had to endure the most
frightful temptations in his cave. The world that he had abandoned
stirred within him, and he was haunted, in particular, by the image
of a woman he had once seen. The more his imagination busied itself with the sweet memory, the greater grew his desire, and he was
on the point of abandoning his self-imposed solitude and returning
to the world when, at the last moment, "seeing many thick briers and
nettle bushes to grow hard by, off he cast his apparel, and threw himself into the midst of them, and there he wallowed so long that,
when he rose up, all his flesh was pitifully torn: and so by the wounds
of his body he cured the wounds of his soul, in that he turned pleasure into pain." [5] Only in this barbarous way could he master temptation.

The father of Western monasticism was a model of balance and
control, but his serenity came to him neither from his temperament
nor as a free gift; it was the fruit of iron self-discipline and an untiring struggle with his own nature. It was there, in the thorny briers,
that he laid the foundations for what he was to become. This contest
unto blood was necessary that he might achieve holiness. Gregory
writes: "From which time forward, as himself did afterward report
unto his disciples, he found all temptation of pleasure so subdued
that he never felt any such thing." [6]

Despite his retirement from the world, rumors of his unusual
life were bruited about the countryside and earned him high regard.
It was thus that the monks of a neighboring monastery, whose abbot
had died, came to ask him to accept that office. At first he refused,
because he was eager to pursue his solitary way of life, and it was
only after repeated requests that he finally agreed.

But this first experiment in cenobitism was to end in abrupt and
unexpected catastrophe. The monks, living in an age of general decay of manners and morals, were unaccustomed to any kind of monastic discipline, and Benedict's strict governance was not at all to their
taste. They looked upon it as an intolerable restraint, and rebelled.

[5] Ibid., chap. ii.   [6] Ibid., p. 55.

Finally, in order to rid themselves of their obnoxious abbot, some of them put poison in his wine. Such crime was possible even among men who had fled the world to lead a life pleasing to God! As we see, Gregory did not choose to gloss over the incident.

Benedict triumphed sublimely over this murderous plot. As he made the sign of the cross over the vessel which, in accordance with monastic custom, had been presented to him for his blessing, the monk who was holding it was overcome by fear and dropped it. Benedict immediately realized what had happened. Rising from the table, he said to the assembled monks: "Almighty God have mercy upon you and forgive you. Why have you used me in this manner? Did not I tell you beforehand that our manner of living could never agree together? Go your ways, and seek ye out some other father suitable to your own conditions, for I intend not now to stay any longer amongst you." [7]

Here, for the first time, we hear the authority in Benedict's voice and glimpse something of that inner majesty of the humble man of God before which all opposition, like the poisoned cup, must fall to the ground. Those who would not suffer Benedict's rebuke, "I intend not now to stay any longer amongst you," must show themselves worthy of his companionship.

The incident marked the close of his first attempt at community life. Even Benedict did not reach his goal in a day, and he had to endure bitter setbacks. But he went on steadfastly, whether his path led him through briers or into the hands of murderers. He returned to his solitude, meditating the lesson of his fateful experience.

And a little later he made a second venture into community living which differed very markedly from the first. He took care to avoid the mistake of joining an already existing community to whose ways he would have had to conform. Instead, he invited several young men who wished to lead a monastic life to join him in founding a new community. The partners in this enterprise would have to conform to his rule, and not he to theirs.

Benedict was now in a position to train his subjects after his own fashion. He was an inspired teacher of men, one of the greatest in the history of Christian spirituality. He possessed the power really

[7] Ibid., chap. iii.

to form young people, to make of them monks who would constitute a rampart against the destructive forces of the age. He knew
exactly where he wanted to go and the way to get there.

In the year 529—the year in which Justinian closed the school
of philosophy at Athens—Benedict moved with his disciples to
Monte Cassino, midway between Rome and Naples. The year
thus marked the end of one era and the beginning of another. And
it was on the ruins of a neglected temple to Jupiter, set on the densely
wooded mountaintop, that Benedict proceeded to lay the foundations of a Christian monastery.

The first task of the monks was to erect their buildings, and their
difficulties were tremendous, for they had little experience in such
matters. Once an inexpertly built wall collapsed, crushing one of
the monks under the masonry. Benedict, however, by the miraculous
power of his prayer, restored him to life.

On another occasion the head of a billhook was torn from its
handle and fell into a near-by lake. Benedict, after causing it to rise
from the bottom of the lake, comforted the monk to whom the mis-
hap had occurred, saying to him: "Behold, here is thy bill again,
work on and be sad no more." [8] A short enough phrase, yet typical
of the Benedictine spirit, a gem to be prized for all times. Instead
of wasting time in pointless reproach, Benedict invites the monk to
work on with a carefree heart. If we ponder these simple words, we
shall suddenly understand something of the grace that flowed from
Benedict. They reflect an attitude as valid today as it was then;
Benedict's way was to deal with a problem without fuss and quietly
to proceed to the next thing. It was this composure which Benedict
planted as a fruitful seed in the monastic foundation of Monte Cassino, and which made of the Benedictine monastery a focus of new
life when Roman civilization was in its death throes.

Benedict's disciples could never quite explain their spiritual father.
For all his humanity, he remained beyond their understanding, and
they credited him with limitless powers. They intimated that he
could read men's hearts and reveal what was hidden from men's
eyes. Gregory's account of Benedict's dealings with the Gothic
king, Totila, is illustrative of this belief.

[8] Ibid., chap. vi.

If we regard this incident as no more than a literary invention of Gregory's, intended to celebrate an easy victory on paper over the hated Goths, we shall miss the point of this unusual encounter. The crafty Totila desired to see Benedict, and announced his arrival. But he wanted first to put the man of God to the test, so he decked out his sword-bearer in his royal attire, gave him the necessary escort, and sent him to Benedict. But hardly had the pseudo-king entered the monastic precincts when Benedict looked at him with penetrating glance and said: "Put off, my good son, put off that apparel, for that which thou hast on is none of thine." [9] The sword-bearer, finding himself unmasked, fell to the ground in fear, and at the same time Totila arrived in person. Benedict spoke to him in the fearless tones that true men of God have always dared use in the presence of the great ones of the world. He admonished the Gothic leader to desist from his wickedness and foretold his unhappy future.

Benedict could foresee the terrible times that were about to befall his country, in which his beloved monastery too was to be engulfed, and his prophetic vision filled him with deep sorrow. His disciples found him weeping in his cell as he looked upon these things. These tears were the unavoidable accompaniment of his terrible prophetic vision.[1] There is no prophecy not linked with tears, for the future is nearly always heavy with nameless terror.

Benedict's prophetic gift was directly linked with his mysticism. And although he said little about his mystical graces, he certainly received them. Gregory relates the following experience: "The man of God, Benedict, being diligent in watching, rose early up before the time of matins (his monks being yet at rest) and came to the window of his chamber, where he offered up his prayer to Almighty God. Standing there, all on a sudden, in the dead of night, as he looked forth, he saw a light which banished away the darkness of the night and glittered with such brightness that the light which did shine in the midst of darkness was far more clear than the light of the day. Upon this sight a marvelous strange thing followed, for, as himself did afterward report, the whole world, gathered as it were together under one beam of the sun, was presented before his eyes." [2]

---

[9] Ibid., chap. xiv.   [1] Ibid., chap. xvii.   [2] Ibid., chap. xxxv.

This radiant vision of light, to which Gregory, in his *Dialogues*, attached a profound significance, belongs altogether to the world of mysticism. Only the greatest mystics have had a like experience of the divine; perhaps we might recall Jakob Böhme's fathomless vision of the center of things. To see "the whole world gathered as it were together under one beam of the sun" denotes a state of rapture in which the soul is incomprehensibly enlarged. To Benedict, apparently so sober and matter of fact in his approach to life, was granted the singular grace of direct vision of the heavenly light. It was Thomas Aquinas's considered opinion that Benedict must have seen God face to face, a grace granted only to Moses and Abraham before him. The understanding of the whole through a part is akin to angelic understanding, and is the aim of all mystical knowledge of being.

A truly delightful incident that Gregory narrates is Benedict's last meeting with his sister, Scholastica, who had also consecrated her life to God. Once a year the two would meet in the vicinity of Monte Cassino, and on this occasion, Gregory tells us, "the holy nun his sister entreated him to stay there all night, that they might spend it in discoursing of the joys of heaven." Benedict was dumfounded at the suggestion that he should spend a night outside the monastery, and refused point-blank. Scholastica did not insist, but folded her hands, bowed her head, and prayed to the Almighty. At once a torrential rain began to fall, so that Benedict was unable to leave. Realizing the connection, he proceeded to reproach her, but she replied: "I desired you to stay, and you would not hear me; I have desired our good Lord, and he hath vouchsafed to grant my petition." And so, Gregory concludes, Benedict, "being not able to go forth, tarried there against his will, where willingly before he would not stay. And so by that means they watched all night, and with spiritual and heavenly talk did mutually comfort one another." [3]

Scholastica died three days later, and Benedict did not long survive her. He had prophetic knowledge of his death, and gave his disciples due warning. Six days before he died, he asked that his grave be prepared; he wished to view the place where his body was to be buried. He was completely fearless in the face of the inevitable

[3] *Ibid.*, chap. xxxiii.

end; he himself had taught his monks that one of the "tools of good works" was "to keep death daily before one's eyes." ⁴ Then fever gripped him, accompanied by torturing heat. In his last hours, Gregory tells us, Benedict had himself carried into the church and, "having his weak body held up between the hands of his disciples, he stood with his own lifted up to heaven, and, as he was in that manner praying, he gave up the ghost." ⁵ The probable date was March 21, 547. The scene is rich in symbolism; the father of the monks of the West, standing in prayer to return his soul to his Maker, had become as a single flame soaring to heaven.

Gregory reports only isolated incidents in Benedict's life, yet, taken together, they make up a singularly impressive picture, which gains in depth if viewed against the historical background of the time. And there could hardly be a more somber background than that of the close of the fifth century, when Benedict was born. It was a time of frightful destruction, leading to a cultural decline without parallel. The decay had spread into every sphere, and threatened to destroy Western civilization altogether. The Roman empire, its strength already undermined, was falling before the onslaught of savage hordes from the East, and the wandering of the nations was as a second flood which, like the first, engulfed everything. Moral and social corruption was accompanied by epidemic disease and famine, which decimated populations and turned the countryside into something more like a wilderness. And, as in all periods of decline, the centrifugal forces were everywhere triumphant.

Against this fearful and widespread devastation, Benedict's constructiveness stands out all the more strikingly. The Abbot of Monte Cassino was a master builder; that is the basic conclusion we may draw from Gregory's hagiographical portrait of Benedict.

For our generation, groaning under the weight of new devastations, this view of Benedict opens up new horizons. We ask: what is the significance of the father of Western monasticism for our times? And we find that it is this: Benedict was, in the first place, the living embodiment of the divine will for man, which is that man should

⁴ *The Rule of Saint Benedict*, ed. McCann (Westminster, Md.: The Newman Press; 1952), chap. iv.

⁵ *The Dialogues of Saint Gregory the Great*, Book II, chap. xxxvii.

build and not destroy. It is both literally and figuratively true to say that Benedict, whose influence has survived the erosion of the centuries, was a spiritual architect. All his words and all his works were directed to the single purpose of building up the City of God on earth. Few other men have been so completely positive in their approach. And it was this approach that enabled him to find the new remedy-which, quietly and imperceptibly, saved Western civilization.

The man of the *pax Christi* remained aloof from theological strife, which serves only to divide men. He refrained equally from controversy, believing it better "to be silent than to speak" of unpleasant matters, and to turn away from them, as he says, "leaving them on one side." [6] His sole concern in the midst of the general havoc was to build up again, to lay a new foundation upon the ruins of the old. The more closely we study him, the more clearly he appears as the saintly adversary of the diabolical nihilism of every century. And his example is of timeless value to all Christians, whose duty it has always been to restore what foul malice has destroyed.

II

The proof positive of Benedict's constructive action lies in his rule, which was his life's main work, second only to the founding of his monastery on Monte Cassino. As a document, it is *sui generis*. The Latin is far from flawless, and the language often leaves a good deal to be desired. The general arrangement, moreover, is unsystematic, and we should not lay too much stress on its much-vaunted legal character. In drafting it, Benedict drew abundantly upon the works of Pachomius, Basil, and Cassian. It would seem, therefore, that the rule lacked originality. And as it contains no trace of emotion, it makes a very stark impression; indeed, its matter-of-fact tone tends to make the first reading a somewhat disappointing experience. Nor is it only the spoiled reader of modern literature who approaches it with false expectations; monks, too, have often admitted that it is not always easy for them to find the right approach to it.

[6] *The Rule of Saint Benedict*, chap. i.

These criticisms both can and must be made, yet the rule possesses one trait that compensates for all these deficiencies. Its epoch-making significance lies in the determination to build up, to restore, which is reflected in every syllable. Benedict's formative spirit permeates his whole rule, concerning which Gregory wrote that "the holy man could not otherwise teach than himself lived." [7] Herwegen, too, in his brilliant commentary on the meaning and spirit of the Benedictine rule, lays particular emphasis on its essentially spiritual basis, touching in this connection on the mystery of constructiveness. [8]

The rule begins with a prologue whose very first sentence has its own characteristic tone: "Hearken, my son, to the precepts of the master and incline the ear of thy heart." With this invitation, Benedict appeals to the power of men's hearts. For men's hearts are needed if the purpose of his foundation is to be fulfilled, a purpose that he states with glorious clarity in the prologue: "Therefore must we establish a school of the Lord's service; in founding which we hope to ordain nothing that is harsh or burdensome." [9] Benedictine spirituality is a training for service in God's army, and that goal can be achieved only through the creation of a new kind of man. [1] The rule is a norm given to the monk, not as an impersonal code of law, but as a trusted guide whose directions he must faithfully follow.

For Benedict, the abbot is the cornerstone of the monastery; he is at the summit of the monastic hierarchy, the pillar that supports the entire edifice; he is the representative of Christ. He will have to give an account to God of the souls entrusted to him, and he must never regard his functions as purely administrative. "He ought to rule his disciples with a twofold teaching: displaying all goodness and holiness by deeds and by words, but by deeds rather than by words." [2] So that the monks may faithfully follow the rule, he must be kind as well as stern, not closing his eyes to insidious faults, yet seeking "rather to profit his brethren than to preside over them,"

---

[7] *The Dialogues of Saint Gregory the Great*, Book II, chap. xxxvi.
[8] J. Herwegen: *Sinn und Geist der Benediktinerregel* (1944), p. 12.
[9] *The Rule of Saint Benedict*, Prologue.
[1] G. Aulinger: *Das Humanum in der Regel Benedikts von Nursia* (1950), pp. 35 ff.
[2] *The Rule of Saint Benedict*, chap. ii.

and to be loved by them more than feared.[3] As the name "abbot" implies, his role is that of a father, not of a military leader or other impersonal authority. His is a holy fatherhood that must prompt him ever to concern himself with the spiritual welfare of his monks and to give them due counsel.

The application of this concept resulted in practice in the development of a new and much warmer relationship than had existed between teacher and student in the academies of antiquity. That spiritual fatherhood implies the duty of spiritual guidance is an idea that Benedict bequeathed to all subsequent generations of monks. There has to be leadership if there is not to be chaos, and in the monastery it issues from one directing source, a man who bears the responsibility for the whole and sets the spiritual tone of the community.

In that age of general disintegration there was a desperate need for clear-cut leadership; and it was from the Benedictine monasteries, where it was practiced at the community level, that a new concept of leadership emerged. Recovery was possible only by this means, and, indeed, there is always something admirable about a person prepared to assume leadership in full consciousness of his responsibility before God, and in whom people are therefore able to place full confidence.

The rule provides that the abbot is to be chosen from among the monastic community by unanimous vote, in accord with early Christian practice. If this cannot be achieved, then "by a minority, however small, if its counsel be more wholesome." [4] Only if this means fails does the right of selection go to the bishop in whose diocese the monastery is situated, although Benedict was otherwise careful to defend his independence from any encroachment of episcopal jurisdiction.

In his actions, the abbot is sovereign. When important business has to be done, the abbot is to summon the whole community and himself set forth the matter. Each monk, from the oldest to the youngest, may express his opinion. After the question has been fully aired, the abbot is to dismiss the monastic family and make his decision alone. The conscientious examination of the various opinions is his duty, but he is not bound to take the advice of his monks.[5] In

[3] Ibid., chap. lxiv.   [4] Ibid.   [5] Ibid., chap. iii.

this way is eliminated the danger that is so prevalent in modern democracy: the choice of the mediocre as a result of the exercise of the right of the majority.

A striking element in the rule is the obstacles placed in the way of admittance to the community. In contrast to the then current practice of glibly talking people into acceptance of the Christian faith, Benedict began by trying to frighten prospective applicants away. "When anyone newly cometh to be a monk, let him not be granted an easy admittance; but, as the Apostle saith: 'Test the spirits, to see whether they come from God.' If such a one, therefore, persevere in his knocking, and if it be seen after four or five days that he bears patiently his harsh treatment and the difficulty of admission and persists in his petition, then let admittance be granted to him. . . ." [6]

Three times during the candidate's year of trial the novice-master must read the rule to him and draw his earnest attention to the hardships of the monastic life. Each time, after the reading, the novice-master must speak thus: "Behold the law under which you wish to serve; if you can observe it, enter; if you cannot, freely depart." [7] If the candidate perseveres to the last questioning, he is to be allowed to make his monastic profession, which is in the nature of a second baptismal rite. He is thereby incorporated in the community, and from that day forward wears the black monastic habit of the Benedictines, consisting of a tunic and hood. The very simple monastic habit in Benedict's time was indistinguishable from the dress of the poorer classes.

It is interesting to study the three vows whereby the monk submits to the authority of the abbot. The fact of undertaking such obligations was in itself something new, and gave the community a much more solid foundation. The Benedictine vows are in the form of a threefold promise made in the presence of God and His saints to observe "stability, conversion of . . . life, and obedience." [8]

Stability or steadfastness takes the first place. The monk commits himself to a particular monastery and undertakes to remain there forever. This is one of Benedict's most important contributions to monasticism. The founder of Monte Cassino had a distaste for va-

[6] Ibid., chap. lviii.　　　[7] Ibid.　　　[8] Ibid.

grant monks who wandered about from one monastery to another, unable ever to stay long anywhere.[9] The urge to be constantly on the move is indicative of a restlessness incompatible with the life of the monastic family.. The Benedictine monk is one who has put down roots in his monastery and has pledged it the allegiance without which there can be no lasting community; hence, he does not leave it of his own accord.

The vow of *stabilitas loci* is doubtless to be understood in its literal sense, but it can also be understood figuratively, and then it acquires unexpected significance for our own times. As monks understand it, Benedict's *stabilitas* means "something inward and spiritual," something like "character" and "unswerving determination."[1] It follows that the first thing to be avoided is spiritual vagabondage—a restless roving subject only to the whims of curiosity, an inability ever to settle down. The constant seeking after the latest novelty is a neurotic trait wholly incompatible with genuine religion. Material stability, on the other hand, is the visible sign of the inner peace of the monk.

"Conversion of life" is an inadequate rendering of the Latin of the second vow, *"conversatio morum suorum."*[2] Rather than a turning-away from an undisciplined life, it signifies a promise to embrace the monastic way of life. For Benedict, like all monastic founders, conceived of Christianity as a way of life in which practice conforms to principle, and this is the alpha and omega of monastic spirituality.

The pursuit of the monastic life implies, among other things, chastity and renunciation of personal property. Benedict does not use the word "poverty," but he is very clear on the subject of personal property. "This vice," he says, "ought to be utterly rooted out of the monastery. Let no one presume to give or receive anything without the abbot's leave, or to have anything as his own, anything whatever, whether book or tablets or pen or whatever it may be; for monks should not have even their bodies and wills at their own disposal."[3] And just as the monk undertakes not to own anything, so he must renounce marriage. The monk is *par excellence* single; it is

---

[9] Ibid., chap. i.
[1] *Vir Dei Benedictus*, ed. Molitor (1947), p. 107.
[2] *The Rule of Saint Benedict*, chap. lviii.
[3] Ibid., chap. xxxiii.

a sacrifice he must make if he wishes to follow his calling, for the practice of the monastic life is otherwise impossible.

Finally, the monk promises his abbot obedience. The rule is explicitly addressed to those who, renouncing their own wills, "take up the strong and glorious weapons of obedience." [4] And St. Benedict further describes monks as men "not living by their own will and obeying their own desires and passions, but walking by another's judgment and orders." [5]

This obedience, which is the primary virtue of the monk, must be rendered without murmuring or objection, but promptly, as to a divine command. What Benedict is concerned with is the inner obedience given with a cheerful heart and proving itself in the performance of disagreeable duties, for it is then that the monk manifests his quiet self-control. "For the obedience which is given to superiors is given to God." [6]

The practice of constant obedience, and not, as is commonly believed, that of chastity, is probably the monk's heaviest burden. Monastic obedience is almost impossible to imagine for those accustomed to act only in accordance with their own wishes. In our own day, with our special emphasis on independence, it is a wholly alien concept; there can hardly be any greater contradiction than between obedience and the exercise of individual autonomy. There is certainly nothing morally objectionable in the endeavor to become a law unto oneself, on the Kantian model; independence is not lightly to be rejected, even at the risk that it may lead to self-conceit. But obedience is a no less respectable position. It takes great strength of character to pledge obedience freely and persevere in it unwaveringly. Without obedience, of course, a monastic community would not endure a single week.

Benedict sought to foster in his monks a consistent and characteristic outlook upon life, and all the chapters of his rule are directed toward that single goal. This outlook is arrived at by the practice of a number of virtues, the first of which is humility. This is the virtue to which the monk, as the man of obedience, must pay particular attention. Benedict, following the monks of the East, compares humility to a ladder by means of which the Christian

[4] Ibid., Prologue.   [5] Ibid., chap. v.   [6] Ibid.

ascends from earth to heaven, and he names twelve rungs, or de-
grees, of this ladder.[7]

The clearest indication of a monk's humility lies in this: that
he "be content with the meanest and worst of everything." Another
indication is his silence, to which Benedict devotes a whole chapter of his rule. The monk keeps silent in order to preserve his
wonderful secret. "It becometh the master," Benedict writes, "to
speak and to teach; but it befits the disciple to be silent and to
listen." And again: "Therefore, on account of the great value of
silence, let leave to speak be seldom granted to observant disciples,
even though it be for good, holy, and edifying conversations." [8] Idle
chatter and laughter are forbidden; the great silence reigns in the
monastery, engendering a salutary atmosphere of peace.

The spiritual healing power of silence is a thing that our times
fail to understand, and it is only as a result of the increasing preva-
lence of noise in modern life that men have come to long once more
for stillness, in which God's voice is audible. This longing is fulfilled in the cloister, where noise and excitement have given place
to the *pax Christi* so characteristic of Benedictinism.

The most detailed description of the monastic outlook is contained in the fourth chapter of the rule, concerning the "tools of
good works," the first of which is the love of God, the second the
love of neighbor.

"Let nothing . . . be put before the work of God." [9] Benedict had completely reversed his earlier position, when he had forgotten even the dates of the feasts of the Church. From the time
he founded his monastery, he was conscious of the value of the
liturgy and gave it precedence over every other activity. "As soon
as the signal for the divine office has been heard, let them abandon
what they have in hand and assemble with the greatest speed, yet
soberly, so that no occasion be given for levity." [1]

The underlying purpose of Benedict's regulations on the liturgy
is that the monks shall take part in the mysteries of grace without
being burdened by too many hours in choir. Praising God is the
center of the Benedictine life, and Benedict therefore admonishes

[7] Ibid., chap. vii.   [9] Ibid., chap. xliii.
[8] Ibid., chap. vi.   [1] Ibid.

his monks: "Let us then consider how we ought to behave ourselves in the presence of God and his angels, and so sing the psalms that mind and voice may be in harmony." [2] The consciousness that in singing the psalms one is standing in the presence of God is a strong antidote to the tedium that can set in with daily repetition. As one writer has said, "There is also a monotony that is so sublime that it grips the whole soul, in its simplicity embracing all things. Those who come to it and who can make of it the framework of their lives are chosen people." [3]

The liturgy has been most sedulously nurtured and furthered in Benedictine monasteries; in fact, this has often been regarded as the characteristic mission of the sons of Benedict. The Gregorian Chant, for all its strictly limited number of tones, possesses a spiritual loveliness that impresses itself more strongly upon the listener with every hearing. There are no solo parts in this sonorous male choir; the subjective element is suppressed in favor of the objective, and the whole is ordered solely in view of God's glory.

The Benedictine liturgy is strongly anchored in the symbolism of light, the declining light of the evening and the slowly rising light of the morning being transformed by the prayerful soul into a mirror of the mystery of death and resurrection. Mysterious silence alternates with triumphant joy, together forming a harmonious whole. For all Benedictines, the daily divine office is the high point of the monastic life. Abbot Cuthbert Butler, for instance, writes that "the essence of a Benedictine vocation is the celebration of the liturgy." [4]

The Benedictines have played a leading part in the liturgical movement right up to the present day, and they have been primarily responsible for the liturgical revival. They are the embodiment of the praying Church. But the praise of God is not confined to the elaborate, solemn celebration of the liturgy. Benedict believed that prayer was the only justification for the monk's existence. Consequently, alongside the divine office, he provided considerable time for private prayer, which was not to be offered with much speak-

[2] *Ibid.*, chap. xix.
[3] Steiger: *Stifter als Dichter der Ehrfurcht* (1952), p. 47.
[4] C. Butler: *Benedictine Monachism* (London: Longmans, Green; 1919), p. 30.

ing, but with "purity of heart and tears of compunction." [5] Monasteries where long school hours and learned pursuits prevent monks from giving sufficient time to prayer would find little favor in Benedict's eyes.

The monk must praise God, and he must also work. "Idleness," Benedict writes at the beginning of his instructions concerning manual labor, "is the enemy of the soul." [6] By manual labor he meant the performance of the duties connected with the life of the monastery, whether in the church, the mill, the workshop, or the garden, all of which were to be contained within the monastic grounds. His aim was to achieve a monastic way of life marked by complete simplicity, yet free from oppressive poverty. As a result, the Benedictine monastery became the model of a balanced, self-supporting economic unit and the home of craftsmanship. Nowadays, choir monks often leave the manual labor to the lay brothers, but Benedict did not consider it beneath his dignity; Gregory describes him as coming home from the fields at the head of the brethren.

Benedict recognized the value of work in itself, and not merely as an ascetic practice; that is the principal significance of his legislation on this subject. He broke with the ancient, pernicious idea that manual labor was something contemptible, and bequeathed to the Germanic peoples, through his disciples who were their teachers, a lofty concept of labor which helped halt the contagion of pagan fecklessness.

Benedict was unable, by his ordinances, to prevent the accumulation of capital, a circumstance that has cost Benedictine monasticism very dear in the course of its history. The personal poverty of the monk has often stood in glaring contrast to the collective wealth of the monastery; that is the somber side of Western monasticism. Yet precisely because Benedict was opposed to the amassing of wealth, he ordained that goods made in the monastery should be sold a little cheaper than they were sold in the world, so that any tendency toward avarice might be stifled from the outset. [7]

[5] *The Rule of Saint Benedict*, chap. xx.   [7] Ibid., chap. lvii.
[6] Ibid., chap. xlviii.

Intellectual work, according to the rule, consists primarily in reading. At a time when literacy was far from general, this was an important requirement and created a higher intellectual level in the monasteries. The daily reading of the Bible made the written word so familiar that it was never again lost. The readings also extended to the writings of the Church fathers, especially Cassian and Basil, as well as to the lives of the monks of the East.[8]

In Benedict's own days, the studies at Monte Cassino appear to have been confined to religious works, for there is no mention of any profane literature. Soon after his death, however, under the regime of his disciples, secular writing was introduced. The Benedictine monasteries became the home of eager copyists who saved many works of classical literature which would otherwise have perished during the wandering of the nations. Benedict's foundation was thus simultaneously the custodian of the ancient learning and the matrix of medieval culture.

The rule contains many provisions concerning the nightly rest, kitchen service, the distribution of offices, and the like. Benedict never confined himself to the abstract and general; he always got right down to the particular and practical, for it is only by this means that the religious life can flourish and prove itself. Yet among these practical ordinances there are some that are timeless—for instance, the wonderful precept concerning hospitality: "Let all guests be received like Christ."[9] To this day, Benedictine hospitality has a marvelously refreshing quality.

If we do not cite all the precepts, it is because they may be read in full in any edition of the rule. Some of them, moreover, have proved to be too much of their own period, and are no longer applied. This is no derogation from the rule; Benedict himself provided that local conditions should be taken into account, thus giving the order the opportunity of adaptation and development in accordance with circumstances.

Benedict's rule has been criticized as conceiving of Christianity principally in terms of ethics, as being too legalistic in character and to that extent opposed to the spirit of the Gospel. In Old Testament days, so runs the argument, such a body of law would

[8] Ibid., chap. lxxiii.   [9] Ibid., chap. liii.

have been in context, but not in the days of the Son, whose advent marked the end of the Law. But such objections take account neither of the religious purpose underlying the rule nor of the historical circumstances of Benedict's times. Instead of indulging in carping criticism, it would be wiser to stress the timeless value of the rule. True enough, it is a hard and fast ordinance, unwavering in its purpose, but its tone is authentically Christian, evocative of eternity in time. In true Benedictine style, it is never blatant or emphatic, and it is precisely owing to its quiet, unassuming character that it conveys so vivid a picture of the essential nature of monasticism.

In his concluding chapter, Benedict writes: "This rule has been written in order that, by practicing it in monasteries, we may show that we have attained some degree of virtue and the rudiments of monastic observance."[1] And he makes clear that the rule is not an exhaustive statement of the requirements for perfection, but merely a "little rule for beginners." Thus the founder himself shows us how, and in what spirit, his rule is to be understood.

Benedict's rule transcends mere counsel; it rises to the heights of positive command. And its originality lies precisely in the monastic unity that it thus achieves. Benedict did not regard Christianity as a benign teaching entailing no obligation, which the Christian might accept or reject at will. He believed that the words of the Lord and of His Apostles were of a binding character that men might not evade with the excuse of having little "talent" for religion. And what he wrote for his disciples was, paradoxically enough, something in the nature of an evangelical law.

The Christian needs clear, practical directions more than ingenious views and profound theories, and Benedict's rule, one authority writes, "is neither a work of edification, nor a textbook, but a firm law, binding upon abbot and brethren alike, upon all and in respect of all things."[2] Hence the lapidary style. It was not by proclaiming the Pauline teaching concerning "perfect liberty" that Benedict could have assured the survival of his foundation. What men needed in those terrible times of wholesale collapse and disin-

---

[1] Ibid., chap. lxxiii.
[2] Hilpisch: *Geschichte des benediktinischen Mönchtums* (1929), p. 65.

tegration was specific rules of conduct to tell them what they must and must not do.

Law is not to be regarded as an intolerable imposition. All of us are subject to some laws that we can ignore only at our peril. We might remember Goethe's dictum on the subject—that men are free only under the law. And there is a grace in freely assuming a duty that helps a man to mold his own life. Through the rule, the Benedictine became the model Christian—a man enormously attractive to others just because he himself was spiritually disciplined—and so it was his destiny to pave the way for the renewal of Western civilization.

By his rule, Benedict was seeking to satisfy that deep-seated longing for order which is characteristic of the West. He was not concerned, of course, with any bureaucratic pseudo-order, nor with the false conservatism that exalts temporal regulations to the status of eternal laws. For Benedict, order meant the leading of an orderly existence in which things are seen in their proper perspective— that is, in relation to God's creative will. Order is a religious concept; this basic tenet of Benedict's thinking cannot be too often stressed. And his idea of order was a Christian order based on the Bible, which tells us that "God is not the author of confusion, but of peace" (I Cor. xiv, 33). The antithesis of divine order is chaos, toward which so many people feel a demonic attraction, only to be hurled to their destruction.

Order requires discipline, and the rule provides for penalties. Their object is to arouse the transgressor to the necessary repentance, which he displays by prostrating himself before the abbot and begging his forgiveness. But only gradually is he restored to grace and to his former office in the community. In cases of sustained obduracy, corporal punishment is prescribed, a measure that Benedict borrowed from the Eastern fathers. If all other penalties prove vain, the monk is to be expelled. Early medieval artists portrayed Benedict rod in hand; they understood him better than those moderns whose susceptibilities are repelled by such an idea, and who make of the author of the rule a figure so measured as to be wholly lifeless. With all his composure, he was much sterner than we usually realize, though free from heartless severity.

We need make no excuses for the penalties prescribed in the rule. Discipline was a *sine qua non* of the spiritual restoration that Benedict had undertaken; only by this means could he hope to hold his own in the general distintegration. The jettisoning of discipline is a symptom not of progress, but of decay; true discipline is a glorious thing because it is grounded in the law that establishes order. And it is this exalted discipline that the Benedictine cherishes, freely submitting himself to its commandments.

All the provisions of the rule breathe moderation, and nowhere more than in connection with ascetic practice. We cannot repeat often enough that Benedict was himself an ascetic and wished to train his disciples in the school of temperance and self-denial. After all, had they not taken upon themselves the yoke of Christ? The Abbot of Monte Cassino would tolerate no pampering, and if he was obliged to make some small concessions, that was, as he explained—a little sadly—on account of the weakness of the brethren. For instance, after endorsing the view that wine is no drink for monks, he adds that "nowadays monks cannot be persuaded of this," and therefore exhorts them at least to drink temperately.[3]

Asceticism was the antipole to the degeneration attendant upon the collapse of the Roman empire. But it was an extreme, and could not be regarded as a remedy in itself, particularly as it had been compromised by the excesses of the Eastern monks. It was a part of Benedict's greatness that he did not confine himself to the beaten track of ascetic practice, but was also aware of its pitfalls. That is why there was no trace, at Monte Cassino, of the kind of asceticism which had prompted some of the earlier hermits to load their bodies with iron weights, to wear verminous rags, and to eat food that had spoiled. On the contrary, the monk must "do nothing except what is commanded by the common rule of the monastery and the example of his superiors."[4]

Benedict would not hear of self-inflicted flagellation or other inhuman macerations, and Gregory reports him as saying: "If thou be God's servant, let the chain of Christ, and not any chain of iron, hold thee."[5] To his mind, there was nothing glorious in difficulty

[3] *The Rule of Saint Benedict*, chap. xl.   [5] Ibid., chap. lxxi.
[4] Ibid., chap. lxx.

per se, and he was opposed equally to record-breaking ascetic feats and to flabby self-indulgence. By this avoidance of both extremes, Benedict was expressing in its most vivid form the positive Western attitude toward life as against the exaggerations of Eastern monasticism.

Benedict combined wise moderation with an assurance that can issue only from a rare sense of reality. And in this ability to keep to the mean lies one of the secrets of his strength. In all his ordinances, whether they concern the measure of food or the number of psalms to be recited in choir, there is the same underlying thought: "Let all things be done in moderation." [6] The monastic way of life at Monte Cassino possessed a clarity, a reasonableness, a luminous quality such as one rarely finds in this life, for it is a gift of the divine Logos. And this wonderful combination of mildness and severity gives the rule its imperishable value.

A final feature of the rule to which we should allude, and one that at the time was something of an innovation, is the reverence it prescribes for all created things. As so often happens in periods of general decadence, people had lost any clear notion as to the proper relationship between man and the rest of creation, and the resulting disorder only bred worse disorder. The rule, however, lays down that "all the utensils of the monastery and its whole property" shall be looked upon "as upon the sacred vessels of the altar." [7] Here is a definition of the relationship of man to things that we constantly seek and so rarely find.

The Benedictine, then, is not to be at the mercy of his own cravings, snatching greedily at things, using them rapaciously, and then casting them aside in disgust; neither is he to suppress all joy in the things that God has made, as though deprivation were the highest Christian virtue. On the contrary, he is to regard things as means to God, and therefore to the ennobling of natural desires. God is to be seen in all His creatures, and reverence is therefore due all things, even the humblest, and all things must be treated with love.

This means that the wall of separation between the religious and the profane must crumble, opening the way for the great work of sanctifying the world of nature. Created things derive their value

---

[6] Ibid., chap. xlviii.   [7] Ibid., chap. xxxi.

from their relation to God, and it was as coming from God's hands that Benedict accepted them, and accepted his part of responsibility for them. Things are in some way signs and symbols of the very fount of being; the natural is a ladder to the supernatural. And when Benedict taught that everything in the monastery was sacred, he was preaching no equivocal mystique of matter, but a doctrine of religious reverence that holds the only answers to destructive cynicism.

According to the rule, the monks are to treat one another with like respect. They are not to address each other simply by name; the young monk is to call his senior "Reverend Father," and the senior in turn is to call him "Brother." [8] All, however, are to observe the same rule of conduct: they must "give one another precedence." [9] This is no empty formula, but a Christian restatement of human relations; it is the foundation on which Benedict built up the life of the monastic family as it has flourished in his monasteries.

Thus, whether we consider the kind of order and discipline he instituted, or his moderation, or his approach to things, we see that Benedict was truly an innovator, a man who gently, unobtrusively, traced a path no less practicable today than it was in his own times.

There is no end to what we could say in praise of the rule. It is, indeed, Benedict's most glorious memorial. In it is transmitted the great monastic style—not in the esthetic sense, of course, but in the sense of a way of life molded by the Christian ethos. The rule is living truth; it builds the monastic life on one foundation—Christ —referring all things, always, to God. Historically speaking, we can say that it marked the beginning of medieval times rather than the close of the early Christian period. It did not, of course, emerge in a day, but was tried and tested through years of experience till it became the Magna Carta of monasticism, a statement of essentials in their simplest form, which yet omits nothing.

Because its provisions are so clear, leaving no room for endless discussion of their meaning, and because they are so evidently inspired by a deep sense of responsibility for souls, the rule has had tremendous educative force. Its psychological insights could have originated only in a man possessing a profound knowledge of hu-

[8] Ibid., chap. lxiii.   [9] Ibid., chap. lxxii.

man nature. Its pedagogy is a pedagogy of the spirit; it is like an echo of the voice of the divine Logos. Some measure of its greatness is the fact that it has survived for over fourteen centuries.

III

Benedict had no intention of founding an order, and the strength of Benedictinism has always resided in the individual abbey. The Benedictines have never really been an order in the usual sense of the word, and the unification that took place several centuries after Benedict's death was a loose affair. As one authority has said, the Benedictines are not an order created for some specific purpose, like modern orders and congregations; their mission is not to render certain particular religious or cultural services; their purpose is contained in the distinctive structure of their rule, which determines their life and action.[1]

Notwithstanding Benedict's modest intentions, his foundation developed and flourished on a prodigious scale. What the world owes to the Benedictines cannot be calculated; let us say simply that the West as we know it would have been inconceivable without them.

Far-reaching changes inevitably have taken place in the course of this long history. Abbot Cuthbert Butler asks this question in his standard work on the subject: "Has Benedictine life become something else, or is it a living growth that has obeyed the laws of a genuine development? Would St. Benedict's perplexity, did he find himself in a modern Benedictine abbey, be different in kind from St. Peter's, did the Apostle find himself present at a papal function in the church which bears his name?"[2] Let us answer that history is essentially a process of transformation, which does not mean that every change is either necessarily for the worse or for the better; the evaluation of the event should not be confused with the event itself.

[1] *Benedictus, Weihegabe der Erzabtei St. Ottilien* (1947), p. 67.
[2] Butler: op. cit., p. 292.

A first change took place at the close of the sixth century, when Monte Cassino was destroyed by the Lombards and the monks were forced to flee to Rome. The consequences were vast and unforeseen. Pope Gregory I involved the monks in his missionary action, and the Benedictine achievements in this field were of capital importance for northern Europe. The great evangelists of those lands, like Wilfrid and Boniface, were Benedictines.

A still more fundamental change took place in the character of Benedictinism when monks began to be priests as well. Just when this transformation from a lay to a clerical community took place we cannot tell; probably it came about gradually.[3] It has been regarded by Benedictines themselves as the most radical departure from the primitive spirit, for it led to the abandonment of manual labor by monks and necessitated the introduction of lay brothers. Benedict could hardly have dreamed of the mighty and prosperous abbeys that were to flourish in the Middle Ages, and he would doubtless have felt closer to the simple lay brothers than to the ranking members of those institutions.

After a somber period of decadence, Benedictinism was given a new impetus at Cluny, the great abbey founded in Burgundy in the early part of the tenth century. The name calls up the bitter struggle between empire and papacy which was to ravage the medieval world. It is often claimed that Cluny was responsible for the struggle which broke out after the Cluniac reforms had really penetrated the Roman Curia; historically, however, this argument is untenable. Nevertheless, the emergence of Cluny was an event of great significance. In other monasteries, too, a new spirit of fervor was awakening, but monastic reform was the very air that Cluny breathed. And it was particularly well placed to spread its reform, being blessed with a series of outstanding abbots—Berno and Odo, Maieul and Odilo— all men of great religious stature who even in their own lifetimes were credited with miraculous powers.

With its fortifications, its mint, and its diplomatic relations with a multitude of courts, Cluny was a mighty institution that could not fail to command respect. Yet Cluny itself did not remain entirely true to the spirit of St. Benedict. It owed more to Benedict of Aniane,

³ Ibid., p. 294.

whose doctrine constituted a mitigation of the original rule.[4] In addition, Cluny placed too great an emphasis on the liturgy, to the detriment of other monastic work, thus destroying the true Benedictine balance.

It was at Cluny that there originated a devotion that penetrated the medieval world and that may be regarded as symbolic of Benedictinism as a whole. It was said of Abbot Odilo that the groans of the souls in purgatory sounded so insistently in his ears that he was moved to perform a deed of Christian compassion to relieve their distress. He ordered, therefore, that at Cluny and in all its dependent monasteries the day following All Saints should be observed to commemorate the faithful departed with Masses, psalms, and almsgiving. Thus it was a monk's love for the whole of sinful mankind that gave expression, through the feast of All Souls' Day, to the hope of salvation for all and for all times. The institution of the feast illustrates the Benedictines' constant concern, despite their seclusion from the world, with the welfare of all Christians, and affords some explanation of the invincible loyalty that monasticism has always been able to command among the laity.

The subsequent history of Benedictinism has been no less glorious. Again and again, great figures have emerged from its ranks. There was Anselm of Canterbury, for instance, whose profound theological speculations made him the father of scholasticism. There were the Benedictine nuns, who gave a new significance to the life of medieval woman and whose convents, at the time of their fullest flowering, were "citadels of the religious life,"[5] producing women of wit and deep spirituality like Hildegard of Bingen, Mechtild of Magdeburg, and the great St. Gertrude. There was the learned Mabillon, in the seventeenth century, to whom science owes so great a debt. The Reformation and the ensuing secularization inflicted severe wounds on Benedictinism, but a revival took place in the nineteenth century, and its effects have continued up into our own day. And so we can say that the Benedictine monk, whose exemplary life in the stillness of his cloister radiates out upon his fellow men, is no stranger to our modern world.

[4] Schmitz: *Geschichte des Benediktinerordens* (1947), I, 103.
[5] Hilpisch: *Geschichte der Benediktinerinnen* (1951), p. 61.

Yet, after surveying the splendid history of Benedict's order, we are always brought back again to Benedict and to his rule, as to the source of renewal. And we are filled with an irrepressible longing for the Benedictine spirituality, mirroring something of that peace of Christ which surpasses all understanding. Would that Benedict the builder were with us still! Would that he could return to us in spirit!

Saint BRUNO

and the Carthusians

Bruno of Cologne was in Paris, so the legend goes, when an experience of unspeakable horror befell him. He was taking part in the obsequies of an honored teacher, Canon Raymond Diocres. The catafalque with the corpse stood in the church, nocturnes had already been sung, and the priest had begun the lesson. At the words "Answer me," the dead man raised his head, the stiff lips began to move, and a dreadful voice pronounced these words: "I have been justly arraigned before the judgment seat of God!" The dead man's head fell back. Screams of terror sounded through the church, and the trembling clergy postponed the office of the dead until the following day. But when they began again the next morning, the canon again raised himself in his coffin and in a tear-filled voice said: "I have been justly judged before the judgment seat of God." Again the service had to be interrupted by the terrified priests, and word of these preternatural happenings spread through the city. In tense expectation, everyone waited to see what would occur on the third day. And indeed, on that day too, to the consternation of all the onlookers, the dead man raised himself up once more and choked out the words: "I have been justly condemned before the judgment seat of God." Whereupon the priests fled, and the mob threw the corpse into the carrion pit.

The whole thing was all the more incredible in that the dead canon had seemed to be a good Christian whose only fault was some degree of ambition. But Bruno thought upon it. Vanity seemed but a minor weakness, yet this small poison sufficed to destroy the life of grace and to merit hell! And in that moment he resolved to renounce all worldly vanities.

Scholars regard the story as pure fantasy, and Bruno's biographers are quick to point out that no contemporary account exists of this "old wives' tale," and that, furthermore, Bruno never went to Paris. The legend appears for the first time in the elaborate chronicle of the first five Carthusian priors, compiled by an anonymous editor one hundred and fifty years after Bruno's death. Even the Sacred Congregation of Rites struck the gruesome tale from the breviary, considering it without any significance for Bruno's sanctity. And, according to Hermann Löbbel's very thorough monograph on Bruno, sound modern scholarship has rejected the authenticity of this miracle out of hand.[1]

Nevertheless, disregarding the Sacred Congregation of Rites and historical criticism, a Carthusian, Le Masson, suggests that in its deepest sense the story is true.[2] And I agree with him. For the discredited legend holds the key to the understanding of St. Bruno, a key that history alone cannot provide. Cardinal Newman, in his *Historical Sketches,* says that if we want to understand a legend, we have to realize that its meaning is above and beyond us, instead of thinking it is within our grasp. Legends, he maintains, contain so much that is deep, impenetrable, and mysterious that at best we can put forward only suppositions about them, not conclusions. Newman's view, then, is that historical fact cannot be regarded as disposing of legend. And, indeed, to make historical reality the only measure of a legend's value is to conform to a positivist prejudice born of an exclusive preoccupation with externals. In the present case, the legend of the dead canon presents us with the only possible motive of Bruno's conversion; it at once symbolizes and sounds the dominant note of Bruno's life. That some revelation concerning death was made to Bruno is clear, and that he dared to face the consequences, even if they should drive him—as they did—to the very edge of

---

[1] Hermann Löbbel: *Der Stifter des Kartäuserordens, der heilige Bruno aus Köln* (Münster: Schöningen; 1899), p. 31. (Translator's note: Cf. also E. M. Thompson: *The Carthusian Order in England* [London: Society for Promoting Christian Knowledge; 1930], p. 3.)

[2] Emil Baumann: *Die Kartäuser*, p. 19.

being, to the point where man can no longer rely on merely human strength.

What sort of man was this Bruno about whom such a legend could arise? There is little to tell. We know nothing about his childhood save that he was born around 1030 in Cologne and came of a good family. As a youth, he went to Rheims to finish his education. There he showed great zeal for learning and devoted himself wholeheartedly to his studies. Having completed them, he began a brilliant career as a teacher at the cathedral school.

His successful teaching activities were interrupted, some twenty years later, when he was appointed chancellor to Archbishop Manasses de Gournai of Rheims. When he assumed the office, he had no idea of his superior's dishonesty, and a dramatic quarrel took place once he learned the true state of affairs. As a result, Bruno was forced to flee the city. Yet even when the wily prelate succeeded, for the time being, in convincing the Pope that he had not obtained his see through simony, Bruno still refused to change his opinion. No earthly authority could make any impression upon him once he had decided as to the justice of a cause. And he was finally to experience the satisfaction of Pope Gregory VII's recognizing the depravity of Manasses and of being reinstated in his chancellorship.

Bruno's bitter experiences in that age of simony made him increasingly conscious of the vanity of the world. He was drawn to an otherworldly existence, and it needed only some decisive experience to serve as the impetus. That experience, according to the legend, occurred when the dead canon spoke to declare his own condemnation, which was at the same time a condemnation of the whole age, with all its simony. Suddenly Bruno saw that ambition and dishonesty had but one end—eternal damnation. It was not enough to fight against this in the world, as he had been doing up to then. In eternity the most minute details would be weighed, the smallest matters would have to be accounted for.

Thus Bruno made his great decision to become a monk. In a letter to Radulf Viridis he clearly states his motives: "You will remember, my dear friend, that one day, when you and I and Fulcius Monocutus were in the garden adjoining Adam's house, where I was staying at the time, and discussing the false delights and pleasures of this world and its transitory riches, that then for some time we spoke of the joys of the eternal splendor. Thereupon, inflamed with divine love, we promised, nay, vowed to the Holy Spirit, that we would flee this worthless world very soon and take the monastic habit, in order to seek only the eternal. We would have done this very soon, too, had Fulcius not been obliged to travel to Rome first, so that we decided to postpone the fulfillment of our vow until his return. . . . Do not be deterred, through false riches, or because of your position as provost, which you cannot hold without en-dangering the salvation of your soul." [3] According to this letter, Bruno's differences with Archbishop Manasses were only the proxi-mate, not the principal, cause of his decision to embrace the monastic life.

Bruno proceeded forthwith to carry out his decision, but he still had to find the particular type of monasticism meant for him. He entered the Benedictine abbey of Molesme, which at the time was governed by Abbot Robert, who later founded the monastery of Cîteaux. But the community at Molesme had been affected by the corruption of the times, and its halfhearted observance of the rule was another great disappointment for Bruno. With the abbot's ap-proval, he left the monastery and retired with several companions into a near-by forest, there to lead a strict life of penance. During that period he spent much time studying the lives of the desert fathers, and he was especially impressed by Simeon Stylites. Thus, early Christian eremitism seemed to provide him both with his goal and with the means of attaining it.

Searching for a place that would be even more isolated, Bruno set out with six of his companions for Grenoble, where Hugh of Châteauneuf, one of his former pupils, was bishop. Bruno told the bishop of his manifold disappointments, not only during his chan-cellorship but also in the monastery, and sought his advice. The pre-vailing decadence, Bruno felt, called for a response of utmost dar-ing. Monasticism as he knew it was not enough; what he aspired to was a "super-monkhood"—the term to be understood in somewhat the same sense as the "super-divinity" of Angelus Silesius. It should

[3] J.-P. Migne, ed.: *Patrologiae Cursus Completus* (Paris, 1877), Vol. CLII, 68, 74.

be realized that the man who proposed this bold plan was in his fifties, not an immature youth. Bishop Hugh had great understanding of the ascetic life, and he did not dismiss Bruno's ideas as mere fantasies. He was all the more ready to accept them because of a dream he had recently had, in which "God built Himself a temple in the desert, accompanied by seven stars."

The two agreed that Bruno should build himself a monastic retreat in the wilds of the Dauphiné mountains. In the year 1084 the little band made its departure, accompanied by some woodcutters. Even the foothills were almost impassable; there were no tracks through the rampant underbrush, and the pilgrims had the utmost difficulty in getting through with their belongings. They were entering virgin forest, but they were not discouraged. Despite appalling obstacles, they kept pushing on till only towering rocks and deep ravines surrounded them. The more inhospitable the mountains, the more somber the region, the happier they became. They stopped, finally, in a wild, uninviting spot where the last pines grew and where only steep cliffs confronted them and a turbulent stream rushed down into a narrow gorge. There they decided to put up some huts. Later the name Chartreuse was appropriately given to the foundation. "There one hears the last sounds of earth and the first concert of heaven," wrote Chateaubriand of this awe-inspiring, almost hostile region.

It is hard for us, in our day, to realize what an extraordinary feat Bruno and his companions performed in penetrating to their mountain fastness. Medieval man shrank from the mountains—as witness the story about the shepherds who implored Petrarch to avoid such deadly peril. It is certain that Bruno's reaction to the majestic sight that met his eye was different from that of Léon Bloy, who wrote, nine centuries later: "The stars shine to God's glory, to His glory the mountain torrent has cascaded for centuries into the deep, and the snowy peaks glisten to His glory!" These are reactions of modern piety, far removed from that of the first Carthusian. We have to recognize the daring, the unassuming heroism that led Bruno to undertake this venture in search of penance, solitude, and union with God.

Bruno's ascent to a trackless place in which no man had set foot before is significant in yet another way. Inspired by the example of the first hermits, Bruno too wished to withdraw into the desert and to imitate their lives. The mighty rock formations piled up before him in all their weird grandeur were Bruno's desert; here he could fulfill his longing. In the heart of Europe, Bruno had found a real as well as a symbolic desert, and his undertaking was no less re-markable than had been Anthony's before him, in third-century Egypt, for it was the same going-forth into the unknown. Bruno could indeed be regarded as a second Anthony; he was filled with the same aptitude for the impossible, and in him the fire of desert Chris-tianity glowed anew.

To be lost to the world—that men should know as little of him as if he were already dead! However, Bruno never sought emptiness for its own sake, but rather the opportunity to remain in close, un-disturbed communion with God. The exterior journey to the moun-tainous desert symbolizes his interior ascent to God. Kierkegaard's words in a different context aptly describe Bruno's ultimate aim in founding his Chartreuse in the mountains: "To exist in the realm of the mental is not easy, especially on the plane of religion. The believer is constantly suspended over the deep, with seventy thou-sand fathoms of water beneath him. No matter how long he may lie there, never will he eventually get to the point where he will be resting on dry land and where he will be able to stretch himself. He can become more calm, more experienced, can reach such security that he will learn to delight in a joke and a gay spirit—but to the very end he will remain suspended over a depth of seventy thousand fathoms of water." [4]

Bruno and his companions immediately set about building a series of very simple cells in the form of ordinary mountain shacks situated at regular intervals one from the other. The cells were built against rocks, and heavy beams protected the roofs against too much snow. The hermits also erected a small log chapel, for which Bishop Hugh made out a deed of foundation, placing the wilderness in their hands. The following year, at the insistence of the bishop, the companions

[4] Sören Kierkegaard: *Stages on Life's Way*, ed. W. Lowrie (Princeton, N. J.: Princeton University Press; 1940), p. 402.

erected a regular convent with cloisters and enlarged the cells to form little houses with three chambers each, all connected by a common passage. This arrangement was not altogether to Bruno's taste, for he feared any mitigation of his solitude, but he accepted Bishop Hugh's counsel. Some decades later, church and convent were destroyed by an avalanche, and the monks were obliged to seek a site farther down the mountainside which would be better sheltered against such calamities.

We are not dependent upon suppositions in describing the extremely simple, austere way of life of the first Carthusians. A contemporary account is extant in the form of a report made by a Benedictine abbot, Guibert of Nogent, who visited the Chartreuse twenty years after its foundation. The church, he wrote, stood near the top of the mountain, and he continued: "There are thirteen monks, having indeed a cloister, sufficiently fit for cenobitic custom, but not dwelling together like others cloisterwise. For they all have cells of their own round the cloister, in which they work, sleep, and eat. On Sunday they receive their food from the dispenser, to wit, bread and vegetable, which, their only pottage, is cooked by each of them in his own quarters. Water, however, for drinking as for other uses, they have by means of a conduit from the fountain, which goes to the cells of all, and through certain holes passes into each of their little houses. Fish and cheese they use on Sundays and high festivals, fish, I should say, not that they buy it for themselves, but as they might receive it from any kind-hearted men. As for gold and silver church ornaments, they have none save a silver chalice; and in the church itself they meet not at the wonted hours as we, yet at certain hours; Mass, unless I am mistaken, they hear on Sundays and solemn days. They almost never speak, for if anything necessary is wanted, it is got by a sign. If they ever drink wine, it is so diluted that it has no strength and no taste for those using it, and to an ordinary man it would be scarcely better than water. They are clad in hair-shirts next to the skin, and the rest of their garments are very mean. They live under a prior; the Bishop of Grenoble, a very religious man, fills the place of abbot or supervisor. Whereas they abase themselves in every kind of poverty, they are amassing a very rich library; forsooth the less they abound in the supply of material bread, so much the more they labor painfully for the food that perishes not." [5]

This earliest description of Carthusian life leaves open many questions that one would like to have answered. However, apart from the mistaken reference to sign language, it agrees substantially with the independent account of Peter the Venerable, Abbot of Cluny.

Eschatological considerations moved Bruno to found his retreat. In another letter to Radulf Viridis, he writes: "I live in the province of Calabria, in a desert, far from all human dwellings, in the company of religious, among whom there are men of wide learning, who remain in nightly adoration to await the return of their Master, so that, when he knocks, they may instantly be able to open to him." [6] The reference here is to the second foundation, but it applies equally well to the first. It is one of the few extant utterances of that lover of silence, and it affords us a glimpse into the depths of his soul, which was ever preparing itself for eternity. Bruno lived in anticipation of the Second Coming of the Lord, which he believed to be imminent.

This eschatological approach remained a characteristic feature of the Carthusians. We find the Carthusian Denis, for instance, writing a work concerning "the last things of man." Later we find a bell of the Grande Chartreuse bearing the incription: "The day of the Last Judgment is approaching, and I count the hours." We are reminded of the first Christians, who also expected the imminent end of the world. This same longing drove Bruno and his companions into the desert, so that the great moment might not find them unprepared. They enunciated no eschatological doctrine, but they truly lived in expectation of the last day.

The new foundation had hardly survived its initial difficulties when an unexpected tragedy came upon it. For the concept of tragedy is not, as is sometimes claimed, peculiar to classical Greece; there is also a Christian form of tragedy, though it is governed by other laws. Such a tragedy, in all its bitterness, faced Bruno six years

---

[5] Migne, ed.: op. cit., Vol. CLVI, cols. 854–5. The English translation of this passage is taken from Thompson: op. cit., pp. 12, 13.

[6] Ibid., Vol. CLII, cols. 543–4.

after his retreat into the mountains, where he believed himself to have been forgotten by all the world. Suddenly he was called by the Pope "to the service of the Holy See." The summons came like lightning out of a clear blue sky and faced Bruno with a well-nigh insoluble dilemma. As a monk, he knew the duty he owed to the Pope, yet at the same time this meant that he had to renounce his own mission. Obedience or solitude—these opposing demands tore at his soul. The sacrifice required of him was all the greater because the young foundation threatened to collapse without him. After mature deliberation, Bruno decided to obey the Pope, and left his monastery, which he was never to see again.

Bruno's departure had catastrophic consequences. His brethren became utterly disconsolate and lost all courage; they felt like children who had lost their father. He had been, for them, the living personification of the rule, and his example had daily fired them with renewed zeal; without him, they felt unable to carry on their struggle for perfection in the Chartreuse. Like a flock of frightened geese, they abandoned their retreat and scattered far and wide.

This deplorable flight is the most inglorious chapter in the whole history of Carthusianism, and it teaches us how precarious human heroism is, even a heroism inspired by the loftiest ideal. Nor should we attempt to gloss over the fact so that all may be attributed to God's glory, and nothing to human vanity. The timorousness of the first Carthusian monks forms a part of the whole picture of Carthusianism, which must be seen in its entirety, just as the disciples' flight belongs to the story of Christ's capture in Gethsemane and forms an essential part of His passion. Some of the fugitive monks eventually went to Rome, to confess their weakness to Bruno. He was anything but pleased to see them there, and encouraged them to return to their monastery. This they did, shamefaced and greatly humbled.

Bruno, for his part, performed whatever duties were assigned to him in Rome. These seem to have consisted, as far as anything is known about the remainder of his life, of preparations for various Church councils. As soon as he had completed all the essentials, he asked Urban II to permit him to return to his Chartreuse, but the Pope flatly denied his request. Here, again, Bruno seems to be a reincarnation of Anthony of Egypt: like the father of monasticism, he was filled with one desire—to live in solitude—but was not permitted to realize that desire.

Bruno's grief at being unable to follow his vocation weighed heavily upon him. He found it impossible to accommodate himself permanently to the papal injunction. At length, after much pleading, he obtained the Pope's permission to return to solitude provided he remained in Italy so that he might be recalled quickly if he were needed.

Bruno searched for a suitable site, and finally built his second monastery on a wooded mountain in the wild countryside of Calabria. In point of harshness of climate, La Torre in Calabria cannot be compared with the Grande Chartreuse in the French Alps; it lies too far south to recall the terrifying wastes of Dauphiné. Nevertheless, in La Torre Bruno was able to take up his former mode of life once more, and he was soon joined by several brethren. He never felt, however, that this was his goal, and his inmost longing was always to return to his first monastery near Grenoble.

When he was in his seventies, he was struck by a disease that his body, weakened by penance, was unable to resist, and on Sunday, October 6, 1101, accompanied by the prayers of his brethren, Bruno breathed his last.

In the church of St. Mary of the Angels in Rome there is a very impressive statue of St. Bruno which has frequently been reproduced. Yet even this lifelike representation is able to convey only a single aspect of that elusive personality, so great in his humility. No physical description of Bruno exists; no one knows what he really looked like. Similarly, little that he said has come down to us, so that we are also unable to form a complete picture of his mental features. Most of the works ascribed to him were actually written by another St. Bruno, Bishop of Segni. Bruno's greatness cannot be fully comprehended; his life is a mystery that no biographer has yet been able to resolve.

The Western world can boast hardly anyone who can be compared to this man, who found the highest human goal not in learning, but in solitude. His silence, writes a modern authority, is broken only by an occasional cry of elation that arises from the very depths of his soul: *"O bonitas!"* This was Bruno's favorite expression, which seems to sum up his inmost sentiments. In its glowing fervor, it lights up his concept of the divine. This man, who had been so painfully involved in the Church's struggle against simony; who, according to legend, had been struck with terror at the sound of a voice from the dead; and who had undertaken, subsequently, that singular ascent into a mountainous desert, there to live a life of utmost self-denial—this was the man to whom God's essence appeared as infinite goodness, in recognition of which man could utter only a humble song of praise! How different was Bruno's reaction from that of so many men who can never find enough fault with the world; he, instead, full of joyous thankfulness, was completely overwhelmed by God's goodness, and his cry is like an echo of Genesis: "And behold, it was very good."

In his silence, Bruno stands out as a man of tremendous spiritual stature. Only indirectly, through the lives of his disciples, can we glimpse the kind of person he really was. But not even in their rule do the Carthusians use many words; like their founder, they wrap themselves in an impenetrable veil of silence. Yet the manner of their lives shows clearly that what Bruno stands for is a Christianity transcending the bounds of ordinary reason. Rationally speaking, such a life is mere folly; other standards are needed by which to measure it.

II

First and foremost, the Carthusians sought to follow the eremitical way of life, and what they achieved was the unexpected revival, in the West, of the Christianity of the desert fathers. But they were not concerned with a merely mechanical revival. The cenobitic life, initiated by Pachomius, had proved to be an advance over pure eremitism, and this they recognized. Their objective, therefore, was to combine eremitism with communal life. They followed the rule of St. Benedict, supplemented by precepts that Bruno had taken over from the desert fathers and the Camaldolite monks. In this way the Carthusians arrived at that synthesis of eremitism and cenobitism to which St. Basil had pointed but which had never previously existed in monastic history.

Hatred of the world as such is not characteristic of the Carthusians; indeed, hatred as an emotion is altogether foreign to their thinking. Their attitude is best expressed in these words of St. James: "whoso-ever therefore will be a friend of the world is the enemy of God" (James iv, 4). Their watchword is to avoid all entanglement with creatures, lest, being so entangled, they should be made captive by creatures; so the Carthusian Guigo de Castro put it.[7] In the Carthusian creed, it is a great fallacy to believe that in loving creatures one is loving God; it means, simply, that one has not yet seen through the false caresses with which the world seeks to ensnare him so that it may utterly destroy his peace.

The Carthusian does not negate; he simply asks, in regard to everything that touches him: "Is this necessary?" If it does not serve the one thing necessary, it loses all significance for him, and he turns from it. That simple question, if honestly answered, saves many a man from vainly beating the air and teaches him to turn his gaze to that which is of lasting value. To be free from any desire for material things is important, but not simply for the sake of achieving emptiness. The Carthusian desires to dissolve all ties with created things so that he may then be free to seek communion with the eternal. He desires an intimate relationship with God, and this demands, in the first place, solitude.

This aspiration is the real reason for the obscurity in which the Carthusian deliberately chooses to pass his whole life. It is all-important to him to remain as little known as possible; any desire for recognition would appear to him as the vanity of vanities. The Carthusian guards his solitude jealously, as a precious treasure. But in order to be able to live permanently in obscurity, a man must have passed through the barriers of death and found eternity within his own soul. No one is better able than the Carthusian to teach us absolute indifference toward the opinion of the world. He has learned to distinguish the blessings of freedom from that personal ambition which only makes man a slave. Only the man who is not concerned with honor or glory or fame of any kind can live with

[7] Ibid., Vol. CLII, col. 608.

God, and something is seriously amiss in a man's religious life if he claims to serve God but is ambitious for recognition. Such a man is really seeking not God but himself.

But such freedom from all self-seeking does not come about naturally; it must be fought for, and it can be received, ultimately, only as a free gift at the hands of God. The Carthusians' desire for effacement is so marked that they do not even seek to institute any process of canonization for their departed brethren. Bruno himself was never formally canonized, and his cult was not authorized for the Carthusians until 1514, four hundred years after his death. In this respect the Carthusians are altogether different from other religious orders, which consider it a permissible source of pride to have produced a galaxy of saints. Undoubtedly there are many holy people in the Carthusian monasteries. Nowhere else, probably, are there as many, for personal sanctification is the only purpose of their existence. But they make no parade of their virtue, lest they should be as the hypocrites of whom Christ said that "they have their reward" (Matt. vi, 2).

III

Carthusianism, paradoxically, is virtually without a history because in the eyes of the world the Carthusians have produced so few great figures. Not, let us repeat, that they have been unable to, but because the monks have no desire for publicity. In the late Middle Ages a *Life of Christ* by Ludolf of Saxony, a Carthusian, was widely read, and the writings of another Carthusian, Denis, likewise enjoyed considerable popularity. The order, however, did little to promote these works, leaving that to others. The reason for this apparent indifference could not have been that Denis was recognized as an imitative rather than a creative thinker; it was rather fear lest the brethren might be distracted by his fame. Subsequently, members of the order were no longer permitted to publish their writings, and the few Carthusian works of modern times have been brought out by members of other orders. This ban on publishing, for all its apparent harshness, possesses profound significance for our times; the voice of silence stands like a rock above the sea of words which flows daily from our presses.

One of the very few things generally known about the Carthusian order is a development originating in the financial difficulties of the monks of the Grande Chartreuse in the nineteenth century. At the time, one of the monks experimented with the preparation of various liqueurs, and finally invented one that has since achieved world-wide fame as "Chartreuse." And that is really all that most men know about the Carthusians. Yet this, of all things, has least connection with the spirit of the order.

Bruno never intended to found an order, and therefore never laid down a formal rule. Nevertheless, his original foundation developed into the Carthusian order as we know it today. Long after Bruno's death, Guigo de Castro, the fifth prior, urged by all the other senior brethren, assembled and set down in writing all the ancient customs of the Grande Chartreuse. In 1133 these *consuetudines* were formally approved by Pope Innocent II. Previously, there had only been Carthusian monasteries; now there was a Carthusian order.

After their foundation, most medieval orders went through a period of rapid growth, which was subsequently eclipsed by a period of fatal decadence. The Carthusian order, however, developed differently. At first there was hardly any growth at all, and what there was became even slower as a result of a minor split among opposing factions in the order—a split, however, which did not assume any great significance. Not until two centuries after Bruno's death did the order really begin to develop, and then not even the great schism of the fourteenth century could halt it. A few of the houses even became fairly wealthy through their cattle-breeding activities—the Carthusians never engaged in the cultivation of the soil—but their wealth never did them any harm.

The history of the order, which is so devoid of external events, can point to one episode most indicative of its spirituality. Pope Urban V greatly favored the Carthusians, and was very much impressed by their penitential lives. To show them his friendship, he ordered a few alterations of their rule, such as the appointment of an abbot general, communal meals, and the use of meat for the sick and the weak. This gracious gesture, however, was greeted with consternation by the brethren, and they decided to send a delegation, under the leadership of Prior John of Neuville, to the papal court. The white-clad monks in their clumsy shoes must have made an unusual sight when, according to the story, they entered the fine chambers of the papal palace.

Urban V received them with great kindness. Addressing himself to the prior, he told him how dearly he loved the Carthusian order, and that for that reason he had granted it new constitutions about which the monks had doubtless heard. All present must have expected a suitable expression of thanks for this papal favor. Instead, Prior John fell on his knees and explained that he had, of course, heard the news, but that if he might be permitted to speak frankly, he would have to say that these constitutions would not profit the order, but rather would bring about its downfall, for they would oblige the monks to break the rules laid down by their founders. He then proceeded, very humbly, to explain to the Pope why these changes would be most unsuitable, and begged him to annul them.

The Pope must have been greatly surprised at this unwonted reaction to one of his favors, but he possessed sufficient magnanimity not to feel offended. After a short deliberation, he decreed that as the Carthusians desired no such mitigation as he had been prepared to grant them, they were to remain at liberty to continue in the strict observance of their primitive austerity.[8]

This seems but a very minor event in Church history, deserving of scant notice because it brought about no earth-shattering consequences. And yet these tranquil monks, as they beg for the retention of their primitive rule in all its strictness, humbly resisting the highest authority of the Church, reveal the true face of Christianity, which more often remains veiled. Christendom thrives on moments like these.

A comparison of the history of the Carthusian order with that of other orders reveals a striking difference. Most orders came into being on a wave of enthusiasm, experienced an early flowering, and then sank into decay. This decline of the orders, this picture of

[8] J. Wenzler: *Kennst du den Kartäuserorden?* (1912), p. 112. Cf. also Thompson: op. cit., pp. 106, 107.

communities dedicated to perfection but indulging in usury, hunting, revelries, and so forth, had catastrophic consequences for Christendom. Some of the orders, however, were able to counter this
process of decline by internal reform, thereby bringing about a new
era in their history. This rhythm of decay and revival can be traced
throughout the history of monasticism, and in that it is very similar
to human life in general.

The Carthusians are the one notable exception to this historical
law. About them it was said that they had never experienced a reformation because they had never suffered a deformation. Indeed,
there has not been the least trace of decadence in the order at any
time, not even during the disintegration of the late Middle Ages.
During the Reformation no Carthusian monasteries were dissolved
of their own accord. Why should they have been? Because they had
not fallen into decay, they offered the Reformation no internal foothold.

The secret of Carthusian stability lies in the order's stern adherence to its ancient discipline. Ever more concerned with quality
than with quantity, this "little flock" has preserved its purity through
all the storms of history. With its fidelity to holy tradition, the
Carthusian order demonstrates that conservatism need not necessarily lead to stagnation. On the contrary, it has done much to
preserve the order in the joy of its youth.

In this way, and without wasting words, the Carthusians have
made a most valuable contribution to the ever lively topic of religious reform. In order to halt the tendency to decay which is inherent in all earthly institutions, the Christian community is repeatedly faced with the necessity of internal reform. Almost every
century has to solve this problem anew, but amazingly few Christians have succeeded in answering it satisfactorily. The discussions
that took place in the late Middle Ages as to whether the reform
ought to begin with the head or with the members is only one
symptom of human helplessness in the face of this problem. Most
attempts to bring about a reform die out before they have even
properly begun because in general they are aimed at a mere simplification. Such a convenient solution achieves only a very temporary result, which in the long run makes matters worse. For it

is always, as Nietzsche says, the things we try to make easier for ourselves that we have to atone for most.[9] Genuine reform differs from mere reforming zeal in that the true reformer always seeks a harder, never a more diluted, form of Christian living.

What the Carthusians have had to say about this problem, in all simplicity, is most impressive. They were profoundly moved by the sad state of religion at the end of the Middle Ages, and in the sixteenth century one of them actually gave voice to these sentiments, sorrowfully declaring that the Pope refused to give up his pomps and revelries.[1] But they did not waste their time on negative criticism. Instead, they acted upon the surprisingly simple dictum: "Reform thyself, not others," which could serve as the device of every genuine reform. For it is only his own person that each man has under his control, and if he changes himself, then the external circumstances, however vitiated, will be improved automatically. But this luminously simple truth has enjoyed little popularity in Christendom.

Naturally the various tendencies of the times found an echo in the Carthusian enclosure. For example, at the end of the Middle Ages, the Carthusian house at Cologne for a while became the center of a renewal of Christian fervor.[2] But the monks soon realized that any attempt to influence the world would divert them from the true Carthusian mission, which was to fight the enemies of the Church not directly, thereby strengthening their resistance, but indirectly, through their own penitential lives. In consequence, the Carthusians refused to accept the humanism of the sixteenth century, and their members were not even permitted to read the writings of Erasmus.

Thanks to this unswerving fidelity to tradition, life in a Carthusian monastery today is essentially what it was eight hundred years ago. Bruno's institutions have proved their worth, and what has justified itself through centuries of trial will not lightly be relinquished. Having found what they regard as the most favorable conditions for a life turned exclusively toward God, the Carthusians are deter-

[9] Nietzsche: *Werke*, Kröner Edition, III, 426.
[1] Lortz: *Die Reformation in Deutschland* (1941), II, 134.
[2] J. Greven: *Die Kölner Kartäuse und die Anfänge der katholischen Reform in Deutschland* (1935), p. 7.

mined to preserve them. Their principle is to accept as few changes
as possible, and they carry this principle into the smallest details of
their lives. For instance, Carthusian monks today use the oldest
keys in Europe!

Hardly anywhere else has medieval spirituality been preserved
with such purity. As far as the Carthusians are concerned, there
might never have been a Renaissance, an age of humanism, a Reformation, a baroque period, an age of enlightenment, a modern
world. Their motto defines their attitude: *Stat crux, dum volvitur
orbis*. History, with its endless vicissitudes, has found no foothold
in a Carthusian monastery, nor are concessions made to the "spirit
of the times." Instead of succumbing to the eroding action of time,
Carthusianism has turned toward the eternal, triumphing over
the "hoary guest." By ignoring all fluctuating fashions, they have
attained a superiority over time which has frequently been postu-
lated but never reached by others. Dedicated to the eternal, they
have recognized the deceptiveness of the fleeting temporal, and this
mastery over time is their characteristic answer to the problem of
man's life on earth.

IV

The visitor to a modern Carthusian monastery meets there not a
lost past, but a living present—though one that may seldom be
seen and to which it is hard to gain access. For who may visit such
a monastery? The curious, who regard a monastery merely as some
form of novelty, are not desired. The Carthusians admit only two
kinds of visitors—friends of the order and notorious sinners. The
regulations expressly bar women, regardless of their age or social
standing, no matter how earnestly they beg admission. The *consuetudines* that impose this rule recall that neither Solomon the
wise, nor David the prophet, nor Samson the judge, nor even Adam,
who had issued directly from the hands of God, had been able to
withstand feminine wiles, and that one cannot carry fire without
burning one's clothes.[8]

[8] Migne, ed.: op. cit., Vol. CLIII, col. 682.

The reaction to the Carthusian monastery will vary according to the attitude of the visitor. The man with a poetic turn of mind will be struck at first glance by the romantic aspect of the whole scene. The solitary landscape, the silence of the cloisters, broken only by the twittering of the birds, the strange little houses connected to each other—all these are likely to awaken romantic sentiments. Whatever the visitor has read in historical novels about monastic life suddenly comes alive and fills him with delight. On the other hand, a Carthusian monastery can make a terrifying impression on the visitor. Carthusian reality is so very different from the realities of the world. All that man loves in the world and holds dear—art and science, sports and fashions—has been left far behind. The Carthusian transcends all these and presses forward into quite different regions. The impression that this makes can be so frightening that the visitor will desire nothing but to return as fast as he can to his familiar haunts, and will often leave again on the selfsame day.

Nevertheless, though both impressions miss what is essential to Carthusian life, the reaction of fear is better than idyllic misrepresentation. For the guest who has been terrified has at least experienced one side of Carthusian life—namely, its rigorousness—whereas the other has been altogether taken in by superficial appearances.

Nothing is more foreign to Carthusianism than the romantic view of life. We do not find brokenhearted men retiring within monastery walls, there to spend their lives in melancholy resignation, as Stendhal would have it in his famous *Chartreuse de Parme*. What we find there is men who resolutely shun delight in any form, believing imagination to be the enemy against which they must be ever on guard. It is no coincidence that poetry is banned from their well-stocked libraries, or that the pictures on their walls are chosen for considerations alien to esthetic merit. Carthusianism can be understood only if it is described in the sober terms that correspond to its austerity. Rhetoric strikes a false note here; the uncompromising detachment of these silent monks makes anything that smacks of flattery utterly repugnant to them. The Christianity practiced in the Carthusian monasteries is so absolute in quality as to make an unforgettable impression on the stranger who spends a few days within their walls.

The Carthusian lives in a small, two-story house consisting of a corridor, an antechamber, and a cell. The hallway gives him the opportunity for taking a little exercise in bad weather. Below the cell is a woodshed, with a very simple workroom. There each monk is bound to perform an hour's manual work every day. But he does not make objects that require expert craftsmanship, lest concentration on his work divert him from his religious duties. Usually he simply prepares kindling for the winter. In front of the house is a small garden surrounded by a high wall that cuts off any possible view of his next-door neighbor. The furnishings of his cell are of the simplest—a bed with a hard straw mattress, wool sheets and blanket, a chest, a *prie-dieu*, and a table with a bookcase. In the middle of the room stands a small iron stove of very medieval aspect. At the side of the cell door is the hatch through which a lay brother silently hands the monk his food, which nowadays is prepared for all in the monastic kitchen. Except on Sundays and feast days, each monk eats alone in his cell.

In this little hermitage, then, the Carthusian spends his whole life. Night and day, he is alone in his cell; he speaks with his brethren only during their weekly walk, which lasts three and one-half hours. The monks are not allowed to visit one another, but permission for such visits may be requested from the prior, who inspects the cells from time to time to see that everything is as it should be.

For the Carthusian, this solitude is not burdensome, for in his opinion a man is never less alone than when he is alone with God: "The poverty of inner vision, that is, of God, is the cause of your going outside yourself so eagerly." [4] The Carthusian is truly wedded to his enclosure, for during his life all his needs are restricted to the four walls of his cell, and all he asks for after that is a few feet of soil. Pascal gives us the key to this austerity so wholly removed from the ways of the world: "All the troubles of men come about from only one thing, that they are unable to remain at rest in their own rooms." [5]

[4] Ibid., col. 617.   [5] Blaise Pascal: *Pensées* (Paris: Nelson; 1932), p. 105.

Three times during the twenty-four hours the Carthusian leaves his cell to go in silence to the conventual church, which, significantly enough, has no pulpit. Every night at eleven o'clock he rises from his bed and proceeds with his little lantern through the long cloister to sing the divine praises in choir until about two in the morning. This interruption of sleep night after night requires an ever new act of self-conquest, and it would be unthinkable for those who, like Solomon, prefer to treat themselves to "yet a little sleep, a little slumber, a little folding of the hands to sleep" (Prov. vi, 10).

Only the chanting in the dimly lit church disturbs the deep silence of the cloister. Emil Baumann, commenting on the impressive sight of the night office, writes: "These men, who send up their pleas to the Almighty while the rest of the world is sleeping or giving itself over to carnal delights, are the watchmen of eternity. They share in the night watch of the angels and shepherds in the fields of Bethlehem." [6] From the point of view of pure reason, it is hard to explain these nightly vigils; like Carthusianism as a whole, they remain above and beyond human judgment. But it should be a singular source of consolation to sufferers from insomnia to know that while they are restlessly tossing on their beds, the white monks are at their prayers.

Their plainchant is unrelieved by any organ accompaniment; indeed, not a single musical instrument is to be found in the entire monastery. The Carthusian liturgy is exactly the same today as it was in the eleventh century, and the old Gregorian Chant falls with almost plaintive earnestness from the lips of these unpolished singers. One of the rules concerning the chant in choir reads: "As the occupation of a true monk is to lament rather than to sing, let us use our voices in such a way that they arouse in our souls that inner joy which comes from tears rather than the emotions called forth by the chords of a harmonic music. To this end, and with God's help, we shall exclude everything that gives rise to these empty feelings and that is not absolutely necessary." [7]

At a given signal during the divine office, the monks suddenly

---

[6] Baumann: op. cit., p. 90.

[7] H. Faber: *Unter den Kartäusern* (1892), p. 35. Cf. also Thompson: op. cit., p. 111.

prostrate themselves. They do not simply sink to their knees, but lie flat on the ground, their cowls over their heads. This sudden prostration is deeply moving. It expresses the very essence of Carthusianism, which is not to hold the head high, but humbly to throw oneself into the dust before the Almighty. The act reminds us of Christ's agony at Gethsemane. This constant spirit of penance is also apparent in the Carthusian's meager diet—a single meal on most days and frequent fasts—in the hair-shirt he wears night and day next to his skin, and in the discipline he takes weekly, a practice that is not of obligation but has become customary.

This mortified life does not permit of any sort of idyllic misrepresentation; to lose any fanciful ideas one might have had about Carthusianism, one need only consider the rod that to this day is kept as a symbol in a corner of the chapter house. The constant solitude, which the monks themselves have compared to a tomb into which they have voluntarily entered, often produces grave spiritual crises that not everyone is able to survive. Again and again novices have to ask to be released, unable to endure the monotony of this way of life.

But the Carthusian who has overcome these difficulties considers his solitary existence a great privilege, for he is sustained by the faith that "our life will be completely transformed and refashioned once the divine indwelling, the presence of God within us, can have free play, without encountering any opposition on our part." [8] His solitude is no longer solitude, for in his silence and his almost uninterrupted prayer he experiences the closeness of God. Prayer is the only art he practices, and for him it is no idle exercise in autosuggestion, as the unbeliever would have it. In prayer the monk speaks with God, and after years of concentration he attains to a great and inexpressible joy wholly distinct from sentimental effusions.

Only in this mystical context can we understand these men of God, and without the experience of divine joy the whole institution would be purest folly. The Carthusian has only one goal—practical union with God—and everything else is subordinated to that. He writes no deep works on mysticism, but he lives it in its sober reality. If by mysticism we mean the life of man with God, then

8 *Das Leben in Gott,* ed. Kronseder, p. 35.

this, and not theology, is the secret of the Carthusian. Neither learning nor the exercise of power interests him. Nor is he concerned
with all that pomp and ceremony which have earned the Catholic
Church alternate praise and blame—blame for its emphasis on externals, praise for its wise handling of the crowd. All the Carthusian
strives for is the perfection of his spiritual life and ever deeper union
with God. In this perpetual dialogue with the eternal the monk
has found the most direct path to his goal, and therefore he no
longer needs the indirect help that nature, music, painting, and the
like can afford.

Because detachment from things is not considered as an end in itself but as a necessary preparation for that ever deepening union
with God, the Carthusians are not troubled by the injunction
against reading newspapers or giving voice to any desires. Happy
the man who is freed from all such needs. For everything falls under this consideration, that "to keep oneself hidden in the secret of
God's presence; to seek to remain in constant colloquy with heaven;
to rejoice in being unknown; to be disregarded by man; in all things
to grasp only at that which leads to a true and deep humility,
which is the root of all virtues and in some way the channel of God's
grace—that, briefly, is the aim of the Carthusian order." [9]

This consuming longing for God explains the customs that the
Carthusians observe at the deathbed of one of the brethren. As
soon as a monk has died, his cowl is pulled over his head, his habit
is firmly nailed to a board, and thus, without a coffin, he is lowered
into his grave. A plain wooden cross bearing no inscription is erected
over the grass-covered mound, as befits a man who wished to remain unknown in this world. After the burial the monks gather in
the refectory for one of their few communal meals, rejoicing that
once again one of their number has reached his goal. Nor is it cal-
lousness that dictates this simple service, for in no other order are
the dead so much prayed for or do they remain so much a part of
the community.

The mystical life with God drives out any tendency to morose-
ness. The monks, many of whom are already old, are marked by a
natural ease, and in their quiet collectedness they possess a surpris-

[9] Baumann: op. cit., p. 39.

ing understanding even of matters outside the sphere of monasticism. There is nothing lifeless about their gaze, but a singular brightness, and this warm light is nothing but the reflection of the divine life within them. The visitor cannot fail to be struck by the contrast between these shining eyes and the misery and discontent written on so many faces in the world; it is a memory that he will carry with him long after the gates of the monastery have closed behind him.

What, we may well ask, is the use of it all? Carthusianism, as far as the world is concerned, is of no practical value. Even from a religious point of view, it can be objected that the Carthusians do not preach, do no parish work, do not engage in missions—in a word, do nothing useful. One might even say that they are pure solipsists, leading self-centered lives in their little hermitages, waited upon by lay brothers. Contemporary man might perhaps be willing to concede some merit to a monastic life that shows such tangible results as the clearing of forests or the founding of schools, but no merit at all to one where men deliberately renounce all external activity.

It would seem necessary, therefore, to point to the fallacy of judging another's way of life by one's own ability or inability to follow it. In matters of religion, such an egocentric approach is doubly out of place. The critic must realize that everybody cannot do everything, and that a way of life which appears strange to him is not, for that reason, wrong. And should we not recall, in this connection, Christ's words about the one thing needful, which form the basis of all contemplative life? The Middle Ages contrasted the *vita activa* with the *vita contemplativa*, giving precedence to the latter because it gave order to the former. Contemplation, which is directed to the divine and not to the human, reaches the highest summits to which the human mind can aspire, and the failure to recognize the need for it has greatly contributed to the chaos of our times.

Should we therefore defend the Carthusians on the grounds that they constitute islets of recollection in our bewildered world? No, there is no need for such an *apologia;* Bruno's spiritual sons have never made one, either. As Guigo wrote, truth needs not to be de-

fended, for it is not truth that needs man, but man that needs truth.[1]
Let those who have never seriously considered the matter and who
judge everything by utilitarian standards claim that the Carthusians
are useless. According to the Carthusians themselves, "not to defend
oneself" is "the great patience."[2] And they are well able to appreciate, with smiles of genuine amusement, the irony of Kierkegaard's aphorisms: "'Had the Apostle Paul any official position?'
No, Paul had no official position. 'Did he then earn much money
in other ways?' No, he didn't earn money in any way. 'Was he at
least married?' No, he was not married. 'But then really Paul is not
a serious man.' No, Paul is not a serious man."[3]

In conclusion, let us recall an event from biblical history. During Israel's battle with Amalek, Moses prayerfully raised his hands
to heaven, and his people were victorious. After a time, the man
of God grew tired and dropped his arms, and the enemy was able
to rush forward, so that Israel was sorely discomfited. But as soon
as Moses raised his hands again, Amalek was beaten back. After this
had happened several times, Aaron and Hur came to his side and
supported the praying hands of their leader, so that they would remain uplifted until the enemy had been overcome (Ex. xvii, 11–
13). This scene may serve as a symbol of the Carthusians' mission.
They intercede for Christendom, as Moses did for Israel; they are
the praying hands raised to heaven for the eternal welfare of all
men.

---

[1] Migne, ed.: op. cit., Vol. CLIII, col. 602.
[2] Ibid., col. 758.
[3] Sören Kierkegaard: *Attack upon Christendom*, ed. W. Lowrie (Princeton, N. J.: Princeton University Press; 1944), p. 181.

Saint BERNARD

and the Cistercians

Y<small>OU ARE</small> the eagle who gazes into the sun," wrote Hildegard
of Bingen to Bernard of Clairvaux. The great German mystic, who
is also the first German woman to rank as a natural scientist, had
penetrated to Bernard's very essence. Whereas the ordinary man
cannot look into the sun without being blinded by its rays, Bernard,
an eagle of the spirit, could gaze directly into the Sun that is God.
Hildegard was granted this understanding of Bernard's soul in a
vision, of which she wrote to him that "I saw you as a man who
looked into the sun and was not afraid, but was very bold." [1]

As intuitive perception of this kind lost currency, Bernard's reputation declined, and by the nineteenth century it had sunk to its
lowest ebb. Schiller was the first to give the derogatory verdict on
Bernard expression when he wrote to Goethe, in a letter dated
March 17, 1802: "It would be hard to find a second clerical scoun-
drel in history who was so worldly-wise and who at the same time
found himself so ideally placed for playing a dignified role. . . .
He hated all progress and repressed it as best he could, encouraging only the crassest monkish stupidities; for himself, he was no more
than a foolish monk, endowed with nothing but cunning and hy-
pocrisy." Without so much as questioning this view, Jakob Burckhardt incorporated it in his *Weltgeschichtlichen Betrachtungen*
(*Considerations on World History*), and felt justified in denying

[1] J.-P. Migne, ed.: *Patrologiae Cursus Completus* (Paris, 1855), Vol.
CXCVII, cols. 189, 190.

Bernard all consequence. Other historians have gone so far as to describe the Abbot of Clairvaux as the typical representative of that system which "looks like a cross but is really a sword." [2] According to this view, therefore, St. Bernard was a bleak reactionary who re-sisted the progress of his day—the worst, by modern standards, that can be said of any man.

We shall not, of course, arrive at a truer view of the man simply by trying to combine the inspired medieval vision with the pitiful modern distortion. Such compromise rarely achieves its purpose. Bernard's significance becomes apparent only if he is seen in the con-text of his own turbulent twelfth century, with its mighty upheavals in many spheres of human activity. Economic concepts were chang-ing, and artistic and religious concepts as well, and in all these changes the Abbot of Clairvaux played a leading part. He was him-self the clearest exponent of the new ideas. He was, in fact, anything but a reactionary; on the contrary, he helped to bring into being a completely new and forward-looking outlook upon the world. The process, nevertheless, was a painful one, and left undeniable scars.

St. Bernard, the medieval, was not the simple soul he is some-times imagined to have been. In him, attitudes that modern man would regard as mutually exclusive could coexist without conflict. If we are to try to fit this great Cistercian monk into any category, we have first to recall Kierkegaard's axiom: "Truth is subjec-tivity." [3] For the new subjectivity—which the medieval was as little inclined to equate with arbitrary caprice as was Kierkegaard him-self—was born with Bernard. But this does not mean that Bernard favored any kind of egocentrism, in which the individual becomes the measure of all things. His subjectivity, on the contrary, was firmly rooted in an objective world; it consisted, essentially, in a personal reliving of the Gospels.

Bernard was born at the close of the eleventh century of a noble Burgundian family. He grew up to be a handsome youth, tall, slim, fair of complexion, with reddish-blond hair and blue eyes. Not un-naturally, he was beset by temptations, but he realized very early

---

[2] Hausrath: *Arnold von Brescia* (1895), p. 40.
[3] Sören Kierkegaard: *Concluding Unscientific Postscript*, ed. W. Lowrie (Princeton, N. J.: Princeton University Press; 1944), Part II, chap. ii, p. 169.

that his must be a life of continence. And once he had made the decision, feminine charms no longer had any hold over him. The story goes that a harlot once came to his bed and lay down beside him, but that his only reaction was to move over to make room for her and then turn on his side and continue to sleep peacefully.[4] His biographer says of him that "he saw that, outwardly, the world offered him much—great things, even greater expectations—but that all were deceitful." [5] This realization of the deceitfulness of the world's allurements pierced Bernard's soul and remained with him all his life. And, in the first place, it triumphed over that love of poetry and letters which still attached the young man to the world. When his family first heard of his intention to become a monk, they used this love of letters as an argument to sway him from his purpose; but the only result of their heated discussions was that all Bernard's brothers came to join him in his enterprise.

The decisive hour in Bernard's life struck shortly before Easter 1112, when he knocked on the door of the little monastery of Cîteaux. Behind him stood thirty companions who also desired admission—an event that is surely unique in monastic annals. He did not seek to enter the wealthy Benedictine abbey of Cluny, as would have befitted a man of his rank, but deliberately begged to receive the monastic habit in the small, necessitous community of Cîteaux, an indication of the new form of monasticism toward which he was moving.

Bernard, first and last, was a Cistercian; monasticism is the key to the understanding of the man, and he cannot properly be seen apart from his entirely new and subjective experience of the monastic life. All the misconceptions that have arisen about him are based on the failure to take his Cistercianism into account, for this it was which governed all his actions and gave unity to attitudes that sometimes appear hard to reconcile.

Three years after entering Cîteaux, Bernard was sent away with several other monks to found a daughter house, of which he was to be the abbot. The little band of thirteen set out to find a suitable site for the new monastery. And the spot they chose was certainly suitable by Cistercian standards—a wild and fearsome valley known

<hr>

[4] Migne, ed.: op. cit., Vol. CLXXXV, col. 230.　　[5] Ibid., col. 231.

as the "valley of absinthe." It has come down to us in history as Clairvaux—"valley of light," for that is what Bernard and his companions made of it.

The obstacles were almost insuperable. Everything had to be begun from scratch. The first step was to clear some of the wild vegetation and cut timber, and during the first few months the monks hardly ever laid down their axes. They suffered much from cold and hunger before they were able to erect even the barest shelter. Their principal foods were black barley bread and millet gruel; they made soup of cooked leaves, and often had only acorns to eat. The hardship was such that the monks finally implored their abbot to lead them out of this vale of bitterness back to Cîteaux. But Bernard would not hear of it; he was not the man to lose heart and retreat in the face of difficulties—on the contrary, they stimulated him to further endeavor. And so the monks labored on, but it was many years before Clairvaux was firmly established as a monastery.

In the light of this first venture in monastic foundation, we can better understand Bernard's comment in a letter to a friend: "Believe me who have experience, you will find much more laboring amongst the woods than you ever will amongst books. Woods and stones will teach you what you can never hear from any master." [6] Yet the words have a strange ring; could they indicate a budding mystique of nature? Such a theory would seem hard to reconcile with the story we are told of Bernard's riding an entire day along the shores of the Lake of Geneva without ever noticing the lake. But although this story underlines the intensity of Bernard's interior life, it does not prove that he had no appreciation of natural beauty. On the contrary, he loved the brilliance of the noonday sun, the awakening of the world in spring, the mountains that reared their heads above the clouds. And he was intensely aware of the animal kingdom; he had compassion for the birds in wintertime, he could save a hare from the pursuing hounds, he could cure cattle pestilence with blessed salt. Nevertheless, his reference to the woods as his teachers stemmed not so much from his love of nature as from his monasticism, whereby he conceived of God as speaking to him, above all, in solitude.

[6] B. S. James, ed.: *The Letters of St. Bernard of Clairvaux* (London: Burns, Oates & Washbourne; 1953), letter no. 107, p. 156.

Bernard taught his monks by the only pedagogical method that never fails: example. He neither preached the moderate Benedictine discipline nor practiced it himself; the new Cistercian abbot was the sternest ascetic of them all. As a young man, he treated himself with terrifying severity, subduing his body without mercy. He fasted so much that he ruined his health and acquired a permanent gastric disorder, and he even lost his sense of taste, so that he no longer noticed whether he was drinking water or oil.[7] A miserable little cubicle beside the stairs, more like a closet than a room, served as the abbot's cell; he could not stand up in it without hitting his head against the ceiling beams, and the narrow window slit allowed very little light to penetrate into this dark chamber. Here he slept at night, with a straw-covered block of wood for a pillow. And thus he lived for thirty years, demanding the same ascetic discipline from his monks.

Most of the young men who had joined him came from the noblest families of France. Bernard regarded the monastic state as one that demanded nobility, and he appealed only to great souls. Nevertheless, he conceived of aristocracy in terms of spirit, not of blood. For him, the monk was, above all, the knight of Christ, a concept already to be found in St. Benedict's rule, wherein the life of the monk is described as a bearing of spiritual arms in the service of Christ.[8] This was the high ideal that Bernard held up before the eyes of his monks, inspiring them to almost superhuman endeavor.

Bernard was always looking for young men to join him in his new monastic apostolate. There was nothing accidental about the rapid growth of his foundation, for he did everything he could to encourage it. He was born to mold other men. In his view, many youths longed to dedicate themselves to a noble purpose but were unable to find it alone and needed guidance. And so he eagerly let down his nets, as became a true fisher of men.

The story of one young postulant, Geoffrey, is typical. The parents of the youth were greatly concerned about his health, and to allay their anxiety Bernard wrote to them: "Do not be sad about your

[7] Migne, ed.: op. cit., Vol. CLXXXV, col. 304.
[8] The Rule of St. Benedict, ed. Gasquet (London: Chatto & Windus; 1936), Prologue, p. 1.

Geoffrey or shed any tears on his account, for he is going quickly to joy and not to sorrow. I will be for him both a mother and a father, both a brother and a sister. I will make the crooked paths straight for him and the rough places smooth. I will temper and arrange all things that his soul may advance and his body not suffer." [9] This reassurance must have been effective, for Geoffrey now set out with his companions for the monastery. On the way, however, he was suddenly overcome with gloom, and when asked what was wrong, replied: "I feel that from now on I shall never be happy again." The words were reported to St. Bernard, who said nothing, but stopped at the nearest church and went in to pray for the youth. Geoffrey meanwhile fell asleep. When Bernard had ended his prayer and Geoffrey his sleep, the youth's mood had lifted, and with a happy expression he told his astonished companions: "Even though I told you just now that I would never be happy again, I now say that I shall never be sad again." [1]

Here we glimpse the essence of Bernard's personality; we perceive the power of a heart whose interior joy could prevail over another's gloom. Who could resist him? Small wonder that, as his contemporaries reported, mothers feared for their sons, wives for their husbands, when Bernard was about.

St. Bernard considered himself responsible for his monks' souls, and he watched over them with truly paternal care. Once, when a monk who had stayed away from Communion explained to his abbot that he lacked faith and expected to go to hell for this, Bernard exclaimed: "What! One of my monks go to hell! Never! If you lack faith, then I command you under obedience to go and communicate with my faith!" The cure was successful. [2]

When Bernard spoke, his words seemed to carry evangelical authority, and his persuasiveness was virtually irresistible. He would even get his way when he pleaded for highway robbers on their way to the gallows, asking that they be released into his custody so that they might learn something of the reforming power of Christianity. [3] Clearly, there must have been something more in this gaunt

[9] James, ed.: op. cit., letter no. 112, p. 169.
[1] Migne, ed.: op. cit., Vol. CLXXXV, col. 331.
[2] Ibid., col. 419.
[3] Ibid., cols. 425, 426.

figure than "crass monkish stupidity," as the exponents of the Enlightenment maintained.

Monasticism was the wellspring of Bernard's action, and he once summed up what he thought of the monastic state in a letter to a friend: "I say it is a good sort of playing, by which we become an object of reproach to the rich and of ridicule to the proud. In fact, what else do seculars think we are doing but playing when what they desire most on earth we fly from, and what they fly from, we desire? Like acrobats and jugglers, who with heads down and feet up, stand or walk on their hands, and thus draw all eyes to themselves." [4] So magnificent a definition could hardly have come from a Cluniac monk of the time, entrenched as he was in his wealth, with his two feet firmly planted on the ground. This was the new Cistercian concept, and it could not have been more tersely put.

In these words St. Bernard reveals the secret of the monk, which lies in the reversal of all worldly values. And suddenly one understands the explosive force that has always been generated by true monasticism, and one realizes that this type of Christian life is not to be measured by standards appropriate to the ordinary life of ordinary men. St. Bernard's soul is contained in this confession, with its gay mockery of all attempts to cling to security in life. And in his spiritual acrobatics we are made clearly aware of the call to a more rational life. Here, too, is the substance of Christ's message, clothed in characteristic Cistercian form. And that is why real, undiluted monasticism can never be understood in purely rational terms. The "natural man" shudders at the thought of these acrobats and jugglers of the Lord, at these authentic Christians with their frightening asceticism, and yet their topsy-turvy way of life makes them supremely happy. Like St. Paul, Bernard chose to be among the "fools for Christ's sake" in order that, as he wrote to the same friend, the Lord at His coming might "gladden us, exalt us, and glorify us forever." [5]

Bernard's new monasticism was most powerfully reflected in the wave of mysticism which swept through western Europe during the twelfth century. Benedictinism, which the Cistercians were seeking

[4] James, ed.: op. cit., letter no. 90, p. 135.
[5] Ibid., letter no. 90, p. 135.

to revive, contained the seed of mysticism; Cistercianism produced the flower. A particularity of Bernard's mysticism is that it was wholly Christian, untinged by any trace of Neo-Platonism; and it was the very foundation of the monastic life as Bernard himself conceived of it.

St. Bernard, who was probably one of the greatest preachers in Christian history, developed his mystical doctrine through his sermons, never elaborating it in any theoretical system. He preached the word of God with astonishing eloquence whenever he felt moved to do so, without confining himself to monastic convention in the matter. The high point of his conventual preaching was his exposition of the *Song of Songs,* which covered a span of many years.

It is no accident that Bernard should have chosen this Old Testament love song, with its passionate protestations that love is sweeter than wine, with its pressing summons to enter the beloved's chamber, as the vehicle for the explanation of his mystical doctrine to his monks. Something within him must have responded most deeply to these ardent declarations. Yet, despite the passion that echoes through Solomon's song, Bernard's language is nowhere cloying, nor is it possible in any of his sermons to suspect him of seeking an outlet for a repressed eroticism. His allegorical interpretations show very plainly that he was concerned only with the hidden spiritual significance underlying the colorful language.

Bernard opened one of his sermons on the text "Let him kiss me with the kisses of his mouth" by telling his monks: "We shall read today in the book of experience. Turn your minds inward upon yourselves, and let each of you examine his own conscience in regard to those things which are to be mentioned. I desire to make examination, whether to any of you it has been given to speak, out of the deep desire of his heart, these words of the text which we are to consider." [6] In this invitation we can already glimpse something of that new, personal approach which was so characteristic of St. Bernard. He believed, he once said, in order that he might experience; and again, "Believe, and thou hast found." [7]

[6] Mabillon and Eales, eds.: *Life and Works of St. Bernard* (London: Hodges; 1896), Vol. IV, *Sermons on the Song of Solomon,* sermon no. 3, p. 17.
[7] Ibid., sermon no. 76, p. 471.

The insatiable hunger for direct religious experience which consumed him is a distinctive feature of the new subjectivity which St. Bernard inaugurated and which brings him so close, in that sense, to modern man. He was not satisfied to know about God as one knows a doctrine; what he wanted was to grasp the reality of the Godhead. We have to go all the way back to St. Augustine, whose teachings St. Bernard had certainly turned to good account, to find any comparable striving after religious experience.

Speaking of what he called the "spiritual kiss," Bernard affirmed that "no one can comprehend what it is, save he who has experienced it." [8] He was expressing a profoundly important principle—namely, that in religion only what one knows by personal experience is of value. As for Bernard himself, it was certainly not from hearsay that he knew of the mystical life. He threw himself into it without reserve, experiencing ineffable ecstasy before his crucifix; one of his monks reported that he had seen Christ Himself detaching His pierced hands from the cross in order to embrace His servant Bernard. [9] This vision colors all Bernard's teachings on the spiritual life and gives them a note of fervor which distinguishes them radically from any purely theoretical speculations on the subject.

And even if Bernard's reference to the book of experience should indicate that his mysticism was a form of piety derived solely from personal experience,[1] why should this be regarded as suspect or undesirable? It is true that the eternal Source can never be experienced as It is in Itself, and that only rays of Its light can reach us; on the other hand, those rays cannot truly penetrate a man who lacks all personal experience of the divine. A Christian has to experience the reality of Christ for himself; only so will his knowledge of God become more than a merely cerebral process by which he spins abstract theological theories, and become instead the driving force of his life.

For St. Bernard, this new world of experience meant a wonderful and mysterious relationship between the soul and its divine Bride-

---

[8] Ibid., sermon no. 3, p. 18.
[9] Migne, ed.: op. cit., Vol. CLXXXV, cols. 119, 120.
[1] J. Schuck: *Das religiöse Erlebnis bei Bernhard von Clairvaux* (Wurzburg, 1922).

groom, who came and went at will, thereby assuring the soul of His divine indwelling. "I confess, then," Bernard tells his monks, "though I say it in my foolishness, that the Word has visited me, and even very often. But although he has frequently entered into my soul, I have never at any time been sensible of the precise moment of His coming. I have felt that He was present. I remember that He has been with me. I have sometimes been able even to have a presentiment that He would come, but never to feel His coming, or His departure." [2] And as for the manner of this visitation: "It is not by the eyes that He enters, for He is without form or color that they can discern; nor by the ears, for His coming is without sound; nor by the nostrils, for it is not with the air but with the mind that He is blended. . . . By what avenue, then, has He entered? Or perhaps the fact may be that He has not entered at all, nor indeed come at all from outside. . . . I have ascended higher than myself, and lo! I have found the Word above me still. My curiosity has led me to descend below myself also, and yet I have found Him still at a lower depth. . . . And thus I have learned the truth of the words I had read: 'In Him we live and move and have our being' " (Acts xvii, 28). [3]

The reality of the Bridegroom's visitation is here almost tangible, even though Bernard is forced to admit that the manner of it is inexplicable. He continues: "You will ask, then, how . . . I could know that He was present? But He is living and full of energy, and as soon as He has entered into me He has quickened my sleeping soul, has aroused and softened and goaded my heart, which was in a state of torpor, and hard as a stone. . . . Thus, then, the Bridegroom-Word, though He has several times entered into me, has never made His coming apparent to my sight, hearing, or touch. It was not by His motions that He was recognized by me, nor could I tell by any of my senses that He had penetrated to the depths of my being. It was, as I have already said, only by the revived activity of my heart that I was enabled to recognize His presence, and to know the power of His sacred presence by the sudden departure of vices and the strong restraint put upon carnal affections." [4]

Where, before St. Bernard, do we find language such as this?

[2] Mabillon and Eales, eds.: op. cit., Vol. IV, sermon no. 74, p. 457.
[3] Ibid.
[4] Ibid., pp. 457, 458.

Had Erigena or Gottschalk, Bede or Anselm spoken of any such subtle experience? The early Middle Ages knew nothing of the visitations of the Bridegroom of the soul, and only with St. Bernard does this new conception of Christianity awaken, with reverberations that have continued through the ages.

The Abbot of Clairvaux did not attempt the hopeless task of formulating the ineffable; like all mystics, he sought to convey the divine reality by means of images. But here we should sound a note of caution; the images must not be transposed into ordinary conceptual terms.

The essence of Bernard's mystical doctrine is expressed in the lovely image of the threefold kiss, which he borrowed from the opening words of the *Song of Solomon:* "Let him kiss me with the kisses of his mouth." This image he applies, in the first place, to the union of the divine and human natures in Christ, and we need only recall it to feel the warmth, the unconstrained ardor, the consuming fire of this man: "Happy the sign, wonderful and stupendous the condescension, in which, not lip is pressed to lip, but God is united to man. There, indeed, the pressure of the lip does signify the union of souls, but here a union of natures joins that which is divine and that which is human, and reconciles those things which are on earth and those in heaven." [5] Then he applies it, analogically, to the union of man with God, consummated, as he puts it, in the ineffable kiss of the mouth.

In the face of such emotion-charged symbolism, how pallid all those theories become which conceive of man's relationship to God simply as one of obligation! Here we have a far more vital, far more powerful relationship, yet one in which due order is not neglected. For Bernard, with his keen sense of hierarchy, believed that the ineffable kiss did not dispense the soul from the intermediary steps. The soul, he taught, must move ever closer to God by an interior process of perfection until there is no longer any barrier separating it from God.

No man is straightway worthy of the highest favors, and Bernard adjured the sinner: "Let him not have the rashness to lift himself so high as to the lips of the divine Bridegroom, but let him, with holy

[5] Ibid., sermon no. 2, p. 14.

fear, lie with me at the feet of that Lord so severe; let him, like the publican, tremble nor dare to lift up his eyes unto heaven." [6]

This prostration St. Bernard calls "the kiss of the foot," and it forms the first rung of the ladder of perfection. Like the sinful woman in the Gospel of St. Luke, the guilt-laden soul must approach the Lord with great humility and throw itself at His feet. The kiss of the foot represents penance, which St. Bernard believed must have its place in every Christian life. The soul must remain in this contrite position, washing Christ's feet with its tears and covering them with kisses, till the divine Bridegroom at last speaks those all-gladdening words: "Thy sins are forgiven thee." The kiss of the foot thus also represents humility, without which no spiritual life is possible.

The soul now ascends to the next rung of the spiritual ladder, but it is not yet ready for the highest reward. "I do not desire to reach the highest point suddenly, but to proceed toward it by gradual steps. For inasmuch as the shamelessness of a sinner is displeasing to God, in the same degree is the modesty of a penitent pleasing to Him. Thou mayst the sooner please Him if thou shalt observe a becoming measure in thy desires, nor seek for thyself the higher degree of privilege." [7]

The soul, then, has received Christ's forgiveness. But what if it should sin again? Then it will make the gracious reassurance void. Precautionary measures, therefore, are needed, and that is the purpose of the "kiss of the hand." This second kiss, which the soul imprints on the hand of the Lord, represents its promise to persist henceforward in its conversion and in its faithful following of Christ.

The final step is the ineffable kiss of the mouth, a gracious condescension of God which ravishes the soul. This kiss is the highest favor a human being can ask for, and represents that real mystical experience in which the soul is united to God. In the spiritual marriage—Bernard is one of the first to use the term—the soul loses all thought of itself. Such ecstasy, doubtless, is only a foretaste of eternal happiness; nevertheless, it gives the enraptured soul the highest degree of bliss which it is capable of sustaining.

This image of the Bridegroom, whose bride is the soul, opens

---

[6] Ibid., sermon no. 3, p. 18.   [7] Ibid., p. 19.

up a new era in medieval thought. Earlier, the concept of bride had been applied only to the Church. Bernard, without rejecting that symbolism, expanded it to include also the individual soul thirsting after God. Here we have one more example of that sub-jectiveness which is so characteristic of Bernard's approach to Christ.

He himself sums up the three stages of which the threefold kiss is the image: "This is the way, and this the order, which must be followed. In the first place, we fall at the feet of the Lord, and lament before Him who has made us, the faults and sins which we ourselves have committed. In the second, we seek His helping hand to lift us up, and to strengthen our feeble knees that we may stand upright. In the third, when we have, with many prayers and tears, obtained these two former graces, then at length we perhaps ven-ture to lift our eyes to that countenance full of glory and majesty, in order not only to adore, but—I say it with fear and trembling—to kiss." [8]

Of the spiritual marriage, Bernard says: "What can be more full of happiness and joy than this conformity [between the soul and the Word]? . . . This is the contract of a marriage truly spiritual and sacred. And to say this is to say too little; it is more than a contract, it is a communion, an identification with the Beloved, in which the perfect correspondence of will makes of two, one spirit." [9] To show the closeness of this union, Bernard employs another image, that of the drop of water that appears to lose its identity when added to a large quantity of wine, taking on the taste and color of the wine.

The operative word here is "appears," for Bernard made it quite clear that what he had said about union must not be given too literal an interpretation: "But be careful not to allow yourselves to think that there is anything imaginary, on the one hand, or corporeal, on the other hand, in this mingling of the Word with the soul of the believer. I am saying only that which the Apostle says, that 'he that is joined unto the Lord is one spirit' [I Cor. vi, 17]. I go on to express, in what words I am able, the absorption of a pure soul into God, or the hallowed and blessed descent of God into the soul, comparing spiritual things with spiritual." [1]

[8] Ibid., p. 20.   [1] Ibid., sermon no. 31, p. 204.
[9] Ibid., sermon no. 83, p. 508.

Bernard was careful, moreover, to safeguard the divine tran-
scendency by explaining that the spiritual marriage was a harmony
of wills, not a blending of substances, and that "this union is to
them . . . a conformity in charity." [2]

"Let not him who has understanding of the truth, but without
love, nor him who loves, without understanding the truth, think that
he has received [the gift of the divine kiss]!" [3] If God is love, as
the Gospels tell us, then love is the indispensable equipment for
man's journey to God. This is Bernard's constant theme. Referring
to his text, the *Song of Songs*, he points out that "love speaks in it
everywhere, and if anyone desires to obtain a knowledge of those
things which are read in it, a spirit of love is necessary to
him. . . ." And he continues: "In vain will one who is without
love attempt to listen to or read this song of love; the cold heart
cannot comprehend or appreciate its language, full of feeling and
fire." [4] And as, in Bernard's words, the way to love God is "to love
Him beyond measure," [5] the Christian relationship to God can be
nothing else than an ineffable relationship of love—a love that is
violent, vehement, impetuous, a love that is careless of convention,
time, reason, or custom. [6]

Bernard's mystical life caused him to experience the reality of
Jesus with an intensity and in a manner altogether novel for his
times. The early Middle Ages were still completely dominated by
the early Christian conception of Christ in His eternal glory, [7] and,
awed by the majesty of the Divinity, men dared not approach the
Humanity too closely. With Bernard, a profound change took place
in the attitude to Christ's Humanity. Bernard himself was captivated
by the lowliness of the Saviour. He beheld a real manger, in which
there lay a real and helpless infant, uttering real and pitiful cries,
and by this vision he restored reality to the miracle of Christmas. Similarly, Christ's passion was for him a real and wholly personal experi-

[2] Ibid., sermon no. 71, p. 438.
[3] Ibid., sermon no. 8, p. 41.
[4] Ibid., sermon no. 79, p. 484.
[5] T. L. Connolly, ed.: *St. Bernard on the Love of God* (New York:
Spiritual Book Associates; 1937), p. 4.
[6] Mabillon and Eales, eds.: op. cit., sermon no. 79, p. 483.
[7] Cf. W. Kahler: *Radbert und Bernhard, zwei Ausprägungen christlicher
Frömmigkeit* (1938), p. 21.

ence. Like an earlier Grünewald, he appeals to his listeners: "Behold Him! covered with rags, livid with stripes, defiled with spitting, pale with the pallor of death!" [8]

Not that Bernard failed to identify the Man of Sorrows with the glorious Son of God, but that he also cherished a personal love for Jesus which was the effect of a new kind of experimental knowledge, so that the Lord became for him not a historical figure but a living and present power. Bernard was the first to present the Middle Ages with the picture of the suffering and dying Saviour, and he did so with such intensity that this conception has been an essential element of Christian piety ever since. Echoing St. Paul, he states: "In a word, my philosophy is this, and it is the loftiest in the world: to know Jesus, and Him crucified." [9]

This devotion to Jesus permeated Bernard's whole life. If anyone wrote to him, he desired to find Jesus in the words; if anyone spoke to him, the name of Jesus must resound in the speaking; and if anyone was troubled, then, Bernard believed, he need only call upon Jesus in his heart and all darkness would immediately be dispelled by the rays of that Light. Above all things, Bernard was eager to apprehend Jesus, and this goal, he believed, could be more speedily achieved by imitating the Lord than by reading about Him.

With his intimate, personal relationship to Christ the Man, Bernard may be regarded as the father of a new, subjective religious approach, which in modern times has been best expressed in Kierkegaard's dictum that "truth is subjectivity." Emotion rather than intellect governed Bernard's relationship to Jesus. "Feeling ruled him; thought lent feeling wings," one authority has said.[1] Bernard's perception was of the emotional and intuitive kind that is sometimes able to penetrate deeper into reality than a rational, logical approach. If ever it was possible to speak of a "metaphysics of feeling," [2] then it is here, of St. Bernard of Clairvaux.

Bernard traced a path that his contemporaries could really follow. For he was concerned with practice, not with theory. What use, he

[8] Mabillon and Eales, eds.: op. cit., sermon no. 25, p. 154.
[9] Ibid., sermon no. 43, p. 269.
[1] J. Bernhart: *Die philosophische Mystik des Mittelalters* (Munich, 1922), p. 98.
[2] Cf. T. Haecker: *Metaphysik des Fühlens* (1950).

once asked, was all philosophy to him? His teachers were the Apostles. In a sermon on the Apostles Peter and Paul, after pointing out wherein their greatness lay, Bernard continued: "Such, dearest brethren, are our masters. They have been fully instructed in the ways of life by the Sovereign Master of all, and what they received from Him they have been communicating to us, even down to the present time. What, therefore, have the holy Apostles taught us, and what are they teaching us still? Not the art of fishing, not the art of tent-making . . . not how to read Plato or how to use with skill the Aristotelian syllogisms or how to be always learning and never arriving at the knowledge of truth. No, what Peter and Paul have taught me is how I ought to live!" [3]

This mystical experience is the context in which we have to view Bernard's participation in the public affairs of his day. For to him, action and contemplation were not two contrary, mutually exclusive operations; they were organically linked together, like the flower and its stem. Contemplation that cannot be expressed in action is a self-consuming inwardness; action that does not flow from contemplation becomes a breathless driving that destroys the soul's life. A man therefore must be truly penetrated with Christianity before he should think of throwing himself into active works. "Why do you act so hastily? Why do you not wait for light? Why do you presume to undertake the work of light before the light is with you?" [4] And again, in another sermon: "If then, you are wise, you will show yourself rather as a reservoir than as a canal. For a canal spreads abroad water as it receives it, but a reservoir waits until it is filled before overflowing, and thus communicates, without loss to itself, its superabundant water. . . . Be thou first filled, then pour forth with care and judgment of thy fullness." [5]

Bernard's political action was undertaken in direct response to the troubles of his times, as reflected in the state of the Church. He was deeply distressed by the situation, and he had no illusions as to its gravity: "The plague of the Church is inward," he cried out in

---

[3] St. Bernard, *Sermons*, translated by a priest of Mount Melleray (Westminster, Md.: The Carroll Press; 1950), Vol. III, First Sermon for the Feast of SS. Peter and Paul, p. 196.

[4] Mabillon and Eales, eds.: op. cit., sermon no. 62, p. 377.

[5] Ibid., sermon no. 18, pp. 101, 102.

one of his sermons, "and it is incurable!" [6] At another time, he spoke of the foul pus that was spreading through the whole body of the Church. It was thus no vain desire for personal glory that prompted Bernard's incessant journeyings all over Europe; by his own admission, only the great need of Christendom had induced him to leave his cloister and to take part in public affairs.

A papal schism had been created by the almost simultaneous election of two popes, Anacletus and Innocent II, and Bernard, aware of the hopeless confusion this situation was causing in men's minds, determined to bring it to an end. He threw the whole weight of his influence on the side of Innocent II—legally, perhaps, the weaker contender but morally the stronger—and did not rest until he had gained him universal recognition.

In this affair, as in his incessant denunciations of the abuses, vices, and disorders of the Church, Bernard was acting strictly from the standpoint of a priest and a monk. And we can get some idea of the spirit in which he carried on these campaigns from the statements he made in the course of them. For instance, this one, which should put courage into oversubmissive souls: "I do not say that subjects should question the orders of their superiors when it is clear that they do not conflict with the divine ordinances, but I say that prudence is necessary to understand whether they do conflict, and freedom too in order candidly to ignore them if they do." [7]

Bernard's political role has always constituted one of the major charges laid against him. Schiller was by no means the first to formulate it; the cardinals of his own day all too often regarded Bernard as a thorn in their side because he was constantly thwarting their private schemes. The prelate who called Bernard a "noisy and importunate frog" was not voicing an isolated opinion; on the contrary, the members of the Curia made their displeasure all too clear. Not Bernard but one of his own monks was elected Pope, as Eugenius III; later, when Bernard was engaged upon his principal undertaking, the Second Crusade, two very second-rate cardinals were appointed legates in his place. Nevertheless, it was proved again and again that his presence was indispensable; Bernard imposed

[6] Ibid., sermon no. 33, p. 224.
[7] James, ed.: op. cit., letter no. 8, p. 33.

himself on his age by the sheer force of his amazing personality.

Inevitably, in the political arena Bernard became involved in
clashes of opinion and doubtful issues. He learned by experience
that politics is not for the fastidious; on more than one occasion his
garments were stained by the mud of this world. Yet we have no
right to condemn Bernard's participation in ecclesiastical politics out
of hand. He was always frank in his action; he did not carefully conceal himself in the background like some medieval "gray eminence."
Nor did he seek any personal advantage; he did not rise a single step
in the scale of ecclesiastical preferment in consequence of his action.
Only his sense of responsibility brought him into politics at all. His
conscience forbade him to shirk situations of fact which needed to
be faced, and he accepted the burden of making political decisions.
So that even if he occasionally erred, he deserves credit at least for
his willingness to assume responsibility.

Bernard's controversy with Abelard belongs to any discussion of
his part in the public affairs of the Church, though it far transcends
any merely political issue. This controversy has earned Bernard
most criticism in modern times. And, indeed, the stubbornness with
which Bernard hounded those who held opinions different from
his own seems to be in glaring contradiction to the melodious language of his commentary on the *Song of Songs*. Nor can the Christian conscience easily justify Bernard's treatment of Abelard. The
manner of Bernard's campaign was certainly out of keeping with
the depth of his knowledge of Christ, and in his hostility to Abelard
he did not scruple to use means more consonant with his violent
temperament than with his sanctity. He foisted conclusions upon
Abelard which could have been deduced from Abelard's arguments
but which Abelard himself had never drawn. And he even resorted
to personal vituperation.

There is no doubt that in all this Bernard was moved by a zeal
more human than divine. In his deep involvement, he could no
longer distinguish between personalities and principles, so that he
was not satisfied with combating the ideas of his opponents, but also
sought to discredit them personally.

Abelard was no puny opponent. The famous lover of the enchanting Héloïse was a man of exceptional brilliance, but his character fell short of his magnificent intellect. The result was appalling tragedy.

Abelard was well on the way to fame when Bernard first crossed lances with him. He was learned and avid of knowledge, keenly interested in philosophy, quick-witted, ambitious. He may also be regarded as one of the first medievals to have had the courage to use his mind to the full. What he desired was knowledge, and in the first place analytical knowledge, which is why he employed the dialectical method. Indeed, it was Abelard who inaugurated that method in medieval intellectual life. Abelard's conviction that doubt was a necessary stage through which men had to pass worked as a leaven throughout the twelfth century and helped to bring about a new era. Many of his ideas were later accepted and became mighty building-stones in the proud edifice of scholasticism.

Although the quarrel was in fact forced upon Bernard rather than chosen by him, it may be said that he had no choice but to oppose Abelard's teachings. For, whatever the unedifying circumstances of the quarrel, the fact remains that ineluctable religious necessity prompted and justified Bernard's stand.

We can see what he found so unbearable in Abelard's approach from this cry in one of his letters: "Who can endure this cold? In it charity grows cold so that iniquity abounds." [8] Abelard's dialectical method seemed like an unexpected frost threatening the first flowering of religious sentiment which Bernard had been stimulating to growth. Thus he accused Abelard: "He speaks iniquity openly. He corrupts the integrity of the faith and the chastity of the Church. He oversteps the landmarks placed by our fathers in discussing and writing about faith, the sacraments, and the Holy Trinity; he changes each thing according to his pleasure, adding to it or taking away from it. . . . He is a man who does not know his limitations, making void the virtue of the cross by the cleverness of his words. Nothing in heaven or on earth is hidden from him, except himself." [9]

Knowledge can easily lead to intellectual pride, which is what

[8] Ibid., letter no. 239, p. 317.   [9] Ibid., letter no. 241, p. 321.

Bernard was fighting in Abelard, as he had early fought and mastered it in himself. That is also why he remained aloof from the theological discussions of his day. For Bernard, there was something repugnant in the rationalistic approach to religious matters, and behind Abelard's dialectical method he discerned the man who, as he once put it, shamelessly presumed to make the content of faith a plaything for the petty minds of men. Earlier than all his contemporaries, Bernard sensed the paralyzing effect of the dialectical approach to religion, and he sounded the alarm the moment the danger reared its head. Abelard's method threatened the very existence of that ordered world which was the precondition of Bernard's monastic way of life. And one cannot follow Bernard's campaign against Abelard without being continually astonished at his exact intuition of the shape of things to come.

It is an intolerable simplification, however, to see in this controversy a conflict between progress and reaction. Both Bernard, with his emphasis on religious experience and emotion, and Abelard, with his daring intellectualism, were moving toward a new conception of Christianity, but, because they were moving in diametrically opposite directions, their collision could not but be violent.

The essential difference between them may be reduced to this: Bernard sought after love, Abelard after knowledge. Not that Bernard despised learning; he expressly denied the charge.[1] He, too, saw something wonderful in a young man's thirst for knowledge, and he was always happy to meet a learned man. His position could perhaps be stated this way: one can never know enough, and ignorance has always been an enemy of the Christian faith. At the same time, knowledge holds a danger; it can easily turn into mere deadwood incapable of serving any salutary purpose. To know, therefore, is not man's highest end, which is why the greatest of mankind have preferred to follow the way of *docta ignorantia*. To love God is a far higher end, to love Him with all the ardor of one's heart and soul, with an all-consuming passion. That was Bernard's doctrine, as it was his aim: to be possessed by love, intoxicated by the superabundant wine of spiritual joy.

How pitiful, in the light of this spiritual ecstasy, is the process of

[1] Mabillon and Eales, eds.: op. cit., sermon no. 36, p. 234.

critical analysis, whose only object is to dissect; to take a gaily colored plumage and laboriously tear out, one by one, each single feather! Such a method is completely ineffective against a man on fire with love, rapt out of the world by the divine Spirit—a man, that is, like Bernard. That is why all the attacks that have been made on him appear as so much petty caviling.

Because it is hard to combine knowledge and love, a man must choose between them and be quite clear as to his choice. Bernard had chosen to throw himself unreservedly into the fire of love, and this it was that gave his personality its marvelous unity. His choice has relevance for our times, too, surfeited as they are with knowledge but starved of that fire of the Spirit which alone can raise men up to heavenly things.

Bernard's final intervention in politics took place in connection with the Second Crusade. Here again he rushed into an arduous enterprise not out of personal enthusiasm, but in response to the urgings of the Pope and the King of France. Once he had accepted the mission, however, Bernard did not confine himself to giving well-meaning advice; he, in fact, assumed the main burden of preaching the crusade. Without subscribing to the view of the contemporary Archbishop Norbert of Magdeburg that the Antichrist had already appeared, Bernard lived in the belief that "now is the acceptable time, now is the day of abundant salvation." [2] And that is why he traveled all over Christendom calling upon Christians to save imperiled Jerusalem.

Another aspect of Bernard's personality now comes to the fore. He appears, in his new role, as a prophet, a messenger of the Lord whom none could withstand. He burst upon his fellow men with the force of a meteor, dazzling them with his brightness. He became, too, a famous wonder-worker, healing the lame and the possessed as he rode from place to place on his humble little ass.

The power of Bernard's exhortations to take part in the crusade bordered on the supernatural. His words had an irresistible emotional appeal, so that many of those who listened to him took the cross, often against their own better judgment. On one occasion, in the cathedral of Speyer, there took place what Bernard himself

[2] James, ed.: op. cit., letter no. 391, p. 461.

described as the miracle of miracles: the German king, Conrad III, scorning all counsels of prudence, himself took the cross, undeterred even by the knowledge of the Pope's disapproval. Even where people did not understand a word of Bernard's language, they were powerless against the fire of his eloquence. This emaciated monk, who had renounced all earthly pleasures but who burned with a sacred fire, made an indelible impression upon his contemporaries. As though hypnotized, princes accepted his orders, bishops did his bidding. His journeys were a triumphal progress: people lined the streets cheering wildly, bells were rung, and the joy in men's hearts seemed to echo some far-off golden age upon the earth. The reverence that Bernard commanded bordered almost on idolatry.

It is difficult to suppress a sense of discomfort upon reading the accounts of all this enthusiasm; was it not exaggerated? Did not Bernard, unconsciously perhaps, employ some form of mass-suggestion, to which he then succumbed himself?

Yet, however much he swayed the crowd, Bernard always remained supremely himself. When he discovered a monk who had set out on a pilgrimage because he lacked stability, Bernard persuaded him to return to his monastery and wrote to the abbot: "So far as I can judge, he is truly sorry for his instability and impudence, and he promises future amendment, rightly deeming it better for a monk, however guilty, to do penance in his monastery than to wander about the countryside. It is the vocation of a monk to seek not the earthly but the heavenly Jerusalem, and he will do this not by setting out on his feet, but by progressing in his dispositions." [3] Bernard was not prepared to undermine the entire monastic institution in order to swell the ranks of the crusaders. All he was concerned with was that those things should be done which were in accordance with the divine will, as he saw it, and that those things should be avoided which were not.

Thus, when a certain Raoul, in 1146, began to incite the people of the Rhineland to inaugurate their crusade by attacking the Jews at home, Bernard indignantly wrote to the Archbishop of Mainz that to murder Jews instead of seeking to convert them was "foul heresy" and "sacrilegious prostitution." [4] And in another let-

[3] Ibid., letter no. 431, p. 503.   [4] Ibid., letter no. 393, p. 466.

ter, addressed to the peoples of eastern France and Bavaria, Bernard wrote: "I have heard with great joy of the zeal for God's glory which burns in your midst, but your zeal needs the timely restraint of knowledge. The Jews are not to be persecuted, killed, or even put to flight. . . . The Jews are for us the living words of Scripture, for they remind us always of what our Lord suffered." [5] Bernard's intervention on behalf of the Jews is unmistakable evidence of his genuine Christianity. To harm the Children of Israel, Bernard believed, was to wound the apple of the Lord's eye. And, according to the Jewish chronicler of the time, without his intervention no Jew would have been spared.

The crusade was launched with heroism and readiness for sacrifice, but with too little political or financial preparation. And when it collapsed in dismal failure, Bernard was regarded as a false prophet. The disappointed crowds were now as ready to stone him as they had been to cheer him in happier times. But Bernard bore his defeat with dignity, preferring that the blame should fall upon himself rather than that the people should despair of God. This was his hour of humiliation, an experience that is a part of every genuine Christian life. Bernard appears greatest in the humility with which he endured his failure.

Toward the end of his life Bernard wrote a book of meditations entitled *De consideratione,* which he addressed to Eugenius III, one of his former subjects and the first Cistercian monk to become a Pope. The bluntness of Bernard's admonitions to the highest authority of the Church is astounding; such temerity would be unthinkable on the part of a present-day Catholic.

The treatise was Bernard's swan song; it may be regarded as his testament, and as such takes on a particular significance. It disposes definitively of any notion that Bernard was paving the way for the temporal sovereignty of the papacy. He wrote, for instance, to Eugenius: "I dread no poison for you, no sword more than the lust of dominion." [6] He saw with starkest clarity how easily power can corrupt men's souls. "We must most carefully observe," he writes

---

[5] Ibid., letter no. 391, p. 462.
[6] G. Lewis, ed.: *St. Bernard, On Consideration* (Oxford: Clarendon Press; 1908), Book III, chap. i, p. 71.

again, "why it is that you have been set above other men. I certainly do not think it is that you may exercise lordship over them.
For even the prophet, when he was in like manner exalted, was told
'to pluck up and to break down, to destroy and to overthrow; to
build and to plant.' Which of these has the ring of pride in it? Is
it not more correct to say that the laborer's task typifies spiritual toil?
And if we are to think highly of ourselves, we should perceive that
a burden of service is laid upon us, not the privilege of lordship
bestowed." [7]

What the Abbot of Clairvaux was doing was nothing less than
disputing the temporal role that Gregory VII had claimed for the
papacy. It is unfortunate that the medieval Church did not follow
St. Bernard in this point. The Church, Bernard believed, must
serve, not demand service; must be poor, not seek enrichment. Let
the Pope, he taught, abandon ambition and cherish humility; let
him not seek display, but rather let him cleanse the temple with
Christ's scourge. "These lower earthly things have their own judges,
the kings and princes of the earth. Why trespass on another man's
province? Why put your sickle into another man's harvest? Not
that men in your position are unworthy, but because to devote yourselves to such matters when you have enough to do with better is
unworthy of you." [8] Again, a Church that serves must be free from
all vainglory. We do not know, St. Bernard writes, that St. Peter
rode on a white steed, arrayed in gold and silks and jewels, and
surrounded by bustling soldiers and attendants. "In all this painted
pomp you are not Peter's successor, but Constantine's." [9]

God's tempest, Bernard, his force in no way spent by age, was
pounding again at the portals of the Church, summoning her to a
new age of Gospel living.

What Bernard taught, that he lived, as he proved once more,
and for the last time, as he lay dying. To the weeping monks who
surrounded him he addressed these very simple words: "I do not
believe that I have any good examples to bequeathe to you from
my religious life, but three things I do recommend to you for your
imitation which I, as far as I have been able, have observed myself.

[7] Ibid., Book II, chap. v, p. 45.   [9] Ibid., Book IV, chap. iii, p. 103.
[8] Ibid., Book I, chap. vi, p. 25.

I have always depended less on my own judgment than on another's. When someone has wronged me, I have never sought to be revenged against him. I have always tried to avoid giving scandal, but if scandal has come, I have tried to assume the burden of it myself." [1] The three endeavors that the dying Bernard singled out are praiseworthy indeed, but they are not what one would have thought to be the central striving of the great mystic. There is no word about the call to a life beyond reason—"head down and feet in the air"— no mention of the threefold kiss, no reminder that love is greater than knowledge, no exhortation to follow the ideal of a serving Church. But words, at such a time, are perhaps not so important; his humble death, lying on a wretched, ash-strewn heap of straw, is far more revealing. Bernard returned his soul to God on August 20, 1153.

The fame of the unpretentious abbot who had sought no honors in his life, and who yet had determined the course of Western Christendom for a generation, continued to spread after his death. The fact is not surprising, for the more one considers him, the more impressive a figure he is seen to be. But we cannot expect to fit him into any standard pattern of sanctity, for he is larger than all patterns. This extraordinary man always did the unexpected, always gave things a new twist. His times bear his name; we speak of the "age of St. Bernard," and studies of his life and works ran into the hundreds soon after his death. His reputation survived even the Reformation; Luther esteemed him higher "than all monks and priests of the whole earth," and Matthias Flacius included him in his *Catalogus testium veritatis.*

But Dante is perhaps our best guide in assessing Bernard. It is already a moot point whether Bernard should not rank with Virgil and Beatrice as a principal personage of the *Divine Comedy.* The poet had perceived the upward flight of the mystic, and in his allegory assigned to him the role of bringing Dante to the goal of his desire in heaven. In so doing, he revealed Bernard's true function. And Bernard's prayer to the Virgin Mary marks the final climax of the *Divine Comedy.*

Thomas Aquinas, in a sermon on St. Bernard, said that Bernard

[1] Migne, ed.: op. cit., Vol. CLXXXV, col. 520.

had intoxicated the whole world with the wine of his sweetness.
That, in fact, is what Bernard did. In his sober intoxication of love,
he awakened in men an irrepressible longing for the direct experience of God. And the wine that the "mellifluous doctor" offers has
this property: once tasted, it can no longer be dispensed with.

II

Cîteaux, when Bernard asked admission there, was a poor, insignificant foundation of obscure origin. It had been founded by a
certain Robert—subsequently known as Robert of Molesme—who
apparently, in his youth, had spent some time in the locality living
as a hermit and had then entered the Benedictine monastery of
Molesme. But the life of the Molesme community was not rigorous
enough to satisfy his zeal for holiness, and he began to consider making a new, stricter foundation. In fulfillment of this plan, he, together with a number of brethren, "joyfully set out for the desert
called Cîteaux" and in 1098 built themselves a little monastery in
the depths of a wild wood. The spot was anything but picturesque;
the ground was overrun with dense brushwood, and wolves inhabited the surrounding wilderness. The monks' poverty was so
extreme that they were sometimes compelled to beg, but Robert
refused to accept endowments. He was unable, however, to carry
out his plans in regard to Cîteaux because the Molesme community
requested his return and he was ordered by his ecclesiastical superiors to accede to that request. Hence, as Robert remained at
Cîteaux for only a little more than a year, he may be regarded as
the founder of the monastery, but not of the Cistercian order.

Robert was succeeded as abbot by Alberic, also a former member
of the Molesme community, where he had supported Robert in his
advocacy of stricter discipline. As Abbot of Cîteaux, Alberic had
to face much opposition, particularly from the monks of neighboring communities, who regarded his austere way of life as a reproach
to themselves. Alberic, however, refused to be moved from his almost excessive severity, and it was from him, probably, that Cîteaux

derived the guiding principles of its monastic life. We can therefore regard Alberic as the spiritual founder of the new movement. There was nothing speculative about his approach; he sought simply to return to the primitive monastic observance. But his activity, too, was short-lived, for he died in 1109.

The monks now elected Stephen Harding as abbot. Stephen, an Englishman, had also come to Cîteaux from Molesme, and he proceeded to carry on Alberic's work with utmost fidelity. But now he had to undergo a trial that would have broken a man of lesser faith: unaccountably, many of his monks died. The neighboring communities were not slow in voicing their comments: what else could Stephen expect if he exacted too much from his subjects? The reproaches were bitter indeed, the more so because no new monks came to replace the former ones. For years Cîteaux appeared on the point of extinction, having apparently proved that its way of life was beyond human strength. Stephen, meanwhile, unceasingly implored God's help. He never lost patience, nor did he mitigate the rule or make any concessions in order to ensure the survival of his monastery. And then, when the situation seemed altogether hopeless, Bernard and his thirty companions knocked at the door.

Robert, Alberic, Stephen—all three were exceptional men who had had the courage to undertake a bold venture. But they are all overshadowed by Bernard, without whom the Cistercian order would never have flourished as it was soon to flourish. While not the first, Bernard was yet the greatest of the Cistercians, who gave the order its distinctive character. He held fast to all the principles of the order, but by his mysticism deepened the spiritual basis on which they rested. That was one of Bernard's major contributions to the Cistercian order.

The primary aim of the Cistercians was the exact observance of the rule of St. Benedict. Ignoring all intervening and often unfortunate developments, they desired to restore the primitive discipline of the sixth century. Indeed, Cistercianism may be regarded as a revived Benedictinism, and to this day the order honors the founder of Monte Cassino as its spiritual father.

In order to return to the rule, the Cistercians sought to isolate the monastic life from the daily life of medieval society. The incorporation of Benedictinism into the contemporary social structure was, they believed, one of the principal causes for the decline of Benedictine monasticism. The earlier monks had believed that their monasteries should be situated on the borders of human society. But in the course of time the monasteries had moved from the periphery and ever more into the center of secular life. This process had been encouraged by the almost total absence of towns in the early Middle Ages. For monasteries, like castles, could give shelter to hundreds of people, and in that respect could stand in lieu of towns. Princes would use monasteries as inns, often staying with their entire retinues for several days at a time and thereby introducing a piece of the world into the cloistered solitude.

The Cistercians put an end to such practices. In accordance with their aim of returning to the primitive Benedictine rule, they insisted that the place for a monastery was in solitude, not on the main street—a principle that was particularly pertinent in the Middle Ages, when the main street played a part in people's lives similar to that of the newspaper in our own day. It was only fitting, they believed, that the penitent monk, having done with the world, should live in a monastery far removed from worldly bustle. Thenceforward there were to be no brilliant knightly joustings in the monastery grounds. Despite the loss of noble patronage entailed, Stephen Harding refused to permit any prince to display his splendor at Cîteaux. He knew that those whom the world abandoned, the Heavenly Father would care for all the more.

For that reason the Cistercians deliberately built their monasteries in solitary, inaccessible places. The monk, in their view, was not to concern himself with secular affairs, nor even with ecclesiastical affairs, unless it were in prayer before God. No schools were to be conducted in the cloister, the monks were not to preach or assume pastoral duties or accept benefices. For all such obligations again drew the monk into the world, even though under the guise of concern for the Church, and rendered his flight from the world wholly illusory.

The restoration of the primitive rule also brought about a return to manual labor, which had been abandoned largely as a result of the Cluniac emphasis on ceremonial choir duties. The Cistercians, on the other hand, recognized the ever valid dictum: "Work, thou idle man!" They were not ashamed to perform the heaviest work, however noble the stock from which they came. In total silence they worked the land, ground the corn, cleared the forests, and drained the swamps, thereby benefiting not only themselves but also the surrounding districts and even future generations. Every kind of work, provided it could be carried out near the monastery, was hallowed for these new sons of St. Benedict. As one scholar has written, their manual labor symbolized one of their basic tenets— namely, that through the *vita activa* they could earn and deepen their *vita contemplativa*.[2]

In theory, the Cistercian movement was simply an attempt to return to the oldest form of Benedictine life. In reality, it was a new creation. For history does not permit mechanical repetitions, and every attempt to revive previous circumstances leads to new and hitherto unsuspected developments. The Cistercian return to manual labor is a case in point, for it went much further; the monks bound themselves never to profit by the work of other men, never to impose land rents or to accept tithes, and never to keep serfs.

These undertakings, which strongly reflect the new spirituality of poverty, show how a movement concerned solely with a return to the past, and which might therefore be considered ultra-conservative, will inevitably have a revolutionary effect on its own times. Had the Cistercians remained faithful to their resolution, the medieval world might have followed their lead, and a new social order might have come into being which would have spared western Europe the brutal crushing of the desperate peasant revolts which marked the end of the Gothic period.

The Cistercians made another new and practical contribution to monasticism by giving its definitive form to the institution of the lay brothers. These *fratres conversi*, as they were called, were recruited from the peasantry, and concerned themselves exclusively with the economic welfare of the religious community. By reason of their lack of training, they were excluded from choir and from intellectual pursuits, as well as from all voting on matters of concern to the

[2] W. von den Steinen: *Bernhard von Clairvaux* (1925), p. 31.

monastery. Yet the term "lay brother" was not a polite fiction for a serf. The Cistercians undertook to consider the *conversi* as themselves in life and in death; they worked with them side by side in the fields; and, under the rules of the order, the *conversi* were to share in all the material and spiritual benefits of the order. And if the modern mind balks at this hard and fast distinction between choir monk and lay brother, it should be remembered that the institution had its origins in the age of feudalism, whose social conscience should not be judged by modern standards. In any case, the Cistercians' attitude toward the lay brothers was a distinct advance over the contemporary attitude of lords toward their serfs.

Another change introduced by the Cistercians was in respect to clothing. They considered the fur-trimmed habit of the Cluniac monk a luxury, and returned to the simple habit of earlier times. But as they would dye neither wool nor cloth, the color of that habit was different—grayish white instead of the customary black of the Benedictines. For the men of Cîteaux, it has been said, the monk's life was not simply one of penance, but resembled the angelic life, and they wore white garments in order to show the spiritual joy of their hearts.[8]

At night the monks slept in an unheated dormitory. They lay fully clothed on their straw sacks so that at the first sound of the bell they might be able to hasten without long preparations into the presence of the Lord. As regards foods, they followed the old ascetical practices, eating two very simple meals daily, prepared as far as possible without fat.

In their churches the Cistercians tried to avoid excessive decoration. Here, too, their love of poverty was very noticeable. In place of the steeple, they put up a little belfry, from which a single small bell called the community together. Originally, no stained glass was permitted, and the church walls were bare. Nor were there any statues. Not even the chalices were made of gold; there was a saying among the Cistercians that the world had been redeemed by a cross of wood, not of silver. Bernard himself pronounced a scathing condemnation of the sumptuously ornamented Cluniac churches. "The walls of the church glitter," he wrote, "but its poor are destitute. Its

[8] Dalgairns: *Der heilige Stephen Harding* (1865), p. 66.

stones are covered with gold, and its children are left naked. At the expense of the needy, the eyes of the rich are gratified. Art-lovers will find there what will delight them, but the wretched do not find anything that will feed them." [4]

The Cistercians' greatest innovation, from the point of view of monastic organization, was Stephen Harding's *Carta Caritatis*.[5] In this short document all the Cistercian monasteries are treated as a single family, of which Cîteaux is the mother, and it thereby makes of the Cistercians the first real "order" of the Middle Ages.

Under the *Carta Caritatis*, the individual houses are encouraged to pursue their independent development under a freely elected abbot who is no mere prior subject to Cîteaux but who enjoys all the rights of his office. At the same time, all the abbots must undertake to follow Cîteaux in the interpretation of the rule. Cîteaux is not permitted to levy taxes on its daughter houses, nor to legislate for them; it may intervene in any house only if the abbot has acted too autocratically or is guilty of neglect of duty. All monasteries are subject to yearly visitation, and the abbots of the four oldest daughter houses—La Ferté, Pontigny, Clairvaux, and Morimond—are to visit Cîteaux, thereby preventing the mother house from gaining a position of unwarranted pre-eminence. The highest authority of the order is the general chapter of all the abbots, which is to be held annually. (This provision was subsequently adopted by most other orders.) In cases of disagreement at the chapter, the Abbot of Cîteaux has the deciding vote, and the other abbots are pledged to rally to his decision.

The *Carta Caritatis* is a veritable masterpiece of simplicity. It safeguards unity without sacrificing individuality; federalism and centralization are admirably balanced. It is a genuinely Cistercian document, anticipating the new ideas of freedom and comradeship of the later Middle Ages. One historian has commented: "It took courage to submit the *Carta Caritatis*, which omits all reference to the Pope or to bishops, and which claims so exceptional a status for the order, for the approval of the head of the Church." Nevertheless, the *Carta Caritatis* was approved by Calixtus II in 1119.

[4] Migne, ed.: op. cit., Vol. CLXXXII, col. 915.
[5] Reproduced, in English translation, in L. J. Lekai: *The White Monks* (Okauchee, Wis., 1953), Appendix II, p. 268.

III

Once the early difficulties had been overcome, the Cistercian reform spread like wildfire. A⁺ the time of Bernard's death there were apparently well over three hundred houses in existence, and five hundred existed by the end of the twelfth century.[6] But this rapid development was not without its hazards, and the order found itself compelled temporarily to stop the foundation of new houses. The whole world, it seemed, was turning Cistercian—emperors sought the order's friendship, Popes gave it their support.

This golden age of the order, as the Cistercians themselves have called it, lasted almost two hundred years. But then a gradual decline set in, resulting from a variety of factors. The Black Death, for instance, and the Hundred Years' War contributed vastly to depleting the monasteries in the fourteenth and fifteenth centuries. Nor were medieval communications equal to the demands of an organization that reached from end to end of Europe. But far more serious than these external factors was the imperceptible fading of the earlier zeal, together with a growing endeavor on the part of the monasteries to conform to the spirit of the age. One of the worst evils grew out of the institution of lay patronage, which made it possible for a layman to become the titular abbot of a religious house with the sole object of enjoying its revenues. Many monasteries succumbed, too, to the Reformation.

Nevertheless, it would be quite wrong to regard the history of the Cistercian order from the end of its golden age onward simply as a process of uninterrupted decay. Ever and again, zealous abbots would seek to restore the primitive spirit. As a result, the order has endured to this day. And even if the choice of names appears arbitrary, let us single out from the eventful history of the order three figures who bear convincing testimony to its continued vitality.

At the close of the twelfth century there lived in Calabria a Cistercian abbot known as Joachim of Floris. One Pentecost morning he was granted a prophetic vision: he saw the history of the world

---

[6] Figures taken from Abbot Cuthbert Butler's article on the Cistercians in the *Encyclopaedia Britannica*, 11th ed., VI, 395.

divided into three ages, that of the Father, that of the Son, and that of the Holy Spirit. This vision made of him one of the most powerful catalysts of medieval spirituality. The expectation of the imminent dawn of the age of the Spirit was like the opening of a passage to a new and greater perfection of human existence—a magnificent concept of human history far removed from any anguished awaiting of the end of the world. Joachim believed, moreover, that the triumph of the Church of the Spirit over the Church of the clergy would result in the creation of new religious orders that would comprise even married persons.

Inevitably, his ideas brought him into conflict with his order, and Joachim eventually founded a new movement of his own, which only rejoined the order several hundred years later. Yet in certain respects—his zeal and his emphasis on love as against knowledge— Joachim bore a resemblance to Bernard. And that is why the order never altogether disowned its extraordinary son and to this day includes him in its prayers.

Women, too, joined the Cistercian order at a very early stage in its history. They came mainly from the houses of the nobility, but because of their complete withdrawal from the world, little was known about them, nor did they seek the limelight. The best known of such Cistercian communities of women was probably Port Royal, reformed by Angélique Arnauld and associated with the story of the Jansenist controversy in seventeenth-century France.

Port Royal has been greatly misjudged and defamed. It should be realized that in its original opposition to worldliness in religion, it was motivated by pure Cistercian zeal, which only later developed into Jansenism. For there were certain obvious and misleading parallels between Cistercianism and Jansenism; not, of course, in respect to doctrine, but in respect to discipline. As a result, the spirit of Jansenism found a foothold in many a Cistercian house in France.

At Mère Angélique's side stood Pascal's courageous sister, Jacqueline, who could write in the midst of the controversy: "I know that it is not for girls to defend the truth, although it could be said, by a strange concurrence, that since bishops have the courage of girls, girls must have the courage of bishops. But if it is not our duty to defend the truth, it is our duty to die for it and to suffer anything rather than abandon it." [7] These were no empty phrases; the nuns were enduring agonies of heart-searching which no religious man can fail to respect, whether or not he shares their point of view.

No, the Cistercians have no reason to be ashamed of the ladies of Port Royal; on the contrary, they can take pride in them as worthy daughters of the fathers of the order. The story of the political intrigues that led in 1710 to the razing of Port Royal forms one of the most tragic chapters in the history of Christian spirituality.

The most momentous episode in the modern history of the Cistercian order is connected with Jean Le Bouthillier de Rancé, a Frenchman of noble birth and exceptional talent, and a godchild of Richelieu. Rancé was ordained a priest in 1651, at the age of twenty-five, but his sole concern was with his pleasures; a daring rider, a popular figure in court society, he lived according to the motto: "Preach like an angel in the morning, live like a devil at night." But the sudden death of his mistress shocked him out of his dissolute life of sin and brought about a radical transformation in his life; now his one desire was to atone for his past. He realized with horror that, although he was a doctor of the Sorbonne, he did not know so much as the ABC of Christianity. And so he decided, at the age of thirty-seven, to give up all his benefices and to embrace what he regarded as the humblest and most arduous form of the religious life, that of the monk.

After a hard novitiate in a reformed Cistercian monastery, Rancé became the regular abbot of La Trappe, a house of which he had long been the titular abbot. There he found what resembled more a band of robbers than a community of monks. Most of these he was able to pension off, and with the rest he proceeded to introduce a strict reform. He could not do anything by halves, and he was therefore particularly attracted to the asceticism of the youthful Bernard, though of Bernard's mysticism he had little understanding.

His endeavors met with tremendous opposition; his religious superiors thought his zeal excessive and declared him mad. And he provided grist for their mill by making statements to the effect, for instance, that study is an enemy of the spirit that should govern the

---

[7] Letter from Jacqueline Pascal to Sœur Angélique de Saint-Jean, June 23, 1661, reproduced in *Œuvres de Pascal* (Paris: Hachette; 1914), X, 108.

whole conduct of a monk. Nevertheless, Rancé succeeded in setting all opposition aside, and brought about a complete reform of his own monastery, a reform that spread to other Cistercian communities and led finally to the creation of the Trappist order.

Although Rancé was aiming only at a revival of authentic Cistercianism, he achieved something altogether new. And one has only to set foot in a Trappist monastery today to be conscious of an atmosphere that is altogether unique. It might almost be described as an atmosphere of sacred sadness, in which, through a life of daily martyrdom, the monk prepares himself for eternal joy. In the Trappist monastery there reigns the silence of the desert—or of the grave—by means of which the monks do penance for all the sins of the tongue. Only in prayer or in song in their soberly furnished church do the monks open their mouths. In every respect their life is unbelievably hard: every natural contact with the world is closed to them; they never take proper rest; they eat their frugal meals perched on one-legged stools so as to avoid even a semblance of comfort. Their constant aim is to humble themselves, in token of which they hold a weekly *mandatum,* at which they wash one another's feet. Under their pillows is a discipline which they administer to themselves every Friday after matins.

All these practices the Trappist accepts with interior joy, knowing that he is doing penance with his whole life. Death he greets as a deliverer: "If it is hard to live as a Trappist, how sweet it is to die as one!" [8]

The Trappists have bridged the centuries that separate us from Bernard of Clairvaux. Like him, they believe that a monk's responsibilities are so tremendous that he should never eat a morsel of bread without watering it with his tears. The bread Bernard was referring to was the ordinary black bread that formed the staple food of his monks, but we may see in it a symbol of that other Bread of which we read in the Gospel of St. John: "If any man eat of this bread, he shall live for ever" (John vi, 51).

---

[8] Ruff: *Die Trappistenabtei: Oelenberg* (1898), p. 101.

Saint FRANCIS

and the Friars Minor

Sometimes Francis would "pick up a stick from the ground and, putting it over his left arm, would draw across it, as if across a viol, a little bow bent with a string; and, going through the proper motions, he would sing in French about the Lord. Oftentimes all this ecstasy of joy would end in tears, and the song of gladness would melt into compassion for the Passion of Christ; and then this holy man would heave continual sighs, and utter repeated groanings, and, heedless of the things he had in his hands, would be uplifted toward heaven." [1]

The scene depicted by Celano [2] is of more than exquisite beauty. It conveys, indeed, the fullness of human sorrow, and at the same time reflects, as in a burning mirror, the essence of this man Francis. For if the "little poor man" could thus use his humble instruments to pour out his soul, it was because he needed music. His was an artist's nature which, at the divine touch, would give utterance to its joy in canticles of jubilation. The famous Canticle of Brother Sun, with its Christian hallowing of the universe, is only the most splendid expression of that ardent spiritual joy concerning which Leopold

[1] A. G. Ferrers Howell, ed.: *The Lives of St. Francis of Assisi by Brother Thomas of Celano* (New York: E. P. Dutton & Co.; 1908), p. 264.

[2] Brother Thomas of Celano was received into the order by St. Francis himself in 1214. After Francis's canonization in 1228, Celano was ordered by Pope Gregory IX to write the life of the saint. In 1246–7 he wrote a second biography, intended to fill certain gaps in the first. For a discussion of the sources, see, *inter alia*, Cuthbert: *Life of St. Francis of Assisi* (London: Longmans, Green; 1912), Appendix IV, and Otto Karrer, ed.: *St. Francis of Assisi: The Legends and Lauds* (New York: Sheed & Ward; 1948).

Ziegler has aptly said that it "again, for a time, preserved the child-hood of Europe." [3]

Francis desired that when his brethren spoke to the people, their words should sound like music. "For what are the servants of the Lord but His minstrels, who should raise the hearts of men and move them to spiritual joy?" [4] Music is closer to the divine superabundance than the dry conceptual language of the theologians, and any preacher of the Gospel would assuredly be glad to halt his discourse could he but play for his listeners some of those eternal melodies which barren words cannot convey.

Needless to say, the silent music that Francis magically drew from his stick was not intended to serve for the distraction of the bored. God's singer believed that "the children of the world do not under-stand God's mysteries; the musical instruments designed to glorify the Lord have been degraded by man's lustfulness to the purpose of flattering his own ears." [5] Francis's aim was to attune the ears of his astonished fellow men to heavenly sounds in order to wrench them from their brutish existence and lift them up to those higher regions where their true home is to be found.

Francis's attitude toward irrational creatures gives us some idea of the nature of this incomparable music. Did he not call the birds his winged brothers and preach to them the word of God? From the stars in the dark vault of heaven to the merest worm at his feet—all creatures were his spiritual kin, and he called upon them all to praise the Lord just as though they had the power of reason. Francis was filled with a burning love that exceeds human understanding; "he was all joy, filled with purest gladness, and seemed in truth to be a new man and one of the other world." [6]

His heavenly joy flowed from an encounter with Christ that al-most literally swept him off his feet. Francis lived in marvelous union with Christ, whose presence was unimaginably real to him. And those who would separate the Poverello from his Lord would sever the sapling from the roots that feed it. Francis's music rang true be-

---

[3] Ziegler: *Gestaltwandel der Götter* (1922), I, 321.
[4] *The Mirror of Perfection*, published with *The Little Flowers of St. Francis* (New York: E. P. Dutton & Co.; 1951), p. 362.
[5] Karrer, ed.: op. cit., p. 54.
[6] Howell, ed.: op. cit., p. 79.

cause of the torrential love of Christ which inspired it. It was indeed music from a higher world, and exerted an irresistible attraction over his hearers.

But the loveliness of the celestial melodies should not blind us to the utter crudeness of the instrument. The external circumstances were in stark contrast with the inner glory. Untiring labor went into the making of the Franciscan canticle, a "practicing" more arduous than any that the most industrious musician would be prepared to undertake. In order to arrive at even an approximate understanding of the Poverello's silent music, we must know what went before it.

Behind that music was, first of all, Francis's consciousness of a wasted youth, of years spent in extravagance and vanity. Then, there was that terrifying encounter with a leper, which began with Francis turning away in revulsion and ended with a magnificent act of self-conquest, so that he was able thereafter to kneel at the feet of such outcasts and tend and kiss their festering and malodorous sores. Again, there was that vision of Christ in the little church of San Damiano, where the Lord Himself ordered Francis to repair His ruined Church. Whereupon Francis, like any Italian bricklayer, proceeded to patch up the tumbledown chapel brick by brick with his own hands. Not long after, there was the irreparable public break with his infuriated father, concerning which Francis later confessed that it had been the hardest of all.

Any one of these experiences would have sufficed to give shape and content to a whole life, and together they helped mold Francis into the extraordinary figure he was to become. Nor shall we correctly interpret a single note of the Franciscan song if we do not give full weight to these significant antecedents. It was a penitent who brought forth the divine harmonies. To conceive of the Poverello as a "holy lark" or as a "primitive nature-child of Umbria" is to indulge in an intolerable simplification. We have to shake off any notion that Francis was merely a gentle and amiable "vagabond," a poet peacefully seated "beside the forest brook." There is just as little resemblance between such romantic images and the reality of Francis the penitent as between the picture of a "gentle Jesus, meek and mild" and the Christ of the Gospels.

Nor was there anything charmingly naïve about the founder of the Friars Minor. We need only recall, on that score, the terrifying simile he used when asked by his brethren to define his conception of obedience; to be obedient, he declared, meant to be as unresisting in all things as a dead man.[7] He was not even particularly attractive; with his low, receding forehead, his prominent ears, and his shaggy beard, his appearance, according to contemporary report, was neither beautiful nor distinguished.

And the supposedly gentle Poverello could punish without mercy. When the Provincial of Bologna, for instance, took it upon himself to modify the rule, Francis put his curse upon him,[8] and all the entreaties of the brethren were unavailing to make him retract his sentence.

Again, Francis cursed a pig that had bitten a lamb to death, even though it was unconscious of the reprehensibility of its deed. For even in regard to irrational creation he was guided by his devotion to Christ, so that, for instance, as Aegidius relates, he could not take any pleasure in ants because they were too anxious about gathering their food.[9]

A no less unexpected trait, in view of his profound humility, was his complete self-assurance. Here, too, one is reminded of Jesus. We read, for instance, that when he "pondered who would be fitted to direct the whole community after his death, and conserve its perfection with the help of God, he could think of no one." [1] In other words, he realized that there was no one like himself. Another example of this self-assurance is the sermon which he, a layman, dared preach before the assembled cardinals, and in which "he said many things about the insolence of the prelates and their bad example, and how the Church was totally confounded through them. . . ." [2]

The heavenly strains that Francis drew from his sticks exerted an almost magnetic attraction on his hearers. Without any prompting on his part, men came to ask whether they might join him. The wealthy Bernard of Quintavalle was the first, and he was soon followed by others. Francis, referring to this fact, said later: "The Lord

---

[7] *The Mirror of Perfection*, pp. 291, 292.
[8] Cf. Karrer, ed.: op. cit., p. 143.
[9] G. Menge: *Der selige Aegidus von Assisi* (1906), p. 77.
[1] Karrer, ed.: op. cit., p. 143.
[2] Ibid., p. 94.

sent me brothers." "Brothers," not "disciples"—the fine distinction here is most significant.

At first the little flock had to contend with a variety of difficulties, and even met with fierce opposition from many quarters. People considered them "mad or drunk," and "they occasioned great sur-prise in all who saw them, because they were so different from every-body else in their dress and their way of life, seeming almost like men from the woods." [3] Again, we are told that though many, seeing their holy manner of life, were filled with respect for them, no one as yet would follow them; on the contrary, "when women or young maidens saw them from a distance, they fled in fear and trembling lest they might be carried away by their foolishness and madness." [4]

Indeed, primitive Franciscanism had a spark of that foolishness in it of which St. Paul wrote in his first letter to the Corinthians. And the movement continued to spread despite the mistrust and even scorn it aroused in its opponents. The sober call to do penance and to keep the peace struck an answering chord in countless hearts, and people from every walk of life came to enlist in Francis's peaceful company.

These first Franciscans were filled with enthusiasm and joy that stood out in sharp contrast to the indifference that had taken hold of so many Christians of that time. Their joy was not the effect of mere high spirits; it was a spiritual joy in the coming of the kingdom, a joy to which they gave outward as well as silent expression, a joy that could triumph over every form of sadness—which state, Francis believed, was the work of the Devil. In his overflowing joy, Francis could kiss sticks and stones and other such things, and would often walk with dancing movements. There is a close parallel between primitive Franciscanism and the pentecostal storm that broke upon the first disciples in Jerusalem.

"Who are these men, and what are these words they speak?" people asked when they saw the brethren coming, drunk, it seemed, with love of Jesus. The perplexity of their contemporaries is not sur-prising; what is far more surprising is the disagreement that still prevails among modern historians as to Francis's real purpose. For Francis himself made that purpose abundantly clear; the Almighty,

---

[3] Ibid., p. 21.   [4] Ibid., p. 19.

he stated, had shown him that he must "live according to the rule of the holy Gospel." [5] One day, when Francis was in church, "he heard the words read out that Christ had spoken to His disciples when He had sent them out to preach, namely, that they should provide neither gold nor silver, nor brass in their purses, nor scrip for their journey, neither two coats, neither shoes, nor yet staves [Matt. x, 9–10]. When he understood this . . . he was filled with ineffable joy. 'That is it,' he cried, 'and I would obey it with all my soul!'" [6] Christ's words brought light into his darkness; they gave expression to his own inmost desire.

It is obvious, therefore, that what the Franciscan movement aspired to was a renewal of life in complete accord with the spirit of the Gospels. That was its primitive aim, that and nothing else. Francis wanted to thrust his way back to the Gospel—not only to preach it, but also to live it. He longed to reach out to the Lord and His Apostles, and not simply to the first Christian community, whose way of life the monastic foundations were seeking to emulate. Francis wanted to follow Jesus as no one had ever followed Him before. He wanted to penetrate to the four corners of the earth with his brethren, just like the disciples whom the Lord had sent to announce the glad tidings to all peoples.

At first Francis and his brethren were known simply as the "penitents from the town of Assisi," for "at that time the devout community was not yet called an order." [7] It is clear from this comment in the *Legend of the Three Companions* [8] that Francis's original aim of evangelical perfection did not include the founding of an order.

The oldest sources confirm this. Celano, for instance, says that Cardinal John Colonna urged Francis to decide in favor of the monastic life, but that Francis, "as humbly as he could, refused to yield to the cardinal's persuasion, not that he despised what had been urged upon him, but in his pious longing for another course of life, he was carried on by a still loftier desire." [9] Thus, while the

[5] Ibid., p. 275.
[6] Ibid., p. 15.
[7] Ibid., p. 21.
[8] Ascribed, probably erroneously, to Francis's three closest friends, Brothers Leo, Ruffino, and Angelo. See Karrer, ed.: op. cit., pp. 1–3.
[9] Howell, ed.: op. cit., p. 32.

brethren still spent their nights in wretched little huts, warming their frozen limbs at the fire of their devotion, Francis had no intention of establishing a monastery. He had received different instructions from the Lord which made it impossible for him to accept affiliation with any existing order.

Celano's account is corroborated by Brother Leo, who reports the following words of the saint: "My brothers, God has called me by the way of simplicity and humility, and this way He has shown me in truth for me and for all those who want to believe me and follow me. And therefore I do not want you to mention any other rule to me, neither that of St. Benedict, nor of St. Augustine, nor of St. Bernard, nor any other way or form of life except this way which has been shown and given me by God's mercy. And the Lord said to me that He desired me to be a new simpleton in this world, and He will not lead us by any other way than by that science."[1]

In this statement Francis himself made a fundamental distinction between monasticism and his aim of evangelical perfection. The Poverello certainly did not intend to disparage the great monastic founders of the past; if he regarded their way as definitely not for him, it could only have been for the weightier reason that he believed God Himself to have taught him another way.

An abyss separates Francis from the earlier founders. Benedict and Bernard, for instance, had been intent upon withdrawal from the world. Francis, for his part, was not at all averse to solitude, and indeed at various times was strongly tempted to embrace the eremitic life. But, except for relatively short periods of time, he did not indulge his longing, for the solitary life, as such, was barred to him; it was incompatible with his new mission of bringing holiness into the market place. His brethren were not to flee the world and retire behind monastery walls. Their mission, rather, was to go out into the world as fools for Christ and to spend their lives among their fellow men as His ambassadors. Francis instituted a movement diametrically opposed to monasticism, deliberately breaking away from the obligation of *stabilitas loci*.

Francis envisaged for his community—which he called a brother-

---

[1] Karrer, ed: op. cit., p. 114.

hood at first, not an order [2]—a far freer way of life than any permitted under any existing rule. Some scholars have concluded, in
consequence, that for a time Francis believed in the possibility of an
institution halfway between the monastic life and life in the world. [3]
And the Franciscan movement certainly inaugurated a new era in
the history of religious orders. Francis himself recognized the fact;
he told Brother Leo of this prayer that he had once heard from the
lips of Christ: "Father, I would that Thou shouldst make and give
to Me a new and humble folk in these last times, unlike to all others
who have gone before them, in humility and poverty, and content
to possess Me alone." [4] Thus, Francis conceived of his brethren
as a new people of God, differing almost as radically from the former
monastic movements in their way of life as Pachomius' cenobites
had differed from the hermits, or even as the first Christians had
differed from ancient Israel.

The Franciscan movement had the effect of an earthquake. To
regard Francis as no more than a religious troubadour is an esthetic
fallacy that leaves wholly out of account the impetuous power that
bore his movement along its way. It would be much more true to
regard early Franciscanism as a form of Christian revolution, by
which we mean that reversal of values with which Christ prefaced
His message concerning the coming of the kingdom. The Christian
revolution is an effect of the Resurrection, which was accompanied,
as the Evangelist relates (Matt. xxviii, 2), by a great trembling
of the earth; it has its roots in those world-shaking words of Christ
announcing that the last shall be first, and that harlots shall enter
the kingdom of heaven before the learned scribes.

Needless to say, there is no relation between this Christian revolution and the social upheavals of modern times. By definition, it
excludes violence, nor does it bring desolation, chaos, or ruin in its
train; rather, it loosens the shackles of convention, sweeps away
heartlessness, revises all values, and transforms the bitter into the
sweet. And if the history of Christianity is considered as a series of

[2] K. Müller: *Die Anfänge des Minoritenordens* (1885), p. 7.
[3] W. Götz: "*Die ursprünglichen Ideale des heiligen Franz von Assisi*,"
in *Historische Vierteljahresschrift* (1903), p. 26.
[4] *The Mirror of Perfection*, p. 269.

mighty religious revolutions, then an important place must be as-signed therein to the Franciscan movement. For it resulted in one of the greatest upheavals of medieval Christendom, and was aimed, as one authority has put it, at changing the face of the earth.[5]

It is no coincidence that the brethren should have chosen to ad-dress themselves by preference to the "common folk" and to live among them. By so doing, they created a close link with the peo-ple—a new departure in monastic history. The unshaven brethren acted as a leaven in medieval society, introducing a radicalism all their own. Understandably enough, the College of Cardinals began by qualifying Francis's activities as something unprecedented in the Church, something impossible, till one of their number pointed out that to reason thus was tantamount to rejecting the Gospel.

The revolutionary character of Francis's doctrine is most apparent in his attitude toward poverty. He began by divesting himself of everything that was his as the son of a well-to-do merchant. He could not be poor enough, for he wanted to call nothing—abso-lutely nothing—his own. It is impossible to define exactly what evangelical poverty meant for Francis. It is certain that it bore no relation to the mass poverty of our own day. Poverty, for Francis, was personified by a beautiful woman to whom he was wed in chaste love. According to the *Fioretti*, which in this respect do not poeti-cally overstate Francis's thought, he strove to possess the "boundless treasure of holiest poverty; for it is a treasure of such exceeding worth and so divine that we are unworthy to possess it in our vile vessels. Yea! this is that celestial virtue whereby all earthly and transitory things are trodden underfoot and whereby every hindrance is removed from the soul that she may be freely conjoined with the eternal God. This is the virtue that maketh the soul, while yet on earth, have communion with the angels in heaven; that com-panioned Christ on the Cross; with Christ was buried; with Christ rose again, and with Christ ascended into heaven."[6]

There was a mystical relationship between Francis and poverty.

---

[5] Dietrich von Hildebrand, ed.: *Der Geist des heiligen Franziskus und der dritte Orden* (1921), p. 83.

[6] *The Little Flowers of St. Francis*, published with *The Mirror of Per-fection* (New York: E. P. Dutton & Co.; 1951), p. 31.

Is it not very strange that, whereas to most men poverty is one of the worst evils, Francis craved it as a most cherished prize and regarded it as abundance?

For love of poverty, he overcame self and went begging his food from door to door. At first the mere sight of the unappetizing scraps that had been poured into his bowl turned his stomach, "but, overcoming his loathing, he began to eat, and it seemed to him that he had never tasted a dish more delicious." [7] Francis saw nothing shameful in begging; on the contrary, he valued alms as a gift that the Lord Himself had acquired for him, and he regarded begging as the highest form of imitation of the poverty of Christ. The Franciscans are appropriately called mendicants.

Francis's evangelical love of poverty involved a ruthless rejection of money. He had an almost physical revulsion against this thing which most men are so desperately eager to possess. Money, he felt, was of the Devil, and he therefore hated it with all the power of his love-filled soul, and even went so far as to curse it. He taught his brethren to have equal regard for money and for dung, and when one of them had merely touched money, Francis sharply reproved him and "bade him lift the money from the window with his mouth, and convey it without the hedge of the dwelling, and put it with his own mouth on the dung of an ass." [8] Here we have an example of the Poverello's terrible severity.

It is hardly possible to imagine a more radical reversal of values than the one implied in Francis's attitude toward money, and it makes one realize that the Christian revolution is not mere dilettantism. And instead of deploring, as some have done, the "tragedy of a saintly but deluded man," thereby denying the Franciscan dynamism, it would be well to remember that Jesus, in His Sermon on the Mount, proposed the same inexorable choice: no man can serve two masters. . . .

Thus, at the very outset of the bourgeois era, Francis, by his devastating condemnation of Mammon, struck more surely at the roots of convention than have all the social revolutions put together. When the Bishop of Assisi raised objections to the total poverty that Francis had chosen for his way of life, Francis made this reply:

[7] Karrer, ed.: op. cit., pp. 13, 14.   [8] *The Mirror of Perfection*, p. 256.

"My Lord, if we were to possess anything, we would have to have arms for our protection, for from having possessions arises all strife, and in many ways they hinder us from loving God and our neighbors; therefore we do not wish to own any temporal thing in the world." [9] From an economic standpoint, this attitude would appear to be utopian, but in the light of the Gospels it is soberest truth.

Francis's passionate cult of humility was another no less radical feature of his reversal of accepted standards. It is true that monasticism, too, had always taught humility, regarding it as the ladder by whose rungs man could ascend to heaven. But Francis made of the practice of humility an undertaking so bold as to strike astonishment into the hearts of all men, both in his own times and ever since. The Poverello's thirst for self-abasement made of him the very embodiment of humility, so that people suddenly began to see that virtue in a wholly new light. "Never should we desire to be above others, but we should rather be their servants and subject to every human creature for God's sake." [1] It was no coincidence, therefore, but rather the necessary corollary of an essential attitude of mind, that he should have called his brethren "minor," or "lesser," brothers. God Himself had revealed to him that they should be the lowest of all.

This abysmal humility proved to be Francis's greatest strength, sweeping everything before it. As one of the "Spirituals," Ubertino of Casale, later put it,[2] Francis knew that humility, because it was flexible, absorbed hardness by giving in to it, whereas when two hard bodies clashed, they destroyed each other.

We find an example of the revolutionary impact of humility in the organization of the first Franciscan community, which excluded any supervisory office. Because a superior occupied a position of authority, he would inevitably slip into an attitude opposed to humility. Rank, therefore, was simply eliminated; among the Franciscans there were to be neither superiors nor subjects, but only Friars Minor. Later, when the growth of the community made it necessary to institute ministers and guardians, Francis characteristi-

[9] Karrer, ed.: op. cit., p. 20.
[1] J. Meyer: *The Words of St. Francis* (Chicago: Franciscan Herald Press; 1952), no. 230, p. 190.
[2] *Die symbolische Franziskuslegende*, ed. Lützeler (1929), p. 119.

cally held up to them the example of mothers. In discharging their office, they should be filled with loving care, not with lust for power.

Here, again, we see the true face of the Christian revolution. Men were being asked to recognize the validity of a wholly new attitude toward life—an attitude that alone can lead to a solution of the problem of class differences in the spirit of Jesus Christ. Every other social revolution must necessarily fail, for all it does is to bring about a change of roles—the lower classes take the place of the higher, and vice versa; it never leads to the creation of a true community of brethren.

According to the *Fioretti*, Francis made Brother Masseo turn himself around and around several times in order to determine the direction in which God desired them to go,[3] a procedure that some of the brethren themselves considered rather silly. In behavior of this kind Francis revealed that simplicity of heart which at first earned him the reputation of being a fool, and which on several occasions during his life caused him to be mocked as a half-wit. The Poverello gave repeated proof of his simplicity, thereby making of his life a wonderful reflection of that ineffable paean of praise in which Jesus gave thanks to His Father for revealing to "babes" what He had hidden from the "wise and prudent" (Matt. xi, 25). Francis was one of those rare "babes"; he possessed that captivating simplicity of a child which is wholly devoid of guile and therefore completely disarming.

Francis sincerely respected scholars of repute, but in his community the learned were treated with evident reticence. In a letter to Anthony of Padua, for instance, Francis wrote: "It is agreeable to me to have you read sacred theology to the brothers, so long as over this study they do not extinguish the spirit of prayer and devotion, as is contained in the rule."[4] The proviso is a clear indication of Francis's feelings on this subject.

Learning has its place in the world, but does it have one in the Franciscan scheme of things? It is hard for a learned doctor to look upon himself as the least of men. The Poverello's view is expressed in this statement: "Let not those who are ignorant of letters care to

---

[3] *The Little Flowers of St. Francis*, pp. 25-7.
[4] Meyer: op. cit., no. 55, p. 62.

ers, but let them consider that beyond all they should desire
the spirit of the Lord." [5]

the Franciscans shunned learning because they believed that
learning lurked the spirit of pride. Knowledge puffs a man
endangers humility. What Francis aspired to was the per-
m of simplicity, not the pride of learning. He set himself
the arrogant claims of the mind, and his life's work is a
example of the way evangelical simplicity can dethrone
nip—even the scholarship that has always, and rightfully,
ltivated and cherished in Christendom.

reversal of values involved in the Franciscan attempt to live
Christ's teachings to the letter confronted the Church with a grave
problem. The Church was the custodian of the Gospels, yet she
was immediately aware that the Christianity practiced by Francis
was shaking her foundations, too, reconciled as she was to the world.

The Poverello, to be sure, was a faithful son of the Church. His
first vision had come to him in a little tumbledown church, where
Christ had ordered him to restore His ruined Church—an order he
had at first taken literally, and subsequently in its broader meaning.
Toward priests, moreover, Francis had an attitude of boundless confidence on account of their Orders, and in true Christian charity he
announced: "I will not see any sin in them." [6] Francis, then, was
not in conflict with the Church, and it would be altogether wrong to
paint his relations with the Curia in terms of the lamb surrounded
by ravening wolves. Such a black-and-white treatment of the facts
only confuses the issues. Francis's attempt to renew the spirit of the
Gospels, far from involving defiance of the Church, meant breach-
ing a gap that the clergy had failed to fill. And the Curia at once
realized the Poverello's fidelity to the Church and treated him with
evident favor.

It was no ordinary event in the history of the Church that took
place when the seraphic Francis stood before the mighty Pope Innocent III. The insignificance of Francis's appearance may perhaps
have begun by drawing a smile from the Pope's lips, but his bound-

---

[5] P. Robinson, ed.: *The Writings of St. Francis of Assisi* (Philadelphia:
The Dolphin Press; 1906), p. 72.
[6] Karrer, ed.: op. cit., p. 274.

less humility did not fail in its effect, and the Pope acceded to his request to be allowed to preach the Gospel, though without any further commitment.

Francis's subsequent dealings at the Curia were mostly with Cardinal Ugolino, who later became Pope Gregory IX. Francis felt drawn to Ugolino, and expressly asked him to be the protec-tor of his order.[7] Ugolino, of course, was of a very different metal from Francis. He was a typical medieval churchman, his sincere piety overshadowed by his concern for hierarchical order and gov-ernment. As a man of good sense, he paid great attention to matters of organization and administration, and his ambitions for the Church were directed to the attainment of results that were tangible rather than intangible.

We should beware, however, of regarding the members of the Curia as having acted in their personal capacity. They represented the Church, and their attitude was to that extent circumscribed. For the Church could hardly have been expected to agree forthwith to all the plans of the youthful Francis. She owed it to herself to show a certain reserve, which was admirably expressed in these words of Innocent III: "My dear sons, your life appears most hard and rude to us; although we believe your fervor to be so great that we have no reason to doubt you, we must consider those who will come after you, lest the way appear too steep for them."[8]

It was the Pope's view that not all men could burn with the same ardor for God as Francis's first company. There have indeed been many Franciscans, but only one Francis. The Church was looking back over centuries of experience that she could not ignore; indeed, she was in duty bound to take that experience into account, even in regard to Francis's passionate desire to live the Gospel without any compromise.

The Curia sought to stay the flood of the Christian revolution. Not that it contested the need for improvement within the Church, but that it was concerned lest the waters of the spiritual renewal overflow their banks. Ugolino personally feared the impetuosity of the reforming spirit, and his ordinances were aimed at checking an

---

[7] Ibid., p 87. Cf. also Cuthbert: op. cit., pp. 253 *et seq.*
[8] Karrer, ed.: op. cit., p. 25.

enthusiasm he considered excessive. Thus, the efforts of Francis's protector were directed toward restraint; but they also, strangely enough, proved useful to the growing Franciscan community.

Ugolino recognized the primary need for stricter organization; the rapidly expanding movement must assume the character of an order if it was not to dissipate its strength for lack of a firm framework. Francis did not oppose this argument, particularly as Ugolino had approved the idea of a completely new type of order—a mendicant order subsisting entirely upon alms—realizing as he had that traditional monasticism, with its emphasis on withdrawal from the world, could not provide the means for realizing the Franciscan ideal.

Throughout his negotiations with his papal protector, the founder of the Friars Minor showed a firm grasp of the realities of life and full awareness of the sociological implications of the existence of his new movement. He also gave proof of flexibility of mind, being able to accept another's views even if they did not wholly coincide with his own. The arrangements made in Rome to adapt his order to the purposes for which it had been created were made with his full consent; he was not forced to accept something against his will.

Far greater harm was done to Francis's Christian revolution by Elias of Cortona. The character of this unfortunate man is hard to understand. The early sources, for obvious reasons, say very little about him, and it is possible that, under the influence of the Spirituals, the portrait of him that has been handed down is too one-sided. He was highly gifted, intelligent, and an able diplomat in the worldly sense. At the same time, he was a tragic figure whose action was disastrous to the whole Franciscan movement.

With his talent for leadership and his practical approach, Elias showed himself far removed from the ideal of "motherliness" that Francis had set before those who exercised authority within his order. Elias aspired to emulate the pomp and ceremony of the Benedictine and Cistercian abbots. At the same time, he was obviously very much impressed by the Dominican order, and he desired to make of the Friars Minor the rivals of the Friars Preachers. His ambitious plan was to capture all these currents. Thus, even if he was not fully aware of it, he was in fact developing into an outright opponent of the Poverello.

Outwardly, Elias showed great concern for Francis, and thus gained his confidence, but after Francis's death he departed ever more radically from the Franciscan ideal. Being very ambitious, he had risen to the forefront of the movement, till he finally assumed the leadership of the order. And, once in power, he proceeded to transform the mystical brotherhood into a great world organization. To quote one authority, Elias "went far toward making the Franciscan order a world power, throwing its influence into the whirl of politics and into the intellectual life of the rising universities and into the mission fields of Moslem territory. . . . In him the spirit of secularism, sullenly clamoring for recognition since the chapter of 1217, developed a titanic force within the fraternity which his ability wrested in large measure from its original purpose." [9]

Elias lived like a prince, kept several horses, and never appeared in public except on horseback. He never ate together with his brethren, having his own cook to prepare his meals. He would not brook contradiction, and in order to avoid facing criticism he refused to convene the general chapter. Immediately upon Francis's death, he embarked on the construction of a grandiose church in his memory in Assisi—an undertaking hardly in the spirit of the Poverello. When some of Francis's original companions smashed the alms boxes in indignation at this un-Franciscan action, Elias ordered them subjected to corporal punishment.

His unbridled ambition and his violent exercise of power led to his eventual dismissal from office, and finally to his expulsion from the order. Subsequently he incurred excommunication on account of his association with Frederick II, and was reconciled with the Church only at his death.

These unfortunate developments were possible only because Elias of Cortona enjoyed the support of a large number of brethren of like mind. Some of those who joined the order after the first flush of enthusiasm were in favor of more "reasonable" ideas, and tried to neutralize the Poverello's teachings. But it would be unfair

[9] Cuthbert: op. cit., pp. 259, 260, 262.

to regard them as evil men who deliberately sought to destroy the Franciscan ideal. They were faced with new problems that necessarily arose out of the unexpectedly rapid growth of the movement, and they were ready to pay its tribute to the weakness of human nature.

Francis, in his ascetic fervor, had sprinkled ashes on his own food, yet had forbidden the brethren to wear belts of thorns next to their skin. Contradictions such as these he had been able to reconcile in his own person, whereas for the majority of the brethren they meant hopeless dissension. And the question arises whether it is possible at all to organize a community on the basis of the seraphic love that burned in Francis, or whether a life of this kind can be lived completely only by the individual. It was a question that the Curia certainly faced, and which explains its hesitations.

Francis observed a first change in the order upon his return from his missionary journey to the East. From Venice, where he landed, he went on foot to Bologna, where he found that the brothers had built themselves a monastery, which the Provincial regarded as the property of the order. The Provincial had thus yielded to that desire for possession which is so deeply rooted in the human heart. Francis deemed his action a shameful violation of the rule of poverty, and indignantly refused so much as to set foot inside the building. Indeed, he ordered the immediate evacuation of the house; even the sick had to be carried out at once.[1] The incident shows Francis at his most implacable; the culprit, in his view, had subverted the spirit of the order, and he wanted nothing more to do with him.

But the acquisition of a monastery in Bologna was only the first sign of the change that was systematically taking place in the character of the order. A no less significant departure from the primitive ideal consisted in the decrees issued by Francis's two vicars during his absence in the East. Francis's faithful followers opposed these ordinances, but were treated in most un-Franciscan fashion for voicing their objections. "Not only were they afflicted with unjust penances, but as men of evil mind they were cast out from the com-

[1] Karrer, ed.: op. cit., pp. 97, 98.

munity of the brethren. . . . Many, fleeing from fury, wandered about here and there, bewailing the absence of their pastor and guide." [2]

This transformation was largely the result of the clericalization of the order. Francis had great reverence for the priesthood, and treated its members with respect; the priest, for him, was pre-eminently the man who administered the Body of the Lord.[3] Francis himself, however, never became a priest, and his first brethren, with the exception of Silvester, were laymen like himself. In this respect the first Franciscan community resembled the earliest monks. Priests, however, soon began to ask for admission to the order, and Francis saw no reason for turning them away. He accepted everyone, and he treated all alike, for the Christian revolution obliterated every distinction. The brethren were not divided into priests and laymen. They shared their meals in fraternal style, sitting anywhere, without thought of precedence. It was Francis's wish, we are told, that the clerics among the brethren should attain to such humility that a Master of Theology would interrupt his discourse at the request of a lay brother who desired to preach.[4]

In time, however, the difference in education made itself increasingly felt. The clerical members of the order, for all their reverence for Francis, had a different way of thinking, and they finally got the upper hand. After Francis's death, an authority writes, the lay brothers were declared incapable of filling the higher offices in the order, which meant, in effect, the final transformation of the brotherhood into an order of priests.[5]

The ascendancy of the clergy also resulted in a changed attitude toward study. Learning played no part at all in the Franciscan community during the first ten years of its existence; evangelical simplicity did not so much as allow any concern with the matter to arise. In Francis's view, the Friars Minor were not to hold learned discourses; and indeed the first Franciscans, intoxicated with the love of God, preached very simple, short sermons, announcing

[2] Quoted in Cuthbert: op. cit., p. 248.
[3] Karrer, ed.: op. cit., p. 274.
[4] Menge: op. cit., p. 37.
[5] F. Ehrle: "*Die Spiritualen, ihr Verhältnis zum Franziskanerorden*," in *Archiv für Literatur und Kirchengeschichte des Mittelalters* (1887), III, 581.

the kingdom of God and the need for penance, and reminding their hearers of the rewards and punishments attendant upon their actions. The clerical members of the order, however, could not accept what they regarded as Francis's almost stubborn attitude toward learning,[6] and they stressed the preacher's need for study. Francis recognized the justice of their claim, but he was nevertheless eager to limit study to the absolute minimum. His warnings, however, went unheeded, and the brethren, we are told, positively stormed the seats of learning.

Francis's reaction to this transformation of his order is of capital importance. He was certainly not unaware of what was going on; on the contrary, his zeal for a revival of the spirit of the Gospel impelled him to watch with utmost care over everything that happened within the order. He soon perceived the alien forces intent upon wrecking his Christian revolution, and he resisted them with a stubbornness that again belies the notion that the Poverello was no more than a gentle dreamer. To start with, he tried to check these forces by means of various rules that he gave his order.

The primitive rule [7] was lost and cannot be reconstructed. According to Francis himself, it consisted merely of some "short and simple words," probably of sentences from the Gospels. In did not, however, have the normative authority of the rule of St. Benedict, for, in the final analysis, Francis was himself the rule. His Christ-like life was the living obligation that constituted both law and example for the brethren. Francis once said to a young man: "I am the breviary"; [8] in the same way, his towering personality was at first the determining rule, which all revered like a sacrament.

The rapid growth of the order—by the middle of its second decade it already had thousands of members and had begun to spread to all parts of western Europe—made it imperative to draw up a second rule, with more specific regulations.

This second rule, issued in 1221,[9] is a marvelous product of Francis's mind, even though the Poverello by temperament was anything but a legislator. His enthusiasm is reflected in every line, as

[6] L. Casutt: *Das Erbe eines grossen Herzens* (1949), p. 114.
[7] Presented by Francis to Innocent III in 1209.
[8] Karrer, ed.: op. cit., p. 106.
[9] Usually referred to as the *regula prima*, or first rule.

witness the opening words, which are the key to all the rest: "This is the life that Brother Francis begged might be conceded to him and confirmed by the Lord Pope Innocent. . . ." And what was that life? "The rule and life of these brothers is this: namely, to live in obedience and chastity, and without property, and to follow the doctrine and footsteps of our Lord Jesus Christ." [1] To imitate Christ —that was his single purpose, which he pursued unwaveringly. The rule speaks constantly of "our life" and "this manner of life." It lays down exactly "how the brothers should go throughout the world." It exhorts the brothers: "Whoever may come to them, either a friend or a foe, a thief or a robber, let them receive him kindly." [2] It provides no test for admission to the order; Francis accepted everyone, like the king in the parable of the great supper.

Francis expressly sent his brethren to the despised and the rejected of the world: "They ought to rejoice when they converse with mean and despised persons, with the poor and the weak, with the infirm and lepers, and with those who beg in the streets." [3] The friars, moreover, should "take care not to appear exteriorly sad and gloomy like hypocrites, but let them show themselves to be joyful and contented in the Lord, merry and becomingly courteous." [4]

Francis's rule contains no threats or severe punishment for infractions, an apparently small yet very significant difference from the rules of earlier founders of religious orders. The Poverello put his trust in the power of Christ, and confined himself to this burning exhortation: "And I entreat all, kissing their feet, to love greatly, keep and treasure up these things. And . . . I, Brother Francis, strictly command and enjoin that no one subtract from those things that are written in this life, or add anything written to it over and above, and that the brothers have no other rule." [5]

It is forever to be regretted that the order did not abide by the second rule, with its fairly general provisions. Before two years were out, the brothers urged Francis to draw up yet another rule containing more definite regulations. The desire for legalistic definition prevailed over the original Franciscan spirituality. Nevertheless,

[1] Robinson, ed.: op. cit., pp. 31, 32.
[2] Ibid., p. 40.
[3] Ibid., pp. 42, 43.
[4] Ibid., p. 41.
[5] Ibid., pp. 63, 64.

even though the third, considerably shorter rule of 1223 [6] does not possess the immediacy of the earlier one, it still bears the unmistakable imprint of Francis's hand. For everything that Francis did was a faithful mirror of his heart, and he could not but bear witness to the Christian revolution which he embodied. It was in the true Franciscan spirit that this rule exhorted the friars "not to despise or judge men whom they see clothed in fine and showy garments, using dainty meats and drinks, but rather let each one judge and despise himself." [7] Pardoning the weakness of others has always been an infallible touchstone of the evangelical spirit, which prompts a man to be stern with himself and lenient with others.

At the same time, this rule also bears the marks of influences far removed from the Franciscan ardor. For instance, although the prohibition to accept money is maintained, no reference is made— Cardinal Ugolino was adamant on this point, to Francis's deep sorrow—to Christ's command to take nothing on the way, "neither staves, nor scrip, neither bread, neither money" (Luke ix, 3). The Poverello regarded this omission as a death blow to that evangelical poverty for which he was prepared to give his life. This example touches a key issue and points to the forces of change which rendered the original purposes of the order impossible of achievement.

As Francis could not prevail against the new majority, he relinquished the direction of the order. His resignation was further motivated by poor health and the desire to sound still greater depths of humility. But the fact that he had abandoned the primary responsibility for the government of the order could still neither his conscience nor his pain. At the following chapter he exhorted his brethren with all the strength remaining to him, with vehemence, but without bitterness, to realize how far removed their views were from the ideal he had set before them.

His own doctrine remained unshaken: the preaching best calculated to move a secularized Christian community was example. As he said to one of the friars: "My son, I love my brothers as best as I can, though if they were to follow in my footsteps I would love them even more and would not alienate myself from them. Now

---

[6] Regarded as the definitive Franciscan rule.
[7] Robinson, ed.: op. cit., p. 66.

there are those among the prelates who draw them toward other things, showing them the examples of ancient rules and despising my counsels. . . ." [8]

Not long after, Francis fell ill. As he was lying in his bed in great pain, he raised himself up and cried: "Who are they who have wrested my order and my brethren out of my hands? If I come to the next chapter, I will show them wherein my will consists!" [9] His anguish was such that it has been compared with the pangs of martyrdom.[1] A sword had truly pierced his heart.

Francis did not confine himself to heart-rending lamentations. The testament that he drew up in the last year of his life is an admirable and courageous statement of his position vis-à-vis an order that was departing ever further from its origins. The flame of Franciscan fervor pierces through the document in purity and strength, lending it a nobility that prompted some brothers to liken it to a text from Scripture. The basic theme is again set out with unmistakable clarity: "To all my brethren, clerics and laymen, I strictly command by holy obedience that they shall make no gloss to the rule or to these words, saying, 'Thus we want them to be understood.' But as the Lord has given me the grace to write the rule and these words purely and simply, you are to understand them just as purely and simply, without any gloss, and observe them by saintly deeds unto the end." [2] Francis realized the dangers of glosses, which often imperceptibly modify the essential character of a text. In his view, the brothers had simply to follow the way of holy poverty— "without any gloss."

But even this powerful protest was powerless to stay the inexorable development of the order in a direction that Francis so deeply deplored. And after Francis's death Pope Gregory IX declared his testament legally invalid because it had been drawn up at a time when Francis no longer held the office of Minister-General.

Was this anguishing consummation of Francis's life's work simply the outcome of the inevitable conflict between ideal and reality? Had Francis in fact been seeking to resolve a problem to which

<hr>

[8] Karrer, ed.: op. cit., p. 135.
[9] Ibid.

[1] Casutt: op. cit., p. 53.
[2] Karrer, ed.: op. cit., p. 276.

there is no solution and found himself crushed between the upper and the nether millstones? If we put too much stress on Francis's "ideals," then the answer must be in the affirmative. But the marvelous secret of the little poor man was that he was grounded in the real, not in the ideal. In Francis the divine was fulfilled, not merely longed for. In contrast to the hearts of most Christians, his was undivided. Once Christ had entered his life, the Poverello no longer felt the slightest hesitation or even uncertainty. The reality of the Gospel was reborn in him and lifted his life into a completely new dimension. He lived in the center of reality; he did not nourish his soul on abstractions. And that reality embraced the paradisal sermon to the birds and the Canticle of Brother Sun as well as the estrangement of his brethren and tears of infinite pain.

Now Francis in his turn was entering the garden of Gethsemane. Christ, too, had been sorrowful unto death. That night in Gethsemane, when the Lord was so changed, having lost, it seemed, His customary majesty, cannot be conjured out of the story of His life. And if Francis was to be like his Lord, then he too had to accept his passion. Jesus' piercing sorrow must needs be reproduced in the Poverello's life, else his discipleship would not have been perfect.

Francis, in his passion, brought the Christian revolution to fulfillment. The way of sorrows that leads to Gethsemane and thence to Calvary excludes defiance or revolt, nor might Francis rebel against the course of events, however much he might suffer from them. Jesus' agony in the garden required that Francis show like obedience, and in his last days he was mysteriously conformed to his Lord. The divine seal of this passion was the stigmata that Francis received in an ecstasy on Mount Alverna. The marks of Christ's wounds which the seraph implanted in Francis's hands and feet and side may be regarded, above all, as God's acceptance of the Poverello's passion.

Francis's weakened physical condition led to his early death. He asked his doctor to tell him the truth, for he did not fear death; in fact, he welcomed it with complete confidence. The dying Francis was again filled with spiritual joy, and he begged his brethren to sing to him of death. Again and again they intoned for him his own Canticle of the Sun, their singing heralding the Easter alleluia that

was to follow his Good Friday. Francis, meanwhile, caused himself
to be laid naked upon the naked earth, there, in perfect poverty, to
await the kiss of God.

The stupendous fact of Francis utterly disconcerted his contemporaries. They could not, of course, understand him fully, but their
rapturous comments are some indication of their feelings. In the
preface of the *Legend of the Three Companions*, for instance, we
find this effusion: "Shining like the dawn and the morning star,
even like the sun flooding the earth with ardent streams of light to
render it fruitful, thus Francis appeared at his emergence, like a
new luminary. At the rising of this sun the earth lay numbed by
the frosts of winter, in darkness and devoid of life. His words and
his deeds were like a clear light, resplendent with truth, flaming with
love and, by virtue, the mother of all merit, awakening a new and
finer life. The three communities he founded [3] blossomed like a
garden containing different trees laden with fruit. How marvelous
was their fruitfulness! It was like the coming of spring to the
world." [4]

Yet it is not really so farfetched to compare the coming of
Francis to the coming of spring. For in his own person he was a
unique embodiment of the creative message of the Gospel, and he
was looked upon as the harbinger of a new era of joy in the world.
There were many, indeed, who could have agreed with the authors of the *Fioretti* that "St. Francis, the true servant of Christ, was
in certain things well-nigh another Christ given to the world for
the salvation of souls." [5]

Francis left to his order a heritage of holiness which his heirs were
unable fully to assimilate. That heritage was further burdened by
his own dark predictions concerning the order's future. Shortly
before his death he had addressed these words to his companions:

[3] The Friars Minor, the Poor Clares, and the Third Order.
[4] Karrer, ed.: op. cit., p. 3.
[5] *The Little Flowers of St. Francis*, p. 18.

"Fare ye well, all ye my sons, in the fear of God, and remain in Him always, for a great trial is coming upon you and tribulation draweth nigh. Happy are they who shall persevere in the things they have begun, for the scandals that are to be shall separate some from them." [6] Not only would there be grief and separation, but "the time will come when, through evil examples, the order beloved of God will be so ill spoken of that it will be ashamed to show itself in public." [7] At the same time, as Francis had told his friends, God had given him the certainty that the order would never come to an end, having comforted him in these words: "Why, thou manikin, art thou distressed? Have I so set thee as shepherd over my order that thou knowest not that I am its chief protector? . . . Be not therefore distressed, but work out thy salvation, for even though the order were reduced to the number of three, it shall ever, through my gift, remain unshaken." [8]

Francis's Christian revolution, we can say, neither triumphed altogether nor failed altogether. He had brought a movement into being which, in part, was more powerful than he, and whose development he was unable to control. But the order could not always have remained at its initial stage; instead of thriving, it would have slowly atrophied. It was its duty to adapt itself to the changing conditions of the times.

The different tendencies within the order which were already apparent in Francis's lifetime gradually crystallized after his death. From among those brethren who sought to remain completely faithful to the spirit of the founder there emerged the group known as the "Spirituals." It was their aim to observe the Franciscan law to the letter, and their attitude is best reflected in the following passage from the introduction to the *Mirror of Perfection*: "And when Brother Elias was near the place where blessed Francis was, Brother Elias called him. To whom answering . . . the blessed Father said, 'What would these brethren?' And Brother Elias said, 'These are ministers who, hearing that thou art making a new rule, and fearing lest thou shouldst make it too harsh, do say and protest that they will not be bound to it; make it for thyself and not for

---

[6] Howell, ed.: op. cit., p. 107.   [8] Ibid., p. 291.
[7] Ibid., pp. 289, 290.

them.' Then blessed Francis turned his face to heaven and spoke thus to Christ, 'Lord, said I not well to Thee that they would not believe me?' Then all heard the voice of Christ answering in the air, 'So do it, there is nought of thine in the rule, but whatever is there is Mine, and I will that the rule should thus be observed to the letter, without a gloss, without a gloss!' And He added, 'What human weakness can do, I know, and how much I wish to help them; let those, therefore, who will not obey it go out from the order!'" [9]

One is tempted, at first, to sympathize wholeheartedly with the position of the Spirituals, who sought so earnestly to preserve the purity of the Franciscan heritage. A spark of the Poverello's fire certainly glowed in them, and they constituted a spiritual left wing of the Franciscan "revolution," causing the constituted authorities of the Church considerable trouble. In Gemelli's view, it is to these bold enthusiasts that we owe the "great Franciscan epic." [1] Yet over them, too, there hangs a shadow. For their watchword—"To the letter"—was in contradiction to the evangelical teaching that the letter killeth, whereas the spirit giveth life. Their fidelity to the letter led them to something approaching bigotry. At the same time, they were themselves not altogether faithful to the teachings of St. Francis, for they emphasized mainly his teachings on poverty, which constituted but a part, albeit an important one, of his evangelical revival.

In 1241 an abbot of the Floris movement fled to Pisa before the advancing troops of Frederick II and deposited all the writings of Joachim of Floris in the monastery of the Friars Minor. The event had the effect of a cap set to dynamite. The Joachimite theories were closely allied to those of the Spirituals; moreover, the Franciscans took Joachim's prophecies concerning the age of the Spirit as having achieved a beginning of fulfillment in Francis. Francis, they believed, was truly "the angel who opens the sixth seal," and they rejoiced in the imminent advent of the reign of the Holy Ghost.

This was the feverish perspective in which the Spirituals looked

---

[9] *The Mirror of Perfection*, p. 240.
[1] Gemelli: *Das Franziskanertum* (1936), p. 61.

upon the world they lived in, and their enthusiasm was not diminished when the premature death of Fiederick II dealt a fatal blow to the Joachimite prophecies. Their leaders, men like Peter John Olivi and Ubertino of Casale, remained ardent heralds of the "eternal gospel," which they distinguished from the Gospel set forth in the New Testament.

The alliance between Franciscanism and Joachimism was disastrous. At its height, it produced an unhealthy exaltation bordering on fanaticism, and it was well on the way to turning the Franciscans into a sect. In addition, the extravagant speculations of the Spirituals were fed by doctrines that were clearly heretical, and this circumstance gave the Curia the legitimate excuse it needed for taking action against them.

The principal difference between the Spirituals and the Poverello whom they claimed to follow so faithfully lay in their lack of love. In their rigorous insistence on poverty, they forgot Francis's own words: "Blessed is the man who bears with his neighbor according to the frailty of his nature, as much as he would wish to be borne with by him if he should be in a like case." [2] And, significantly enough, they did not even achieve their primitive aim of strict poverty themselves; they were too much preoccupied with their apocalyptic yearnings.

Posterity nevertheless owes the Spirituals a debt of gratitude, for it was they who gave the world its most beautiful literary monuments to Franciscan spirituality. The "symbolical Franciscan legend" is largely their work, in particular the *Fioretti*, which are quite untainted with Joachimite ideas and contain only very veiled allusions to their own leanings.

The fact that the *Fioretti* date only from the fourteenth century does not detract from their value as legends, and as such they are perhaps even better able to convey the essence of Franciscanism than the more prosaic account of the first biographer, Celano. In any case, Celano could not have known everything. The *Fioretti* are certainly not to be regarded as mere fables. Only a document that bears the stamp of Franciscan authenticity could ascribe to the Poverello this answer to the question of what constitutes perfect

[2] Robinson, ed.: op. cit., p. 15.

joy: "When we are come to St. Mary of the Angels, wet through with rain, frozen with cold, and foul with mire and tormented with hunger; and when we knock at the door, the doorkeeper cometh in a rage and saith, 'Who are ye?' and we say, 'We are two of your friars,' and he answers, 'Ye tell not true; ye are rather two knaves that go deceiving the world and stealing the alms of the poor; begone!' and he openeth not to us, and maketh us to stay outside hungry and cold all night in the rain and snow; then, if we endure patiently such cruelty, such abuse, and such insolent dismissal without complaint or murmuring, and believe humbly and charitably that that doorkeeper truly knows us, and that God maketh him to rail against us; O Friar Leo, write—there is perfect joy." [3]

Another current in the order was represented by those who put the main emphasis on the idea of "community," and who later became known as "Conventuals." They too were earnest Franciscans, and they were profoundly impressed by the example of Francis's stupendous humility. Indeed, it was their view that the founder had reached such heights of sanctity that his way of life could not be generally imitated. This led them to adopt measures of relaxation which were clearly detrimental to the order. With them, the Christian revolution was deliberately brought to an end; they sought to soft-pedal Francis's religious radicalism so as to attract more people to the order. As their aims were supported by the Curia, they were more easily able to achieve them.

It would be unfair to reproach the Conventuals with complete disregard for Francis's rule and testament. Certainly some among them were scandalously lax, but many of them were worthy religious who emulated their seraphic model to the best of their ability.

St. Bonaventure was close to the Conventuals, but he cannot be identified with them. The manner of his life placed him above criticism, he had remarkable intellectual gifts, and he was filled with such compassionate love of God that it was said of him that Adam did not seem to have sinned in Bonaventure. With his conciliatory approach, he sought to remain outside all factions, and he was clearly the man best suited to restore much-needed peace to the divided order. He was appointed general of the order, and in that

[3] *The Little Flowers of St. Francis*, pp. 20, 21.

capacity he neither added to nor took away from the rule of St. Francis.

It might, of course, be objected that by his teaching activities in Paris he was himself going counter to the founder's intentions, but the spirit in which he pursued those activities was the authentic Franciscan spirit of peace. It has been said, indeed, that Bonaventure put his intelligence at the service of adoration. Learning, for him, was but a means to a much deeper end. What he sought was not so much knowledge as wisdom illuminated by love.

Himself a "man of desires," he wrote these words: "No man is in any way disposed for divine contemplations . . . unless he be, like the prophet Daniel, a 'man of desires.' In two ways are such desires enkindled in us: through the cry of prayer that ascends from anguish of heart, and by the splendor of high thought which turns the eyes of the mind directly and intently upon the rays of divine light. Wherefore, to the groanings of prayer to God through Christ crucified, in whose blood we are cleansed from the defilements of sin, I first of all invite the reader, lest he should perchance think that reading will suffice without unction, speculation without devotion, research without admiration, circumspection without exultation, industry without piety, knowledge without charity, intelligence without humility, study without divine grace, or speculation without divinely inspired wisdom." [4]

Bonaventure's teachings constitute a mental climate rather than a logical system, and are directed, in the last analysis, toward action. This accounts for the Franciscan opposition, prior to the emergence of scholars of the caliber of Bacon and Duns Scotus, to the scholasticism normally taught in medieval universities. "What is the use of knowing much and experiencing nothing?" Bonaventure did not believe in knowledge *per se;* knowledge separated from action must lead necessarily to sterile words. Bonaventure desired to know in order to become good, and he believed that a man should know only so much as he is able to apply in his own life. It is a point of view that deserves serious consideration in relation to the mortal crisis of knowledge in our own age of intellectualism.

[4] St. Bonaventure: *Itinerarium mentis in Deum,* tr. and ed. by B. S. James (London: Burns, Oates & Washbourne; 1937), pp. 11, 12.

The bitter discord between Spirituals and Conventuals forms a painful chapter in the early history of the order, and constitutes, as it were, a continuation of St. Francis's passion. It is surprising that the order was able to survive at all. The heirs of the seraphic Francis, who had enjoined his brethren to greet men with the words "The Lord give thee peace," were now split into opposing factions that fought each other with unbridled violence. They were wrangling about Francis's legacy to them, forgetful altogether of his commandment: "And love those who oppose thee."

The intervention of the papacy occasionally succeeded in calming tempers on both sides, but only for a time. In the end the Conventuals, being in the majority, got their way. At the general chapter in 1262 it was even decided to destroy all the old histories of Francis, save one by Bonaventure which was to replace all earlier legends, so as to obliterate any disturbing memory of the original Poverello. Fortunately, this fateful decision was not generally carried out.

Thanks to papal decrees, the Conventuals succeeded in relaxing the strict rule of poverty, and, as many of their communities had established themselves in towns, even the principle of accepting only gifts in kind was waived, being too difficult to apply. Henceforward Franciscans might accept alms in the form of money.

Spirituals who refused to conform to the new rules were sentenced to perpetual imprisonment, and some were even burned at the stake. Finally the whole left wing of the order was excommunicated. This eradication of the Spirituals is a grim drama in the history of the order, and the responsibility weighs heavily on both sides.

In 1430 there was a further split, the Conventuals, or "black" Franciscans, opting for the possession of monasteries, while the reformed Observants,[5] or "brown" Franciscans, chose to retain the rule against property, though they too regarded Francis's testament as not binding upon them and continued to devote themselves to study.

[5] The party of the "Observant" reform grew up in the middle of the fourteenth century in opposition to the laxity of the Conventuals. Like the Spirituals, whom they largely superseded, the Observants favored a stricter adherence to the rule, but, unlike the Spirituals, they did not incline to heterodox views.

The Capuchins may be described as constituting the synthesis between the opposing movements of reform and relaxation. They go back to Matthew of Bascio, who once, when at prayer, heard a voice telling him to follow the rule faithfully, to the very letter. To obey the divine call, he secretly left his monastery early in 1525, sought audience with the Pope in Rome, and begged to be allowed to adopt a new way of life.[6] His wish was granted. That may be considered the founding day of the Capuchin order. Despite the consistent opposition of his former fellow Observants,[7] Matthew succeeded in gaining a rapidly increasing number of brothers to his side. The Capuchins—the name was coined by children who greeted the hooded friars with cries of *"Cappucini!"*—were yet a new kind of Spirituals as far as reforming zeal was concerned. They too desired to follow the rule in all its severity, and regarded Francis's testament as binding; and Rome endorsed their decision.

Thanks to the fervor of its preachers, the Capuchin order grew rapidly, and its influence would probably have been even greater in the sixteenth century had its general, Ochino, a brilliant but unstable man, not fallen away from the Church, thus heavily compromising the young reform movement. Ochino's flight to Geneva jeopardized the very existence of the Capuchins as an order. They survived this mortal crisis only by doubling their efforts to be utterly faithful to the rule, and they eventually regained their popularity. To this day the Capuchins are popular missionaries among the people, adapting their sermons to the needs of their listeners and expressing themselves forcefully, clearly, and practically.

The Poor Clares, or Second Order of St. Francis, constitute the female branch of the Franciscan movement, and may claim to have been the most faithful custodians of the Poverello's legacy. The credit for this goes to their founder, the noble lady Clare, one of Francis's earliest followers and one who, aided by true feminine intuition, seems really to have penetrated his soul and made his ideals her own. The bonds uniting Clare and Francis were of a spiritual tenderness seldom equaled in history.

[6] Cuthbert: *The Capuchins* (London: Sheed & Ward; 1930), Vol. I, chap. i.
[7] By this time the Observants themselves had become much more lax.

The ability of this defenseless woman to resist all the efforts of the Curia to move her from her strict conception of poverty was truly remarkable. When Pope Gregory IX offered to free the sisters from their vow of poverty, Clare answered: "Holy Father, absolve me from my sins, but I shall never wish to be dispensed from following our Lord Jesus Christ." [8] And she succeeded in securing papal approval of her position. From that time on, the Poor Clares have possessed the right to possess nothing.

Francis's spiritual daughter passed to eternity with this magnificent affirmation: "Since I experienced the grace of our Lord Jesus Christ through the merits and teaching of our father Francis, no suffering has been hard for me, no exertion or penance or illness painful." [9]

God alone, Who sees all hidden things, knows how much good the Poor Clares have done through the centuries, in their own hidden way, for churches and schools.

Finally, we should mention the "lay community of penitents," as the Third Order was originally called. This was no mere substitute for a monastic order; on the contrary, it played a tremendous part in bridging the gap between the spiritual and the worldly attitudes toward life, and may be regarded as an integral part of the whole Franciscan movement. [1] The emergence of the Tertiaries was a fulfillment of Francis's own dearest desire to penetrate the world once more with the Gospel. As Benedict XV said on the occasion of the seventh centenary of the founding of the Third Order, "Francis conceived the project that no founder of a regular order had yet imagined, to cause the religious life to be practiced by all." [2]

The members of the Third Order, whether married or single, and following their respective avocations, have done much to imbue Christian life with the spirit of St. Francis. Tertiaries, for instance, were originally forbidden to bear arms, and it is not hard to imagine

[8] Quoted in N. de Robeck: *St. Clare of Assisi* (Milwaukee, Wis.: Bruce Publishing Company; 1951), p. 81.

[9] Ibid., p. 132.

[1] F. van den Borne: *Die Anfänge des franziskanischen dritten Ordens* (1925), p. 102.

[2] From the encyclical *Sacra Propediem* of January 24, 1921.

what a salutary effect their compliance with this rule must have had on the war-torn society of medieval Europe.

The purpose of the Third Order is to show persons living in the world a way to perfection accessible to all Christians. The Tertiaries "should really and essentially break with the world in spirit, just as members of orders do externally and literally." [3] The Third Order is really a new state of life, and as such differs from all previous fraternities. It is neither an attempt to turn laymen into monks nor an attempt to laicize monasticism; were either the case, the Third Order would not have produced its wonderful galaxy of genuinely Franciscan saints—people like the lovable Elizabeth of Thuringia or the unforgettable curé d'Ars. The Third Order may boast, indeed, of many eminent members; we need mention only such diverse men as Dante, Columbus, and Pasteur.

Whether we consider the first, second, or third order, it is certain that the disappearance of any one of them would leave the Christian world much the poorer. And it is equally certain that the members of the three orders are filled with a truer love for Francis than his uncommitted admirers among modern esthetes, their practice of poverty affording constant proof of their kinship with the Poverello. Nevertheless, we cannot fail to see the shift in emphasis which has taken place in the First Order. Preaching and pastoral duties, which originally were only incidental to the total personal practice of the evangelical precepts, now absorb most of the Franciscans' time. And this means that Francis's primary goal of integral Gospel living has been to some extent pushed into the background. Yet only if this ideal is accepted can a religious renaissance come about, and with it that Christian revolution in which modern man can find an answer to the anguishing social problems that have him by the throat. The noblest task of the sons of Francis today is to lead men back to the source of Francis's inspiration and to Francis himself, the little poor man who was bold enough to throw himself headlong into the arms of Christ.

[3] Hildebrand, ed.: op. cit., p. 60.

Saint DOMINIC

and the Order of Preachers

MANY misconceptions are still current about the Middle Ages. Some talk, as in the Age of Enlightenment, of the "dark" Middle Ages, bedeviled by superstition, while others wax romantic, like Novalis, about the glorious days when Europe was still Christian. But it is impossible to generalize in this manner about the Middle Ages, a period characterized not by unity but by vast divergency. The thirteenth century, in particular, saw society on the defensive against a multitude of disruptive trends. It was one of those times which evidence with startling clarity the truth that power is often not powerful at all. The Church, for instance, had a great appearance of power. She was governed, at the beginning of the century, by Innocent III, one of the mightiest popes of all times, a man conscious of his ability to rule and determined to make her strong. Yet behind the façade of strength the Church was in a state of marked debility, and Innocent was well aware of the fact.

The Church's own representatives, in Innocent's view, were chiefly to blame for the deplorable state of affairs. The clergy were manifestly and shamefully ignorant and were therefore little able to command respect; moreover, being themselves uninstructed, they were unable to teach others. Still worse was the un-Christian manner of living of many of the clergy, which inevitably confused the faithful as to the precepts of the Church. When the shepherds flee, the sheep are scattered. The resulting worldliness of the Church was the main reason for the rapid defection of the faithful, which, particularly in southern France, had already begun to assume alarming proportions.

As the influence of the Church waned, so the tide of heresy mounted. The heretics openly defied the papacy. They had cut themselves off from the life of the Church and established their own way of life, more in keeping with their particular religious leanings. Nor was it merely a handful of obscure devotees who had embraced Catharism; the nobility of southern France openly favored it and offered it every encouragement, and it swiftly gained ground among the rest of the population. Indeed, in some areas the majority of the inhabitants had fallen away from the Church.

Side by side with the Albigensians, as the Catharists were called in southern France, were the Waldensians, not so far removed in doctrine from the Church as the gnostic Catharists, yet still in increasing opposition to her. The Waldensians preached a simple form of Bible Christianity, and their emphasis on virtuous living made a powerful impression in that age of clerical decadence. Their own practice was in accord with their teaching; their itinerant preachers lived truly apostolic lives. The heretics were sincere in their strivings, and their zeal stood out in marked and favorable contrast to the laxity and luxury of so many of the clergy.

This was the situation when in the year 1206 the Bishop of Osma, Diego, accompanied by the subprior of his cathedral chapter, Dominic Guzman, arrived in Rome. Diego wished to resign his see and to request the Pope's permission to go to Russia, together with Dominic, to evangelize the heathen Cumans.

Little is known about Diego, but that little is enough to indicate that he was a remarkable, deeply religious person. Concerning Dominic's early years in Spain we also have scant reliable information. One thing, however, is certain: he was filled with zeal. As a student, he would spend most of his nights poring over his books. Yet it is also told of him that when famine broke out in the region, he promptly sold his precious books, which were covered with notes he had made in his own handwriting, and gave the proceeds to the poor, being unwilling, as he said, "to prize dead skins when living skins were starving and in want." [1] Only genuine religious fervor could occasion such a deed in one so young. And it was with the same devotion that he became a canon and then a priest of the cathedral chapter of Osma, where he lived in close contact with Diego. That was how Dominic came to accompany his bishop to the Eternal City.

Their journey took them by a roundabout way through Languedoc, in southern France, where they made what was for them a surprising discovery. In their own native Spain the Church presented a united front against a common and constant foe, Islam. Because of the menace of the Saracens, Christianity had always to be striven for anew, could never be taken for granted. In southern France the position was exactly reversed. There the Church was languishing in dull indifference; indeed, she seemed to be on the point of expiring altogether.

The religious decadence of this neighboring country, which stood out in such sharp contrast to the militant Christian atmosphere of Spain, affected both Diego and Dominic very keenly, and their dismay was augmented by the very evident success of the heretical teachings. They felt personally involved as Christians. This was undoubtedly the decisive moment of Dominic's life; the realization of the Church's need shook him to the depths of his soul and determined his entire life's work.

In Rome the Pope refused Bishop Diego's request, and the two returned, instead, to southern France. It seems clear that both Diego and Dominic were by now convinced that their missionary field was here rather than among the far-off heathen.

Dominic was a man of courage, and did not shrink from bold solutions. He realized that new methods were needed to meet the situation, the old ones having proved ineffective. Men do not use old cloth to patch a new garment. The method he chose was far in advance of his age; it must have occasioned no little alarm in many a timorous breast.

It so happened that Dominic's first night in southern France had been spent in the house of a heretic. The two had entered into a dis-

---

[1] Quoted in B. Jarrett: *The Life of Saint Dominic* (Westminster, Md.: Newman Press; 1955), p. 11.

cussion on religious topics which had continued the whole night through. Finally, by daybreak, Dominic's host had been won back for the Church. Dominic regarded this experience as an indication from heaven as to the means he was to use to counter heresy. That means was debate—honest, unaffected talk between one man and another, without aversion or condescension. The realization of the absolute necessity of religious discussion had, we might say, been forced upon him.

Discussion with heretics was not, of course, a novelty in Church history. In the first centuries of the Christian era, Christians had frequently engaged in controversy with their opponents. St. Paul himself, as we see in the Acts of the Apostles, disputed vehemently with the Jews. The apologists conducted their controversy in writing, and as late as the fifth century St. Augustine, for instance, would meet the Donatists face to face to argue specific points of difference. Subsequently, however, religious discussion fell into desuetude, to be replaced by methods of compulsion. We have only to recall, in this connection, Charlemagne's policy toward the heathen Saxons.

Dominic was the first, many centuries later, to revert to Christian controversy in full consciousness of the superiority of his cause. It was a portentous moment in the history of the Church: at long last Christians and non-Christians were talking together and seeking to justify their beliefs instead of simply forcing them upon their opponents.

The two Spaniards took real trouble to go into the heretics' arguments before refuting them. Without scorn or hatred, they sought to win back the Albigensians and the Waldensians by exhaustive exposition. This manner of talking was a radical departure from the appeal to force—"compel them to come in"—which had so disastrously taken the place of the evangelical approach.

Naturally, Dominic's new methods were also influenced by the situation in southern France, where Catholics and heretics were almost equally strong. Yet Dominic was not afraid to appoint a heretic to arbitrate a debate and to adjudicate the victory. Nor did he resort to such strategy only on heretical terrain merely because he had no other choice; he employed it out of a sovereign certainty that his faith must triumph.

9

The value of such discussion is permanent even if, in the event, it does not always lead to the desired result. As was to be expected, both sides often claimed the victory, whereas in fact the argument had merely been inconclusive. That, however, does not detract from the value of discussion as a method. Controversy, like everything human, has its shortcomings. Nevertheless, just as democracy, for all its defects, is still the most satisfactory form of government the human mind has yet devised, so honest debate between confessions also remains the method that most closely accords with the spirit of the Gospels.

These discussions gave Dominic a far deeper insight into the minds and lives of the heretics than was possessed by any other churchman of his day. As to the error of heresy, he was in no doubt at all, and he certainly never wavered in his faith or contemplated going over to the heretics. At the same time, he could not but inwardly admit that the Waldensians—the Albigensians were another matter—conducted themselves, in many respects, with exemplary virtue. They were not the pestilential heretics that they had been made out to be. Their main objection, after all, was to priests who cherished riches and led unapostolic lives. And had not Pope Gregory VII, in his campaign against simony, just over a hundred years earlier, denounced the bloated benefice-hunters as unworthy of the priesthood?

At closer quarters the Waldensians revealed themselves as Christians who took the Gospels seriously, who originally had not been heretics at all, and who had been brought into conflict with the Church only in consequence of an imprudent prohibition to preach. They made great sacrifices for Christianity as they understood it. Peter Waldo, the founder, had been a wealthy man who had distributed his entire possessions among the poor. A movement of this sort could not be deserving of wholesale condemnation.

Dominic made no secret of his admiration for certain features of the Waldensians' lives, nor did he hesitate to adopt them himself. As Scheeben writes, "Dominic, in his reform, is the successor of Peter Waldo. Throughout his plans for his order, we can trace the influence of Waldo. . . . It must be repeated again and again that St. Dominic's reforming movement arose out of the Waldensian movement; it has no parallel with the reforms of Cluny or Cîteaux." Scheeben is further of the opinion that "Dominic came to the conclusion, from his contact with the Waldensians, that they could not simply be stamped out by force. Their teaching contained too much that was Christian simply to disappear overnight. For Dominic it was clear that the heresy could be overcome only if the Waldensians' just claims, purged of all heretical excrescences, were recognized and given effect within the Catholic Church." [2]

This view—which, in our opinion, is very well founded—might appear to detract somewhat from Dominic's originality. In fact, it is simply one more indication that heresy is often a creative element in the history of the Church, producing and developing new ideas that are then taken over by the Church in a purified form. And to admit Dominic's debt to the Waldensians is not in any way to diminish his stature: he gains as a model of Christian virtue what he seems to lose as an innovator. In his humility, he did not esteem himself too wise to learn from his opponents. Not many are capable of a similar open-mindedness; they are blinded by their prejudice, and they cannot summon up the humility that alone could dispel their blindness.

It is to Dominic's credit that, instead of hurling insults at the Waldensians, he tried to understand them. He listened calmly as they inveighed against the well-fed clergy, and sought to determine what was justified in their arguments and what consequences should follow from them. Without this fruitful reflection, Dominic would never have come to undertake his life's work. His greatness lies precisely in his readiness to investigate the heretical position and to use whatever was good in it for the Church. That, of course, has always been the only satisfactory way of combating adverse doctrines.

An incident narrated in an early account of Dominic's life admirably illustrates his new approach. A southern French bishop wished to accompany the two Spaniards to a disputation with the heretics arrayed in great pomp. But Dominic said to him: "Not so, my lord and father, must we act with the children of pride. The foes of truth must be convinced by examples of humility, patience, religion, and every virtue, and not by the pomp of grandeur and outward,

[2] Scheeben: *Der heilige Dominikus* (1927), pp. 142-3, 135.

worldly show. Let us arm ourselves with prayer, and with external marks of humility advance barefooted to meet these Goliaths." [3]

These words give us food for thought. Dominic realized how distrustful people always tend to be of priests who live in ease and opulence, and he regarded it as a matter of conscience to approach the heretics in the proper way. It was not prudent, he felt, to counter heresy without due preparation; nor was every cleric equipped for the task. It is no easy matter to confront apostates with true Christian charity. Dominic realized that a pompous manner could vitiate the best arguments. Words needed to be backed by example. And in a land where the luxurious living of the clergy had caused people to forsake the Church, that example had to be one of humility and self-denial. Whatever else one might say, no one could deny that the Waldensians practiced what they preached. Such consistency of life and works has always had great power of attraction. Among the clergy, on the other hand, there was scant evidence of genuine Christian living, and it was for that reason that they had not been able to make much headway against the heretics.

Dominic realized the need for a change. Churchmen, in his view, must live simply and set a good example. As soon as they did that, they would again enjoy the respect of the people, and the apostasy would be brought to a halt. This approach would undoubtedly have inaugurated a new chapter in Church history had it been properly followed up.

Unfortunately, it never got beyond the initial stages. Bishop Diego died after a short illness, and his death made Dominic's task much harder. Diego had been a Christian of exceptional piety, and had contributed considerably to the development of the new approach. Moreover, the bishop had enjoyed a different standing with the southern French clergy from that of the humble subprior.

But Dominic's mission was far more seriously affected by the outbreak, at this time, of the terrible Albigensian war. It was a conflict of unparalleled savagery, which inflicted appalling wounds upon the entire territory. Both religious and secular interests were involved, and the action soon developed into a regular war of conquest, gov-

[3] Quoted in H. D. Lacordaire: *Life of Saint Dominic* (London: Burns & Oates; 1883), pp. 82-3.

erned solely by political considerations. The debate that had barely
started between orthodoxy and heresy, and which had held so much
promise, was abruptly brought to a stop; there was no place for
calm discussion amid the sound and fury of war.

Where was Dominic? He seemed to have disappeared from the
face of the earth. Throughout the entire duration of the Albigensian
war his name is not so much as mentioned in any extant document.
"It will doubtless have been remarked that no mention is made of his
taking part in the war. He is absent from councils, conferences, rec-
onciliations, sieges, and triumphs; and the letters from Rome make
no allusion to him." [4] Was Dominic too unimportant? Or had he
simply been forgotten? No. Dominic withdrew deliberately from
the scene of bloodshed because, as a priest, he wanted to have no
part in it. He was not the kind of cleric who blesses arms, bringing
scandal upon the Gospel. Dominic realized that the true Christian
cannot further his cause by violence, and the only arms he ever used
against heresy were those of debate and instruction, of prayer and
patience. Dominic's deliberate dissociation from the Albigensian war
has been described by Catholic historians as "a dumb protest against
the policy of the Curia"; he could not reconcile himself to Rome's
"excessive mingling of secular and spiritual interests." [5]

In that hour of darkness Dominic withdrew to Prouille. His en-
forced inactivity weighed heavily upon him, but he did not waste his
time. While the surrounding countryside was being laid waste, he
founded there a convent for women, realizing the value of their example for the revival of Christianity in a war-torn land. Even more
important was the opportunity for reflection that Dominic's time in
Prouille afforded him. Ever since he had set foot on French soil,
events had crowded in upon him, and they needed to be inwardly
digested. During those years in the newly established convent
Dominic meditated continually on the plight of Christianity in his
time.

Out of this assiduous reflection was born a project of startling
novelty: the foundation of an order of preachers. No documents exist
to indicate the detailed steps of Dominic's thinking. The project was
born and matured in the silence that was so dear to him.

[4] Ibid., p. 80.   [5] Scheeben: op. cit., p. 225.

There was nothing romantic about it; Dominic was an intensely practical person. In his quiet retreat at Prouille he had discovered a new answer to the old question: Am I my brother's keeper? That answer was the creation of a new order. It must be completely new if it was to relieve the great distress of Christendom, and it must use completely new methods. In addition, it must be an order of priests. Because the negligence of the clergy was responsible for the decadence of the Church, it was from the clergy that the remedy should come. The various monastic orders that had flourished had all started as lay foundations, and had only gradually become clerical communities. But Dominic needed priests to carry out his plans; laymen would not serve the purpose. Nor were the members of his order to withdraw from the world, like the monks, to lead contemplative lives.

Thus St. Dominic broke with the established forms of monasticism just as radically as St. Francis; he did not so much as use the term "cloister." The sole and compelling purpose of his order was to retrieve for the Church the souls that had fallen away.

Preaching was to be the specific task of the new order, whence its name, Fratres Prædicatores. For Dominic, to proclaim the word of God was to wield the piercing sword of the Spirit. Dominic himself wielded that sword mightily, and he was convinced that he could lay no more urgent charge upon his brethren than to preach, preach wherever they could. Here Dominic was returning to the very earliest Christian practice. Jesus and the Apostles had used preaching as a method of instruction, and the practice had never altogether died out. Nevertheless, in the early Middle Ages it had been largely relegated to the background. In the thirteenth century, preaching was reserved to the bishops, who in general were not equal to the responsibility. Occasionally an itinerant preacher would announce the Word, but monks did not preach. For Dominic, preaching was a witnessing to the Spirit, and it was the Dominicans, not the men of the Reformation, who first restored to the sermon its full dignity and value.

The brethren were to devote their entire effort to the proclamation of the word of God. Dominic believed in the effective power of words to sway men's actions; in his day, unlike our own, human speech had not yet suffered inflation.

The first duty of the preacher, in Dominic's view, was to expound Christian truth, not to refute heresy. Consequently, the main theme of the Dominican preachers was Holy Scripture, which they explained in methodical fashion, avoiding the homiletic form as being too dull. They preached wherever they could—in cemeteries, in the street, in the open fields—nor did they seek, at first, to be admitted to the parish pulpits. The single, overriding goal was to win souls by eloquent persuasion.

This required educated men, and Dominic therefore declared study a duty. In this respect his brotherhood differed sharply from the Waldensians, who set no store by learning and were therefore often at a loss for arguments. The Order of Preachers derived its initial impetus from the Waldensians, but it was no mere orthodox copy of a heretical movement; it was a new creation with an entirely new life process all its own. Dominic considered study to be indispensable to preaching, and no member of the order was to assume to preach without having acquired the requisite knowledge. In order to give the brethren time for study, Dominic freed them from the obligation of manual labor, which devolved exclusively upon the lay brothers.

Dominic was thus the first founder of an order to make study the principal occupation of its members, and to give it an importance equal to that of prayer. Study, of course, was always to be governed by the requirements of preaching, and was not to extend to the secular field. Dominic never advocated learning for its own sake; what he wanted was not scholars, but men of deep conviction eager to learn that they might be more effective heralds of the Gospel. This attitude toward study was one of the points in which the Friars Preachers differed most markedly from the Friars Minor who came into being, as an order, at the same time.

But a preaching based on thorough knowledge would still not have availed to bring about what Dominic had in view. Dominic demanded of his brethren a manner of life in conformity with their preaching. Experience had showed him that the people's main grievance against the clergy was their self-indulgence, and he was fully persuaded of the justice of the complaint. He therefore made poverty mandatory for his order. The brethren were to have no fixed source of income, and were to beg the food they needed in order to live. The Order of Preachers was to be an order of mendicants.

This insistence on poverty was not, as with Francis, the fruit of mystical experience. Purely practical considerations led Dominic to regard poverty as a principal arm against the heretics, the means to take the wind out of their sails. Poverty was as little an end in itself as study; "It was to be the handmaid of preaching; its purpose was to make it easier for the brethren to devote themselves to preaching without hindrance of worldly preoccupations." [6]

The personal poverty of the preacher was to give added efficacy to his teaching and to remove any occasion for the scandal that so readily arises when preaching and practice fail to coincide. Hence also the prohibition, in the original rule, of begging during sermons.

Although, in Dominic's estimation, poverty was of secondary importance, the emphasis he laid upon it was nonetheless novel for his time. A wave of enthusiasm for poverty was sweeping through Christendom, but it had claimed few adherents among the clergy. A cleric without a benefice, or a monastery without communal property was an unthinkable innovation. To beg for one's bread seemed incompatible with the dignity of the priesthood; not even the monks of the old orders stooped so low. In this respect, too, Dominic was blazing a new trail.

Nor was poverty, for St. Dominic, mere window-dressing; the Apostles, proclaiming the Gospel, had been poor, and the brethren were to be poor likewise. Dominic's aim was to make the Gospels a reality in people's lives, not to proclaim an interesting theory. He wanted a poor Church, and his views on this point were astonishingly bold. One of the witnesses at the process of canonization testified that Dominic insisted on simplicity in buildings and churches, in church utensils and ornaments. All his life, according to the same witness, he sought to ensure that the brethren wore neither purple nor silk in their churches, and he wished them to observe the same rule in regard to the altar cloth. Silver and gold vessels were forbidden, with the single exception of the chalice. [7]

[6] Cambermond: *Der Armutsgedanke des heiligen Dominikus und seines Ordens* (1926), p. 16.

[7] Hofmann, ed.: *Sankt Dominikus, Zeugnisse seines Innenlebens* (1935), p. 44.

Dominic would permit none of the brethren to take money with them on their journeys; they were to live on alms. Once, when a rich citizen had presented the order with some property and certified the transfer by deed, Dominic tore up the document and refused the gift. Preaching, study, and poverty were to be the pillars of his order.

It is hard, today, to realize the extent of the novelty of an order of this kind in the thirteenth century. It signified a veritable revolution in monastic history. Some idea of the impression it made on men's minds may be gathered from the reaction of Innocent III. The Pope was indubitably a man of vision, and not one to be swayed by any petty considerations, yet he refused point-blank to confirm Dominic's project as it stood. He felt, apparently, that Dominic was going too far and aiming too high, and he could not countenance such a radical departure from established monastic practice.

For Dominic, the Pope's disapproval was a shattering blow. It placed his whole work in jeopardy. But, unlike Peter Waldo, he was never tempted to set the papal authority aside and proceed on his own, in opposition to the Church. His work was a holy work, and he clung to it tenaciously, but humbly. The salvation of souls, he believed, belonged together with the Church, not apart from her. Nor had Innocent deprived him of all hope; he had requested a modification of the plan. And Dominic, to meet the Pope's wish, chose a monastic rule that was ready to hand: the Augustinian rule that was already familiar to him as a canon of the chapter of Osma. He took it over unchanged, but completed it by what are known as his Constitutions.

The main drawback to the Augustinian rule, from Dominic's point of view, was its insistence on prayer in choir. Not that Dominic, for his part, was opposed to such prayer, but he feared that it might prove an obstacle to the main task of his order, and he therefore prescribed that superiors might dispense from choir on grounds of preaching or study—an unheard-of innovation in the thirteenth century.

The order consisted of priests and lay brothers, but they were not so sharply divided as in the old orders. They prayed together in chapel and ate together at table. Dominic, in his magnanimity, de-

9*

sired to leave the entire management of the order to the lay brothers, so that the preachers might not have to busy themselves with
material concerns at all. But the idea came to nothing, owing to
the opposition of the priests, who feared that they would find themselves in tutelage to the lay brothers. In refectory the lay brothers
were to be served first, and the superior last. Each house of the order was directed by a prior, assisted by a conventual council. Candidates for admission had to undergo a period of novitiate. These
regulations made of the Order of Preachers a link between the old
and the new, and the Dominican rule received papal sanction from
Honorius III.

Dominic regarded Rome's confirmation as merely a starting-point,
and he labored tirelessly for the expansion of his work, allowing
himself no respite, never satisfied with the results achieved. His
solicitude extended to the spiritual needs of other countries, and he
was eager to meet them, too, despite the opposition of local nobility
and episcopate alike. Nothing could shake his conviction that the
work must spread. When friendly prelates and even his own companions opposed his plans for expansion, he answered them with
the words: "My lords and fathers, do not oppose me, for I know
very well what I am about." [8] If Dominic, so slow to speak, could
speak so sharply, it was surely because he sensed a challenge to the
very foundations of his whole work. It was enough that he should
have to overcome the resistance of an obtuse and worldly clergy—
an undertaking in which he could succeed only thanks to the papal
decree—and he would tolerate no obstruction from within the order.

Dominic went forward with his plans unperturbed, his enthusiasm undimmed. He gathered many new disciples, particularly in
the university cities, and he spent the last six years of his life—he
was in his forty-fifth year when the order was confirmed—traveling
from place to place to make sure that all was well and the order
securely established. Toward the end he stayed mostly in Bologna,
and it was there that the illness overtook him from which he was
never to recover.

During his years of activity Dominic the man is obscured, for

---

[8] Quoted in A. T. Drane: *History of St. Dominic* (London: Longmans,
Green & Co.; 1891), p. 177.

the most part, by Dominic the founder of the Order of Preachers. Now, on his sickbed, we have a singularly moving picture of the man. According to an eyewitness, Dominic "bore the pains of his sickness with such patience that never a complaint nor a sigh issued from his mouth; indeed, he appeared joyful and even merry." [9] His composure in the face of terrible pain cheered and comforted his companions.

As his strength ebbed, he assembled his brethren to give them his final instructions. "These are, beloved ones, the inheritances that I leave you as my sons: have charity among you; hold to humility; possess voluntary poverty!" [1] With his last breath, he forbade them again to accept any kind of property. Then he made this confession to the brethren who stood around his bed: "God has in his mercy kept me till this day in pure and unstained virginity. . . . [But] I must admit that I have taken more pleasure in conversation with young women than I have with old." [2] A little while later Dominic began to fear lest his words concerning his spotless purity should be regarded as self-laudatory, and regretted having uttered them. The commission charged with the process of canonization, on the other hand, struck out of the record the other part of his statement, deeming that his reputation might be damaged if it were known that he had preferred speech with young women rather than with old. In reality, this self-accusation is a moving testimony to the unspoiled humanity of the saint.

After he had received extreme unction, he told his brothers to prepare to say the prayers for the dying, and he again comforted them with the words: "Do not weep, beloved ones; do not sorrow that this frail body goes. I am going where I can serve you better." [3] Then he said to them: "Begin," and to the sound of the prayers for the dying Dominic passed into eternity. The date was August 6, 1221.

Because of St. Dominic's reserve, it is hard to portray his personality in a way that really does him justice. He was not a man who loved to display his brilliant parts. In his modesty, he always withdrew into the background. Nor do our historical sources trans-

[9] *Acta Sanctorum*, August, Vol. I, para. 827.   [2] Ibid., pp. 165, 166.
[1] Quoted in Jarrett: op. cit., p. 166.   [3] Ibid., p. 167.

mit many authentic sayings of Dominic's which would throw a more vivid light on his personality. Consequently, most biographies of Dominic are slightly disappointing, and his best biographer complains: "No one has portrayed St. Dominic's spiritual struggle. No one has told us how Dominic became what he was, no one has described the process by which he took root in the supernatural." [4]

Dominic's individuality cannot be seen apart from his religion; the flame of his Christianity consumed his whole being. His companions observed again and again that he never indulged in idle talk, but spoke always with God or about God. He was a man turned wholly to the essential, unconcerned with what was merely entertaining. He shunned vain desires and always led a sternly ascetical life. He wore an iron chain about his hips, and he would spend entire nights standing with his arms outstretched, lost in prayer. His personal poverty was such that he did not possess so much as a cell of his own. It was said of him that "to others he very glady gave dispensations, to himself never." [5]

But the most admirable trait of Dominic's personality was his great love for his fellow men. By his own admission, he had studied "chiefly in the book of charity, for that teaches everything." [6] Yet he never spoke of it in honeyed tones. His was a dry, restrained love, a strong, boundless, and unsentimental love that extended not only "to all the faithful, but to unbelievers, and even to those suffering in hell, for whom he shed many tears." [7]

Dominic gave many proofs of this all-embracing love. It was said of him that he had a marvelous compassion for the sins of man, and that when, for instance, he was drawing near a village or a town, the thought of all the human misery and sin there would make him weep.[8] It was this compassionate love for his fellow men which prompted his ardent zeal for souls, and which freed him of any desire for personal glory. On several occasions he was chosen to be a bishop, and each time he declined the honor with the utmost firmness. For him, the only thing that mattered was his mission. The order was central to his thoughts, and his every thought served

[4] Scheeben: op. cit., pp. 6, 7.
[5] Quoted in Jarrett: op. cit., p. 148.
[6] Quoted in Lacordaire: op. cit., p. 199.
[7] Ibid., p. 187.
[8] Ibid., p. 199.

its interests. At the same time, he never identified it with himself. He was the founder, he made every sacrifice for the order, but the order, for him, was above his own person.

II

Dominic's burial was a very quiet affair, nor did the brethren proclaim his death an irreparable loss. His grave received scant care; according to Jordan of Saxony, one of his first biographers and his successor as Master General of the order, it was exposed to wind and weather. A thick stone slab, bearing no inscription whatsoever, covered the tomb, and there was nothing to indicate that the founder of the Order of Preachers lay buried there. Such neglect finally struck some of the brothers as unseemly, and twelve years after his death they decided to transfer his remains to a worthier grave.

The decision was not taken without considerable hesitation. A day was set for the ceremony, and the slab was removed. To the inexpressible amazement of those present, a sweet odor streamed out from the coffin. Both priests and lay folk stood there speechless and rejoicing; none of them had been prepared for the experience, but none could doubt the reality of it. At the process of canonization some of the brothers who had been eyewitnesses of the event testified under oath that they had personally smelled the pleasing scent.

At the time, the episode was regarded as a miracle that served to prove St. Dominic's holiness. But the miracle is at the same time a symbol. The sweet odor streaming out of the tomb symbolizes the order of the Friars Preachers, whose action gave forth an odor of sweetness that eventually penetrated into every corner of Christendom.

Because of its emphasis on study, the Order of Preachers was early connected with the nascent universities. Despite some initial opposition, the friars were soon securely established, and they eventually directed numerous schools and held important chairs in the various universities. It was no small service that they rendered to the medieval university, and they played a decisive part in the development of scholasticism.

The notion of scholasticism as a dry-as-dust system concerned exclusively with the elaboration of foolish sophistries has died hard. It is a notion born of prejudice and ignorance; the merest acquaintance with any of the mighty "summas" suffices to show how totally unfounded it is. The scholastics regarded thought as a form of divine worship, and believed in the validity of a reason enlightened by faith. By the central period of the Middle Ages, people had begun to ask for proofs of the truths of faith, and the Dominicans were concerned to supply them; the reason they served, after all, was a reason illumined by the divine Word. Dominic's sons stressed the importance of not sundering faith and knowledge; rather, they desired to reconcile the two. And they sought by reason to bring all the multifarious aspects of life into a single system of belief. Such an ambitious undertaking cannot be denied admiration, even though by its very nature it could never altogether succeed.

The friars' entrance into the universities was inevitably fraught with grave dangers to the order. Many of them succumbed to intellectual pride, ambition, and desire for honors, a state of affairs which was certainly not in the spirit of the founder. But there was an even graver problem: that this active concern with scholarship might bring about a change in the very character of the order. For the order's main concern now appeared to be with the study and teaching of theology, whereas the function on which Dominic had laid principal stress had been preaching. But this evident shift in emphasis was not in fact a defection from the primitive ideal; it was determined by the historical situation, and the manner in which the Order of Preachers dealt with that situation was certainly not contrary to the spirit of St. Dominic, who had always urged his brethren to cherish reason.

The irruption of a non-Christian philosophy into the West in the latter part of the thirteenth century constituted no less a danger to Christendom than the gnostic Catharist creed; it was a philosophy of skepticism, skillfully propounded by Averroës, and it was poisoning the sources of Christian belief. This was the danger that the sons of St. Dominic now sought to combat, and the weapon that brought them victory in their mortal struggle with Averroës was the scholastic philosophy which they helped to develop. This achievement alone should earn the Dominicans the gratitude of all who see in skepticism the forerunner of nihilism. The schoolmen of the thirteenth century were fighting in the front lines, and their passionate participation in the intellectual life of their times was completely in accord with the ideal of the order—namely, the saving of souls.

The transition originated with Albertus Magnus, a German, and one of the most impressive scholars of the age. He is regarded as the greatest student of natural history of the Middle Ages, and it has been said that "he felt the world was great because he was great himself." In the history of the order, however, he has been eclipsed by his pupil, Thomas Aquinas.

Young Thomas joined the order despite the violent opposition of his family, for at that time the mendicants were still regarded as a somewhat disreputable band of vagrants. Thomas, however, did not share his family's class-consciousness, and was determined to wear the Dominican habit.

When he first entered the order, no one so much as guessed at the stupendous intellect of this taciturn young man. His fellow friars called him the "dumb ox," and took his silence as evidence of stupidity. But his teacher, Albertus Magnus, perceived the depths that were hidden under the surface of Thomas's mind, and prophesied of him: "You call him a dumb ox; I tell you this dumb ox shall bellow so loud that his bellowings will fill the world." [9] The prophecy proved true in the most literal sense. Thomas Aquinas was the man who "baptized" Aristotle—a feat that took no mean courage at a time when the pagan philosopher was still so suspect in the eyes of most churchmen.

There is a Gothic loftiness about Thomist rationalism, a quality stemming from the man's own inner freedom to weigh and to assay every theory before accepting or rejecting it. The importance of his "summas" resides principally in their unique power to harmonize opposites in a single whole. His marvelous sense of balance is well

[9] Quoted in G. K. Chesterton: *Saint Thomas Aquinas* (New York: Image Books; 1956), p. 71.

exemplified, for instance, in his own statement that grace does not destroy nature, but rather fulfills it. Thomas sought to build a bridge between faith and knowledge, and he set the human reason the noble task of providing theology with the arms it needed to combat false doctrine.

This, of course, was wholly in keeping with Dominic's ideas. But Thomas went a step further and inaugurated a Christian philosophy. Thomas neither made a fetish of the intellect nor regarded his work as the effect of revelation; he was simply trying to discuss the problems of Christianity in philosophical terms. Nor was his tremendous achievement a source of danger to him personally; in his most successful teaching activity he remained ever filled with a humble piety, and he was able to say: "I give thanks to God that neither my learning, nor my professorial chair, nor any public disputation has ever been to me a source of vainglory." [1]

And at the end of his life this titanic thinker realized in starkest clarity the insufficiency of all his labors. Returning to his cell from church one morning, he appeared strangely altered. He laid his goose-quill aside and, in reply to the insistent questioning of his friend, Brother Reginald, said only: "I can no more; such things have been revealed to me that what I have written seems but straw." [2] A more shattering assessment of his own life's work by a great thinker is hard to imagine. Thomas's weighty expositions appeared to him as straw in the light of the radiant vision of God which had flooded his soul in church.

From this time on, the mighty wielder of the pen was silent. This conclusion of his philosophical labors indicates better than many words that the prince of the schoolmen was no prisoner of his own system, and bears conclusive testimony to his truly Christian spirituality.

Aquinas was not immediately accepted as the final authority for scholasticism. His predilection for Aristotle at first aroused open opposition among the traditionalists, and some passages of his writings were condemned by the Archbishop of Paris. Eventually,

---

[1] *Acta Sanctorum*, March, Vol. I, *Vita S. Thomae*, chap. v, para 25.
[2] Quoted in M. C. d'Arcy: *Saint Thomas Aquinas* (Dublin: Clonmore & Reynolds; 1953), p. 36.

however, his work imposed itself by the well-nigh irresistible force of his reasoning, and his order refused to countenance any hostile criticism of "the holy Thomas." Indeed, as early as the beginning of the fourteenth century Thomas's teaching was declared to be the firm rule for study, and subsequently all preachers of the order were required to take this oath: "I swear, vow, and promise that I will not depart from the sure teaching of the Angelic Doctor, St. Thomas, so help me God and this holy Gospel of God." [3]

The Dominicans have identified themselves with Aquinas, and his authority in the order is on a level with Dominic's. As the Angelic Doctor, he became the supreme church teacher, a position that was confirmed by Pope Pius XI in his encyclical, "*Studiorum ducem,*" of June 29, 1923.

The order's pride and joy in its great son are easy to understand, but the propriety of the oath its members are bound to take in regard to his teachings remains questionable. Would he himself have sanctioned it, he who at the end of his life adjudged his writings to be as so much straw? In his own humble estimation of himself, there was nothing sacrosanct about his work, and to make it so is to negate its essential vitality. The canonizing of Thomas's doctrine has written a kind of *finis* to his work which should never have been written. The door must always remain open, because the Christian may always hope to penetrate still deeper into the heart of truth. It is doubtful, too, whether the newer, specifically modern problems can be resolved by means of Thomas's Christian philosophy, which does not so much as envisage them. And if his philosophy does hold the key to their solution, then it is only on condition that his followers do more than repeat what Thomas thought, and instead think ahead, as Thomas himself thought ahead. [4]

If the order made a significant contribution to Christian thought, it made a no less significant contribution to Christian spirituality. It is customary to speak of a German mysticism, thereby characterizing as national a phenomenon that is supranational, but it would be far more fitting to speak of a Dominican mysticism, because it was largely within the order that it originated.

[3] From the *Constitutions* of the Dominican Order.
[4] W. Dirks: *Die Antwort der Mönche* (1952), p. 194.

In characteristic Dominican fashion, the Dominican mystics responded to the religious distress of their times by the radiance of their divine joy. Theirs was the triumphant reply to the growing skepticism that surrounded them. They showed men the way back into their own hearts. They were men athirst for God, consumed in their longing for union with the Almighty. Their goal was to be ever closer to God, nor did they ever feel that they had achieved that goal. And the divine dwelt in them not merely as an ardent longing, but as a reality, as an all-absorbing presence. Like the early Christians, these mystics knew something of the tenderness and the intimacy of the eternal, and to this day a radiance proceeds from their writings which warms and rejoices all souls that thirst for God and desire to possess Him otherwise than through the halting language of theological textbooks. Here, in their mysticism, is revealed as nowhere else the inmost secret of monasticism, the power by which monasticism is able to subsist. It is hard to conceive of any more eloquent testimony to God's presence in man than was given by the Dominican mystics.

At the summit of the movement stands Meister Eckhart, who takes rank beside Dominic and Aquinas as the third great figure of the order. One would have to speak with the tongues of angels to speak fittingly about Meister Eckhart—the man "from whom God hid nothing." A magnificent preacher, he never feared to proclaim his heavenly message in all its fullness, whether before persons practiced in the interior life or before the simplest congregations, whom he addressed in the vernacular. His mystical doctrine is enveloped in the language of theological speculation. Eckhart certainly took part in the scholastic movement and, while remaining faithful to tradition, displayed an almost revolutionary boldness —the fruit of his towering aspirations.

It was his assumption that "he who wishes to see God must desire it mightily." [5] The exuberance and even rashness of his language make it impossible to classify his spirituality in any narrow categories. A statement such as "I defy God, or the angels, or any creatures, to separate the soul from its origin, in which it is one with

[5] *Meister Eckhart's deutsche Predigten und Traktaten*, ed. Schulze-Maizier, p. 359.

God" [6] reflects his passion for paradox and explains why the more pedestrian minds among the clergy were quite unable to follow him.

Yet, whatever his extravagances, Eckhart was a man wholly dedicated to God. Everything that he taught, whether about the knowledge of creatures as they are in themselves and in their relation to God, or about withdrawal from the world and the birth of God in the soul, had only one aim: to lead people back to their lost homeland in God. This ineffable "fool for God" was so completely penetrated by the desire to be with God and in God that his writings must not be looked at askance even if their language is sometimes inappropriate.

This sense of being at home again with God inspired all his glowing sermons: "On no account let anyone suppose that he is far from God because of his infirmities or faults or for any other reason. . . . It is most mischievous to set God at a distance. Man goes far away or near, but God never goes far off; he is always standing close at hand, and even if he cannot stay within he goes no farther than the door." [7]

Eckhart penetrated regions that can only be described as the summit of Western Christian spirituality. And, coming as they did from those dizzy heights, some of the notes of his song of God sounded false in the ears of his hearers. He was believed to be talking heresy, whereas he was merely using the language of Neo-Platonism. Sometimes, too, his statements came too close to the recognized frontiers of dogma, and he was suspected of pantheism.

At first the Order of Preachers remained faithful to its venerated *lector biblicus*. In the end, however, spite and envy triumphed; Eckhart's name was dragged into disrepute, and he ended his days under a heavy cloud. After his death a number of his statements were condemned by the Pope, a tragic and most regrettable step. Once the stigma of condemnation had been attached to his writings, the order could no longer defend him publicly, and—to the great loss of Christian culture—Eckhart's influence could spread only through unofficial channels.

[6] Ibid., p. 391.
[7] C. Evans, ed.: *The Works of Meister Eckhart* (London: John W. Watkins; 1952), II, 23.

One of the men most strongly influenced by Eckhart's teaching was Johannes Tauler, who also possessed the characteristic Dominican gift of preaching. He could speak with such power that a Dominican nun of the period, Christina Ebner, wrote of him: "Tauler is the man most dear to God on earth. He has set the world ablaze with his fiery tongue."

With Tauler, Dominican mysticism is directed against empty ceremonial. Not that he scorned ceremony, but he wanted people to give their participation a spiritual content: "We must keep many rules. We must go to choir to sing and to read office; this we must do, whether we like it or not. Well, then, let us do this with a festive and joyous soul, rather than with a spiritless observance, dragging ourselves to the task. Let us be faithful to our rules in order not to forfeit the eternal festival day in heaven." [8]

Concerning external poverty, Tauler taught that it must lead to interior poverty; the Christian must leave all things and overcome all things so that he may return again to the source of being: "Men will come to thee . . . telling thee high-sounding and subtle things of the intellect, as if they thought they were Christ's apostles. Dear child, get away from them and sink into thy inmost soul, into thy nothingness, and let these men talk on like the ringing of the bells in a church steeple. Nay, if all the devils in hell were turned loose upon thee, and all other creatures with them—it will all help thee wonderfully, if thou wilt but turn inward to the study of thy nothingness: that is the 'best part.' " [9]

One hour in God's quiet hiddenness, we read again, is a thousand times more profitable than many years spent in acting according to one's own desires. And in order to attain to peace in the midst of turmoil, the Christian must first suffer a spiritual death: "Nature must die many a death. By many a wild and desert way does God lead the soul as He teaches it to die. But, O children, what a noble life is born of this death—noble and joyous and fruitful!" [1]

Tauler's sermons are filled with profound insights. His central

    [8] W. Elliott, ed.: *The Sermons and Conferences of John Tauler* (Washington, D. C.: Apostolic Mission House; 1910), Second Sermon for the Fourth Sunday of Lent, p. 214.
    [9] Ibid., First Sermon for the Thirteenth Sunday after Trinity, p. 501.
    [1] Ibid., Third Sermon for the Feast of *Corpus Christi*, p. 385.

and constant theme is the soul's life in God, of which he speaks so eloquently that only a heart of stone could remain unmoved. And only a slight acquaintance with this genuinely Dominican mysticism is needed to understand why Matthias Claudius, with childlike simplicity, would "doff his hat whenever he read Tauler."

The third member of the great trio of Dominican mystics was Henry Suso, also a disciple of Eckhart, to whom he remained faithful even after it was no longer expedient to mention his name. Suso is often regarded as overly sentimental, but the charge is unjustified. He was the born seeker after God, and his hunger for the eternal caused him to make this confession:

"Beloved, gentle Lord, since the days of my childhood my heart has sought for something with an ardent thirst. Lord, what that is I cannot yet fully understand. Lord, I have pursued it for many a year eagerly, and I have never yet succeeded, because I do not rightly know what it is, and yet it is something that draws my heart and soul toward itself, and without which I can never find true peace. Lord, in the first days of my youth I tried to find it in the creatures, as I saw others do; but the more I sought, the less I found it, and the nearer I went to it, the farther off it was. For of every image that appeared to me, before I had fully tested it, or abandoned myself to peace in it, an inner voice said to me: 'This is not what thou seekest.' And I have always had this revulsion from things. Lord, my heart now yearns for it, for it would gladly possess it, and it has often experienced what it is not; but what it is, my heart has not discovered. Alas, beloved Lord of heaven, what is it, or of what nature is it, that it should so mysteriously make itself felt within me?" [2]

To find what he was seeking, young Suso entered the Order of Preachers, where he was eventually to make his glorious discovery: "A detached man must be unformed from the forms and images of creatures; he must be formed upon Christ, and transformed into the Godhead." [3]

When we consider the stern asceticism by which Suso subdued

[2] Henry Suso: *Little Book of Eternal Wisdom*, ed. James M. Clark (London, Faber & Faber; 1953), pp. 47, 48.
[3] T. F. Knox, ed.: *The Life of Blessed Henry Suṣo by Himself* (London: Methuen & Co.; 1913), p. 219.

his frail body we realize how truly he practiced detachment from all creatures. But one cannot be "formed upon Christ" without being prepared, also, to suffer with Him, and Suso consequently ascribed to suffering an indispensable function in the Christian life. In his *Life* he describes a vision he had of a seraph with six wings: "on the two lowest wings was written, 'Receive sufferings willingly,' on the two middle wings, 'Bear sufferings patiently,' and, on the two highest wings, 'Learn to suffer after Christ's pattern.'" [4] The final aim of the perfect man is transformation into the Godhead, concerning which Suso writes of himself that "his soul was caught up in ecstasy . . . and he saw and heard what no tongue can tell. It was without form or mode, and yet it contained within itself the entrancing delightfulness of all forms and modes," after which he appeared to himself "like a man who has come from another world." [5]

This threefold aim contains the essence of Suso's mystical teaching, and, like his fellow Dominican, Tauler, he loved to give it the generic name of detachment. He never wearied of speaking of the detached man: "The highest school, and the craft which is taught there, consist simply in an entire and perfect detachment from self; that is to say, how a man may attain to such an abiding spirit of self-renunciation, no matter how God treats him, either directly by Himself or indirectly through creatures, or how he feels, whether joyful or sad, the one object of his strivings shall ever be to continue always the same by a perpetual giving up of self, as far as human frailty will allow, and to make God's honor and glory his sole aim, just in the way that the dear Christ acted toward His heavenly Father." [6]

Suso's spirituality proved itself in his pastoral work. He was an inspired director of souls. Few clerics have been so adept at consoling men in their spiritual distress as this tenderhearted Dominican, with his gift of putting himself in the other man's place. This, he tells us in his *Life*, was the fourfold rule he sought to fulfill when called to the convent door: "first, to receive everyone with kindliness; secondly, to dispatch the matter with brevity; thirdly, to send the person away consoled; fourthly, to go back again free from

---

[4] Ibid., pp. 190, 191.   [5] Ibid., p. 10.   [6] Ibid., p. 66.

attachment." [7] A short enough precept, yet one that contains every-thing needful to Christian conduct.

The mystical life was not some esoteric enthusiasm of a handful of Dominican friars; it penetrated the entire order, and was partic-ularly marked in the convents of Dominican nuns. A graphic ac-count of the intense spiritual life cultivated in one such convent, that of Toss, near Wintherthur, has been left to us by Elsbeth Stagel, a member of the community and a devoted friend of Suso's. But the most outstanding of the women mystics of the order was undoubtedly Catherine of Siena. "Without love," she wrote in one of her eminently readable letters, "the soul cannot subsist," [8] and this was the theme of her life. She was granted ineffable ecstasies, and received, mystically, the marks of the Crucified. Christ, for her, was as fire, and she would allow nothing to stand in the way be-tween her soul and her Lord. She was devoted to her order, and would kiss the ground the Friars Preachers had trod. And she was filled with an authentically Dominican zeal for souls, offering herself unreservedly for their salvation. In characteristic fashion she wrote to one of her correspondents, a papal nuncio: "I, your unworthy daughter, have taken the guilt of your sins upon me; that we may burn them, yours and mine together, in the fire of sweet charity, where they will be consumed." [9] At the same time, this frail young woman could address sharp expostulations to the ecclesiastical au-thorities, and did not shrink from comparing the conduct of certain prelates to that of parasites. Her ardent apostolate brought her into the center of the arena of Church politics, and she did not rest till she had persuaded Gregory XI to return from Avignon to Rome.

Art, too, bears the imprint of Dominican mysticism, particularly in the work of Fra Angelico, of whom it is said that he never painted his Christs otherwise than on his knees, with tears streaming down his cheeks. The angelic figures that he painted on the walls of the cells of his convent of San Marco, in Florence, are like a call to prayer, their external beauty signifying inner greatness of soul. Angelico's people seem to ignore earthly cares; clothed in

---

[7] Ibid., p. 46.

[8] *Le lettere di S. Caterina da Siena*, ed. Tommaseo (Siena: Libreria Giun-tini & Bentivoglio; 1913), Vol. IV, letter no. 299, p. 321.

[9] Ibid., Vol. II, letter no. 109, p. 188.

light, they seem already to have attained beatitude. "He had the rare ability to transcend matter, which is why he was able to see things with a purity such as only children possess—and those who are so pure of heart that they will see God." [1]

There is a fresco over the entrance to the cloister of San Marco depicting a monk standing with his finger on his lips. This too is from the hand of Fra Angelico, and the figure represents Peter Martyr. But it also represents the inmost secret of monasticism. For here we sense the life of contemplation in the monastic cell, and the gesture points to the ineffable that dwells in the man who has dedicated himself wholly to God. Gazing at Angelico's monk, we may perceive something, perhaps, of the soul of monasticism, and it may inspire us, too, to a love of silence, which is the condition of all mystical life.

We have spoken of Dominican mysticism, a region of light, clearer than the clearest summer day; we are obliged now to descend into regions of unutterable darkness, for it behooves us, in fairness, to refer to the complicity of the Dominican order in the bloody work of the Inquisition.

The picture of Dominic as the first inquisitor is without historical foundation; it originated in a later endeavor to justify what had become one of the principal functions of the order. [2] In point of fact, the Inquisition was in diametrical opposition to the spirit of St. Dominic, who had made it abundantly clear that force was not the way to deal with heresy. Indeed, the least complicity in the vile operations of the Inquisition was a violation of Dominic's deathbed testament to his children: "Have charity among you." It was as a humble preacher, and not with weapons in hand, that Dominic had sought to win back those who had fallen away from the faith, thereby tracing a new path for Christian endeavor. Hence the inquisitorial method was the worst betrayal of all that Dominic stood for: Dominic's idea was to convince his opponents by well-founded argument, whereas the use of force in matters of faith is a Mohammedan principle—the Prophet having prided himself on receiving from the Almighty the mission of the sword.

[1] *Beato Angelico*, ed. Ciaranfi (1947), p. 6.
[2] Scheeben: op. cit., p. 92.

The order's complicity in the work of the Inquisition became possible only after Dominic's original aim had been lost sight of and the erroneous view had arisen that the founder's primary purpose had been to "wipe out heresy," as the brutal saying went.

The alliance between the Inquisition and the Dominicans originated with the Curia. Because the bishops had become too remiss in dealing with heresy, the papacy saw itself compelled to take more stringent measures and took over from the state the inquisitorial apparatus that had previously been operated by the secular authorities.

Strange as it may sound, the Inquisition started out as an "improvement"—by comparison, that is, with the method of "trial by ordeal" previously in vogue. For the Inquisition, unlike the earlier practice, based its operations on the principle of confession of guilt, and at first the Church opposed the use of torture.

The new endeavor to convince heretics by argument made the presence of theologians imperative, and the obvious persons to call upon in those times were the Dominicans. Hence, rather more than ten years after Dominic's death, Gregory IX, on grounds of ecclesiastical policy, detailed the brethren for the struggle against heresy [3] and charged them with the operation of the Inquisition. Only a moment of unguardedness on the part of the order, and the evil was upon it; the Order of Preachers allowed itself to be misused for a purpose alien to its very essence.

Mankind seems to be incapable of stamping out the execrable spirit of the Inquisition; the activities of modern totalitarian states in the field of criminal jurisprudence are only another manifestation of the same horror. It is a spirit that witnesses to the incursions of the Devil in human affairs. How right Vladimir Soloviev was to call the Inquisition a "hellish betrayal of the spirit of Christ." The principle of the stake is altogether incompatible with the Gospel, and two more different worlds can hardly be conceived of than the Inquisition and mysticism, in both of which the Order of Preachers was involved.

It would be unfair, however, to identify the entire order with the Inquisition. At all times there were Dominicans who had nothing

[3] Scheeben: *Jordan, der Sachse* (1937), p. 199.

to do with it and who remained true to the primitive aim of preaching. At the time of the Spanish conquest of South America, for instance, members of the order were the first to protest against the bloody adventure and to qualify it as a mockery of Christianity. The noble humanitarian Bartolomé de Las Casas, who took up the defense of the oppressed Indians, was a Dominican.

Another incident that casts a shadow on the history of the order is the tragedy associated with the name of Savonarola. And it can be rightly understood only against a background of decadence within the order. Discipline had long been growing slack, and this had led to the temporary split between "Observants" and "Conventuals." A major evil that had affected the order since the time of the great schism was the so-called *vita privata*, which meant that the members of a community would at most live under a single roof, but each at his own expense and according to his own good pleasure, and that in many cases a friar was authorized to enjoy his patrimony during his lifetime. The legend goes that once, when some Dominicans were singing the verse "Fulfill, Father, what thou hast promised" at the grave of their founder, a voice replied: "Neither am I your father nor are you my sons!"

Yet despite this decadence—accentuated by the depopulating of the Dominican houses as a result of the plague that swept Europe in the fourteenth century—there always remained men in whom the primitive spirit burned bright. One of these was Savonarola, a man with a true Dominican gift for preaching. To get an idea of the spiritual power of Dominican preaching, it is sufficient to read Savonarola's sermons.

Savonarola was concerned with the other side of the Renaissance, which the modern art-lover is only too prone to overlook: he realized the appalling loss in the substance of Christianity which was the price of the rediscovery of antiquity. Like St. Dominic, Savonarola saw the forces of corruption of his times and threw himself into the lists against them with all the resources of his fiery eloquence. It is worth remembering that it was Dominican spirituality that first took up the struggle against the depletion of Christianity which was in full swing by the end of the fifteenth century. Savonarola, however, differed from Dominic by his passionate diatribes against the corrupt clergy, whose inadequacy Dominic had sought to remedy by other means.

The people of Florence were visibly shaken by Savonarola's thunderings concerning the judgment to come, and were led to establish a Christian republic. But his very efficacy in public affairs made him many political enemies, who sought his removal. They joined forces with the Pope to silence this tiresome monk. It was not the Church that was responsible for Savonarola's destruction; the blame falls squarely on the shoulders of his political foes. What is distressing, on the other hand, is the way his own order abandoned him after his secular enemies had seized him. The monks of San Marco took the incredible decision that Savonarola and his two companions in misfortune should forever be denied admission to the monastery—whether alive or dead, whether openly or secretly. Later they were ashamed of this decision and therefore omitted to record it in their chronicle. [4]

This attitude is significant of the conflict between the two tendencies that divided the order at the time. Savonarola the reformer, who advocated a return to renunciation of all personal and communal possessions, was a thorn in the side of the moderate elements. This explains why, after Savonarola's body had been broken on the rack and just before he was executed, on May 23, 1498, the Master General of the Dominicans, Jerome Torrigiani, ordered that his habit be stripped from his body with ignominy—a command that the prior willingly obeyed.

In the face of this outrage it is hard to say anything more about Savonarola, and yet a final verdict is essential. The erstwhile prior of San Marco was filled with Christian ardor, but he does not deserve uncritical admiration. His apostolate knew nothing of religious joy. Only the terrifying vision of the visitation of judgment breaks through the thundering sermons in which he summoned his hearers to repentance. His cry to God: "Pour out thy wrath upon the peoples!" squares ill with the Lord's rebuke to the sons of Zebedee: "Ye know not what manner of spirit ye are of" (Luke ix, 55).

[4] J. Schnitzer: *Savonarola in Streite mit seinem Orden und seinem Kloster* (1914), p. 89.

These are notorious limitations. On the other hand, we should pay due recognition to the prophetic element in the man. Savonarola was inhabited by the spirit of prophecy, which led to an awakening of the Christian conscience—something that Christendom cannot forgo without courting disaster. The Florentine Dominican remained faithful to the dictates of his Christian conscience at all times and in all circumstances, and he paid for his message with his own blood.

The martyr of San Marco was no heretic; had there been anything heretical about his writings, saints like Philip Neri and Catherine Ricci would not have defended them so passionately. Savonarola's crime was disobedience to the Pope—and that Pope was Alexander VI. He was not a rebel against the apostolic see; he was torn between the claims of obedience to God and submission to the orders of an unworthy Pope. At all times Savonarola has been held in great veneration by many of his fellow Dominicans, and his final rehabilitation is a duty that the order has yet to fulfill, if only in order to show that within the Church, too, people may speak a Christian language to their superiors, a language that today is too seldom heard.

Because the Order of Preachers did not learn the lesson of the tragedy, the chastisement that Savonarola had predicted overtook the Church only too speedily and the Dominicans were among the most severely affected. Under the onslaught of the Reformation, the order lost more than half its houses in Germany. Even worse was to come in the Age of Enlightenment and the French Revolution; the order was virtually wiped out in most countries.

It was not until the middle of the nineteenth century that an attempt was made by Lacordaire to reinvigorate the order. That great preacher achieved something, but he was not able to carry through his plans for reform completely. The great renewal of the order will come only if it endeavors to remedy the religious and social distress of the present times with as much open-mindedness as St. Dominic displayed when he triumphed over the decadence of his own day by the new solution that he offered. Then a new era will dawn for the Order of Preachers, and the ancient prophecy of the illuminated Mechtild of Magdeburg concerning the Dominicans will be fulfilled: "When the ancient mantle becomes old, it no longer covers and warms every part; therefore it is necessary that I should cover and protect my bride, the Church, and it is through the preachers of the latter times that I clothe her and shield her against the snares and the wickedness of anti-Christ." [5]

[5] Mechtild of Magdeburg: *Das fliessende Licht der Gottheit*, Book VI, chap. xxi. The English translation of Mechtild's *Revelations* by L. Menzies (London: Longmans, Green; 1953) is presumably based on a different manuscript from the one used by the German editor, as it does not include the passage quoted.

Saint TERESA

and Carmel

THE SCENE was Avila, in the dark hours before dawn of November 2, 1535. A veiled figure was hurriedly making her way through the streets, evidently anxious to avoid discovery. It was Teresa, the twenty-year-old daughter of Don Alonso Sánchez y Cepeda, who was leaving her father's house without his consent in order to become a nun at the convent of the Incarnation.

She was trembling in every nerve as she pulled the bell-rope at the convent door. She had had to do utter violence to herself to make this fateful decision, and the strength to carry it out, she believed, could have come to her only from God. She must, it seems, even then have had some premonition of what her step was to entail. Many years later Teresa described her feelings at that moment: "I remember—and I really believe this is true—that when I left my father's house my distress was so great that I do not think it will be greater when I die. It seemed to me as if every bone in my body was being wrenched asunder." [1]

But the convent of the Incarnation at Avila was no Jacob's ladder leading to perfection. It had been founded not long before, and it was remarkable neither for its fidelity to venerable tradition nor for its religious fervor. It cultivated an atmosphere of agreeable domesticity, and was more like a boarding-school for the daughters of the well-to-do than a convent. The nuns prettied themselves with necklaces, bracelets, and rings; they arranged delightful gatherings in

[1] *Complete Works of St. Teresa*, ed. E. Allison Peers (London: Sheed & Ward; 1944), Vol. I, *Life*, p. 20.

their private rooms, at which they served sweetmeats to their guests. Yet there was nothing positively evil about the community, nothing that warranted its dissolution. It had simply slipped, imperceptibly, into a state of mediocrity which affected every detail of the religious life. Religious houses of this kind, where nothing particularly reprehensible takes place, but likewise nothing exceptional, are to be found in every clime.

In the failure to do great things greatly there lies an insidious evil which becomes increasingly deadly as long as it remains unrecognized. Easy living, too, which the world prizes so highly, holds a danger. Apparently so innocuous, it is the enemy of the religious life, a stumbling-block in the path of spiritual progress. Indeed, attachment to comfort can be worse than outright sin, which can be easily recognized, grieved for, and repented.

The ladies of the Incarnation, for instance, saw nothing to repent of in their way of life, and so there was little prospect of improvement. The result was a generalized sclerosis of the religious life. To quote the prioress in Bernanos's *Dialogue des Carmélites*, "The position of an unworthy nun seems to be more deplorable than that of a brigand. The brigand can be converted, and it will be as a second birth for him. The unworthy nun, for her part, cannot be born again. She has been born, but she has missed her birth, and without a miracle she will always remain an abortion." [2]

Teresa was fully aware of the debilitating effect of habit on the religious life: "Custom," she lamented, "is a terrible thing in human nature." [3] Religious practices mechanically performed must necessarily degenerate into mere formalism, which slowly enmeshes the soul and renders it incapable of rising to higher things. For formalism is but another name for that lukewarmness concerning which St. John's Revelation contains the terrible warning that the Lord will spew forth from His mouth them that are neither hot nor cold (Rev. iii, 16).

It was only to be expected that the young novice in a community that cherished ease and cultivated gossip should develop into but a

[2] G. Bernanos: *The Fearless Heart*, tr. M. Legat (Westminster, Md.: The Newman Press; 1952), p. 30.
[3] *Complete Works of St. Teresa*, Vol. III, *Method for the Visitation of Convents of Discalced Carmelite Nuns*, p. 240.

mediocre nun. The sisters recited only those prayers which were of obligation; they preferred to spend hours on end in the parlors chatting with gossip-loving friends and relatives, whose idle tattle for empty heads, as Teresa put it later, provided the necessary color in their rather humdrum lives. Teresa, being of a very lively temperament, eagerly took part in these social activities; moreover, like the other nuns, she often left the convent for days at a time to stay with relatives, for the rule of enclosure was not observed. No one, apparently, saw any inconsistency between this easygoing way of life and genuine monastic practice; indeed, the nuns hardly seemed to know the meaning of a binding rule. Teresa, who took full advantage of the freedom the convent afforded her, differed from her sisters only to the extent that she entertained occasional doubts about the propriety of such an unmonastic life.

At an early age Teresa had experienced spiritual favors that seemed to summon her to a higher kind of life. The memory of these graces disturbed her; hence her repeated decisions, after she became a nun, to lead a more nunlike existence. But her good intentions foundered again and again on the rocks of mediocrity. Often she would neglect religious practices, in particular mental prayer, for long stretches of time, till suddenly she would find herself stirred to renewed endeavor.

The first years of her religious life, in consequence, were anything but happy; they were, indeed, extremely painful. Once again the time-honored spiritual maxim was proved true: negligence in religion necessarily rends the soul. No one could have experienced this bitter truth more acutely than the Teresa of this period, as she hovered irresolutely between heaven and earth. Having fled the world to enter a convent, she heard God's call clearly in her soul, and at the same time she clung with every fiber of her being to the fascinations of the world. And so she strove with might and main to reconcile two irreconcilables—the spiritual life and a life of agreeable leisure. For twenty years she remained bound in the toils of mediocrity, and she could not make good her escape.

The ladies of Avila were charmed with Sister Teresa—she was such an excellent storyteller, she had such a gay laugh. . . . But their opinion only underlines the incongruity of her life as a nun.

Later, when she wrote her autobiography, she laid bare with ruthless candor the religious ambivalence that was the fruit of her
spiritual indiscipline. Only a book written in prayer could present
such a lucid analysis of the workings of the soul.

As we consider this first phase of Teresa's life as a nun, we are
reminded of Sanvert's dictum that Teresa "discovered the laws of
spiritual gravity just as her contemporary, Kepler, discovered the
laws of physical gravity." [4] Teresa, indeed, has much to teach us
of the pressures that bear upon the soul; she had probed the matter
long before Simone Weil reflected upon it in our own day.[5] Nevertheless, the formula is not altogether satisfactory, for what Teresa
really did was to disprove the "law" of spiritual gravity. She was only
too well aware of the well-nigh irresistible pull of the earth on the
soul, but she also knew what it was to resist that pull. For it is not
man's destiny to creep ignominiously upon the earth. Teresa's writings in effect proclaim the powerlessness of "gravity" to impede the
soul's flight to God.

The victory over "gravity," however, took place only in the second phase of Teresa's religious life, when her soul was pierced, as
she herself relates, by an angel's spear.[6] The transformation is staggering; here was a nun who had almost come to terms with a life of
spiritual dichotomy, who seemed forever barred from crossing the
threshold of the absolute, and who now was suddenly swept up by
angelic powers into the supernatural. This irruption of the divine
into her life took place without warning. Upon coming into the
chapel one day, she found there a new picture representing Christ
at the Pillar. The Lord seemed to be looking into her very soul,
and with such power that suddenly her hesitations ceased, her lukewarmness was banished forever. What Teresa had not achieved in
years of struggle, God had done for her in an instant. This, then,
and not the hour of her impetuous flight from her father's house, was
the climactic hour of her life.

Teresa now found herself endowed with extraordinary visionary
powers, to her own great alarm. However prone she might be to

[4] M. Virnich: *Teresa von Avila* (1934), p. 110.
[5] Simone Weil: *Gravity and Grace* (New York: G. P. Putnam's Sons;
1952).
[6] *Complete Works of St. Teresa*, Vol. I, *Life*, p. 192.

wax enthusiastic, she also had a very critical turn of mind which prompted her to subject all her experiences to careful scrutiny. She was particularly afraid lest her visions might be the work of the Evil One; instances of diabolical deception were common enough in sixteenth-century Spain, with its not inconsiderable crop of pseudo-mystics. She discussed the matter with her various confessors, and analyzed herself mercilessly. Indeed, this penetrating self-analysis has led certain modern authorities to claim that Teresa took a scientific interest in her raptures. One such pundit has gone so far as to maintain that Teresa would have made an ideal subject for a modern psychiatric institution.[7] Teresa would probably have laughed heartily at the suggestion. For her ecstasies had nothing whatsoever to do with psychology; her conversation was with angels, and the heavenly powers led her soul to the divine. The essence of Teresa's life was union with God.

A passage in her commentary upon certain words of the *Song of Songs* is relevant in this connection: "I have often noticed that, as far as we can understand, the soul appears here to be speaking with one person and asking for peace from another. . . . I do not understand how this can be, and I am very glad not to do so. For really, daughters, the soul should not so much meditate upon or be taught to meditate upon or reverence her God in the things that with our lowly intelligence we can apparently comprehend in this life, as in the things that are quite incomprehensible."[8]

Teresa recognized, in other words, that many things must necessarily elude man's understanding, and she revered the mystery. From this reverence flowed that vital approach which caused her to marvel at every manifestation of being and to rediscover it afresh at every encounter. This childlike sense of wonder was one of her greatest gifts. She rejoiced in the unfathomable mysteries that surround man on every side, and this joyous realization gives her writings their inimitable charm. In her *Interior Castle*, for instance, she writes: "In all things that have been created by so great and wise a God there must be many secrets by which we can profit, and . . . I

---

[7] A. Mager: *Mystik als seelische Wirklichkeit* (1946), p. 144.
[8] *Complete Works of St. Teresa*, Vol. II, *Conceptions of the Love of God*, p. 359.

believe that in every little thing created by God there is more than we realize, even in so small a thing as a tiny ant." [9] In the ant under her feet, as in a moving portrayal of Christ's passion, Teresa was ever aware of the divine reality that transcends human understanding and is also the only foundation of a genuine monastic life.

Teresa's mystical life was the fruit of her visions, and it is very hard to understand, as she herself declared, without personal experience of such favors. However, as Teresa was very clear as to the difference between mere talk about mysticism and the real experience of suprasensual union with God, she was well able to act as a guide to others in their aspiration toward the ineffable intimacy of the divine. Every line betrays a detailed and experimental knowledge about the soul's ascent to God. As for her visions, she never craved them; they came upon her with such overwhelming power that she was simply unable to withstand them.

Teresa, with her inspired understanding of the spiritual life, stands at the apex of that line of medieval women mystics which includes such eminent figures as Hildegard of Bingen, Mechtild of Magdeburg, and the great St. Gertrude. Her soul ascended to inaccessible regions, and she enjoyed moments of bliss so intense as to rob her, for a time, of consciousness. Even her body was sometimes mysteriously raised up from the ground. The skeptics may shrug their shoulders, but these levitations are a fitting and unmistakable symbol of the movement of Teresa's whole life from earth toward heaven. There was no trace of familiarity in her communion with the God who was the exclusive object of her love; she was careful always to refer to Him as "His Majesty." Her mystical prayer was akin to the adoration of the angels whom Isaiah saw in his vision in the temple crying "Holy, holy, holy, is the Lord of hosts!" And Teresa, obedient to her Master's command that she converse henceforth with angels and not with men, herself became, as it were, an angel.

Remarkably enough, this angelic mysticism did not lead Teresa to scorn life on earth. All her desire, as she repeatedly said, was to do the divine will, not to be rapt in ecstasy. "The highest perfection," she writes, "consists not in interior favors or in great raptures

[9] Ibid., Vol. II, *Interior Castle*, p. 236.

or in visions or in the spirit of prophecy, but in the bringing of our wills so closely into conformity with the will of God that, as soon as we realize He wills anything, we desire it ourselves with all our might, and take the bitter with the sweet, knowing that to be His Majesty's will." [1] Therefore, precisely because Teresa's whole being was now directed toward the supernatural, she felt a far keener sense of responsibility for her actions in this world.

If proof were still needed that mystical union with God never means sensual or selfish pleasure, Teresa provides it. In her principal work on the mystical life, *The Interior Castle*, she makes herself quite clear on this point: "For if the soul is much with God, as it is right it should be, it will very seldom think of itself; its whole thought will be concentrated upon finding ways to please Him and upon showing Him how it loves Him. This, my daughters, is the aim of prayer; this is the purpose of the spiritual marriage, of which are born good works and good works alone." [2]

This emphasis on good works frees Teresa of any suspicion of quietism. Certain of her statements concerning the prayer of quiet might lead one to see in her one of the first of the quietist mystics, but that conclusion would be wholly erroneous. Teresa consistently maintained that mystical favors imposed corresponding obligations on their recipients, and that Martha's action must be combined with Mary's contemplation if the Lord was to be properly served. Teresa's thirst for action stamps the whole of this second part of her life as a religious. A mysticism that did not lead to good works, she believed, was not genuine mysticism at all; conversely, all works must stem from the mystical life if they were not to degenerate into the aimless activism that spells death to the Christian life.

This balance was admirably realized in her own life; a well-nigh irresistible stream of activity seemed to issue as naturally from her angelic adoration as the fruit from the vine. And because, for her, action and contemplation were mutually interdependent, she could take comfort, in her anguish for the souls of pagan multitudes, in the Lord's words: "Wait a little, daughter, and thou shalt see

[1] Ibid., Vol. III, *Book of the Foundations*, p. 23.
[2] Ibid., Vol. II, *Interior Castle*, p. 346.

great things." [3] For those "great things" were to be the founding of a Carmel—and then of many more—of the primitive observance. This was to be her means of working for the salvation of souls.

She was strengthened in her resolve by a seemingly trivial incident. One evening when some of the nuns of the Incarnation convent were gathered in Teresa's cell for a chat, Teresa began to tell them about the austere lives of the first hermits on Mount Carmel. Suddenly her youthful niece, María de Ocampo, interrupted her in mid-sentence, crying: "Then let us go away, too, all of us here! Let us seek out a place where we can live in solitude, like the hermits! If you feel the courage to live as the discalced Franciscan sisters, we can found a convent!" Teresa regarded this spontaneous reaction of youthful generosity as a heavenly directive, and from that time forward pursued her project with even greater earnestness.

Six months later Teresa was in Toledo, where she made the acquaintance of Mary of Jesus, a pious woman who also desired to found a reformed convent of the order. Mary was not a very impressive person, and she was handicapped by her illiteracy, but she had remarkable zeal for penance. As they talked, she told Teresa more about the earlier Carmelites, and how they had followed a much stricter rule than the one now in force, with much greater emphasis on contemplation. Because nuns in those days received no instruction about the history of their orders, Mary's words were a revelation for Teresa. It suddenly became utterly clear to her that the only remedy for the evil of mediocrity which was sapping the vigor of the order was absolute poverty. She resolved, therefore, that her new foundation should possess no settled revenues, and that it should observe a very strict rule of enclosure—without which, she later wrote, there could be no salvation for communities of women.

Teresa began by laying her plan before her confessor, Fr. Alvarez, who at once raised all kinds of objections. A convent without revenues, whose members would have to live on alms, made no sense to him; it could easily mean exposing the nuns to starvation, for under the new regulations about enclosure they might not beg from door to door. Teresa, however, did not waste time on her con-

[3] Ibid., Vol. III, *Book of the Foundations*, p. 4.

fessor's objections, which she regarded as savoring too much of purely human calculation. Brushing his hesitations aside, she turned with her plan to Fr. Luis Bertrán, who had much greater sympathy with her ideas and who wrote to her: "Now I bid you, in the name of the same Lord, arm yourself with courage to undertake so great an enterprise. He will help and support you in it, and I assure you, as from Him, that before fifty years are out your order will be one of the most famous in the Church, who keeps you in her holy protection." [4]

After such encouragement there could be no more hesitation, and Teresa went forward with her plans with prodigious energy—and also, or so she believed, with discretion. Despite her precautions, however, word leaked out prematurely, and Teresa found herself the butt of her community's displeasure. The sisters of the Incarnation accused her of shameful disloyalty to her convent and of questioning the quality of their religious life. In order, doubtless, to still the voice of their own consciences, they accused Teresa of acting out of a desire for novelty and self-assertion. Teresa, however, bore with their abuse in silence, and held fast to her purpose.

And so it was that a new convent was finally founded, dedicated to St. Joseph, in a small and poorly equipped house purchased through the aid of friends. On her way from her old convent to the new one, an incident occurred which at first glance would hardly appear to deserve notice; Teresa stopped in a church, took off her shoes and cast them in a corner, and instead put on *alpargatas*, the hemp-and-rope sandals of the Spanish poor. Henceforward, Teresa was to live as a discalced Carmelite. The incident symbolizes the renewal of the Carmelite order.

The little convent of St. Joseph was insignificant enough. Was this, then, the sum of the "great things" that Teresa had been promised? No one could have suspected that this small and necessitous community of fewer than half a dozen nuns would play any part in the spiritual renewal of Christendom. Its importance lay in this: that by its very existence it inaugurated the Carmelite reform.

[4] *Butler's Lives of the Saints*, ed. H. Thurston and D. Attwater (New York: P. J. Kenedy & Sons; 1956), IV, 73.

As Teresa put it, God could again "show forth His greatness in these poor weak women." [5] Here, at last, was a Carmel that depended for its daily bread not on any settled revenues, but on the providence of God.

The nuns' only income was from the sale of their handiwork; the price, however, was left to the discretion of the purchaser. They themselves made their brown habits out of coarse cloth, and used old straw-filled sacks for bedding. They permitted neither visiting in one another's cells nor close friendships between sisters. In their uncompromising Christianity they were true spiritual descendants of the first hermits of Mount Carmel, who had sought in their divine madness to storm the gates of heaven.

Teresa was not content with the foundation of a single convent. Barely was one little house ready when she would proceed to establish another. Christ had told her in a vision "that this was no time for me to rest; I was to make haste to found these houses, and He would feel rested when there were souls living in them." [6] In consequence, she traveled from place to place at a well-nigh modern speed, and with a tireless energy reminiscent of St. Paul.

The convents she founded were small—no community was to number more than thirteen—but their establishment cost her untold effort. Even Teresa could not settle everything by the wave of a wand; she had to write every letter in her own hand, arrange for every appointment well in advance. As a result, she was constantly having to embark on long journeys, for which she had always had a strong distaste. It could, indeed, have been no pleasure to travel in Spain in those days, given the terrible state of the roads, especially if one's conveyance was an unsprung wagon and one's way led through seemingly endless and trackless wasteland. Moreover, because of the sharp contrasts in climate between different parts of Spain, Teresa and her companions suffered alternately from scorching heat and piercing cold. Often the travelers would lose their way, and once they were preserved from a disastrous accident only by a miracle. But nothing could dampen Teresa's ardor; she simply

---

[5] *Complete Works of St. Teresa*, Vol. III, *Book of the Foundations*, p. 17.
[6] Ibid., Vol. I, *Spiritual Relations*, p. 338.

recalled the Lord's assurance to her: "Make no account of the cold, for I am true heat." [7]

On these incessant journeyings Teresa was always faithful to the monastic rule. Enclosure was observed by hanging thick curtains over the windows of the conveyance, and when the nuns reached an inn they would remain in their room till it was time for them to go on again, one of them going to the door to receive their food at mealtimes.

To the hardships of travel others were added. For instance, the civic authorities of the places to which she came to make her founda-tions would refuse point-blank to countenance the establishment of convents without fixed revenues, fearing that they might become a charge upon the public purse. Teresa therefore had to overcome their objections, one after another, before she could so much as begin to carry out her plans. And although her health was always very poor—she suffered from various forms of paralysis, rheumatism, and constant nausea—her incredible tenacity enabled her to elimi-nate each successive obstacle.

She showed the same indefatigable energy in regard to the in-ternal organization of her convents. Her visionary gifts were accom-panied by equally astonishing good sense—one is reminded, in this respect, of St. Pachomius, the founder of the first monastery. Her conversation might be in heaven, but this did not remove her from earthly concerns; on the contrary, she retained her marvelous understanding for all things human. She was equally at ease at the washtub and at the kitchen range; in fact, she was a splendid cook, and the sisters were always glad when it was Teresa's turn to pre-pare the meals. No task was too menial for her, but at the same time she never allowed the details of housekeeping to absorb her.

Teresa never lost sight of the principal aim of her foundations, the spiritual welfare of the nuns. She deliberately opposed any merely numerical expansion; convents, she believed, served for the salvation of souls, and nothing else. The prioress, therefore, must not imagine that she could easily read a soul, but must humbly leave its secrets to God, Who alone knows them. Teresa herself had a knowledge of souls which puts modern depth psychology into

[7] Ibid., Vol. III, *Book of the Foundations*, p. 188.

the shade, but she nevertheless believed that it was supremely difficult to understand a soul because the interior life has its variations of climate just like the physical world.

In order to help her nuns follow the hard road of perfection, Teresa wrote a set of maxims for them into which she poured the fruit of all her experience, illumined by grace. She admonished her sisters, for instance, to avoid singularity and never to exaggerate, and: "Do everything as though you really saw His Majesty before you." [8]

Her inspired realism is marvelously exemplified in her instructions for the visitation of convents of Discalced Carmelite nuns. Here Teresa lays great stress on the need for the perfect ordering of every detail of the conventual life. A prioress, she writes, may be very holy yet still incapable of governing a community, and in that case she should simply be removed from office. [9] Any consideration of her feelings would be out of place, for the whole community might suffer from it. The Visitor, she writes further, "should always examine every part of the house to see if proper provision is made for seclusion. For it is well to remove occasions of sin and not to rely too much upon sanctity that is visible." [1] He must inspect the confessionals no less than the parlor grilles; this is a duty, and should not be regarded as evidence of distrust. In addition, "the accounts of the convents must be examined with great care and attention, and the Visitor must not pass them over lightly." [2] Income and expenditure must balance even in a convent. No detail should be overlooked, for "temporal conditions can have a harmful effect on spiritual conditions, and are thus most important." [3]

It is worth remembering that the Teresa who wrote these words was the same Teresa who never prayed for any temporal goods and who always sought the way of greatest perfection. The paradox is only apparent; for Teresa, perfection applied to everything. "It is for this reason," she wrote, "that religious houses, and even re-

[8] Ibid., Vol. III, *Maxims*, p. 257.
[9] Ibid., Vol. III, *Method for the Visitation of Convents of Discalced Carmelite Nuns*, p. 240.
[1] Ibid., p. 242.
[2] Ibid., p. 241.
[3] Ibid., p. 241.

ligious orders, have in some places fallen into ruin: little heed is paid to trifling things, and so they run into great error." [4]

Teresa's sweeping reforms met with violent opposition within the order. For it is probably easier to found a new order than to reform one that has fallen into lax ways, the law of inertia operating in favor of habit, which comes to be regarded as an inalienable right. The Calced Carmelites wished to preserve their accustomed liberties and passionately rejected the idea of following the primitive rule, to which they had not committed themselves on entering the order. They called Teresa a foolish troublemaker, an obstinate and conceited female, a scorner of the Pauline doctrine forbidding women to teach, and so forth. Nor was the opposition merely verbal; some of the contestants actually resorted to force. The conflict between Calced and Discalced Carmelites rocked the order to its foundations, so that their common membership of the order was completely forgotten, to say nothing of the commandment of charity.

The Calced Carmelites resorted to disgraceful machinations, which they were later to recall with shame. The leader of the reforming movement among the friars was thrown into jail, and the nuns who declared themselves in sympathy with the movement were excommunicated. Teresa, too, was temporarily confined in a convent. Her comment on all this is characteristic: "The Lord now showed me what a signal blessing it is to suffer trials and persecution for His sake." [5]

It is a moot point whether the reformers conducted themselves in more Christian fashion than those of the mitigated observance. The Discalced were not all saints, but they certainly tried at first to meet the opposition in a Christian spirit. Nevertheless, they too were soon divided by profound disagreements—the conflict between Nicolas Doria, for instance, and Teresa's devoted collaborator Jerónimo Gracián ended with the latter's expulsion from the order. Even St. John of the Cross was finally relieved of his office by his fellow reformers and cast into a corner—as he himself put it—like an old dishrag.

[4] Ibid., p. 245.
[5] *Complete Works of St. Teresa*, Vol. I, *Life*, p. 225.

The following incident is indicative of the passions aroused by the issue of reform. A provincial of the order, in the course of a visitation, appointed Teresa prioress of the convent of the Incarnation without the consent of the community. When the appointment was announced in chapter, pandemonium broke out. Forgetting the reverence due to the sacred precincts, the nuns jumped up from their seats, weeping and gesticulating in their indignation at this violation of their voting rights. The provincial could not even make himself heard; the uproar was such that several of the nuns fainted. Only Teresa remained calm and collected. She neither defended herself nor played the part of outraged dignity. Instead, at the first opportunity she escaped to the chapel, threw herself down at the altar steps, and prayed: "Lord, I beseech you, give this house peace. Send them another superior who will be less burdensome to them, or else bend their wills to obedience."

The provincial, however, was adamant, and Teresa had to assume the office of prioress. The manner in which she carried out the duties that had thus been laid upon her is yet another revelation of her greatness. Not for a moment did she reproach the nuns for their unseemly behavior or their hostility toward her. Nor did she seek to introduce her strict reforms, as they had feared. Instead, she tried to acquaint herself with every detail of the community's life, to bring the nuns to a realization of the value of the monastic life, and to restore peace.

At the second chapter meeting she set a statue of the Virgin on the raised chair reserved for the prioress, placed the keys of the convent in Mary's hands, and herself took the next seat. Then, without so much as referring to the previous disturbances, she opened the chapter with these words:

"My ladies, mothers and sisters: Our Lord has sent me to this house, by virtue of obedience, to hold this office, which I had never thought of and which I am far from deserving.

"This election has greatly distressed me, both because it has laid upon me a task which I shall be unable to perform, and also because it has deprived you of the freedom of election which you used to enjoy and given you a prioress whom you have not chosen at your will and pleasure, and a prioress who would be accomplishing a great deal if she could succeed in learning from the least of you here all the good that is in her.

"I come solely to serve and please you in every possible way that I can, and I hope that the Lord will greatly assist me to do this—in other respects I could be instructed and improved by anybody. See, then, my ladies, what I can do for each of you; even if it be to give my life-blood, I shall do it with a right good will.

"I am a daughter of this house and a sister of you all. I know the character and the needs of you all, or, at least, of the majority of you, so there will be no necessity for you to make a stranger of a person who is so eminently one of yourselves.

"Have no misgivings as to how I shall govern you, for though I have thus far lived among, and governed, nuns who are Discalced, I know well, through the Lord's goodness, the way to govern those who are not. My desire is that we should all serve the Lord in quietness, and do the little that our rule and constitutions command us for the love of that Lord to Whom we owe so much. I know well how very weak we are; but if we cannot attain in deed, let us attain in desire. For the Lord is compassionate and will see to it that gradually our deeds become commensurate with our desires and intentions." [6]

Clearly, Teresa had the situation well in hand.

Her contemporaries reacted to Teresa either with boundless admiration or with violent hostility. Only three weeks before she died, the prioress of one of her convents showed her the door, and at about the same time another prioress treated her in so unfriendly a manner that she spent only one night in the convent and left the following morning, fasting, and greatly weakened by illness, fatigue, and undernourishment. A few days later she arrived half dead at the convent at Alba and at once went to bed. She knew that death awaited her here, and she longed for it because it would bring her to complete and definitive union with her Lord. She would have wished, of course, to die in her first foundation, the convent of St. Joseph at Avila, but she considered it presumption to express such a wish, and when someone asked her whether she wished her body to be taken to Avila, she replied: "Is that for me to decide? Have

[6] Ibid., Vol. III, Appendix III, pp. 337, 338.

I anything of my own? Will they not give me a little earth here?" [7]

The sixty-seven-year-old woman who now lay dying had indeed seen "great things." She had founded eighteen convents; she had launched the reform of an order. Yet her achievements were not a source of pride or self-satisfaction to her. On the contrary, she was filled with a sense of her own unworthiness, and her final exhortation to the nuns assembled around her sickbed echoed her profound contrition. "My daughters and ladies," she said to them, "forgive me for the bad example I have set you, and do not imitate me, who have been the greatest sinner in the world and the most lax member of the order in keeping the constitutions. I beg you, for the love of God, to observe them perfectly and to obey your superiors. If you do this, as you are bound to do, no other miracles will be required for your canonization." [8]

There was no false modesty about this confession. Teresa was far too brilliantly endowed to serve as a model for the cloistered nun. This great ascetic, with her doctrine of silence and withdrawal from the world, was constantly involved in talking, writing, exhorting, persuading. We have only to recall her delightful relations with children, her love for artistically executed handicrafts, her countless dealings with persons outside the cloister. No one was better aware of the contradiction between the monastic life on the one hand and the effervescent natural disposition of a Teresa on the other. Those last words were an expression of her inherent honesty and of that deep sense of reality which comes at death to those whose souls have really been moved by God. On October 4, 1582, Teresa was caught up in an ecstasy, her face "glowing and shining like the sun," [9] and in that ecstasy she died.

What is Teresa's permanent significance—for our times as well as for her own? Some discussion of the question might be not unprofitable.

Teresa was given this threefold encomium while she was yet alive: that she was beautiful, intelligent, and holy. Regarding the

[7] *Minor Works of St. Teresa*, tr. Benedictines of Stanbrook (London: Thomas Baker; 1913), pp. 213, 214.

[8] Ibid., p. 211.

[9] Ibid., p. 215.

first two qualities, she admitted that she had once believed in them, adding that this had been great vanity on her part; as to the third, however, she had never succumbed to that delusion. The comment is typical of Teresa's matter-of-fact attitude toward herself; she could analyze herself without indulging in any form of egocentrism.

She was unquestionably beautiful in her youth, with her black curls and flashing eyes, and she was much admired. She also knew how to handle such admiration; the story is told, for instance, that once, when a man complimented her on her dainty feet, which he had glimpsed as she was getting into a carriage, she replied with great equanimity: "Take a good look, sir, for this is the last time you will see them!"

As she grew older, she lost her beauty—she became stouter, and her lower lip tended to droop—but only to acquire another, inner loveliness that made her even more attractive. The spiritual life that she cultivated with such tender care gave her a marvelous radiance; she became, as it were, the living representation of a soul that has received the Kingdom for its portion. In her we see something of metaphysical beauty, and so she leads us back to a truth which we are all too prone to ignore: that beauty is a reflection of God Himself.

As to intelligence, Teresa gave any number of proofs of her possession of that quality, which she also valued very highly in others. Once, when the mother of a postulant was expatiating on her daughter's great devotion, Teresa asked her whether the girl also had good sense, and added: "Even though our Lord should give this young girl devotion and teach her contemplation, if she has no sense she never will come to have any, and instead of being of use to the community, she will be a burden." [1] And a learned contemporary of hers, Fr. de Castro, admitted that he would rather argue with all the theologians than with "Mother Teresa."

Hers was not the intellectual slickness that spreads a mortal chill around it, but rather a warm and stimulating good judgment. Eternal wisdom spoke through Teresa, and her writings reveal spiritual depths that are still unplumbed. Although she did her writing in a cell without a table or chair, and although, as she said, her head felt too weak to permit her to read through what she had written, her

[1] *Butler's Lives of the Saints*, IV, 120.

language has the evocative power of great poetry. Such works can proceed only from rare natural intelligence enlightened by a super-intelligence beyond human understanding. Teresa's works are the immediate fruit of her prayer, and may be called inspired; by her own admission, she did not seek to know what she had written, setting words to paper as though they were not her own.

Finally, there is the question of her holiness. Teresa was not born a saint; she had to pull herself painfully out of the slough of mediocrity before she could attain to holiness. Even then, as she put it dryly, it was only a semi-holiness—without feet or a head! Her denial of the attribute is no argument against her possession of it, however, but rather the reverse. Above all, she was free from any posturing; she was not given to gazing heavenward with rapt expression, and she was genuinely pleased when someone told her: "Maybe you are a saint, but you don't look like one to me!"

Teresa's holiness took nothing away from her gay femininity. She loved to laugh, and her infectious humor triumphed over many a difficult problem. And as she lived always in joy, so she desired her sisters "to have a reasonable amount of enjoyment." [2]

This was the woman who restored the Carmelite order to its primitive austerity—a woman who could laugh, who could dance to the sound of the tambourine, whose mind was open to every facet of reality. The paradox is not susceptible of merely rational explanation; it is bound up with the extraordinary richness of Teresa's nature and with her sense of chivalry, which impelled her to seek high adventure, to make generous decisions. Pettiness could find no place in a heart filled with such "holy temerity"; and she dearly loved the words of the psalmist: "Thou hast enlarged my heart" (Ps. cxix, 32). Nor was there any conventional "this is not done" about her actions. The clue to the mystery lies in the "glorious folly" that had captivated her soul, so that she could write to her confessor: "I beseech your Reverence, let us all be mad, for the love of Him Who was called mad for our sakes." [3]

Fr. Luis de León, Spain's greatest lyricist, paid this tribute to

---

[2] *The Letters of Saint Teresa of Jesus*, ed. E. Allison Peers (Westminster, Md.: The Newman Press; 1952), II, 721.

[3] *Complete Works of St. Teresa*, Vol. I, *Life*, p. 99.

Teresa in his first edition of her works: "It is a miracle in itself that one woman alone should have restored perfection to a whole order, both of men and of women." [4] It is the more extraordinary in that women in sixteenth-century Spain possessed so little freedom of movement. For the most part, they were confined to their houses, whose windows looked out upon ornamental inner courtyards and were shuttered to the street. And as far as religion was concerned, their position was defined by the scriptural teaching that women must be silent in church.

Teresa was only too conscious of all these impediments, but she did not let them distress her. Her contemporary, Fr. Hernández, said of her that she was much more manly than any man he had ever known, but the epithet is not a happy one; Teresa was first and last a woman, and it was precisely as a woman and a nun that she brought her great work to fruition.

There is a quality of greatness about a true nun. And this quality may be posited not only of the nun who tends her suffering fellow men in hospitals for no other reward than God's approval, and whose merit is universally recognized, but also, and perhaps even more, of the woman who spends her whole life in an enclosed convent, having renounced human love in order to give all the powers of her heart to Christ. As the bride of Christ, she wears her veil every day of her life, unlike her sister in the world who wears it only on her wedding day. In her readiness for sacrifice, she has transcended time, and may therefore fittingly be called the "eternal woman."

There could be no more striking illustration of this truth than the one afforded by St. Teresa of Avila. By her own admission, she had been profoundly hostile, in her youth, to the very notion of being a nun, yet in fact she ennobled the cloistered life for all time and earned it widespread esteem. Teresa channeled all her powers heavenward. Not that she did less combat with the Evil One than St. Anthony of Egypt, for instance, but hers was essentially an upward movement. She literally threw herself into the arms of the eternal. Her visions and ecstasies are, above all, symbols of this angelic flight. She was a supremely strong woman, totally directed

[4] Ibid., Vol. III, Appendix VII, p. 369.

to eternity; that, indeed, is what has earned her the regal title of "the seraphic nun."

She stands before us, like a seraph in human form, revealing her deepest secrets for our instruction. We read—and rightly—the works of Dostoevsky and Kafka, of Pascal and Kierkegaard, but why do we not steep ourselves in Teresa's writings? A serious Christian approach is hardly possible without her guidance. Not that she offers a mystical system; she simply directs our attention to the spiritual substructure of all things. "I certainly find secret things in ourselves," she writes concerning the human soul, "which often amaze me—and how many more there must be!" [5]

But with all her emphasis on the interior life, Teresa never sank into mere subjectivism, being ever mindful of the divine command: "Seek thyself in Me!" She returns constantly to the problem of man's soul and to God's mysterious relationship with the soul. The marvel of it overwhelmed her, and no one could speak with greater understanding of the nature of the spirit which God has breathed into man, and which becomes intelligible only when seen in its dependence upon its Creator. "O Jesus, how wonderful it is when two souls understand each other!" she wrote in one of her letters.[6]

Teresa herself possessed rare spiritual perception, and her works convey an overpowering sense of the reality of the spirit. The immortality of the soul is borne in upon one with complete certainty; the soul's divine origin ensures that it shall not simply vanish like a puff of smoke. And is not this conviction something that modern man needs desperately to recapture?

There is a final aspect of Teresa's personality and action which we must touch upon as having significance for ourselves—her reaction to the events of her own times. The seraphic nun, enlightened by her visionary experience, saw deep into the tragedy of her age; with horror she recognized the demonic forces at work in her stormy century, and the infinite need of Christendom.

We can draw many parallels between our own twentieth century and the war-torn sixteenth century of Teresa, its blood-red sky portending the destruction of a civilization. But whereas our

---

[5] Ibid., Vol. II, *Interior Castle*, p. 237.
[6] *The Letters of Saint Teresa of Jesus*, I, 368.

own judgment is often confined to externals, Teresa looked into the substance of things. It seemed to her that heresy was like a raging fire seeking to destroy the Church, to profane the Sacrament. Jesus is crucified anew! she cried in anguish. "O Christians, it is time to defend your King and to stand by Him in His great loneliness. For very few of His liegemen have remained faithful to Him, whereas following Lucifer there is a great multitude. And, what is worse, they declare themselves His friends in public, yet secretly betray Him: there is scarcely one whom He can trust." [7]

Although, as a cloistered nun, Teresa was too much withdrawn from the world to have an accurate over-all picture of the situation, she had an intuitive perception, enlightened by grace, of the deepest need of her times—personal experience of the divine. While most of the protagonists in the great struggles of her day were arguing with all the panoply of sterile erudition concerning the need for a root-and-branch reform, this woman penetrated to the central problem: a return to the Source. This alone, she believed, could prevent the impending cataclysm.

Teresa was not content merely to diagnose the malady of her times. She believed the remedy to be the creation of "interior castles"; what, she asked, would become of the world if God did not spare it for the sake of those who consecrated themselves to Him in religious orders? If we do not understand this question, we shall never understand Carmel. It may be restated thus: God has mercy on Christendom for the sake of the monks and nuns who are making atonement, who have withdrawn from the world in order the better to intercede for the world. This was the conviction that prompted Teresa to exhort her fellow religious to further expiatory endeavor. Like a Christian Deborah, she summoned a Christendom sunk in apathy to renewed battle:

> *All ye who with our Master fight,*
> *And 'neath His banner take your stand,*
> *Oh, sleep not, sleep not, 'tis not night:*
> *There is no peace in all the land.* [8]

---

[7] *Complete Works of St. Teresa*, II, 410.
[8] *Ibid.*, Vol. III, *Poems*, no. 29, p. 309.

Through her monastic foundations, Teresa sought to erect im-
pregnable fortresses for God which would be able to resist all the
forces of disintegration. The Carmels were to be strongholds of
Christian mysticism: "I would the evil were not so great and I did
not see more souls being lost every day. O, my sisters in Christ!
Help me to entreat this of the Lord, who has brought you together
here for that very purpose. This is your vocation this must be your
business; these must be your desires; these your tears; these your
petitions. . . . The world is on fire. Men try to condemn Christ
once again, as it were, for they bring a thousand false witnesses
against Him. They would raze His Church to the ground—and
are we to waste our time upon things which, if God were to grant
them, would perhaps bring one soul less to Heaven? No, my
sisters, this is no time to treat with God for things of little importance." [9]

Teresa wanted no sumptuous buildings for her new convents,
which would only crumble to the ground in the wrath to come,[1]
and she deliberately established houses that were small, poor, and
unprotected. Still less did she look for help to the "secular arm,"
like the Church in the Middle Ages. Here we have another instance of her essentially evangelical approach: any reliance on force
was ruled out *a priori*. She relied solely on the defenselessness of a
life of pure prayer. This conviction of the spiritual power of weakness is one more lifeline that Teresa extends to humanity in its
present peril; this, then, is the final aspect of her significance for
our times.

II

The Carmelite order traces its descent back to the prophet Elias,
a highly controversial claim that has been rejected as historically
untenable. As a symbol, however, it is most apt; Carmel takes its
motto from Elias's words: "I have been very jealous for the Lord
God of hosts" (I Kings, xix, 10), and in Carmel's cloisters there
dwells that zeal in the service of God which consumed the prophet.

[9] Ibid., Vol. II, *Way of Perfection*, pp. 4, 5.   [1] Ibid., pp. 8, 9.

According to the oldest historical account, Bertold of Calabria founded the first Carmel in Palestine in 1155. Little is known about this first foundation, and not much more about Bertold's successor, Brocardus. We know, however, that Brocardus requested the Patriarch of Jerusalem, Albert, for a rule, and that this rule was confirmed by Pope Honorius III in 1226.

What is significant about these meager details is the fact of Carmel's Eastern origins. Eastern Christianity put its seal on Carmel, and this non-European ancestry explains many of the characteristics of the order.

The order had flourished in Palestine for less than a century when its monasteries fell before the onslaught of the Saracens. Only a few of the monks escaped the carnage and made their way to the West, where at first they were looked upon askance and had some trouble finding a monastic habitation. The migration created other problems for the order, too, which an English hermit, Simon Stock, was largely instrumental in resolving by obtaining the Pope's approval for a rule more suited to Western conditions. From then on, the Carmelites were a mendicant order, exercising pastoral duties at the side of the secular clergy. Simon, however, who eventually became the general of the order, never lost sight of its original eremitical character, and in his own person constituted a strong counterweight to the new trend. It was to Simon, too, that the Virgin appeared, bestowing upon him the scapular, the shoulder garment that to this day is worn by every member of the order, and which symbolizes Carmel's particular devotion to Mary.

Through its contact with the universities, the order continued to lose its primitive eremitical and contemplative character. Imperceptibly it grew more lax in its observance until finally, in February 1432, at the request of a general chapter of the order, Pope Eugenius IV formally sanctioned a mitigation of the rule. This mitigation affected primarily the regulations concerning solitude, fasting, and abstinence. Twenty years later the first Carmel for women was founded, but the event did not infuse new life into the order, having issued from the spirit of the modified rule.

Teresa of Avila lifted the order out of its lethargy and opened up a new era. For the order, therefore, Teresa's significance is even greater than that of the founder, whose personality, in any case, is shrouded in the mists of time. Teresa redirected the order, restoring it to its origins and at the same time making possible its further expansion.

Another person who contributed very considerably to the reform of the order was Juan de Yepes, better known as St. John of the Cross. Teresa's reform would probably not have had such wide repercussions had it remained confined to the communities of women. The male communities had to be associated in the reform, and this was the task that the young John of the Cross undertook, with Teresa's encouragement.

Their friendship was based perforce on conversations at the parlor grille; nevertheless, in their spiritual unity they are reminiscent of St. Francis and St. Clare. Both by nature and by temperament they were as unalike as possible; in their monastic ideal, however, they were as one. On either side the relationship was purely practical and disinterested, yet in their mystical ardor they felt a strong attraction toward each other. Once, as they were talking together at the parlor grille, they were both caught up in ecstasy, to the consternation of a nun who chanced to enter the parlor at the time. This simultaneous rapture may be regarded as symbolic of the unity of Teresa of Jesus and John of the Cross.

St. John of the Cross was a mystic and a poet whose exquisite verse reveals his inmost aspirations. More than anything else, he was the man of silence: "The greatest necessity we have is to be silent before this great God with the desire and with the tongue, for the language which He alone hears is the silent language of love." [2] John of the Cross believed it impossible to make spiritual progress without wrapping oneself in silence, which he regarded as a condition *sine qua non*, not as a distinct virtue.

A modern Carmelite writes of St. John of the Cross that he saw the world irradiated in a supernatural light because the Incarnate Word had looked upon it. [3] For proof, we have only to read such verses as these:

[2] *Complete Works of St. John of the Cross*, ed. E. Allison Peers (Westminster, Md.: The Newman Press; 1951), III, 272, 273.

[3] François de Sainte-Marie: *Initiation à Saint Jean de la Croix* (Paris: Aux Editions du Seuil; 1945).

O woods and thickets
Planted by the hand of the Beloved!
O meadow of verdure, enameled with flowers,
Say if he has passed by you!
Scattering a thousand graces,
He passed through these groves in haste,
And, looking upon them as he went,
Left them, by his glance alone, clothed with beauty.[4]

But John of the Cross did not remain seated at the "table of creatures." His soul longed for union with the eternal, and to fulfill this longing he undertook that laborious "ascent of Mount Carmel" which involves a complete reversal of human thought and feeling. It begins with the "dark night," into which he entered and which led him to formulate these staggering precepts: "Strive always to choose, not that which is easiest, but that which is most difficult; not that which is most delectable, but that which is most unpleasing; not that which gives most pleasure, but rather that which gives least. . . ."[5]

Neither his artistic temperament nor his mystical absorption prevented him from throwing himself wholeheartedly into the movement for the reform of the Carmelite order. For his efforts in behalf of the monastic ideal he suffered severe penalties in a prison in Toledo, but none of this could modify his resolution. At Duruelo he founded a monastery in which the friars lived, under unbelievably primitive conditions, according to the constitutions of the Discalced. Teresa visited the monastery on one of her journeys, and thus describes her impression: "I went into the little church and was amazed to see what spirituality the Lord had inspired there. And I was not alone in this, for two merchants, who were friends of mine, and had come as far as this with me from Medina, did nothing but weep. There were so many crosses about, and so many skulls! I have never forgotten one little wooden cross, above the holy water, on which was stuck a piece of paper with a picture of

---

[4] *Complete Works of St. John of the Cross*, Vol. II, *Spiritual Canticle*, stanzas 4, 5.
[5] Ibid., Vol. I, *Ascent of Mount Carmel*, p. 61.

Christ: it seemed to inspire greater devotion than if it had been a crucifix of the finest workmanship." [6]

This little picture of Christ pasted on a wooden cross can be regarded as an image of the reformed Carmel. Instead of the accumulations of art treasures which had been a feature of the earlier monasteries, there rose from these humble buildings the searing flame of divine love, which both consumed and replaced all earthly goods.

The Discalced Carmelite order bears the clear stamp of its Hispanic origins, yet it was not a merely national phenomenon, and it soon spread far beyond the Pyrenees. Its first home outside Spain was France, to which it came, characteristically enough, in consequence of a vision. The visionary in this case was Barbe Acarie, a well-born and very devout French lady to whom St. Teresa appeared, commanding her to bring the reformed Carmel to France. Not surprisingly, Mme. Acarie was considerably frightened by the commission; nevertheless, thanks to her connections, she succeeded in arranging for an embassy to leave for Spain under the direction of Cardinal Bérulle. After lengthy and troublesome negotiations, the strange caravan returned with six Spanish nuns, headed by the venerable Anne of Jesus, who had been personally associated with both St. Teresa and St. John of the Cross.

Anne lacked Teresa's unique holiness, and the French nuns groaned at first under her stern rule, but her intimate knowledge of the spirit of the reformed Carmel made her the person best fitted for the task, and she soon gave evidence of her considerable ability. Under her supervision, the first community of Discalced Carmelite nuns in Paris came into being in 1604, and other foundations followed shortly thereafter in other parts of France and in Flanders. Barbe Acarie entered the order after her husband's death, but not as a choir nun; she preferred to be a simple lay sister and to perform the most menial duties in the Carmel that she had helped to create in France.

The migration from Spain to France involved a certain risk, for it meant that the Carmelite nuns, who were the first of the order to

[6] *Complete Works of St. Teresa*, Vol. III, *Book of the Foundations*, p. 66.

leave Spain, were placing themselves under non-Carmelite spiritual direction. Fortunately, Cardinal Bérulle, a man of prayer and great piety, himself assumed the direction of the new community and introduced no alien conceptions. The French Carmel stood the test marvelously well, and exercised a profound influence over a country rent asunder by calamitous wars of religion.

Communities of Discalced Carmelite friars soon followed. An outstanding product of the French Carmel was Brother Lawrence of the Resurrection, who joined the Paris community as a lay brother in the second quarter of the sixteenth century. His "conversion" at the age of eighteen had been precipitated, as he told a friend, by his realization of God's providence: "One winter day he noticed a tree stripped of its leaves, and reflected that before long leaves would appear anew, then flowers, and then the fruit, and this consideration gave him so striking an idea of the providence and might of God that it had never since been effaced from his soul." [7] Some of his sayings and letters were collected and published after his death under the title *The Practice of the Presence of God.*

For the humble lay brother, prayer was the consciousness of the continual presence of God. This realization never left him, whether he was cooking eggs in the kitchen or kneeling in the sanctuary. In order to be with God, he said, it was not necessary to remain constantly in church; man's heart, too, could be his oratory. "I have given up all devotions and pieties that are not of obligation, and instead try to keep myself always in God's holy presence by simple attentiveness and a loving gaze upon Him." [8]

Brother Lawrence experienced neither visions nor ecstasies; his spirituality, nonetheless, in its very simplicity, is essentially Carmelite. He made no attempt to achieve intellectual brilliance either in his conversations or in his writings, and this, too, is in the spirit of the order and reminiscent, indeed, of the Gospels. His little book is extraordinarily consoling precisely because he himself, through his constant communion with God, had found the joyous peace of para-

[7] Brother Lawrence of the Resurrection: *The Practice of the Presence of God* (London: Burns, Oates & Washbourne; 1948), p. 1.
[8] Ibid., pp. 29, 30.

dise even in this life. To the man who earnestly seeks to live a religious life, Brother Lawrence gives this advice: "We should try unceasingly to allow each one of our actions to become a moment of communion with God: not a studied act, but just as it comes from purity and simplicity of heart." [9] And elsewhere he writes: "If I were a preacher, I would preach nothing else but the practice of the presence of God." [1]

Brother Lawrence was a contemporary of Descartes, who did so much to wrench humanity from its moorings by his philosophy of skepticism. The humble lay brother, by contrast, hidden though he was from the affairs of the world, offered Christians their firmest support in life by his conception of prayer as attention to the presence of God.

Since the Teresian reform, the women Carmelites have played an even more significant part in the life of the order than the men. Not because the order is more especially suited to women; the reason is simply that the nuns have been able to remain closer to the teachings of St. Teresa and St. John of the Cross than the friars, whose pastoral duties make it impossible for them to lead a truly eremitical life.

Let us look a little more closely at some of these Carmelite nuns.

Italy, in the latter part of the sixteenth century, gave Carmel an extraordinary mystic, Mary Magdalen dei Pazzi. She entered the Florentine Carmel at a very early age, and was granted remarkable visions. Once, for forty mornings in succession, she was rapt in ecstasy, and conversed with the Almighty, while her sisters, unknown to her, wrote down her words. During these ecstasies, which lasted several hours at a time, Mary Magdalen felt nothing, her appearance was completely altered, and her weight increased so greatly that her companions were unable to move her.

And yet the essential thing about this Florentine nun was not her raptures, indicative though they were of marvelous grace, but her burning devotion to the divine love. "O Love," she would cry, "love is not loved, not known by His own creatures. O my Jesus! If I had a voice sufficiently loud and strong to be heard in every

---

[9] Ibid., p. 53.　　　　[1] Ibid., p. 23.

part of the world, I would cry out to make this love known, loved, and honored by all men as the one immeasurable good." [2] Christ, for her, was pain and assuagement, labor and repose, and her love for Christ affected even her bodily health. Yet she was no *exaltée*, and her ecstasies did not prevent her from fulfilling her monastic duties in exemplary fashion. She arrived at a state of inwardness in which it became absolutely indifferent to her, as she said, whether she was told to go to choir or to perform some distracting task; indeed, she affirmed, she was able to find God more easily in external activity than in prayer itself.

Mary Magdalen's holiness is attested, finally, in her mortal remains, which to this day have remained incorrupt.

The thirst for martyrdom which characterizes Carmel is not an effect of romantic enthusiasm. It is a sentiment directed to deeds, not words, as the sixteen Carmelite sisters of Compiègne so gloriously demonstrated at the time of the French Revolution.

Defying the decree issued during the Reign of Terror forbidding all religious practices, these Carmelites continued to live the monastic life in the world after the dissolution of their convent. No threat could move them because it was their belief that the continued existence of Carmel was justified only by a readiness for total sacrifice. They were all arrested and thrown into jail, where they received their death sentences with joyful faces. On the day of their execution they were driven through the streets of Paris in a tumbril, erect, hands bound behind their backs, loudly reciting their prayers; they made a deep impression on the gaping crowd. They sang as they mounted the scaffold, laid their heads upon the block without constraint, and died for Carmel. The bodies of the martyrs of Compiègne were thrown into a lime kiln, but their heroic death ensured the continuation of Carmel in France.

The religious ardor of Carmel has remained undimmed right up to our own day, as evidenced by a number of outstanding Carmelites of relatively recent times. The best known, perhaps, is St. Theresa of the Child Jesus, whose *Story of a Soul* has given rise to two contradictory but equally erroneous portrayals of her. At first she was presented as a figure of almost saccharine sweetness;

[2] *Butler's Lives of the Saints*, II, 418.

now there is so much emphasis on her theological significance that the real Theresa is again in danger of becoming obscured. Both approaches miss the essential point: the complete self-mastery that Theresa achieved by means of her childlike purity. Her teaching was of the "little way," the way that consists not of doing extra-ordinary things but of doing ordinary things extraordinarily well. This young Carmelite declared that of herself she had not the power to merit eternal life in heaven, and that she stood empty-handed before God. Here she touched on the deepest mystery of Christianity—everything is an effect of grace. She died very young, after a protracted illness and in great pain, which she endured with exemplary courage, promising on her deathbed to spend her heaven doing good on earth.

III

The convents of the Discalced Carmelites cultivate their own char-acteristic spirit, which, it has been said, reaches majestically, per-suasively, often almost compellingly, almost seductively, toward the invisible, toward the mystery behind the veil.[3] The life is one of utter austerity, yet it exercises an extraordinary attraction. Anything savoring of womanish sentimentality is strictly ruled out. St. Teresa, for instance, after urging her daughters to avoid the use of certain "loving expressions" as being too effeminate, continues: "I should not like you to be that, or even to appear to be that, in any way. . . . I want you to be strong men. If you do all that is in you, the Lord will make you so manly that men themselves will be amazed at you." [4] Neither pampering nor sensibility is compatible with the mysticism that thrives in Carmel's bare cells. Again, St. John of the Cross writes that the Carmelite has entered the cloister in order to become holy, and that he must not, therefore, tolerate in his soul anything that does not lead to holiness.

The spirit of Carmel is immediately in evidence in the furnishing of the cell, which is a small room with an uncurtained window. A

[3] *Schwester Elisabeth von der Dreifaltigkeit* (1952), p. 6.
[4] *Complete Works of St. Teresa*, Vol. II, *Way of Perfection*, p. 35.

sack of straw resting on a wooden board supported by two blocks
serves as a bed, and it is covered with woolen blankets. The rest
of the inventory consists of a wooden stool, a water pitcher, a sew-
ing-basket, and a plain trestle.

Even more significant than this wretched furnishing is the naked
cross that hangs on the bare wall. This cross is a compelling symbol;
it is an invitation to the Carmelite to nail herself to the gibbet.
Truly a terrifying invitation, yet one that expresses the very essence
of Carmel. The mystical nuptials between the soul and Christ are
accomplished in the night of the cross; that is the truth taught by the
naked cross that overshadows Carmel, reminding all who look
upon it that they must fill up in their own bodies what is wanting
in the sufferings of Christ (Col. i, 24).

The naked cross also signifies solitude. "Alone with the Alone"—
these words accompany the novice to her cell. Carmelite solitude
is a lesson to which the nun must apply herself her whole life long.
"For the whole manner of life we are trying to live," writes St.
Teresa, "is making us, not only nuns, but hermits, and leading us to
detachment from all things created." [5] The Constitutions contain
strict provisions concerning the solitary life with God. Carmel is a
desert, and he who enters it buries himself in God. It is a hard thing
to enter into the living silence, and the solitariness of the Carmelite,
in life and in death, is almost unimaginable. Yet it is not solely a
thing of bitterness and horror. The daughter of Carmel is battling
her way through to an inner solitude of heart in which she can find
her beatitude, which is God. That is why she reverently kisses the
floor of her solitary cell each time she goes in or out.

With solitude goes silence. In Carmel there is little time for
talking. Only rarely during the year may the nuns visit one another
in their cells, like the desert fathers of old. St. John of the Cross
writes: "One word spake the Father, which Word was His Son,
and this Word He speaks ever in eternal silence, and in silence must
it be heard by the soul." [6] This metaphysical justification of silence,
in its turn, is bound up with the naked cross.

---

[5] Ibid., p. 56.
[6] *Complete Works of St. John of the Cross*, Vol. III, *Points of Love*,
p. 251.

With solitude and silence goes poverty. Not a vestige of comfort is tolerated in Carmel. The foundress even objected, at first, to the practice of admitting lay sisters, and today three such sisters at most are permitted to serve any single community. Apart from the dowry that a nun brings with her, the monastic family lives on alms, for which it does not beg, but waits till they are brought. The Carmel eschews all decoration; its furnishings are of the umost simplicity and sobriety. The nuns eat their meals from earthenware bowls, using wooden spoons and sitting at a bare refectory board. Flowers are used only to adorn the altar. The fundamental aim is always to recapture the spirit of the first Carmel, and in this connection we might recall these words of St. Teresa:

"O God, how little have buildings and outward comforts to do with the inward life of the soul! For love of Him I beg you, my sisters and fathers, never to be other than very modest in this matter of large and sumptuous houses. Let us bear in mind our true founders, those holy fathers from whom we are descended, for we know it was the road of poverty and humility which they took that led them to the fruition of God. I have really seen greater spirituality, and even inward joy, in places where there has seemed to be no kind of physical comfort at all than later on, when there has been a large house and comfort in abundance." [7]

As in all religious orders, great emphasis is placed on obedience. St. Teresa gives this example ot the way obedience was practiced in her convents: "On one occasion [the nuns] were all looking at a pond in the garden and the prioress said to them, of a nun who was standing close by: 'What would she do if I told her to throw herself in?' She had hardly spoken when the sister was in the water, with the result that she had to go and change her habit." [8] The incident smacks of comedy, but it illustrates the importance the Carmelite attaches to obedience. The Carmelite is one who submits to obedience in all circumstances; she lives her conviction that from obedience there flows the strength by which she can surpass herself.

Solitude and silence, poverty and obedience—all these are fruits

---

[7] *Complete Works of St. Teresa*, Vol. III, *Book of the Foundations*, pp. 65, 66.
[8] Ibid., p. 77.

of the naked cross. They are bound together in suffering, which the Carmelite deliberately takes upon herself. Teresa herself uttered this almost superhuman prayer: "To die, Lord, or to suffer! I ask nothing of Thee for myself but this." [9] Those who choose to live in Carmel are not simply lost in admiration of the divine mystery—an attitude of wonder that marks every religious awakening—they go a great step further. What we find in Carmel is the desire to share in the passion of Christ, to be nailed with Him to the cross.

The soul that has become a Host—the expression is that of another nineteenth-century Carmelite, Mary of Jesus—suffers with a joyous readiness for suffering: "To be strong in suffering," she writes, "we must know how to keep it between God and ourselves. Jesus held His peace: that is what made His pain so majestic. Let us make ourselves strong Carmelites, silent and rejoicing under Christ's cross." [1] The Carmelite sets out deliberately to offer herself in sacrifice. Instead of grasping at life for herself, she loses it and prays: "Help me, Lord, to forget myself completely." All her striving is to overcome herself: "Yes, I believe that the secret of peace and happiness is to forget oneself, to cease to be concerned with oneself." [2]

The naked cross of Carmel conceals a terrible reality. For what Carmel offers is an experimental knowledge of the cross, and not merely a "theology of the cross" as against a "theology of glory." It is a daily following of the road to Calvary. St. John of the Cross gives us the key to the mystery: "In order to arrive at having pleasure in everything, desire to have pleasure in nothing. In order to arrive at possessing everything, desire to possess nothing. In order to arrive at being everything, desire to be nothing. In order to arrive at knowing everything, desire to know nothing. . . ." [3]

But Carmel's stark doctrine of total detachment—to enjoy nothing, to possess nothing, to know nothing, to be nothing—must not

[9] Complete Works of St. Teresa, Vol. I, Life, p. 297.

[1] A Carmelite of the Sacred Heart, tr. M. E. Arendrug (New York: Benziger; 1923), p. 120.

[2] Sister Elizabeth of the Trinity: Praise of Glory, tr. Benedictines of Stanbrook (New York: Benziger; 1914), p. 73.

[3] Complete Works of St. John of the Cross, Vol. I, Ascent of Mount Carmel, pp. 62, 63.

blind us to that other part of its teaching—to enjoy all, to possess all, to know all, to be all—which is the whole purpose of detach- ment. For Carmel's aim is not negation as such, but affirmation; "no" is but the threshold to the loftiest "yes." This other side of Carmel is bathed in light; indeed, were it not so, there would not be so strong an accent on the joy that comes through pain. The cross hangs naked, indeed, upon the bare wall of the cell, but its ulti- mate meaning, for the Carmelite, is deliverance.

This joy in salvation is most fully expressed in the prayer that is central to the life of Carmel. Carmel is a citadel of prayer; its whole duty is uninterrupted prayer for others and in place of others. "It is the prayer of agony which saves the world," wrote Mary of Jesus. "Our prayers, even in great suffering, never leave us without a divine strength." [4] Prayer is the substance of Carmel, the justifica- tion for its existence. In prayer—not in ecstasy—the creature at- tains to union with the Creator. Brother Lawrence, for instance, told a friend that "it was a great delusion to imagine that prayer-time should be different from any other, for we are equally bound to be united to God by work at work-time as by prayer at prayer-time." [5] And Sister Elizabeth of the Trinity wrote with no less conviction: "A Carmelite's life is a communing with God from morning till night and from night till morning. If He did not fill our cells and our cloisters, how empty they would be! But we see Him through all, for we bear Him within us, and our life is an anticipated heaven." [6]

The consciousness of the indwelling of the Trinity in the souls of men—this is the secret of Carmel, this the blessedness that flows from the naked cross. And the fruit of this abiding presence of God is an outpouring of love that fills everything. The Carmelite knows the meaning of the burning love of God. Faith is not enough; above all else, man must love. "At eventide they will examine thee in love," wrote St. John of the Cross. [7] Theresa of the Child Jesus, for instance, regarded it as her vocation to love; she knew of no

[4] *A Carmelite of the Sacred Heart,* p. 125.
[5] Brother Lawrence of the Resurrection: op. cit., p. 15.
[6] Sister Elizabeth of the Trinity: op. cit., p. 21.
[7] *Complete Works of St. John of the Cross,* Vol. III, *Spiritual Sentences and Maxims,* p. 247.

other means to perfection than love, she sought no other knowledge than that of love. Mary of Jesus expressed the same thought very clearly: "In a Carmelite, love takes the place of all else. . . . One is a Carmelite in order to love our Lord to the point of folly, and to let all the rest go. . . . We were made to love more than others; it is to love more that we are here." [8]

The Carmelite proves her love by her constant dying to self, and she longs for the death that will bring her to perfect union with Christ. But this stern spirit of expiation is wholly unmixed with gloom, for Carmel enjoys the happiness that flows from divine love. Sadness, in Carmelite thought, signifies preoccupation with self; he who abides in God abides in joy. "Spiritual joy," to quote Mary of Jesus again, "is the radiance of love, it is the flower of charity, it is the delight of him who loves and of him who is loved. . . . Joy gives wings to the soul, raising it above the earth, its trials and its sufferings, to soar to God alone." [9]

This inextinguishable joy of love fires the apostolic zeal that reigns in these secluded cloisters. To save souls: that was the second compelling reason—the first being personal salvation—which motivated the reformers of Carmel. But the astonishing thing about the Carmelite apostolate is the manner in which it is conducted. Carmel sends out no missionaries; it has no confidence in human activism, and even refrains expressly from taking part in the Catholic Action movement sponsored by Rome. For the Carmelites, the salvation of Christendom will come through prayer and penance. The Carmelite apostolate can be defined only by a paradox: to act in the world by not acting. This strange contradiction is the deepest mystical wisdom: Carmel's passivity is finally revealed as the highest action.

---

[8] *A Carmelite of the Sacred Heart*, pp. 126, 127.
[9] Ibid., p. 129.

Saint IGNATIUS OF LOYOLA

and the Society of Jesus

In the story of his conversion which Ignatius dictated to Fr. Gonzáles de Cámara, he tells of his love for the shimmering, star-studded night sky. "It was his greatest consolation," he says, writing of the time when he was convalescing from his wounds after the Battle of Pamplona, "to gaze upon the heavens and the stars, which he often did, and for long stretches at a time, because when doing so he felt within himself a powerful urge to be serving our Lord." [1] The picture of Ignatius gazing upon an unending sea of stars is a vivid symbol of the mystery of that profound soul. And if we are to encounter the real Ignatius, then it is only by raising our mind's eyes, too, to those metaphysical heights where men's noblest purposes meet and earthly differences of opinion are reconciled.

The story of his life begins with a prelude—the first twenty-five years, which Ignatius tersely dismisses as having been given over to worldly vanities.[2] According to Fr. de Polanco, his secretary, those vanities were gambling, sundry affairs of the heart, and vexatious affairs of honor of the kind that residence at court and his rank as an officer inevitably brought in their train. But while Ignatius did not regard this period of sinful living as deserving of a long description, his honesty would not permit him simply to ignore it. Indeed,

[1] *St. Ignatius' Own Story*, ed. William J. Young (Chicago: Regnery; 1956), pp. 11, 12.
[2] Ibid., p. 7.

11

some time after his conversion he returned to his native Azpeitia and, standing in the pulpit of the parish church, told the people how once, as a youngster, he had taken part in an orchard robbery for which another man had suffered punishment; [3] he was more concerned to humble himself than fearful lest his reputation suffer from such an avowal.

Then came the blow that jolted him out of his dissolute existence. He was in the family castle of Loyola at the time, nursing the severe leg wound he had received during his defense of Pamplona. His courage, let it be said, had not only fired the little garrison to offer a stiff resistance, but had also aroused the admiration of the beleaguering French, some of whom, after their victory, had carried Ignatius back to Loyola on a litter. There the doctors broke his leg a second time, with the intention of improving on the crude work of the field surgeon, but their lack of skill was such that after they had finished a piece of bone protruded from the leg. This deformity was so offensive to Ignatius that he ordered it removed. Throughout these agonizing operations he exhibited a self-control indicative of unique strength of character; never once did he utter so much as a cry, his only expression of pain being his clenched fists.

But the boredom of the sickroom was harder for him to endure than the butchery of the surgeon's knife. To shorten the time, he asked for some of the romances of chivalry which enjoyed such vogue in sixteenth-century Spain, and which were also to turn the head of the youthful Teresa of Avila. His family, however, was unable to accede to his wish, the whole castle boasting of only two books, both pious works: the *Life of Christ* by the Carthusian Ludolf of Saxony, and the *Golden Legend* by Jacopo de Voragine. Since Ignatius was ready to do anything to escape his own thoughts and the endless tedium that afflicted him, he snatched eagerly even at this unaccustomed literature.

At first his worldly manner of thinking made it difficult for him to find his way about this strange world of holiness. From time to time he would lay aside the legends of the saints and give himself

[3] F. Thompson: *St. Ignatius Loyola* (London: Burns & Oates; 1909), p. 93.

over to pleasant daydreams. Only when he got to the stories of St. Francis and St. Dominic was his imagination stirred; with his cult of courage, he could not fail to be impressed by the daring deeds of the fathers of the mendicant orders. He began to see a parallel— though it is doubtful whether any such parallel exists in fact— between the heroes of religion and the heroes of war, and to compare the two kinds of lives. His ideas on the subject were altogether hazy, for at this time he conceived of holiness as being simply a series of extraordinary feats of daring. In his inordinate ambition, he came to think to himself: "Suppose that I should do what St. Francis did, what St. Dominic did?" The question so fascinated him that he answered it with an all too simple conclusion: "St. Dominic did this; therefore I must do it. St. Francis did this; therefore I must do it." [4] From a religious point of view, this boasting was of little consequence; it showed only that Ignatius had not yet the faintest awareness of the part the divine had played in the deeds of Francis and Dominic.

Through this idle daydreaming there nevertheless penetrated a first call to higher things. For the wounded knight made an interesting psychological discovery: he found that when he indulged his longings for his lady love, they filled him for a time with delight, only to leave him more depressed than ever, whereas when he thought of spiritual things, his thoughts left him cheerful and satisfied. For Ignatius, this accurate observation of the workings of his soul revealed more than a valid psychological theory; like the late medieval that he was, he naturally thought in terms of metaphysical categories, and he therefore "came to recognize," in the contrary effects of his two moods, "the difference between the two spirits that moved him, the one being from the evil spirit, the other from God." [5]

This discovery was to be the real starting-point of his religious development; indeed, it had revolutionary consequences. Ignatius was on the point of receiving one of the most marvelous charisms of his life—a priceless gift of grace without which he could never have fulfilled his mission in his own troubled times. He was now learn-

[4] *St. Ignatius' Own Story*, pp. 9, 10.
[5] Ibid., p. 10.

ing the rudiments of that high art of the discernment of spirits of which both St. Paul and St. John speak in their epistles, and which was to become one of the central themes of his life.

By early in 1522 Ignatius had sufficiently recovered, although one leg was to remain permanently shorter than the other, and he resolved to leave home in order to lead the life of a wandering penitent. The exact mode of this new life was still unclear to him, and he gave his family no hint of his intentions. So he set out one day, riding his mule, and, like another Knight of the Sorrowful Countenance, leaving it to his beast to choose the way at crossroads.

Ignatius was fired, indeed, with the knightly ambition to do great deeds for the love of God,[6] but his conversion was as yet only in its beginnings. Not so easily does a pleasure-loving youth turn into a knight of Christ. The story of the Moor, as Ignatius told it to Gonzáles de Cámara, is strikingly illustrative of the spiritual blindness that still afflicted him at this time. As he was riding along, Ignatius relates, he fell in with a Moor, "and the conversation turned on our Lady. The Moor admitted that the Virgin had conceived without man's aid, but could not believe that she remained a virgin after once having given birth. . . ." After a heated argument, the two men went their separate ways. But now Ignatius fell into a rage, and "a desire arose [in him] to go in search of the Moor and give him a taste of his dagger for what he had said."[7] Thus, according to Ignatius himself, the thought of Mary and the thought of the dagger thrust were indissolubly linked in his mind at that point. Fortunately, his mule, like Balaam's ass, showed greater sense than its master, and obstructed his plans by choosing to follow a different road from the one taken by the Moor.

He continued on his way to Montserrat, a shrine made famous through its connection with the legend of the Holy Grail and most dear to the hearts of Spanish Christians. There he made a general confession to a monk of the Benedictine monastery, after which "he arranged with the confessor to have the mule taken away and his sword and dagger hung in the church at the altar of our Lady."[8] Then the noble knight gave his fine clothes to a poor man and put

[6] Ibid., p. 15.   [7] Ibid., p. 14.   [8] Ibid., p. 15.

on, instead, a rough tunic of sackcloth, slung a gourd over his shoulder, and took a pilgrim's staff in his hand. Thus attired, he spent the night in vigil before the shrine of Mary. This was his final break with the world, after which he never again looked back.

Ignatius threw himself into his new life of immeasurable penitence with all the ardor of a knight seeking adventure. But this adventure was God's, which made all the difference. We find a similar view of Ignatius, for instance, in Unamuno's commentary on Don Quixote, whom he regards as a knight of Christ and who constantly reminds him of the founder of the Society of Jesus.[9] It is a view that comes much closer to the reality of the elusive Basque than the more pedestrian conception of the superb psychologist with his amazing power of self-analysis. For Ignatius, like the immortal lover of Dulcinea del Toboso, was indeed gripped by a divine madness that lifted him right outside any conventional categories of being.

Ignatius had considered joining the Carthusians in Seville, but now he gave up the idea and set out from Montserrat for Manresa. And it was there that he sustained his decisive spiritual struggles. Everything that had gone before had been at most but a preparation for that irruption of the divine into his life which was about to transform him. Manresa saw the birth of his life's work; it holds the key to his entire development. Ignatius himself, whenever he was asked anything about his life, always answered with reference to Manresa. In Manresa, Ignatius came face to face, as it were, with the Being of God; there the Eternal hammered his soul mercilessly into its providential shape. There the truth about the diverse effects of diverse spirits that he had glimpsed upon his sickbed took on existential reality, and he became immediately and painfully aware of the conflict between good and evil of which his soul was both the terrain and the prize.

Ignatius lived in the hospital of Manresa or the Dominican priory, or stayed at the houses of various pious ladies. Most of the time, however, he lived in a cave, where he employed himself in ascetic practices worthy of any of the desert fathers. Besides attending all the religious offices in the church, he spent seven hours a

---

[9] Miguel de Unamuno: *Ensayos*, ed. B. G. de Candamo (Madrid: Aguilar S. A. de Ediciones; 1951), *Vida de Don Quijote y Sancho*, Part I.

day in prayer on his knees. He abstained from meat and wine, flagellated himself thrice a day, wore an iron chain about his hips, and slept on the bare ground. He stopped combing his hair or cutting his nails, and even refrained from washing, so that he soon presented an appearance of shocking neglect. No trace remained now of the well-groomed gentleman who had danced attendance upon the ladies. For Ignatius was in bitter earnest about his penance; the days of idle dreaming about doing what St. Dominic had done were gone forever. Whatever he did, that he did completely; halfheartedness was not an Ignatian trait.

Ignatius was assailed, in his cave, by frightful temptations. In the literal sense of the word, hell broke loose about him; the powers of evil raged and stormed, seeking to crush him under the weight of their wrath. At the same time he was afflicted by every form of the spiritual malady of scrupulosity, which tortured him to the point of desperation. Once, in his despair, he was violently tempted to throw himself out of the window of the cell in the Dominican priory where he was staying. This call to suicide was the climactic point of the diabolical assault; it showed, too, something of the nature of the dark forces against which Ignatius was battling so valiantly.

Ignatius spoke of his problems to various spiritual persons, but none was able to help him, as none had dealt with the adversary at such depths. In the end he triumphed over his scruples only by resolving firmly not to confess again sins which he had confessed before—to treat the past as really past. And because he had himself suffered the spiritual martyrdom of scruples, he was able, later, to help others in their struggles. In one of his letters, for instance, he writes: "We must then be very careful; and if the enemy lifts us up, we must lower ourselves, counting our sins and miseries; if he lowers and depresses us, we must lift ourselves up in true faith and hope in the Lord, counting over the benefits received, and with how much love and kindness He waits upon us so as to save us. . . ."[1]

[1] A. Goodier, ed.: *Letters and Instructions of St. Ignatius of Loyola* (St. Louis, Mo.: Herder; 1914), letter to Jacobo Cazador, pp. 22, 23.

Ignatius derived great help in his temptations from Thomas a Kempis's *Imitation of Christ*. No other work contributed so much to his spiritual development. All his life he kept it beside him and read it over and over again. This is not difficult to believe, for the *Imitation* has something of the quality of daily bread: it never wearies the spiritual palate, and always nourishes. Ignatius's love for this humble work speaks in his favor; only a real Christian can be so attracted to Thomas a Kempis's sober teachings, wholly devoid, as they are, of artifice or equivocation.

The *Imitation* produced a profound change in Ignatius. He realized now that holiness consisted in inner purification rather than in external mortification, as he had thought before. Gradually, therefore, he relaxed his excessive austerity, cut his hair and his nails, and reverted to a more normal appearance. But this change of direction must not be misconstrued. Ignatius continued as before to cultivate asceticism, a virtue no member of a religious order can dispense with. The mortified man remained his ideal, because only a controlled person can be master of his own passions. What Ignatius was rejecting now was not asceticism, but only a blind ascetic urge that stifles man's creative powers. For excessive self-castigation merely suppresses the outward tendency to sin without quelling the inner desire. From this time forward, Ignatius no longer confused the supernatural with the unnatural, or a love that was purified with a love that was merely benumbed.

By this victory over negative asceticism, Ignatius achieved far greater spiritual depth. More than anything else, he now desired to attain to joy in God. And later, wherever he found a tendency to excessive mortification, he always opposed it. To a noble lord who had joined the order, he wrote: "As to fasts and abstinences, I would advise you to be careful and strengthen your stomach for our Lord, and your other physical powers, rather than weaken them. . . . I should like very much to see your Lordship imprint in your soul the truth that as both body and soul are a gift from your Creator and Lord, you should give Him a good account of both. To do this you must not allow your body to grow weak, for if you do, the interior man will no longer be able to function properly." [2]

In Manresa, too, Ignatius had his first taste of heavenly joys. Visions came upon him, unsolicited, irresistible, as they have always come upon the great visionaries of Christian history. Mostly they were trinitarian visions; as he himself relates, one day "his understanding began to be elevated as though he saw the Holy Trinity under the figure of three keys." [3] Again, in his spiritual diary, he noted: "I saw the divine being, or essence, in the form of a sphere, a little larger in appearance than the sun." [4]

These visions constitute an impenetrable mystery, unsusceptible of investigation. For visions are an indication not only of unusual spiritual activity, but also of some participation in the world of the transcendental. Ignatius's consolations clearly show him as a man touched by the hand of God. And it was out of his supernatural union with the divine that he drew the power to follow his difficult vocation.

Closely connected with these consolations was the gift of tears, which he also received at Manresa. Again and again he would note in his diary that he had wept so greatly from devotion that his eyes hurt him. Prayers accompanied by tears remained henceforward the weapon with which he strove before God. This gift of tears, which many saints have enjoyed, is wholly unconnected with sadness; it is a purely mystical phenomenon: Ignatius's tears were the effect of his spiritual joy, which rarely left him during the rest of his life. Later, when he was in Paris, for instance, he was filled, he relates, with "so great a joy and spiritual consolation, that he began to cry out through the fields and to talk with God." [5] Incidents like these are all too often forgotten. But it was joy of this kind, accompanied by tears, that sustained this spiritual Don Quixote, however often he might splinter his lance against the dull opposition of the world.

[2] Letter to St. Francis Borgia, appended to *St. Ignatius' Own Story*, pp. 95, 96.
[3] *St. Ignatius' Own Story*, p. 22.
[4] *Obras Completas de San Ignacio de Loyola*, ed. I. Iparraguirre (Madrid: Biblioteca de Autores Cristianos; 1952), p. 309.
[5] *St. Ignatius' Own Story*, p. 55.

Sometimes, in his raptures, he would also hear an interior voice. All these phenomena point to a fact not sufficiently recognized: that Ignatius was in the first place a Christian mystic, which description of him is even more apt than that of a spiritual Knight of the Sorrowful Countenance.

While he was still at Manresa, in the throes of his prayerful struggle, Ignatius received the great illumination of his life. So profound an impression did it make on him that when he dictated the account of those early days to Cámara, at the age of sixty-two, he could still remember the exact hour and circumstances of that unique experience. He was on his way to the church of St. Paul, about one mile from Manresa, and he sat down for a moment at the roadside, looking toward the river that flowed below. "As he sat, the eyes of his understanding began to open. He beheld no vision, but he saw and understood many things, spiritual as well as those concerning faith and learning. This took place with so great an illumination that these things appeared to be something altogether new." [6]

This wholly unexpected experience was pivotal for Ignatius's whole development. He himself used the strongest possible terms to describe it, saying that it had made of him "another man," with a "new understanding." All the spiritual insights he had received during his whole life, he said later, could not compare with this single illumination. And he told Laynez once that he had learned more in that hour than a hundred professors could have taught him. Ignatius, indeed, should be numbered not among the official theologians of the Church, but rather among the great visionaries who are granted a spiritual understanding of the mysteries of the Christian faith. The art of the discernment of spirits, first perceived but not yet learned at Loyola, was now gloriously consummated. Everything appeared new to him: this lapidary experience encompasses the whole of that "illumination of existence" which modern philosophy vainly strives for. As for Ignatius, it caused him to fall on his knees in boundless thanksgiving before the nearest wayside cross.

But his new knowledge had to be given form, lest it dissolve again into uncertainty. It took Ignatius almost ten years of inner

6 Ibid., p. 24.

11 *

preparation to achieve that goal. Meanwhile, the impression he had
received was so powerful that he was compelled to put his thoughts
on paper. He filled a whole notebook in this way—this was the
first draft of the Spiritual Exercises. The final version was to come
much later, but in their original conception the Exercises are the
fruit of the Manresan period. The truth of this statement is in no
way affected by Ignatius's own statement that "the Exercises were
not composed all at one time, but things that he had observed in his
own soul and found useful and which he thought would be useful
to others he put into writing. . . ." [7]

The Spiritual Exercises are not intended to provide a spiritual
training; Ignatius was aware that many things in the spiritual life
are not susceptible of training. They may rather be regarded as a
manual for the transforming of one's life. In masterly fashion, Ignatius teaches how one may overcome oneself and order one's own life
—the aim, indeed, of all founders of religious orders. The Exercises make it absolutely clear that a thorough examination of conscience is an essential preliminary to the reordering of one's life.
Ignatius also believed that if a man was to become master in his
own house, he must gain control of his imagination, which determined his will.

In all these teachings, the former officer showed himself a born
director of souls. But the Spiritual Exercises will disappoint the
merely curious reader. They are not intended as a book of edification. Just as swimming cannot be learned by reading about it in a
book, but only in the water, so the Exercises reveal their content
only to those who carry them out for the prescribed period of thirty
days.

The Exercises propounded a new, analytical method of meditation. In consequence, many objections were raised against them,
and even after they had received papal sanction, the Archbishop of
Toledo was able to point to more than a dozen offensive passages
in the little book. By an irony of Church history, it was the Dominican Prior of Manresa who saved the Exercises from the Index.
Later the Exercises were connected with a movement of "illumi-
nati" suspected of heresy. But Ignatius succeeded in rescuing his

[7] Ibid., p. 69.

book from all perils. He firmly believed that God had given him the Exercises, that they were really His work, and this conviction has received its confirmation in the enduring quality of the Exercises, which have been practiced to this day.

When Ignatius left Manresa a year later, with the Spiritual Exercises in his pocket, he knew that he was still at the beginning of his road. This realization prevented him from congealing, so to speak, in his new-found devotion. It was clear to him, as he put it in his Exercises, that "man was created to praise, reverence, and serve God our Lord, and by this means to save his soul; and the other things on the face of the earth were created for man's sake, and in order to aid him in the prosecution of the end for which he was created." [8] But, while he never doubted God's general providence, he was not yet clear about his own particular vocation. He found himself very much in the position of St. Paul on the way to Damascus, asking: Lord, what wilt thou have me to do?

But he had already realized, at Manresa, that God's will is not revealed to men for the mere asking: it must be sought that it may be found. To find out God's will was the central endeavor of Ignatius's life. All his actions from this time forward were governed by that single aim, and can be explained only in terms of that aim. We have to emphasize this point: Ignatius never acted willfully, never did what he happened to feel like doing, but sought always to find out what God wanted him to do in a particular situation.

In his constant prayer to determine God's will, Ignatius gives us a wonderful illustration of what we may call, for want of a better expression, the "mysticism of the way." Needless to say, we are not referring here to any intellectual theory, but rather to a spiritual life of extraordinary intensity directed to the highest Christian relationship with God. The "mysticism of the way"—let us not forget that the Christian teaching, in the Acts of the Apostles, is often referred to as "the way"—leads men to the center of the divine life. And the religious passion with which Ignatius conceived and followed this ideal makes him one of the great figures of Christian

[8] *The Spiritual Exercises of St. Ignatius* (Westminster, Md.: The Newman Press; 1949), p. 12.

spirituality. There is nothing farfetched, therefore, in the close parallel that has been drawn between St. Ignatius and St. Francis of Assisi.[9]

Ignatius believed that he would be doing God's will by fulfilling his vow to make a pilgrimage to Jerusalem. And so he set out for the Holy Land, limping slightly on account of his shortened leg but wholly undeterred by the length or the difficulties of the journey. This pilgrimage is symbolic of an interior attitude; Ignatius conceived of himself as a pilgrim, and indeed was later to refer to himself under that name in the story of his conversion. That was one of the things he had understood during his great illumination outside Manresa: that the Christian's life on earth is really a pilgrimage to eternity.

Begging his bread as he went, the scion of the noble house of Loyola made his way to Venice, and thence set sail for the Holy Land. Throughout this pilgrimage he was granted visions that greatly consoled and encouraged him. Thus, in Jerusalem, for instance, "he had great consolation from our Lord, Whom he thought he saw above him all along the way." [1] He was filled with joy as he finally arrived in the Holy City and gazed with love and reverence at the places where the Supernatural had taken on natural form. With deep fervor he knelt before the footprints in the rock in the Garden of Olives, and he returned again and again to look upon them. This naïveté, unclouded by the merest suspicion of doubt, betrays a marvelously childlike quality with which Ignatius is rarely credited, yet which was just as much a part of his personality as his extraordinary mental acumen. Indeed, it was this rare combination of gifts which made him so attractive.

Ignatius's great desire was to stay in Jerusalem and work among the Moslems there. The Franciscan Guardian of the Holy Places, however, refused to accede to his request, owing to the prevailing tensions in Palestine, and Ignatius had to leave. The pilgrimage, nevertheless, had not been fruitless, for it had enabled Ignatius to see for himself something of the situation in the East, and to arrive at the conclusion that the old orders were incapable of dealing effec-

---

[9] F. Heer: Das Experiment Europas (1952), p. 60.
[1] St. Ignatius' Own Story, p. 34.

tively with unbelief. His cherished dream of working among the Moslems in Palestine continued to haunt him for many years, and led, among other things, to an ambitious scheme for the creation of a Mediterranean fleet.

Back in Spain, Ignatius was again faced with the crucial question of knowing what God wanted him to do. He longed to help others deepen their religious experience, but his attempts to form little groups for that purpose were frowned upon by the ecclesiastical authorities. Thus he came to recognize the absolute necessity of study—"so as to be able to help souls." [2]

The decision was not easy for a thirty-three-year-old man; it meant, for instance, having to sit on a bench beside schoolboys to learn the rudiments of Latin. And there were other difficulties, which he had not foreseen; for instance, as he relates in his little autobiography, "there was one thing that stood very much in his way, and that is that when he began to learn by heart, as had to be done in the beginning of grammar, he received new light on spiritual things and new delights. So strong were these delights that he could memorize nothing, nor could he get rid of them however much he tried." [3] Thinking it over very thoroughly, Ignatius recognized it as a temptation, and he resolved that he would let nothing deter him from his studies. So, by sheer strength of will, he persisted in an undertaking that would doubtless have defeated a less determined man.

The spiritual influence he exercised on those about him during this period brought him under suspicion of heresy, and the dread Inquisition inquired on more than one occasion into his activities. Once he was kept in chains in a dark prison of the Inquisition for a month and a half. Such proceedings throw light on the novelty of Ignatius's methods. What he had undertaken did not fit into any known framework, and was consequently regarded as highly suspicious. That, in fact, was the only reason why the Inquisition was stretching out its tentacles toward him. As for Ignatius, he conducted himself in this dangerous situation with exemplary courage and confidence, as only a man sustained by God can conduct himself. Even when he could easily have escaped, he remained in

[2] Ibid., p. 36.   [3] Ibid., p. 39.

his prison, telling the Cardinal of Burgos: "I will tell you that there are not bars enough or chains enough in Salamanca but I would desire more for God's love." [4]

Ignatius was able, in the end, to prove the groundlessness of the suspicion of heresy, and regained his freedom. But the experience left him with a profound dislike, not to say hatred, for the Inquisition: never might a Jesuit, in later days, sit on an inquisitorial tribunal.

As a result of this affair, Ignatius decided to leave Spain and complete his theological studies in Paris. There he remained for nearly seven years, and there he met the men who were to be his first companions and lifelong friends, Peter Favre and Francis Xavier. In August 1534, Ignatius and a little band of friends gathered in the underground chapel of St. Denis on Montmartre and, after Fr. Favre had celebrated Mass—he was the only priest among them—they pronounced the vow they had agreed upon beforehand. They promised to go to Jerusalem, renouncing their families and all worldly goods except money for their journey, in order to help their neighbors in the Holy City. If, however, war with the Turks stopped shipping for a year, or if they were sent back by the Guardian of the Holy Sepulchre, they would go to Rome to place themselves at the Pope's disposal for the welfare of their fellow men. [5]

The content of this twofold vow deserves attention. We can discern in it, first of all, Ignatius's constant endeavor to determine the divine will. His plans were more specific now, but far from definitive. The terms of the vow would seem to reflect a compromise between the view of the members of the group. Ignatius seems still to have held fast to the idea of the Palestine mission, whereas the others were already thinking in terms of what they could do in Europe. The fact that this difference of opinion could be given expression in the Montmartre vow is evidence of the democratic spirit that prevailed in the original Ignatian circle.

Some time later the companions—ten in all—met in Vicenza, where they decided that, as they were unable to find passage to

[4] Ibid., p. 50.
[5] Cf. Thompson: op. cit., p. 85; P. Dudon: *St. Ignatius of Loyola*, tr. William J. Young (Milwaukee: Bruce Publishing Co.; 1954), p. 154; P. Van Dyke: *Ignatius Loyola* (New York: Scribner; 1926), pp. 132, 133.

Jerusalem, they would go, in fulfillment of their vow, to Rome.[6] And it was on the way to Rome that Ignatius finally received the clarity he had so greatly longed for concerning his vocation. Laynez, one of the original band, who was with Ignatius at the time, has left us this account: "When we were going to Rome by the road through Siena, the Father had many spiritual sentiments. . . . Then he said to me that it seemed to him that God impressed on his heart these words: 'I will be propitious to you at Rome,' and our Father, not knowing what these words might mean, said: 'I do not know what will become of us at Rome, perhaps we shall be crucified.' Then another time he said that he seemed to see Christ with the cross on His shoulder and the Eternal Father near by, who said: 'I wish you to take this man for your servant' and so Jesus took him and said: 'I will that thou shouldst serve me.' And gaining from that vision great devotion to the name of Jesus, he wanted his congregation called the Company of Jesus." [7]

This vision, of which Ignatius in his memoirs gives a very sum-mary account, while confirming to Cámara that he had told it in greater detail to Laynez,[8] took place at La Storta. In it we find a new tone, heralding the birth of the hitherto only dimly perceived notion of a new order. Now, at last, Ignatius saw clearly what he was to do. The struggle that had begun at Manresa was over; the "mys-ticism of the way" had led Ignatius to his goal. This, then, was the divine confirmation of his deepest desire. The great dream of his life —to help souls—was about to become a reality. The chapel of La Storta saw the birth of the Counter-Reformation.

When Ignatius and his companions arrived in Rome in mid-November 1537, they at once began to preach in the streets, car-ing less for polished phrases than for spiritual fervor. Their unor-thodox conduct again brought the little group under suspicion of heresy, but the investigation, undertaken at Ignatius's own request, ended in their triumphant vindication. Ignatius succeeded in gaining audience with Pope Paul III, and explained to him in detail what he wished to do. This conversation, carried on without witnesses,

[6] *St. Ignatius Own Story*, p. 67.
[7] Quoted in Van Dyke: op. cit., pp. 120, 121.
[8] *St. Ignatius' Own Story*, p. 67.

decided the future of Ignatius's work. The wise Pope could not resist the inner power of the fervent Spaniard, and declared himself
won over to his cause. Inevitably there were still innumerable difficulties to be surmounted, but from then on Ignatius enjoyed papal
favor, and proceeded to put his plans into effect.

God's will, he believed, was that he should constitute a little
compañia de Jesús, a mobile unit that would always be prepared for
service in any field. And by a papal bull of September 27, 1540,
the new order was confirmed, but with the limiting clause that it
should consist of no more than sixty members. This clause shows
that Rome took no exaggerated view of the importance of Ignatius's
project; no one suspected that the new congregation would henceforward bear the main burden of the Counter-Reformation.

The Company—or Society, as it later came to be called—had
to begin by choosing a leader, and the choice fell naturally upon
Ignatius, who emphatically declined the honor. In so doing, he was
acting not merely out of humility, but also out of the belief that
he lacked the necessary health for the office. His companions, however, insisted, and when the matter was brought before Ignatius's
Franciscan confessor, the latter stated forthwith that Ignatius must
accept the post. So far, Ignatius had simply been first among equals;
only now, after his election as General of the Society, did the relationship become one of authority. Democratic equality gave place
to absolute supremacy. But this elevation in rank in no way affected
Ignatius's personal humility, and he began his generalship by spending several days performing the most menial tasks in the kitchen.

St. Ignatius devoted the remaining sixteen years of his life to
directing the new congregation—a task that demanded gigantic
efforts, not the least of which were involved in the elaboration of
the Constitutions. In this legislative work he displayed not only an
astonishing talent for organization, but also such an unerring eye
for the essential as is possessed only by a man who refers every decision to the will of God. Ignatius was interested in every detail of the
life of the order; nothing was too trivial for his attention. The twelve
volumes of his correspondence alone bear eloquent testimony to his
gift for leadership. It should be remembered, moreover, that he was
operating on the difficult terrain of Rome, where particular cir-

cumspection was required; but Ignatius had extraordinary diplomatic ability. He had a marvelous way of dealing with people, so that he got what he wanted without letting the other man feel that he had been short-changed. His was truly a great heart, as witness that wonderful maxim of his: "Never let anyone leave you unhappy." [9]

Ignatius's tireless action as General of the Society of Jesus places him among the great "fishers of men" in the history of the Church. This Gospel expression best renders the inner significance of his achievement, for, like the disciples whom Jesus called to follow Him, Ignatius was concerned with one thing only: to save souls. And because of his own bitter struggles, he was admirably equipped to help other people.

Ignatius never tried to treat all men alike, whether within the order or outside it, but always took individual characteristics into account. He combined finished courtesy with great firmness, leaving full freedom of decision to the person he was speaking to. His extraordinary practical ability derived precisely from the fact that he was infinitely more than a mere diplomatist. Ignatius impressed upon his followers that in their zeal to combat the new doctrines, they should not forget to deal lovingly with those of different faith.[1] He was always concerned to put the most favorable construction on the statements of others, and one of his maxims was that one should not dwell on a neighbor's faults, but should rather seek to excuse them, and, conversely, that one should always be quick to accuse oneself.[2]

Even during his student days in Paris, Ignatius's spiritual power made itself felt. On one occasion, for instance, being suspected of engaging in undesirable activities at the university, Ignatius appeared of his own accord before the rector to refute the charge. The heated conversation ended with a strange scene: the rector, who had been

[9] *Obras Completas de San Ignacio de Loyola,* letter no. 51, p. 766.

Translator's note. There exists no complete English translation of St. Ignatius's letters. Most of the quotations from his letters in the original German version of the present work are taken from the critical selection by Otto Karrer, revised and supplemented by Hugo Rahner, which appears under the title *Ignatius von Loyola, Geistliche Briefe* (Einsiedeln/Cologne: Benziger; 1942).

[1] Karrer and Rahner, eds.: op. cit., p. 169.

[2] Ibid., p. 283.

hopelessly prejudiced against Ignatius, fell on his knees before him and asked his pardon.

The most varied persons found themselves under the spell of Ignatius's Christian radiance. And he, in his turn, was prepared to do the most astonishing things for his sons. Ribadenaira, another of the early Jesuits, says that there was never a mother more concerned about her children than Ignatius about his sons, particularly the sick and weak.[3] The story is told that once, when one of his friends was suffering from depression, Ignatius, after considering for a moment how he might help him, sprang to the middle of the floor and began to dance a Basque folk dance.[4] A ridiculous performance? Far from it, but rather proof of the greateheartedness of this inspired fisher of men. Needless to say, the remedy was immediately effective. Ignatius's actions all stemmed from his wonderful gift of being "all things to all men"; few Christians have given such substance to that Pauline maxim.

The antithesis of Ignatius's striving to be all things to all men would have been reliance on cunning stratagem and tactics. His attitude held no trace of cool calculation, nor was his way of handling people something that one can simply learn. He had been granted the charism of being a fisher of men, and this alone explains the irresistible attraction he exerted over his followers. Men as dissimilar as St. Philip Neri and Michelangelo were devoted to him, and the prodigious St. Francis Xavier could weep at the mere sight of a letter from "Father Ignatius." González de Cámara once wrote that "to see and hear Fr. Ignatius is like reading a chapter in the *Imitation of Christ*."[5] That is how he appeared to his sons, and for his sake they were prepared to go through fire.

A sacred sadness casts its shadow over Ignatius's death. Realizing that the sickness that had long held him in its grip was about to reach its fatal paroxysm, Ignatius asked his secretary, Polanco, to go to the Pope and request his last blessing. Polanco could not believe that Ignatius's condition was as serious as he seemed to think; moreover, he was alone, and was anxious to finish some letters in time

[3] Huonder: *Ignatius von Loyola* (1932), p. 68.
[4] Thompson: op. cit., p. 116.
[5] Quoted in Thompson: op. cit., p. 192.

for the next overseas mail. So he asked if the errand might wait till the following day. "The sooner you go, the more satisfied I shall be," Ignatius replied. "However, do as you wish." [6] Those were the last words he spoke, save for occasional exclamations of "Ah, my God!" during the night. At daybreak on July 31, 1566, Ignatius died—without receiving the last sacraments, without bidding farewell to his sons. He endured his agony alone; the desired consolation was denied to him. His death was one of utter desolation.

Modern man has lost the art of elaborating those colorful legends in which our forebears were able to capture the essence of a personality. And because our enlightened minds have no understanding for symbols, we have swept symbol away—and substituted fables. No one has fared worse in this respect than St. Ignatius of Loyola. He has been characterized as a cunning schemer, a man who introduced the barracks regimen into religious education in order to get young men into his clutches. He has been called a master of intrigue who governed his congregation with the iron hand of a dictator. He has also been described as a hopeless fanatic whose action spelled a new dark age for Europe. Even within the Catholic communion he long remained a controversial figure, and Protestants have always regarded him with strong aversion.

It is obvious that such prejudiced views effectively bar the way to any understanding of the real Ignatius. Actually, if we take the term "Jesuit" in its vulgar acceptation, then Ignatius was the very antithesis of a Jesuit. And this paradoxical statement comes much closer to the truth than all those fables which, when confronted by historical facts, must scatter like clouds before the sun. The propounders of the fables have never lifted their eyes high enough to find a common viewpoint with Ignatius himself. Ignatius's own letters, memoirs, and diaries show him in so different a light that he needs no other defense against their charges.

Within the last fifty years a radical change has taken place in the field of religious history. For instance, Denifle's or Grisar's venomous portrayals of Luther as an evil man, a psychopath, a man untouched by anything divine, have today been recognized by Catholic historians as untenable distortions of fact, and have been replaced by

[6] Quoted in Dudon: op. cit., p. 428.

the far more justified approach of historians such as Josef Lortz or Johannes Hessen, who no longer deny the religious power of the Wittenberg reformer.

A similar correction of the Protestant attitude to Ignatius of Loyola is long overdue. Gothein and Böhmer made a beginning along these lines by going to the sources and using them dispassionately, but they never saw anything beyond Ignatius's psychological ability, so that their work cannot be regarded as altogether satisfactory. It is necessary to go a step further and to explore the religious depths of the founder of the Society of Jesus, for they constitute the core of his personality. If we approach him from this religious point of view, we shall be able to see through the sterile polemics that savor of the literature of the *Kulturkampf*, where Ignatius is represented as having founded his congregation in order to combat Protestantism. The historical inaccuracy of that argument has been easily proved by Bernhard Duhr in his *Hundert Jesuitenfabeln*.

We are not trying, here, to introduce some kind of veiled philo-Jesuitry or crypto-Catholicism. Any such suspicion would be too ridiculous to deserve an answer. The issue is simply one of historical justice, which religious historians should surely be the first to respect. And since the beginning of the First World War we have in fact been seeing metaphysical problems in a new light; we have tried to shed our confessional blinkers and to understand the great truths of Christianity in all their depth, regardless whether they are presented by Catholics or Protestants. The religious affiliation of the person who propounds a statement of religious truth is secondary; what matters is whether that statement leads to the center of life.

Such a strictly matter-of-fact approach is the only tenable one at the present time, an approach stripped as far as possible of all prejudice and concerned primarily with the religious substance of a personality. Ignatius of Loyola stands so deep in divine reality that half of Western Christendom cannot afford to cling to a deliberately distorted picture of the man. In his timelessness, Ignatius has a message for the whole of Christendom.

Ignatius's Spanish—or, rather, Basque—ancestry should be given due account in any assessment of his person, but its importance should not be overrated. What moved him primarily, and we might almost say exclusively, was his religious conviction. The truth is that, while Ignatius shows us how the Gospel can be mirrored in a Basque soul, the emphasis is on the Gospel. It is worth noting, too, as Francis Thompson notes in his book on St. Ignatius, that "Spain was not to afford him even a theological training. With all his persistence, Ignatius had tried to force on it a great saint and a great order; and it had refused to assimilate the saint except without his order." [7]

No national categories, indeed, could contain the man. And his mystery is heightened by the very complexity of his spiritual and psychological make-up. His roots struck deep into the Middle Ages; at the same time he looked forward boldly into modern times. He was a man of extreme sensibility, who could not bring himself, for instance, to pluck a flower, yet he was a man of iron self-possession. He once said that if he should receive the hardest blow of his life— the dissolution of the Society of Jesus—it would take him but fifteen minutes of recollection in the presence of God to resign himself to the divine will. And this proud Spaniard once said that he would regard it as a signal honor to have been of Jewish birth, so that he might have been more like the Saviour in this respect, too, by being of His race. [8]

The question remains, however, whether St. Ignatius did not also inculcate harmful doctrines. Were not some of his views tarred with the brush of equivocation? Take, for instance, this counsel of his: "In all conversations by which we hope to win over others, and bring them into the net for the greater service of God our Lord, let us follow the same course that the enemy follows with regard to a good soul, he all *ad malum*, we all *ad bonum*. For the enemy enters in with the other and comes out with himself. . . . In the same way, we may *ad bonum* approve or agree with someone in regard to some one thing that is good, passing over other bad points, and thus by winning his confidence we further our good object; by going in with him we come out with ourselves." [9]

[7] Thompson: op. cit., p. 60.
[8] R. Blunk: *Der schwarze Papst* (1937), p. 211.
[9] Goodier, ed.: op. cit., pp. 57, 58.

We can only answer by saying that the emphasis in Ignatius's action as a fisher of men—in contrast to that of the earlier monastic founders—was on the human rather than on the divine, and that so long as such precepts are practiced by a saint like Ignatius, who lived and moved only in the presence of God, they cannot prove harmful. The trouble comes when they are applied by men who no longer base their action on holiness, but on their own powers, unaided by grace. And in fact, wherever Jesuits have lost their sound religious foundation, the change of emphasis from divine to human has had disastrous consequences.

Rubens has given us a pictorial representation of Ignatius's essential role: he shows us the founder of the Society of Jesus healing a demoniac before the altar of a church. And rather than shrug off the scene as a hagiographical absurdity invented by Ignatius's sons, we would be well advised to look at it more closely. For the artist is endowed with an intuitive perception which enables him to penetrate far more deeply than the scholar into a personality. Rubens, in his realistic and dramatic portrayal, in fact captured the real meaning of Ignatius; the picture of the exorcism symbolizes the action of the author of the Spiritual Exercises.

Like St. Dominic in his day, St. Ignatius perceived with utter clarity the terrible sickness of his times; he saw men's total indifference to Christianity and their readiness to see it engulfed in the waves of a new paganism. With his singular ability to "prove the spirits," Ignatius was powerfully aware of the satanic assault, opposed it with determination, and sought to heal a humanity possessed by the evil spirit of the times. Ignatius really was, as Rubens conceived of him, one of the great exorcists of Christendom. At a time when the extravagant Renaissance claims for freedom were leading to the dissolution of all the bonds of Christian living, Ignatius saw the salvation of the West in the creation of new bonds. The prevailing disintegration could be checked only by a new type of integration. Ignatius is thus to be numbered among the architects of Christendom, not among its subverters.

The strength that enabled St. Ignatius to perform his mighty task he drew from his mystical life. The founder of the Society of Jesus ranks with St. Teresa of Avila and St. John of the Cross among the classic exponents of Spanish mysticism. We may speak, indeed, of a specific Ignatian piety, characterized by the immediacy of the creature's relationship to the Creator. And there is also a close connection between Ignatius and the German mystics, whom he met through his reading of the works of Ludolf of Saxony, Thomas a Kempis, and Johannes Tauler. In many ways he took his inspiration from them, but without ever becoming their slavish imitator.

Ignatius was a man who had abandoned himself to the eternal, who was dissolved in God, as it were, "like a snowflake." He reveals his mystical doctrine very clearly in his letters, as for instance in the following instruction concerning the spiritual life of students: "They should practice the seeking of God's presence in all things, in their conversations, their walks, in all that they see, taste, hear, understand, in all their actions, for His Divine Majesty is truly in all things by His presence, power and essence." [1] This is only another name for "constant prayer." And here we reach the very substance of Ignatius's personal life; God spoke to him always "without the sound of voice." [2] One of his closest companions, Fr. Jerónimo Nadal, wrote of him: "He was privileged to feel and to experience God's presence in all things, actions, and conversations, and to have a taste for spiritual matters, so that in his active life he was a contemplative. This grace and this light of his soul were revealed in the radiance of his countenance and in the unction and assurance of his actions—to the marvel and great spiritual consolation of us all, for some of this seemed to be reflected in us." [3] And Fr. Polanco, Ignatius's secretary, emphasized the fact that Ignatius "approved more of a man's seeking in all things to find God than of his spending much time" in prayer. [4]

The accuracy of this first-generation view of St. Ignatius is confirmed by modern Jesuit research. Fr. Przywara, for instance, sees in the endeavor to find God everywhere "the very essence of Igna-

---

[1] Letter to Fr. Antonio Brandão, appended to *St. Ignatius' Own Story*, p. 103.
[2] Goodier, ed.: op. cit., p. 26.
[3] Quoted in Huonder: op. cit., p. 55.
[4] *Obras Completas de San Ignacio de Loyola*, p. 796.

tius's piety," [5] and Fr. Hugo Rahner characterizes it as "the summit of Ignatian devotion and holiness." [6]

Ignatian spirituality has much in common with that of Meister Eckhart; it is impossible, indeed, to approve the one while rejecting the other. Both men were prepared to set their visions aside—"it is great spiritual gain to leave God for the sake of God"—in order to do their daily work in a spirit of service. For the author of the *Spiritual Exercises*, as for the *lector biblicus* of Cologne two hundred years earlier, everything, in the end, was turned to prayer.

But the art of finding God in all things is no easy one to learn. It is the goal, not the starting-point, of the "mysticism of the way." Much practice, spiritual discipline, and interior recollection are necessary if one is really to find God in things instead of being merely distracted by them. It is a free gift of heaven which is granted only to those who, in Ignatius's own words, "abandon themselves to belong to their Creator." [7]

II

We may well begin our short sketch of the Society of Jesus with Franz Overbeck's comment that he could not speak of the Jesuit order otherwise than with the respect that was owing to so sublime a monument of Christian life in the Church. [8] Overbeck, that most faithful friend of Nietzsche, was also the most independent-minded Protestant ecclesiastical historian of the nineteenth century, and his view concerning the Jesuits lifts the whole question to a much higher level than that of acrimonious controversy. On this level we are equally far removed from Novalis's enthusiastic exaltation of the Society of Jesus as a "model of all societies" and from any spine-chilling tales of Jesuit iniquity. At the same time, we shall not discount the difference between Ignatius and his later followers. If we complete Overbeck's attitude of respect by considering the question

---

[5] Przywara: *Majestas Divina* (1925), p. 70.
[6] Karrer and Rahner, eds.: op. cit., p. 53.
[7] Letter to Francis Borgia, Duke of Gandia, appended to *St. Ignatius' Own Story*, p. 90.
[8] Franz Overbeck: *Christentum und Kultur* (1919), p. 276.

from a religious point of view, we shall come closer to the position where it becomes possible to speak of the Jesuits with Christian decorum instead of in terms of friend and foe.

The Society of Jesus inaugurated the Counter-Reformation, which might better be described as the second Reformation, for it embodied the heavenward striving of fifteen hundred years of Christendom, and at the same time opened up new religious horizons. The Counter-Reformation was not simply a movement of reaction, determined by resentment against the first Reformation. It was carried along by its own consuming religious devotion. Indeed, we might call it, by a paradox, an almost tempestuous movement directed toward the most profound rest in God. The Society of Jesus was only a part of the newly dawning Christian spirituality that came to the Church's aid in her hour of greatest peril. However timely its creation, the order that Ignatius founded was directed through the temporal to the eternal.

The life of the Society of Jesus is governed by its Constitutions. These were Ignatius's own work, and rank beside the Spiritual Exercises in importance for the order. The way Ignatius set about his task was without precedent. He certainly looked at the rules of earlier orders, but there was never the remotest question of adapting any of them to the needs of the new order. When the time came for the actual drafting, Ignatius spent days in prayer in order to discover God's will in this matter too. The only books he kept in his room at this time were the New Testament, the *Imitation of Christ*, and the Missal. Each completed sheet he laid on the altar during Mass, imploring God to enlighten him further. Over some questions he wrestled in prayer for more than a month before final clarity was vouchsafed him. In this manner the Constitutions came into being.

At their head, we find this clause: "The purpose of this Company is not simply to attain, by divine grace, to the salvation and perfection of their own souls, but with equal zeal to seek to further the salvation and perfection of their neighbors." [9] Ignatius's burning apostolic zeal is clearly apparent in this provision. The fundamental purpose of the Society of Jesus is "to help souls." Christianity, in the Jesuit view, is primarily service of God, and only secondarily per-

[9] *Constitutiones Societatis Jesu* (Avignon, 1827), p. 2.

sonal experience of God in the soul. Nevertheless, the fathers of the Society are warned not to stray from the presence of God. The rules enjoin upon them to proceed with caution in their commerce with their sinful fellow men, just as the would-be rescuer of a drowning man must take great care lest both go down together. If the Jesuit succeeds in putting his neighbor on the right path, he must not take any credit for it for himself. Even in the most successful action he is only an unworthy instrument, like the ass's jawbone in Samson's hand.

So exacting a vocation is not for everybody; neither is ordinary zeal sufficient. Hence the stringent requirements that must be met before a candidate can be admitted to the Society. The Jesuits were the first to face the capital and very difficult problem of the creation of a religious elite, and they themselves came to constitute a religious and intellectual aristocracy that placed itself at the service of the Church. And in this way they came to grips with a problem that was particularly important for Christendom in an age of vulgarization.

An essential characteristic of the Jesuit order is its complete departure from the old monasticism. Not that Ignatius himself had any personal objection to the monastic life or any desire for the abolition of the old orders. The change was determined by the needs of the times. St. Ignatius founded the Society of Jesus at a time when the old orders were in a state of fatal weakness. Instead of breasting the tide of corruption, they had become engulfed in it, and their degeneration had brought them into disrepute among many religious persons. Ignatius had no illusions about this unfortunate state of affairs. Nothing could be expected from the old orders in this mid-sixteenth century, and Ignatius was convinced of the need for starting out on an entirely new path. He never swerved from that view, and as a result this conservative resolved on the bold step of founding a new kind of order.

This order was not to be some new form of monasticism: hence its members were to wear neither habit nor tonsure. The Jesuit is indistinguishable, in his clothing, from the secular priest. There is no external badge of membership; Ignatius himself did not even wear his rosary upon his person when he went about his affairs, but always left it at home.

Even more striking was the omission of any provision for the chanting of the divine office in choir—an essential element in the life of every existing order. Ignatius believed that the fulfillment of the obligation to attend choir would take up too much of the fathers' time, which they could devote to other duties. At the time this abandonment of the sung office created a storm of protest; it was regarded as a well-nigh intolerable innovation.

Ignatius also objected to any changing of name upon admission to the Society, as had been the practice hitherto in religious orders. Similarly, there is no reference in the rules to "cloisters" or "convents," but only to "houses" and "colleges." Ignatius, in fact, reversed the old monastic vow of *stabilitas loci;* "the spirit of the Company," he wrote, "is to move from city to city, and from one place to another; in all simplicity and humility, without binding ourselves to any particular place." [1] Such availability for action rules out any possibility of living for any length of time in a secluded cloister.

The Jesuit's vocation is constant action in the service of the Church rather than contemplation. The Society of Jesus is determined to give the world no quarter; it regards itself as in a state of unremitting warfare against all anti-Christian forces. That, of course, is what has given the Jesuits their reputation for aggression. Ignatius saw the monastic orders as the cuirassiers of the Church militant, who must remain at their appointed posts without ever abandoning them, while the Society of Jesus was the light cavalry that must be ever at the ready for attack or for defense wherever it was needed.

Not all sixteenth-century churchmen could reconcile themselves to this radical departure from monasticism. There was much venomous comment, much friction. Nevertheless, the Jesuits were proof against all opposition, defending themselves strenuously and successfully against any attempt of the papacy to assimilate them to the old monastic ideal. The verdict of the Sorbonne, that the Society of Jesus was "subversive of monasticism," was in fact justified. The

---

[1] *Obras Completas de San Ignacio de Loyola,* p. 716.

Jesuit order went a great step further than the Franciscans or the Dominicans, who had begun the break with the old form of monasticism. Indeed, it is hardly possible to go any further in this direction.

Ignatius's work constitutes the most radical change in the history of monasticism; his overriding concern with the apostolate writes *finis*, so to speak, to the monastic way of life. And because the Society of Jesus took the last remaining step in the development of monasticism, some account of it had to be included in the present work, even though it transgresses the frontiers of monasticism proper. We are thus enabled to see more clearly the process that took place within Western cenobitism, leading ever more compellingly from the type of the Benedictine monk to that of the Ignatian "cavalryman" of Christ.

Although the Society of Jesus does not belong to monasticism, it is quite untrue to maintain, as the Dominican contemporary of Ignatius, Dominic Soto, maintained, that without the observance of the monastic rule a congregation could not be a religious order.[2] On the contrary, if ever there has been a real order, then it is the Society of Jesus, which is characterized by a unique sense of membership, or *esprit de corps*. The Jesuit is penetrated with the idea of living exclusively for his order. And precisely to prevent any weakening of this sense of corporate membership, the fathers of the Society are not permitted to accept ecclesiastical dignities. Ignatius regarded personal ambition as the worst plague of monasticism in his day, and he also believed that the acceptance of episcopal sees was the surest way to destroy the spirit of a religious order.

The esprit de corps that is so marked a trait of the Jesuits is particularly apparent in their conception of obedience. All orders require a vow of obedience. A monastic community without any obligation of obedience is simply unthinkable; the obligation is as old, at least, as the cenobitism of St. Pachomius. But in the Society of Jesus, obedience is carried to the highest possible pitch. It is stressed from the first day of the novitiate. The Jesuit has to place himself at the disposal of the order blindly; he must learn to obey its commands without asking why. He must not rely on his own judgment, which can deceive him. Ignatius, in the "rules for thinking

[2] Thompson: op. cit., pp. 141, 142.

with the Church" which he appended to his Spiritual Exercises, included this famous and much debated statement: "To attain the truth in all things, we ought always to hold that we believe what seems to us white to be black, if the hierarchical Church so defines it. . . ." [3]

The fully professed members of the Society are bound in obedience not only to their superiors, in whom they are to see Christ, but also, and in particular, to the Pope. Their vow of obedience is thus twofold in character, and this special relationship to the papacy gives the order its distinctive Catholic note. The Society has often given proof of its utter fidelity to the Pope. Ignatius himself wrote: "We may . . . allow other religious orders to surpass us in the matter of fasting, watching, and other austerities in their manner of living, which all of them devoutly practice according to their respective institutes. But in the purity and perfection of obedience and the surrender of our will and judgment, it is my warmest wish, beloved brethren, to see those who serve God in this Society signalize themselves." [4]

The Jesuit is the obedient man who always and in all circumstances defers to the orders of his superior. The strictness of Ignatius's conception of obedience comes out very clearly in a letter which he wrote to all the members of the Society, and which may be regarded as his testament on the subject of obedience. He wrote: "I may not belong to myself at all, but to my Creator and to His vicar; I must let myself be directed and moved about just as a little ball of wax lets itself be kneaded; . . . I must behave as one dead, who has neither will nor understanding; like a little crucifix, which lets itself be moved about without offering resistance; like a stick in the hand of an old man, to be placed wherever he will and as he can use me best." [5]

Such unbounded obedience is often contemptuously dismissed as mere servility. But the analogy of obedience to the passivity of a corpse goes right back to St. Francis of Assisi, who would certainly have subscribed to the Ignatian definition. Hence, any objections on

[3] *The Spiritual Exercises of St. Ignatius*, p. 123.
[4] Letter to the brothers of the Society of Jesus in Portugal, appended to *St. Ignatius' Own Story*, p. 111.
[5] Karrer and Rahner, eds.: op. cit., p. 249.

this score must be laid at the door of the Poverello no less than of Ignatius. Yet the total obedience that Ignatius demanded was not intended to break the personality of the would-be Jesuit; the order would have been ill served, indeed, by men without backbone. Obedience was intended to produce the controlled man whose inward and outward discipline would enable him to meet any situation.

In individual cases the special emphasis on obedience was felt to be too hard to bear, and many, finding it oppressive, left the Society. But in considering the yoke that obedience lays upon a man, we must not forget the powers that it releases. The Jesuit's obedience is the burnt offering, as it were, that he makes to God, for through it he throws himself into the flames of love; he believes that in obeying his earthly superior he is obeying Christ. The Jesuit training in obedience teaches men to rise above the daily turmoil, to look upon events and things from a higher vantage point. And the ability to distinguish between subjective feeling and objective fact helps the Jesuit to gain the mastery in a given situation. His training in obedience enables him to disregard his personal preferences and instead to tread unfalteringly the path traced for him by his superiors. The history of the order clearly shows the advantages of this training. As for the dangers involved in such total obedience, the Jesuit believes they can be countered by the endeavor to perform every action "to the greater glory of God."

The Society of Jesus is characterized by intelligence placed at the service of religion. And the fear the Society has so often engendered would appear to derive largely from the sense of intellectual inferiority of its adversaries. Yet real intelligence, of which the Jesuits have given countless proofs, is surely an advantage, the world being unable to boast of any superfluity in this respect. Nor is intelligence in any way denigrated in the New Testament; Jesus, after all, exhorted His disciples to be wise as serpents. This is the Jesuits' motto, so to speak; they might also cite in their own favor St. Paul's "wisdom in Christ." Needless to say, there is no question here of worldly wisdom. The order displays its religious wisdom in this: it never regards a person's intellectual endowments as the most important thing about him, but always recognizes something that is higher than all reason. Ignatius declared that one could go too far along the road of the intellect, and that people who were too clever rarely accomplished great things or glorified God as they ought.[6] The man who is aware of the limits of intelligence is indeed a man who is deeply rooted in religious wisdom.

III

The Society of Jesus expanded rapidly. Its help was solicited on all sides, and within a very short time it had moved into many and varied fields. On the Catholic side, the Jesuits were the first, in the sixteenth century, to find their feet and to know exactly what they wanted. They did not suffer from the kind of paralysis that afflicted those who failed to perceive the significance of the movement in the north. Instead of allowing themselves to be driven by events, they followed a clear program of action adapted to the changed circumstances. Thus, for instance, they made use of the weapons that the new humanism had placed in their hands to champion the old medieval position. By such unprecedented methods, the Jesuits became the architects of the most fundamental revival of Catholicism. They it was who inaugurated what the old orders were incapable of effecting at that point: the inner reformation of the Church.

In order to fulfill its purpose of conquering the world for Christ, the Society turned its attention to the sadly neglected problem of the pagan missions. And here we meet St. Francis Xavier, prince of Jesuit missionaries and one of Ignatius's original band. He, too, came of a noble Basque family, but the two first met in Paris. Francis proved refractory at first to Ignatius's influence, but was eventually won over and became one of Ignatius's most loyal and devoted friends. Something of the quality of the man may be gauged from his conception of what the Jesuit order should be: it must be, he once wrote to Ignatius, the company of love and inner unity, not of severity and servile fear.[7] His missionary zeal is reminiscent of St. Paul's; like the Apostle, he was constrained by the love of Christ

---

[6] Huonder, op. cit., p. 42.
[7] Karrer and Rahner, eds., op. cit., p. 182.

to move forward with giant strides, conscious that the world could be gained for God only through the sacrifice of self.

Francis fashioned his own finest memorial in his letters, of which a contemporary declared that they contained only strong hope, heart, fire, storm, and dynamite. Their magic lies not only in the exotic fragrances which they seem to waft from the distant Orient, and which he was one of the first Europeans to convey to the West, but also, and especially, in the personality they reveal. They testify to an interior life that continued to soar heavenward whatever the difficulties with which he had to contend. In the midst of all his trials and sufferings, this man of great heart was able to experience the priceless peace of Christ, because for him there was only one real calamity: to be unworthy of the cross.

The first Jesuit missionary was one of those holy adventurers who are undeterred by long sea journeys or scorching sun, and whose heroic temper prefers danger to security. In his zeal for the conversion of the heathen, he undoubtedly moved too fast: in one month he baptized over ten thousand persons, and once he put his arm out of action by so much baptizing. At the same time, we should remember with admiration how strongly he protested to the King of Portugal against the shameless exploitation of the heathen natives by the Portuguese colonizers.

This apostle to the heathen realized that Christian missionary action could be effective only if conducted with humility, and without display. To a nobleman in Lisbon who offered him a servant to attend to his needs on his journey, Francis retorted that striving after esteem and authority had brought the Church of God to the sad pass in which she now found herself, and her prelates with her, and that the way to gain esteem and authority was to wash one's clothes and prepare one's meals oneself, and at the same time to devote oneself to the work of saving one's neighbor's soul. By his proclaiming of the Gospel, Francis sought to remedy the spiritual hunger of the Orient, not to bring European civilization to the Asiatic peoples.

St. Francis Xavier died at the very gates of China, completely alone, lying upon a heap of straw in a little hut. Like his beloved Ignatius, he endured his last agony in utter desolation.

Francis was the first, but by no means the only, Jesuit to penetrate to Asia. The missionary methods of the Society, like all things
human, may be criticized for their emphasis on immediate results,
rather than on the laying of a durable foundation. And the Jesuits'
tolerance of certain pagan rites was the subject of violent controversy
within the Church. Yet, whatever doubts may attach to their action,
the "Jesuits beyond the seas," with their utter selflessness and abnega-
tion, contributed an honorable chapter to their order's history.

An equally remarkable achievement was the Christian-Socialist
state that the Jesuits created in Paraguay. Its theoretical bases had
been laid by a Dominican, Thomas Campanella, in his *Country of
the Sun*,[8] but the Jesuits turned theory into practice. In point of fact,
the Paraguayan settlements—or reductions, as they were called—
never constituted an independent state, but remained an integral
part of the Spanish colonial empire. Nevertheless, the Jesuits protested vehemently—like the Dominican Las Casas—against the
cruel Spanish oppression of the natives, and this early earned them
the hatred of the colonizers.

Ignatius's sons had the merit of being the first to solve the problem of converting the Indians to Christianity without delivering
them to slavery. In their reductions, money, and with it the inevitable profit motive, was simply dispensed with. Drunkenness was
brought to a halt, the practice of abandoning children was stopped,
the death penalty fell into desuetude. Naturally there were corresponding disadvantages, in particular the curtailment of personal
freedom; these are the inevitable concomitants of theocratic gov-
ernment. But it is sheer calumny to maintain that the Jesuits merely
spread superstition and propagated empty ritual. No one who studies
the history of the Jesuit reductions in Paraguay with any degree of
impartiality can deny the Society the admiration its great endeavors
deserve.

Extraordinary courage was required to make the experiment, and
it has no less a title to be regarded as a holy venture than the Quaker
settlements in North America. Its great merit was recognized by
men like Montesquieu, Herder, and Gothein. The Jesuits made a

[8] See *Civitas Solis*, by Tommaso Campanella (1568–1639), in *Ideal
Commonwealths*, ed. H. Mosley (New York: The Colonial Press; 1901).

serious attempt to solve the social problem of the South American natives, and that is why their Christian-Socialist state in Paraguay deserves a lasting memorial. Even today it is worth pondering, for the unresolved problem of the life of men in community remains the source of all disturbances. Had everyone devoted as much attention to these questions as the Jesuits devoted to them in Paraguay in the eighteenth century, Christendom would doubtless not have failed so miserably to grapple with social problems in the nineteenth century.

Although the Society of Jesus was the creation of Ignatius, it must not be identified with him. For in its later developments it has often diverged considerably from his intentions—a fact that Jesuits themselves are understandably loath to admit. Every order desires to believe in its fidelity to its founder, yet every order must necessarily develop in ways the founder never anticipated. In the case of the Jesuits, the order gradually acquired certain characteristics alien to the original Society. It is hard to determine just where the change set in, but the facts are notorious. Organizational measures constantly encroached on the domain of the spirit, driving it ever further into the background. Sacchini, one of the first historians of the order, found himself compelled to observe that there had gradually crept into the Society, by what means he knew not, a spirit very different from the loving-kindness that had marked the early days. The nature of this spirit was first analyzed and openly stated to the order by one of its generals, Fr. Tamburini, who defined it as the intrusion of natural conceptions, the loss of a certain manliness, and the indulgence of effeminate cravings for pleasure and comfort.

This deterioration resulted in part from the Jesuits' residence at the courts of princes, for although Ignatius had exhorted his sons not to meddle in affairs of state, they did not always heed his advice. To retain the favor of the ruling families, certain concessions had to be made to their way of life. The early Christian spirit of austerity and penance which had filled Ignatius did not appear to be reconcilable with the nascent bourgeois age, and so the Jesuits began to make minimum demands. Baltasar Gracián's *Truthtelling Manual* is symptomatic of the new attitude. This grossly overrated little book on the "art of worldly wisdom" teaches, for instance, this basic principle:

"Employ human means as though there were no divine, and divine means as though there were no human." [9]

Jesuit conformism to the world provoked opposition within the Catholic Church, spearheaded and voiced by Blaise Pascal. There was nothing Protestant about Pascal's antagonism to the Jesuits; the supporter of Port Royal stood firmly on the ground of Catholicism. The quarrel was an internal one, and this gives it its exceptionally absorbing, even tragic, character. And it would be an altogether unwarranted simplification to suggest that all the right was on one side and all the wrong on the other: right and wrong, indeed, are inextricably intertwined in Pascal's violent polemics against the Society of Jesus.

Pascal's *Provincial Letters* against the Jesuits were written after the mystical experience that led to his "second conversion." They are thus the direct fruit of Pascal the Christian, not of the philosopher or scholar or scientist that he was too. But it is significant that in all his attacks on the Jesuits he never so much as mentioned the person of St. Ignatius. Clearly, Pascal drew a distinction between Ignatius and his order. As for the sons of Ignatius, Pascal wrote in his *Pensées* that "the Inquisition and the Society are the two scourges of the truth." [1] A terrible indictment of a situation that Pascal could endure only because, as he believed, the Church was innocent of the Jesuits' "corruptions." [2]

Pascal did not rush heedlessly into the conflict against the Jesuits. A great Christian, he was well aware of his responsibility in launching his attack upon the then powerful Society, and he did so only at the behest of his conscience. But the fact that Pascal's letters are filled with religious pathos does not mean that all his statements should be accepted as eternal verities. Understandably enough, in the heat of controversy he took a one-sided view of the order, condemning it for its faults while deliberately overlooking its great achievements.

[9] Baltasar Gracián: *A Truthtelling Manual, and the Art of Worldly Wisdom*, ed. and tr. Martin Fischer (Springfield, Ill.: Chas. C. Thomas; 1945), pp. 232, 233.

[1] Blaise Pascal: *Pensées* and *The Provincial Letters* (New York: Modern Library; 1941), no. 919, p. 319.

[2] Ibid., pp. 499, 500.

Pascal's brilliant irony was only at the surface of his argument. Beneath it lay the deep conviction that made him the friend of Port Royal. He was scandalized by the attitude of the Jesuits of his day, or, rather, their position appeared to him too poor a defense against the emerging theories of deism. With his sense for the essential, he concentrated on the Jesuit teaching on grace. To understand his *Provincial Letters*, we have always to remember the anguished cry that sprang to his lips after reading certain Jesuit works: "Are these really religious, and priests, who talk in this manner? Are they Christians?" In Pascal's view, there could be only "children of the Gospel" or "enemies of the Gospel"; "you must be ranged either on one side or on the other," he tells the Jesuits, "for there is no medium here." [3]

It was this radical "either-or" position, in which the complexities of life are reduced to overly simple formulas, which prompted Pascal's feud with the Society of Jesus. His main grievance against the order was that in its contact with the world it sought unjustifiably to adapt the Gospel to the spirit of the world. That was, indeed, the basic problem—conformity to the world, not morality. As regards morality, Franz Overbeck, for instance, maintained that it was the Jesuits' least transgression to have questioned the bases of the accepted standards.[4] Moreover, the Jesuits' approach to moral problems is usually misrepresented. They were, after all, religious men who subjected their consciences to careful scrutiny; they were not irreligious nihilists. This fact inspired Nietzsche's comment that "people speak of the cunning and villainies of the Jesuits, while disregarding the self-conquest that the individual Jesuit undertakes and the fact that the less arduous way of life which the Jesuit manuals preach is intended not for the benefit of the authors but for the benefit of the laity." [5] In any case, concessions to human weakness were made in the Church long before, and outside the Jesuit order, and they may also be observed in modern Protestantism.

The Jesuits still take the view that Pascal was unfair to their order, and that it is the Society's fate to be misunderstood. Contrary to their principle of bearing injuries in silence, the Jesuits of the time

[3] Ibid., p. 528.   [5] Nietzsche: *Werke*, Kröner Edition, II, 77.
[4] Overbeck: op. cit., p. 124.

turned their heaviest artillery against Pascal and, having succeeded in proving that his quotations contained inaccuracies, they had his book placed on the Index. But the question is not whether Pascal sometimes went too far in his remarks. The basic problem, which must be considered in the light of the facts, and dispassionately, is rather this: Is it really true to say that the Jesuits adapted their teaching too freely to the spirit of the world? Did they not sometimes, in their concessions, make too great allowances for modern mores? These are questions that every religious man must face, for they conceal a danger which threatens all Christians, and which they can elude only by deliberately defending themselves against it. But the Jesuits were reluctant to pass through Pascal's fire, and therefore the controversy did not avail them for purification. Pascal's hostility inflicted only grave wounds on the order; it did not bring healing.

The Jesuits fell into increasing disfavor during the decades that followed this great controversy, but for reasons wholly unrelated to those which had moved Pascal. The Society became the butt of ridicule and suspicion. It was abhorred for its real or alleged intervention in politics, and this abhorrence was soon translated into action. One hundred years after Pascal's attacks, the Jesuits were expelled from the Romance countries. Portugal led the way, followed by Spain and France; even Naples and Parma expelled their Jesuits. A veritable persecution set in, launched by governments in what was intended to be a diversionary maneuver, with the Jesuits as scapegoats for all the ills that assailed the peoples. The pressure of the Catholic powers on the Pope was so great that Clement XIV was compelled, in 1773, to order the dissolution of the order. Not since the last days of the Knights Templar had such measures been taken by the Church against any of her orders, and here, by a strange irony, the papacy was turning against an institution that had been created for its own specific support.

The Society bore its disgrace with singular dignity, proving its willingness to serve as the seed that must fall into the earth and die if it is to bring forth fruit. It would have been impossible, in any case, for the Jesuits to have been as bad as their calumniators made out in their polemics, inspired as they were by political, not religious, motives. A genuinely Christian note rings through the solemn protestation of the innocence of the order made by its last general, Fr. Ricci, five days before his death in the Castel Sant'Angelo, where he had been forcibly detained. It reads in part:

"Believing that the time has now come when I must stand before the tribunal of infallible truth and justice—for such is the tribunal of God—after having long and maturely reflected, and after having humbly begged my merciful Redeemer and terrible Judge not to let me be swayed by passion, or bitterness of spirit, or by any unholy affection or object, solely because I judge it my duty to render justice to truth and innocence, I make these two declarations and protestations: 1. I declare and protest that the suppressed Sociey of Jesus gave no grounds whatever for its suppression. I declare and protest this with the moral certainty that a superior can have who was well informed as to the state of his order. 2. I declare and protest that I have given no grounds whatever, not even the slightest, for my imprisonment. I declare and protest this with the absolute certainty and evidence that each man has concerning his own actions. And I make this second protestation solely because it is required to vindicate the good name of the suppressed Society of Jesus, of which I was the Superior-General." Then he pardoned the authors of the suppression and those who had injured him and his brethren.[6] Except in its earliest days, the order was never so near the divine as during the years of its ignominy.

Protestant Prussia and Orthodox Russia offered a refuge to the banished Jesuits, enabling the order to hibernate, as it were, on non-Catholic soil. And forty years later, after the charges laid against the Jesuits had been shown to be manifest slanders, Pope Pius VII restored the Society. Since Clement XIV had acted under duress in sacrificing his most loyal sons, a later pope was entitled to revoke the decree. And the Society, upon its restoration, quickly recovered from its wounds and resumed its leading role within the Church.

But the prejudice against the Jesuits was not thereby dispelled. Impartial Protestants have always combated such prejudice—for instance, that truly Christian writer Jeremias Gotthelf, who protested against the order's dissolution—but an *idée fixe* about the Jesuits

[6] M. P. Harney: *The Jesuits in History* (New York: The American Press; 1941), pp. 342, 343.

nevertheless remains as stubbornly engraved in men's minds as the absurd stories about the Freemasons. Yet one conclusion that must necessarily arise from any unbiased examination of the order is that there exists no Jesuit "type," despite the iron discipline that every Jesuit must undergo. At no time has any such type existed. The order has always included the most diverse personalities; we need only mention, from its early history, two such men as St. Francis Borgia and St. Aloysius Gonzaga. Jesuits—foremost among them men like Tanner and Spee—were the first to oppose the horrible custom of witch-hunts. Nor has there been any lack of such diversity in our own day.

If we are to posit any general concept applicable to the Society as a whole, it is that of the Christian warrior. It corresponds most closely to the essence of the Jesuits; indeed, St. Ignatius himself, in his life story, refers to himself as a new warrior of Christ. Yet this concept is seldom understood; the Christian warrior is confused with the soldier, so that many people have been led to see the Society of Jesus primarily as a kind of military body. This misconception derives from the spirit of secularism, which takes into account only the cultural significance of any historical development. But it is equally false to regard the Christian warrior as a theological polemicist. The concept of the warrior of God is an eminently Christian one. It goes right back to the New Testament, where we read those mysterious words of Christ, that He had come to bring not peace but the sword. And St. Paul, in his Epistle to the Ephesians, was most emphatic on the subject of the armament suitable to the Christian warrior. All through history we find traces of the warrior of Christ: he lives in St. George as he slays the dragon; in the medieval knight; in St. Joan of Arc. In modern times the concept has tended to fade, yet without the warrior of Christ there can be, in the long run, no Christendom. St. Ignatius recognized this truth, and his little company of Christ was nothing else than a last great attempt to re-create the Christian warrior, who was to wage a spiritual war under Christ's leadership against the kingdom of Satan. Only in this perspective shall we understand the secret of the Society of Jesus. The Jesuit is to feel himself "a noble warrior of Christ," whose duty, Ignatius tells him, is to "go, set all afire and aflame!"

INDEX

INDEX

Index

Faith: and knowledge, 264, 266; and philosophy, 35, 264; and reason, 264

Fallmerayer, Jakob Philipp, *quoted*, 84

Fanaticism, 88

Fasting, 24, 41, 46–7, 52, 115

Fellahin: first monks from, 58

Feofan, *staretz, quoted*, 13

Feudalism, 209

Fioretti di S. Francesco d'Assisi, 241–2

Fischer, Martin, 349 *n*

Flacius, Matthias, 204

Flanders, 305

Flight: and monasticism, 39, 72, 74, 108

Florence, 277

Floris, 240

Food: of hermits, 40–1; of monks, 78, 113, 161, 176, 209

Foran, E. A., 108 *n*

Fornication, 87, 88

France, 249, 250, 251, 305, 306, 351

Francis Borgia, St., 322 *n*, 338 *n*, 353

Francis of Assisi, St., 9, 215–40, 241–2, 244, 246, 247, 256, 258, 303, 317, 326, 343; *quoted*, 225, 226, 227, 233, 235–6, 239, 241; and brethren, 218–19, 220–1; Canticle of Brother Sun, 215, 237; character of, 217–18; and Christ, 216–17; and Church, 227–9; and Clare of Assisi, 245, 246; death of, 237–8; and evangelical perfection, 219–21; early life of, 217; in *Fioretti*, 241–2; and founding of order, 229–31; and humility, 225; and learning, 226–7, 232–3; mission of, 221–2; and poverty, 223–5; and priesthood, 232; rules of, 233–5; and simplicity, 226; spiritual joy of, 215–16; stigmata of, 237; testament of, 236–7, 244, 245

Francis Xavier, St., 328, 332, 345–7

Franciscans, 218–47, 257, 342

Fratres conversi, 208–9

Fratres Praedicatores, 256; *see also* Dominicans

Frederick II, Holy Roman emperor, 230, 240, 241

Free will, 126

French Revolution, 3, 278, 308

Friars Minor, 218–45, 247, 257

Friars Preachers, 229, 257, 263; *see also* Dominicans

Frundsberg, Georg von, *quoted*, 12

Fulcius Monocutus, 157, 158

Gemelli, A., 240 & *n*

George, St., 353

Germany, 17, 278

Gertrude, St., 153, 285

Gethsemane, 163, 176, 237

Gilson, Etienne, 107

Gluttony, 113

God: and demons, 29, 30; as hunter, 98; love of, *see* Love, *s.v.*; mercy of, 122–3; presence of, 337–8; and soul, *see* Soul, *s.v.*; and things, 149–50; union with 17, 41, 43–4, 51, 59, 75, 126, 160, 176–7, 190, 268–9, 284, 286; word of, 256

Goethe, Johann Wolfgang von, 147, 180

Gogol, Nikolai, *quoted*, 8

Gonzáles de Cámara, Luis, 315, 318, 323, 329; *quoted*, 332

Goodier, A., 320 *n*, 335 *n*, 337 *n*

Gospel, eternal, 241

Gothein, Eberhard, 334, 347

Gotthelf, Jeremias, 352

Gottschalk, 123, 190

Götz, W., 222 *n*

Grace, 123, 126, 127, 266, 309

Gracián, Baltasar, 348–9; *quoted*, 349

Gracián, Jerónimo, 292

Grail, Holy, 318

INDEX

INDEX

Index